Historical Evolution and Contemporary Challenges

INTERNATIONAL AIR AND SPACE LAW

FIRST EDITION 2026

Alsayedissa Alhashmi L.L.M

Reviewed by Sudeesh Robert

notionpress.com

INDIA • SINGAPORE • MALAYSIA

ISBN
Paperback 979-8-90342-852-6
Hardcase 979-8-90431-290-9

For those who look upward and dare to imagine the law that follows.

"The Earth is the cradle of humanity, but mankind cannot stay in the cradle forever."

– Konstantin Tsiolkovsky, 1911

"Outer space, including the Moon and other celestial bodies, is not subject to national appropriation by claim of sovereignty, by means of use or occupation, or by any other means."

– Article II, Outer Space Treaty, 1967

CONTENTS

Preface 7

PART I FOUNDATIONS **9**

1. Humanity's Dream of Flight and the Birth of Aerospace Law 11
2. Airspace, Sovereignty, and the Limits of the Sky 43
3. What is Outer Space? Science, Law, and the Boundary Problem 71

PART II LEGAL ARCHITECTURE OF SPACE GOVERNANCE **97**

4. Outer Space as a Legal Domain: Res Communis or Common Heritage of Mankind? 99
5. The United Nations and the Architecture of Space Governance 125
6. State Responsibility and Liability for Space Activities 153
7. Military Uses of Outer Space and the Law of Armed Conflict 179

PART III ACCESS, EQUITY, AND COMMERCE **207**

8. Developing States, Access to Space, and Capacity-Building 209
9. Commercialization of Outer Space and the Role of Private Actors 235
10. Space Resources, Utilization, and the Future of Property Rights in Outer Space 263

PART IV CONTEMPORARY CHALLENGES, CYBERSECURITY AND ARTIFICIAL INTELLIGENCE **287**

11. Environmental Protection, Sustainability, and Space Traffic Management 289
12. Dispute Resolution and Conflict Management in International Space Law 315

13. The Future of International Air and Space Law: Convergence, Challenges, and Opportunities 341

14. Artificial Intelligence and Autonomous Systems in Space 367

PART V FUTURE FRONTIERS, FROM THE CISLUNAR ECONOMY TO HUMAN SETTLEMENT ON MARS 383

15. Convergence, Expansion, and the Future Legal Order 385

16. The Cislunar Economy: Governance Beyond Low Earth Orbit 399

17. The United Arab Emirates and the Future of Mars 413

18. Conclusion: Toward a New Legal Imagination 431

About the Author 443

PREFACE

This book traces the arc of international law from the earliest human dreams of flight to the complex governance challenges of the twenty-first-century space age. It is written for space enthusiasts, scientists, students, professors, and professionals who seek to understand not merely what the law says, but why it evolved as it did—and where it might be heading.

The story of aerospace law is, at its core, a story about humanity's relationship with boundaries. From the moment the Montgolfier brothers ascended in 1783, every advance in flight has forced societies to confront fundamental questions: Who controls the sky? Who is responsible when things go wrong? And can domains beyond national territory be governed at all?

Air law answered these questions by extending sovereignty upward. Space law answered them by deliberately refusing to do so. This divergence—one of the most remarkable in modern international law—forms the central narrative of this book.

The eighteen chapters that follow are organized in five parts. Part I lays the historical and conceptual foundations. Part II examines the legal architecture of space governance. Part III addresses access, equity, and commerce. Part IV confronts contemporary challenges, including cybersecurity and artificial intelligence. Part V looks toward future frontiers, from the cislunar economy to human settlement on Mars.

Each chapter is designed to be self-contained yet interconnected, allowing readers to engage with the material sequentially or by topic. Throughout, the text draws on treaty law, state practice, scholarly commentary, and emerging developments to present a comprehensive picture of a field in rapid transformation.

The law of air and space is not static. It is being written today—by governments, private companies, international organizations, and the choices of individuals. This book invites you to understand, question, and ultimately participate in that ongoing process.

Part I
FOUNDATIONS

Chapter 1

HUMANITY'S DREAM OF FLIGHT AND THE BIRTH OF AEROSPACE LAW

From the mythic flight of Icarus to the silent orbit of Sputnik, humanity's ascent into the sky has always been inseparable from the question of governance. This chapter traces the arc from dream to law—from the pre-legal sky to the birth of international aerospace regulation.

Part 1

Myth, Philosophy, and the Pre-Legal Sky

Long before the emergence of law as a formal system of rules, humanity's relationship with the sky was shaped by imagination, symbolism, and metaphysical inquiry. The desire to rise above the Earth—to transcend physical limitation and observe the world from above—appears consistently across civilizations separated by geography, culture, and time. This universal impulse reveals something fundamental about the human condition: flight was not initially conceived as a technological problem to be solved through engineering, but as a philosophical and existential question about the boundaries of human agency and the nature of the cosmos itself.

In virtually every ancient civilization, the sky occupied a position of profound significance. It was not merely empty space stretching above the horizon; it was a realm of meaning, a domain inhabited by gods, celestial bodies, omens, and moral order. The movements of stars and planets were read as messages from the divine. Eclipses provoked fear and reverence. Thunder and lightning were interpreted as expressions of supernatural will. To enter the sky, therefore, was to cross a boundary between the human and the divine—an act laden with symbolic weight far exceeding any physical challenge.

Early narratives of flight served as moral instruction rather than technical speculation. They warned of the dangers of hubris, the limits of human agency, and the catastrophic consequences of transgressing boundaries established by nature or the gods. These stories were not idle fantasies; they reflected deep anxieties about power, control, and the proper relationship between human beings and the forces that governed their world.

Figure 1: Early Human Imagination of the Heavens

Source: Generated using OpenAI Sora.

The Myth of Icarus: A Legal Parable

The Greek myth of Icarus remains the most frequently cited illustration of this theme, and its resonance extends far beyond literary criticism into the foundations of aerospace governance. According to the myth, Daedalus, a master craftsman, constructed wings of feathers and wax for himself and his son Icarus so they could escape imprisonment on the island of Crete. Daedalus warned Icarus not to fly too close to the Sun, lest the wax melt, nor too low over the sea, lest the feathers become damp. Icarus, intoxicated by the freedom of flight, ignored his father's counsel, soared toward the Sun, and fell to his death when the wax binding his wings dissolved.

The conventional interpretation treats this myth as a simple cautionary tale against excessive ambition. Yet a more nuanced reading reveals a lesson with striking relevance to modern aerospace law. Flight itself is not condemned in the myth. Daedalus flies successfully by respecting the constraints imposed by his materials and environment. What leads to catastrophe is not ascent, but unregulated ascent—flight without restraint, foresight, or structure. Icarus perishes not because he dared to fly, but because he flew without discipline.

> ■ **The Icarus Principle in Law**
>
> The Icarus myth anticipates a central tension that later aerospace law would seek to resolve: how to enable ascent while preventing harm. Modern air and space law embodies this tension—permitting increasingly ambitious activities while imposing frameworks of responsibility, safety, and oversight to prevent catastrophic outcomes.

In this sense, the myth functions as a proto-legal parable. It establishes two foundational ideas that would later animate aerospace regulation: first, that access to new domains creates new risks; and second, that managing those risks requires rules, adherence, and accountability. Daedalus's instructions to Icarus represent an early form of operational guidance—flight within defined parameters. Icarus's failure to comply represents the consequences of regulatory non-compliance. The parallel to modern aviation safety standards, with their emphasis on defined operational envelopes and mandatory compliance, is difficult to ignore.

Figure 2: The Myth of Icarus – Early Symbol of Humanity's Aspiration to Fly

Source: Generated using OpenAI Sora.

Flight Myths Across Civilizations

Similar motifs appear well beyond the Western canon, revealing that humanity's preoccupation with flight transcends any single cultural tradition. In the ancient Indian epic texts, particularly the Ramayana and the Mahabharata, celestial vehicles known as vimanas are described as instruments of divine or royal power. These vehicles were capable of traversing vast distances, hovering, and ascending to the heavens. Importantly, the vimanas were associated with sovereignty and authority: they were tools of kings and gods, not of ordinary individuals. The implicit message was that access to the sky was a function of legitimate power, not universal right—an idea that would later find expression in the principle that airspace access requires sovereign authorization.

In Chinese mythology, the theme of ascent takes a different form. The legendary Emperor Shun was said to have been carried aloft by dragons, while the Daoist tradition taught that immortals could ascend to the heavens through spiritual cultivation and harmony with the cosmic order (the Dao). Unlike the Greek tradition, which emphasized transgression and punishment, the Chinese tradition framed ascent as achievable through alignment with natural principles. This distinction carries philosophical weight: it suggests that access to new domains is possible when conducted in harmony with the underlying order of things—a concept that resonates with the modern legal emphasis on due regard and non-interference in space law.

In Islamic intellectual history, the heavens were objects of rigorous astronomical study rather than mere theological abstraction. The Quran contains numerous references to the heavens as signs of divine creation, but Islamic scholars went further, developing sophisticated mathematical models of celestial motion. During the Islamic Golden Age (eighth to fourteenth centuries), scholars such as al-Khwarizmi, al-Biruni, and Ibn al-Haytham advanced astronomical knowledge to levels unmatched in the medieval world. The heavens were understood as governed by mathematical regularity—ordered, predictable, and intelligible. This emphasis on the knowability of celestial phenomena contributed directly to the later scientific understanding that would make flight possible.

■ **Cross-Cultural Flight Narratives**

Greek (Icarus): Flight as transgression; unregulated ascent leads to catastrophe.

Indian (Vimanas): Flight as sovereign power; access tied to legitimate authority.

Chinese (Daoist Immortals): Ascent through harmony with natural order.

Islamic (Astronomical Tradition): Heavens as ordered, mathematically intelligible domain.

These diverse traditions collectively shaped an understanding of the sky as navigable, governable, and subject to rules—anticipating the legal frameworks that would emerge millennia later.

Abbas Ibn Firnas and the Birth of Experimental Flight

A critical shift occurred when speculative imagination gave way to empirical curiosity and practical experimentation. While philosophers debated the nature of the heavens, a small number of individuals attempted to enter them physically. The most significant of these early experimenters was Abbas Ibn Firnas (810–887 CE), a ninth-century Andalusian polymath whose contributions to the history of flight have only recently received the international recognition they deserve.

Ibn Firnas was a scholar of extraordinary breadth, working across fields including chemistry, optics, astronomy, and engineering. In approximately 875 CE, at the age of sixty-five, he constructed a set of wings from silk and feathers and launched himself from a hill near Córdoba, Spain. Contemporary accounts report that he managed to glide for a significant distance before landing heavily, sustaining injuries to his back. The consensus among historians is that he achieved a form of controlled glide but failed to account adequately for the mechanics of landing.

The significance of Ibn Firnas's experiment lies not in its technical success—which was partial at best—but in its conceptual reframing of flight. Unlike the mythical figures who preceded him, Ibn Firnas approached flight as a problem of design, balance, and descent. He studied bird anatomy, experimented with materials, and analyzed the aerodynamics of wing surfaces. His flight was not an act of divine inspiration or mystical communion; it was a deliberate, planned, and analyzed human technical endeavor, subject to improvement through knowledge and further experimentation.

> ■ **Historical Citation**
>
> The Algerian scholar Ahmed Mohammed al-Maqqari, in his seventeenth-century work Nafh al-Tib (The Breath of Perfume), provides the most detailed historical account of Ibn Firnas's flight, describing his use of feathered wings and his observation that birds use their tails as braking mechanisms—an insight he failed to incorporate into his own design.

Ibn Firnas's experiment also occurred in a complete legal vacuum. There were no rules governing ascent, no claims of jurisdiction over the space above Córdoba, and no conception of airspace as a regulated domain. The sky remained a commons by default, not by design. Yet even at this stage, the seeds of future legal questions were present, if unrecognized. Who may ascend? Who bears responsibility if an experiment causes harm to persons below? Does flight threaten the social or political order? These questions would remain dormant for centuries, awaiting the technology that would make them urgent.

Figure 3: Abbas Ibn Firnas and Early Experiments in Human Flight

Source: Generated using OpenAI Sora.

The Enlightenment and the Conceptual Transformation of the Sky

The transition from medieval to modern thinking about the sky was gradual but transformative. Beginning in the sixteenth century, the Scientific Revolution dismantled the Aristotelian cosmology that had dominated Western thought for nearly two millennia. Copernicus, Galileo, and Kepler demonstrated that the Earth was not the center of the universe, that celestial bodies obeyed the same physical laws as terrestrial objects, and that the heavens could be studied empirically rather than merely contemplated theologically.

This conceptual revolution had profound implications for the later development of aerospace law. By stripping the sky of its sacred character and revealing it as a physical domain governed by natural laws, the Scientific Revolution created the intellectual conditions for treating the sky as a space subject to human intervention—and, eventually, human regulation. A sky inhabited by gods is not a domain for human governance; a sky explained by physics is.

Enlightenment philosophers reinforced this transformation. Thinkers such as John Locke, Immanuel Kant, and Jean-Jacques Rousseau emphasized reason, progress, and the mastery of nature. Flight, once symbolic of transgression against divine order, became emblematic of human advancement and the triumph of reason over superstition. This shift in attitude was crucial: once flight was accepted as a legitimate aspiration rather than a forbidden act, law would inevitably follow. As history repeatedly demonstrates, law does not precede capability; it responds to it.

The Global Commons in Pre-Modern Thought

Before formal legal doctrines emerged, diverse cultures developed sophisticated approaches to shared resources and common spaces. The concept of commons—domains belonging to no individual but available to all—appears in virtually every legal tradition. In English common law, village commons provided pasture and wood for all residents. In Islamic law, the doctrine of hima designated protected communal grazing areas, while water rights were governed by principles of shared access and equitable distribution. These terrestrial precedents established a pattern of thinking about shared domains that would eventually extend upward.

The sea offered the most relevant analogy. For millennia, coastal communities understood the sea as simultaneously dangerous and essential, exploitable yet unconquerable. Roman law classified the sea as res communis omnium—a thing common to all—recognizing that its vast, fluid nature made exclusive ownership impossible. This classification would later prove foundational when jurists confronted the analogous challenge of governing the sky and, eventually, outer space.

What these diverse traditions shared was a recognition that certain domains, by their nature, resist exclusive control. The sky—boundless, intangible, and traversed by winds that respect no borders—belonged instinctively to this category. Yet as long as humans remained on the ground, the question of governing vertical space remained purely theoretical. Only the advent of actual flight would transform it from philosophical speculation into urgent legal necessity.

Philosophical and Jurisprudential Foundations

The foundations of international air and space law are deeply rooted in classical jurisprudence and political philosophy. Long before human flight became technologically feasible, legal thinkers grappled with the question of how vertical space above the Earth should be treated under law. These early debates, though seemingly abstract, shaped the conceptual architecture upon which modern air and space law would later be constructed.

In Roman law, the principle cuius est solum, eius est usque ad coelum et ad inferos—"whoever owns the land owns it up to the heavens and down to the depths"—reflected an early assumption of vertical sovereignty. This maxim, attributed to the medieval glossator Accursius and later adopted into common law through Coke and Blackstone, posited that property rights extended indefinitely upward. For centuries, this notion posed little practical difficulty: no individual could occupy or use the airspace above land in any manner that interfered with surface ownership. The heavens were theological and metaphysical spaces, not operational domains.

> *"Cuius est solum, eius est usque ad coelum et ad inferos—Whoever owns the land owns it up to the heavens and down to the depths."*
>
> – Roman legal maxim, attributed to Accursius (c. 1260)

As scientific understanding progressed, particularly during the Enlightenment, thinkers began to question absolute vertical ownership. Natural law philosophers argued that certain domains—especially those incapable of exclusive control—should remain res communis, shared by all humanity. Hugo Grotius, writing in 1609, applied this reasoning to the seas in his seminal work Mare Liberum, arguing that the oceans, being vast and inexhaustible, could not be appropriated by any single state. This intellectual framework would later prove remarkably adaptable, providing the conceptual foundation for the legal status of outer space.

The emergence of international law in the nineteenth century introduced new tensions. Sovereignty became the organizing principle of the international system, formalized through the Peace of Westphalia (1648) and refined through subsequent practice. Yet technological advances increasingly challenged sovereignty's territorial limits. Telegraph wires, submarine cables, and radio waves crossed borders without physical impediment. The law was forced to confront a central dilemma that would define the coming century: how to reconcile absolute sovereignty with the practical realities of new domains.

■ Technology as a Driver of Legal Change

International air and space law exemplify technological determinism in lawmaking. Unlike many legal fields that evolve through gradual social or economic pressures, air and space law emerged directly in response to technological breakthroughs. The invention of powered flight and later rocket technology forced states to confront domains previously unregulated and conceptually undefined. The law did not anticipate flight; it reacted to it.

This reactive pattern explains why air and space law developed as functional regimes, shaped less by abstract theory and more by operational necessity. Early aviation accidents, military overflights, and commercial ambitions compelled states to establish rules governing safety, sovereignty, and liability. Similarly, space law emerged not from gradual legal evolution but from sudden geopolitical necessity when Sputnik transformed outer space from a theoretical concept into a strategic reality overnight.

***

Part II

The Scientific Revolution, Balloons, Early Aviation, and the First Legal Questions

The transition from imagination to sustained human flight was neither sudden nor accidental. It emerged from the broader Scientific Revolution, a period marked by systematic experimentation, mathematical modeling, and the rejection of purely metaphysical explanations of natural phenomena. As scientific understanding of air pressure, gravity, and motion deepened, the possibility of controlled ascent moved decisively from speculation into engineering reality. With this transition came the first practical legal questions concerning flight—questions that societies were initially unprepared to answer.

The Physics of Ascent

Seventeenth-century advances in physics fundamentally altered humanity's understanding of motion and forces. Galileo Galilei's observations and experiments challenged Aristotelian physics, demonstrating that objects of different masses fall at the same rate and that projectile motion follows predictable paths. Isaac Newton's Principia Mathematica (1687) provided a comprehensive mathematical framework for understanding motion, gravity, and force. Newton's laws of motion and universal gravitation explained not only why objects fall to Earth but also how objects might remain aloft—and, crucially, how they might orbit.

Concurrently, developments in fluid dynamics began to explain how objects could be supported by air. Daniel Bernoulli's work on fluid pressure (1738) established the relationship between the speed of a fluid and its pressure—the principle that would later explain aerodynamic lift. Robert Boyle's experiments with air pressure demonstrated that the atmosphere had weight and could be manipulated. These insights did not immediately produce aircraft, but they transformed flight from a mystical aspiration into a solvable scientific problem, amenable to experimentation and engineering.

Figure 4: Early Scientific and Technological Developments in Aviation

Source: Generated using OpenAI Sora.

The Balloon Revolution: 1783 and Its Aftermath

The first decisive breakthrough came not with heavier-than-air machines, but with lighter-than-air flight. On 4 June 1783, the Montgolfier brothers—Joseph-Michel and Jacques-Étienne—demonstrated an unmanned hot-air balloon flight at Annonay, France. On 21 November of the same year, Pilâtre de Rozier and the Marquis d'Arlandes made the first manned free flight in a Montgolfier balloon over Paris, traveling approximately 9 kilometers in 25 minutes. Just ten days later, on 1 December 1783, Jacques Charles and the Robert brothers made the first manned hydrogen balloon flight, also from Paris, demonstrating an alternative approach to lighter-than-air aviation.

Almost immediately, ballooning captured the imagination of Europe and beyond. Flights were conducted over cities, countryside, and national borders, often without regard for political boundaries. Balloonists became celebrities; spectators gathered in their thousands. The sky, once largely unused and uncontested, was suddenly populated—albeit sporadically—by human presence. The practical implications were immediate and far-reaching.

> ■ **The First Flight: Key Facts**
>
> 21 November 1783: First manned free balloon flight (Montgolfier), Paris, France.
>
> 1 December 1783: First hydrogen balloon flight (Charles), Paris, France.
>
> 7 January 1785: First crossing of the English Channel by air (Blanchard and Jeffries).
>
> These flights demonstrated that national borders were permeable from above—a realization with profound implications for sovereignty, security, and the future of international law.

This development revealed a striking legal gap. Existing legal systems were built around land and sea. Property rights extended horizontally across the Earth's surface, governed by well-established principles of ownership, trespass, and jurisdiction. Maritime law governed navigation beyond territorial waters, distinguishing between coastal sovereignty and the freedom of the high seas. Vertical space, however, remained legally undefined. No legal tradition had contemplated the systematic use of the air above land.

The immediate legal questions were practical and urgent. Did land ownership extend upward indefinitely? If so, every balloon passage over private land constituted a trespass. Could a landowner shoot down a balloon flying over his property? Could a sovereign state object to a balloon entering the air above its territory? What happened when a balloon, driven by wind rather than controlled navigation, drifted across an international border? Who bore liability if a balloon crashed and caused damage to persons or property below?

Early responses to these questions were ad hoc and inconsistent. Some jurists argued that the Roman maxim usque ad coelum compelled the conclusion that any aerial intrusion constituted a trespass, regardless of intent or altitude. Under this view, even the most innocent balloon passage violated property rights. Others rejected this interpretation as absurdly impractical, noting that it would make not only ballooning but all aerial activity impossible. A balloon driven by wind could not choose its course; holding its operator liable for trespass over every parcel of land traversed below would impose impossibly burdensome obligations.

The tension between these positions reflected a deeper jurisprudential challenge that would recur throughout the history of aerospace law: the conflict between established legal principles and new technological realities. Legal systems are inherently conservative institutions, built on precedent and tradition. Technology, by contrast, is inherently disruptive, creating capabilities and risks that existing categories cannot accommodate. The history of aerospace law is largely the history of this tension—and the creative, sometimes awkward, compromises devised to resolve it.

Courts in France, Germany, and England began developing pragmatic distinctions. French courts generally held that landowners could object to balloon operations that caused actual damage or interference with the use of their property, but not to mere passage at altitude. This functional approach—focusing on impact rather than abstract rights—anticipated the later development of aviation easements and the distinction between sovereignty (a state right) and property (a private right) in airspace law. English courts, influenced by the common law tradition, were initially more protective of property rights but gradually adopted similar pragmatic limitations.

Security Concerns and Military Reconnaissance

The legal uncertainty surrounding balloon flight was compounded by growing security concerns. Balloons could observe military installations from above, cross borders undetected, and potentially deliver weapons or incendiary devices. These capabilities were not merely theoretical. During the French Revolutionary Wars and the Napoleonic period, the French military employed balloons for battlefield reconnaissance, most notably at the Battle of Fleurus in 1794, where the balloon L'Entreprenant provided aerial observation of Austrian positions.

During the Franco-Prussian War of 1870–71, balloons carried mail, dispatches, and even passengers out of besieged Paris, demonstrating their utility as instruments of communication in wartime. The Prussian forces attempted to intercept these balloons, raising early questions about the permissibility of attacking aerial vehicles during armed conflict. While these incidents did not produce formal legal doctrine, they planted the seeds of awareness that flight had military implications that existing law was ill-equipped to address.

> ■ **The Paris Balloon Post (1870–71)**
>
> During the Siege of Paris, 67 manned balloon flights carried approximately 2.5 million letters out of the city. Several balloons were captured or lost, including two that drifted as far as Norway. This episode demonstrated both the potential and the unpredictability of aerial navigation—and the inadequacy of existing international law to govern it.

In response, some states attempted to regulate balloon flights through permits, restrictions, or outright prohibitions, particularly during times of heightened tension or conflict. These measures, however, were local, reactive, and inconsistent. There was no coherent international framework governing aerial navigation. The sky remained a space of experimentation, governed more by custom, tolerance, and the practical limitations of the technology than by law.

From Balloons to Powered Flight

The nineteenth century saw steady progress toward controlled, heavier-than-air flight. Sir George Cayley, often regarded as the father of aeronautics, identified the fundamental principles of aerodynamics in the early 1800s, distinguishing between lift, drag, thrust, and the functions of different control surfaces. He constructed and flew model gliders, and in 1853, his full-sized glider carried a human passenger across a small valley in Yorkshire—the first recorded heavier-than-air flight carrying a person, albeit unpowered and uncontrolled.

Later in the century, Otto Lilienthal in Germany conducted over two thousand flights with hang gliders, systematically studying the relationship between wing shape, angle of attack, and lift. Lilienthal's meticulous documentation of his experiments provided invaluable data for subsequent researchers. His death in a glider accident in 1896 underscored both the promise and the peril of human flight—and the absence of any safety standards or regulatory oversight.

By the late nineteenth century, the prospect of powered, sustained, controlled flight was widely anticipated. The missing element was a reliable, lightweight power source. The invention of the internal combustion engine, combined with advances in materials science and structural engineering, provided the final piece of the puzzle.

The Wright Brothers and the Dawn of Aviation

On 17 December 1903, at Kitty Hawk, North Carolina, Orville and Wilbur Wright achieved the first successful powered, controlled, sustained heavier-than-air flight. The first flight lasted just twelve seconds and covered 37 meters, but it marked the beginning of a new era. Within five years, aircraft were flying for hours at a time, covering hundreds of kilometers, and crossing national borders. Within a decade, aviation had become a serious commercial and military enterprise.

The arrival of aircraft fundamentally altered the legal calculus. Unlike balloons, which were slow, largely uncontrollable, and dependent on wind currents, airplanes were fast, maneuverable, and capable of precise navigation. They could penetrate deep into national territory within minutes, observe or photograph military installations, and potentially deliver weapons. This capability posed an unprecedented challenge to traditional notions of sovereignty and territorial control.

■ **The Legal Impact of Powered Flight**

Speed and Control: Unlike balloons, aircraft could navigate deliberately and cross borders intentionally.

Military Potential: Reconnaissance, bombing, and troop transport transformed national security calculations.

Commercial Promise: Mail delivery, passenger service, and cargo transport created economic incentives for international cooperation.

Legal Urgency: The combination of capability and vulnerability forced states to assert control over their airspace.

States reacted swiftly to the implications of powered flight. Concerns over espionage, smuggling, and military vulnerability prompted governments to assert authority over the air above their territory. The earlier tolerance extended to balloons—largely because they were uncontrollable and posed limited threat—gave way to a far more restrictive attitude toward aircraft. By the early twentieth century, a consensus began to emerge among governments, military planners, and legal scholars alike: the sky could no longer be treated as legally free.

The pace of aviation development was breathtaking. By 1909, Louis Blériot had flown across the English Channel, demonstrating that natural barriers no longer guaranteed protection from aerial incursion. By 1911, aircraft were being used in military operations for the first time during the Italo-Turkish War, when Italian pilots conducted both reconnaissance and bombing missions over Libya. These developments compressed decades of potential legal evolution into a few short years, forcing governments and jurists to respond with unprecedented speed.

This consensus, however, was far from unanimous. Legal scholars engaged in intense debate over the appropriate framework for regulating aerial navigation. One school of thought, drawing analogies to the high seas, advocated for the freedom of the air. Another, emphasizing the direct relationship between airspace and territorial security, insisted on sovereign control. The resolution of this debate would define the structure of international air law for the next century.

Figure 5: Wilbur and Orville Wright with Their Early Flying Machine

Source: Library of Congress Prints and Photographs Division (Public Domain).

***

Part III

War, Sovereignty, and the Codification of Airspace (1910–1945)

If the scientific and technological advances of the late nineteenth and early twentieth centuries revealed the possibility of flight, it was war that revealed its consequences. Armed conflict transformed aviation from an experimental curiosity into a decisive instrument of state power, forcing governments to confront the legal implications of flight with urgency and clarity. Between 1910 and 1945, airspace moved decisively from a zone of ambiguity to one of asserted sovereignty, laying the foundation for modern international air law.

Figure 6: The Role of Aviation in World War II

Source: Generated using OpenAI Sora.

The Freedom of the Air vs. Territorial Control

The debate over the legal status of airspace in the early twentieth century was among the most consequential in the history of international law. It pitted two fundamentally opposed visions against each other, each reflecting different assumptions about sovereignty, security, and the nature of technological progress.

Advocates of the freedom of the air drew their primary inspiration from maritime law, particularly the doctrine of mare liberum articulated by Hugo Grotius in 1609. The most prominent champion of this position was the French jurist Paul Fauchille, who argued at the 1902 and 1910 sessions of the Institut de Droit International that airspace, like the high seas, should be open to navigation by all states. Fauchille proposed that states should have only limited rights to regulate aerial traffic immediately above their territory, while the upper air should remain free for passage. He emphasized the practical benefits of unrestricted aerial navigation for commerce, communication, and scientific cooperation, warning that the alternative—territorial fragmentation of the sky—would stifle innovation and isolate nations.

> *"The air is free. Only the owners of the surface may, to the extent that it is necessary, utilize the air space above their property."*
>
> – Paul Fauchille, proposing freedom of the air at the Institut de Droit International, 1902

Opposing this view were proponents of absolute airspace sovereignty, chief among them the British jurist John Westlake and his intellectual successors. They argued that airspace was qualitatively different from the high seas. Ships at sea operate at a distance from national territory, on a medium that no state can physically possess. Aircraft, by contrast, operate directly above sovereign territory, with the ability to observe, photograph, and potentially attack everything below. The speed and altitude of aircraft made them difficult to intercept, amplifying their strategic value. From a security standpoint, unrestricted overflight posed risks that maritime navigation did not.

This debate was not merely academic. States expressed their positions through practice, and practice consistently favored sovereignty. As aircraft began crossing borders in the years before the First World War, governments required prior authorization for foreign overflight, established prohibited zones around military installations and sensitive areas, and reserved the right to intercept or force down unauthorized aircraft. These measures, taken independently by multiple states, reflected an emerging consensus that whatever academic arguments might suggest, governments were unwilling to relinquish control over the skies above them.

The First World War and the Militarization of Airspace

Even before the outbreak of war, international law had begun to address aerial matters in limited ways. The Hague Peace Conferences of 1899 and 1907 produced declarations prohibiting the discharge of projectiles and explosives from balloons—an early, if rudimentary, attempt to constrain military use of the air. These declarations, while limited in scope and poorly enforced, represented the first formal acknowledgment in international law that aerial activities could have military significance requiring legal regulation.

The First World War (1914–1918) transformed the debate from theory to urgency. Aircraft were used extensively for reconnaissance, artillery spotting, bombing, and aerial combat. Airships conducted strategic bombing raids over London and other cities. For the first time, military operations routinely penetrated the third dimension, demonstrating that control of the air could decisively influence outcomes on land and sea.

Neutral states faced acute dilemmas. Foreign aircraft passing overhead could compromise neutrality, expose military vulnerabilities, or provoke retaliation from belligerents. In response, neutral states such as the Netherlands, Switzerland, and Denmark asserted the right to control, intercept, or deny access to their airspace. These assertions had profound legal significance: even in the absence of comprehensive treaties, states behaved as though airspace was an extension of territorial sovereignty. Unauthorized overflight was treated as a violation of neutrality and, by extension, of sovereignty itself.

The Paris Convention of 1919

The aftermath of the First World War provided the first opportunity to codify these emerging norms in a comprehensive international agreement. The Paris Convention Relating to the Regulation of Aerial Navigation, signed on 13 October 1919 as part of the broader Versailles settlement, represented the first multilateral treaty dedicated to aviation.

Its most consequential provision was unambiguous and deliberate. Article 1 of the Paris Convention declared: "Every Power has complete and exclusive sovereignty over the airspace above its territory." This formulation resolved the long-standing debate between advocates of free air and proponents of sovereignty decisively and permanently in favor of the latter. The language left no room for residual freedom of the air as a general principle. Airspace was firmly territorialized.

> *"Every Power has complete and exclusive sovereignty over the airspace above its territory."*
>
> – Paris Convention Relating to the Regulation of Aerial Navigation, Article 1, 1919

The choice of language was deliberate. The drafters of the Paris Convention were acutely aware of pre-war academic debates and wartime practice. The devastation caused by aerial bombardment—and the fear of future attacks—had underscored the strategic importance of airspace control. Sovereignty over the air was seen as essential to national defense, border integrity, and public order. By codifying this principle in treaty form, the Convention aligned international law with the prevailing security realities of the post-war world.

Figure 7: Delegates at the Paris Peace Conference, 1919

Source: Phot. Isabey, Paris (Public Domain).

At the same time, the Paris Convention recognized that absolute sovereignty could not operate in isolation. International aviation required cooperation. Accordingly, the Convention established rules on aircraft nationality and registration, airworthiness certification, the recognition of foreign certificates, and the rights of innocent passage for civil aircraft. It also created the International Commission for Air Navigation (ICAN) to oversee implementation. This approach introduced a pattern that would define air law for decades: absolute sovereignty in principle, tempered by negotiated freedoms in practice.

Date	**Event**	**Legal Significance**
1783	First manned balloon flight	Revealed the legal gap in vertical space regulation
1852	First powered airship flight	Extended flight capability beyond wind dependence
1903	Wright brothers' powered flight	Triggered urgent demands for aviation regulation
1914–18	World War I aerial warfare	Demonstrated airspace as national security domain
1919	Paris Convention signed	Codified "complete and exclusive" airspace sovereignty
1926	Madrid Convention (Ibero-American)	Extended sovereignty principles to Latin American states
1939–45	World War II strategic bombing	Entrenched airspace sovereignty through devastation
1944	Chicago Convention signed	Established ICAO and the modern air law framework

The Interwar Period and the Growth of Commercial Aviation

Despite its significance, the Paris Convention had important limitations. Its membership was incomplete, excluding significant aviation powers such as the United States and the Soviet Union. Its provisions reflected the political realities of the immediate post-war period rather than universal consensus. Moreover, aviation technology continued to advance at a pace that frequently outstripped the legal framework.

During the 1920s and 1930s, commercial air travel expanded dramatically. Airlines established regular routes connecting major cities across Europe, the Americas, and eventually the globe. Airmail services accelerated international communication. Aircraft range, speed, and carrying capacity increased with each successive generation of technology. By the mid-1930s, flying boats operated transatlantic routes, and aviation had become a significant industry generating employment, revenue, and international connectivity.

The Havana Convention on Commercial Aviation (1928), adopted among Pan-American states, reinforced the sovereignty principle while introducing provisions for commercial aviation in the Western Hemisphere. The Warsaw Convention (1929) established the first international framework for airline liability to passengers—a landmark development that created predictable legal rules for an inherently international industry. These instruments demonstrated that air law was evolving rapidly, developing specialized sub-regimes to address the growing complexity of commercial aviation.

This expansion necessitated a growing body of bilateral air service agreements between states, supplementing the multilateral Paris framework with specific arrangements governing commercial routes, traffic rights, and safety standards. The proliferation of bilateral agreements, while pragmatic, also introduced complexity and inconsistency into the international aviation system. The need for a more comprehensive, universally accepted regime became increasingly evident.

The Second World War and the Chicago Convention of 1944

The outbreak of the Second World War intensified every trend that had characterized the preceding decades. Air superiority became a central objective of military strategy on every front. Strategic bombing campaigns—from the Blitz to the bombing of Dresden, from the firebombing of Tokyo to the atomic attacks on Hiroshima and Nagasaki—demonstrated the devastating consequences of airpower. Civilian populations were exposed to aerial attack on an unprecedented scale. By the end of the war, there was no conceivable scenario in which states would voluntarily relinquish sovereignty over the air above their territory.

Remarkably, even before the war had concluded, states convened to design a post-war framework for international civil aviation. The Conference on International Civil Aviation, held in Chicago from 1

November to 7 December 1944, brought together representatives of fifty-four states to negotiate the foundational document of modern air law: the Convention on International Civil Aviation, known universally as the Chicago Convention.

Figure 8: Signing of the Chicago Convention on International Civil Aviation, 1944

Source: ICAO (Public Domain).

Like the Paris Convention before it, the Chicago Convention reaffirmed the principle of complete and exclusive sovereignty over national airspace. Article 1 stated unequivocally: "The contracting States recognize that every State has complete and exclusive sovereignty over the airspace above its territory." The language was deliberate, echoing the Paris formulation and signaling continuity rather than rupture in the fundamental legal principle.

Where the Chicago Convention differed dramatically from its predecessor was in its institutional ambition. It established the International Civil Aviation Organization (ICAO) as a permanent specialized agency of the United Nations, tasked with promoting safe, orderly, and efficient international air navigation. ICAO was given the mandate to develop international standards and recommended practices (SARPs), to facilitate information-sharing among states, and to coordinate global aviation policy. This institutionalization transformed air law from a static set of treaty provisions into a dynamic, evolving regulatory system capable of adapting to technological change.

> ■ **The Chicago Convention: Key Achievements**
>
> Reaffirmed complete and exclusive airspace sovereignty (Article 1).
>
> Established ICAO as a permanent global aviation governance institution.
>
> Distinguished between scheduled and non-scheduled international air services.
>
> Created the framework for technical Standards and Recommended Practices (SARPs).
>
> Adopted the Five Freedoms of the Air as a separate agreement (International Air Transport Agreement).
>
> As of 2025, 193 states are parties to the Chicago Convention—virtually universal membership.

The Convention also distinguished clearly between scheduled and non-scheduled international air services, granting states greater discretion over the former. This distinction reflected a pragmatic balance between the commercial interests of airlines and the sovereign prerogatives of states. A separate instrument, the International Air Transport Agreement (also known as the "Five Freedoms Agreement"), enumerated specific traffic rights, though it was adopted by fewer states than the Convention itself.

The Five Freedoms of the Air—the right to fly over foreign territory without landing; the right to land for technical purposes; the right to carry traffic from the home state to another state; the right to carry traffic from another state back to the home state; and the right to carry traffic between two foreign states—became the vocabulary of international aviation commerce. Additional "freedoms" were later articulated in practice, extending to cabotage and beyond, though these remained far more controversial and were rarely granted.

> ■ **The Five Freedoms of the Air**
>
> 1st Freedom: The right to fly over a foreign country without landing.
>
> 2nd Freedom: The right to make a technical stop (e.g., refueling) in a foreign country.
>
> 3rd Freedom: The right to carry passengers/cargo from the home country to a foreign country.
>
> 4th Freedom: The right to carry passengers/cargo from a foreign country to the home country.
>
> 5th Freedom: The right to carry passengers/cargo between two foreign countries, on a route originating in the home country.
>
> These "freedoms" are not automatic rights but must be negotiated through bilateral or multilateral agreements—a process that reinforces the sovereignty principle.

The Chicago Convention's enduring influence lies in its successful combination of legal principle and institutional innovation. It acknowledged that absolute sovereignty, standing alone, would produce paralysis; yet it refused to compromise the principle itself. Instead, it created mechanisms through which sovereignty could be exercised cooperatively, enabling global connectivity while preserving national control. This achievement—the institutionalization of sovereignty-based air governance—remains the foundation of international air law eight decades later.

***

Part IV

Sputnik, the Legal Rupture, and the Birth of Space Law

The launch of Sputnik 1 on 4 October 1957 marked a moment of profound technological achievement—and an equally profound legal rupture. For the first time in human history, an artificial object entered orbit around the Earth, traversing the skies above multiple sovereign states at an altitude of approximately 230 kilometers, circling the globe every 96 minutes. The tiny satellite, weighing just 83.6 kilograms, emitted a simple radio signal—a steady beep that was heard by radio operators around the world. Its significance, however, was anything but simple.

Under the sovereignty-based framework of air law that had been painstakingly constructed over the preceding four decades, Sputnik should have triggered immediate and vehement objections. If sovereignty extended indefinitely upward—as the Paris and Chicago Conventions implied without specifying an upper limit—then the satellite's passage over national territories constituted repeated, unauthorized violations of sovereign airspace. Every ninety-six minutes, Sputnik traversed the airspace of dozens of states, none of which had granted permission for overflight.

> ■ **The Legal Significance of Silence**
>
> No state protested Sputnik's overflight of its territory. This absence of objection was not an oversight or a failure of legal vigilance—it was legally decisive. In international law, consistent state practice accompanied by a sense of legal obligation (opinio juris) creates customary international law. The universal acceptance of satellite overflight established, virtually overnight, the principle that outer space lay beyond the reach of territorial sovereignty.

The silence was not accidental. It reflected a calculated convergence of interests among both superpowers and non-spacefaring states. The United States, despite being caught off guard by the Soviet achievement, recognized that objecting to satellite overflight would undermine its own ambitious plans for reconnaissance satellites—plans that would soon produce the Corona program, providing invaluable intelligence on Soviet military capabilities. The Soviet Union, for its part, had no interest in establishing a precedent that would restrict its future space activities. Non-spacefaring states, lacking the capability either to launch or to intercept satellites, had little practical basis for objection.

This convergence produced a rare moment of tacit consensus in Cold War international relations. Both superpowers effectively agreed, without formal negotiation, that the legal regime governing airspace would not be extended into outer space. This agreement was all the more remarkable for being implicit—expressed not through diplomatic notes or treaty provisions, but through the simple absence of protest. State practice, once again, preceded formal legal codification.

Figure 9: Sputnik 1 – The First Artificial Earth Satellite, 1957

Source: NASA (Public Domain).

The Impossibility of Extending Sovereignty

The practical reasons for this legal accommodation were compelling. Satellites in orbit travel at velocities of approximately 28,000 kilometers per hour. They cannot hover, cannot change course on demand, and cannot request permission from each state whose territory they overfly. Their orbital paths are determined by physics—by altitude, inclination, and gravitational mechanics—not by political boundaries. Any attempt to subject orbital flight to territorial authorization would have fractured orbit into a patchwork of national permissions, rendering satellite operations impossible and halting space exploration before it had truly begun.

Moreover, the concept of sovereignty itself depended on the capacity for control. A state asserts sovereignty over its airspace because it possesses the means to monitor, intercept, and regulate activities within that space. Aircraft can be tracked by radar, contacted by radio, intercepted by military aircraft, and forced to land. In 1957, no state possessed the capability to track satellites with precision, communicate with them reliably, or interfere with their operation. Sovereignty without the capacity for control was a legal fiction—and states, however reluctantly, recognized this.

From Practice to Principle: COPUOS and the 1963 Declaration

In the years following Sputnik, the United Nations became the central forum for articulating the emerging legal principles of outer space. In 1958, the UN General Assembly established an ad hoc committee to study the peaceful uses of outer space. In 1959, this was converted into the permanent Committee on the Peaceful Uses of Outer Space (COPUOS), which remains the principal international body for space governance to this day.

Early debates within COPUOS reflected deep ideological divisions between the Western and Soviet blocs. Yet they also revealed shared concerns that transcended Cold War rivalries: the fear of militarization, the desire for stability, and the recognition that space activities required some form of international coordination. Despite these divisions, COPUOS achieved a remarkable degree of consensus on foundational principles.

The Committee's working methods merit attention because they would define space governance for decades. COPUOS adopted the practice of consensus decision-making—no vote is taken; decisions are reached only when all member states agree or at least do not object. This practice was born of necessity: in a bipolar world, any regime that could be imposed by majority vote would lack legitimacy with the losing side. Consensus ensured that whatever norms emerged would carry the weight of universal—or at least broad—acceptance. This practice continues to this day, conferring both strength (legitimacy) and weakness (slowness, lowest-common-denominator outcomes) on space governance.

COPUOS was organized into two subcommittees that reflected the dual nature of space governance. The Scientific and Technical Subcommittee addressed questions of capability—what was technically possible, what hazards existed, and what standards were needed. The Legal Subcommittee addressed questions of authority—who could do what, under what conditions, and with what accountability. This institutional separation of technical and legal analysis would prove remarkably productive, enabling specialists in each domain to develop recommendations that could then be integrated into coherent governance frameworks.

A crucial milestone came on 13 December 1963, when the UN General Assembly unanimously adopted Resolution 1962 (XVIII)—the Declaration of Legal Principles Governing the Activities of States in the Exploration and Use of Outer Space. Although not legally binding, the Declaration articulated principles that would later be codified in treaty form: freedom of exploration and use, non-appropriation, the conduct of activities in accordance with international law, state responsibility for national activities, liability for damage, and international cooperation. These principles represented the normative core of a new legal regime.

The Outer Space Treaty of 1967

The culmination of these efforts was the Treaty on Principles Governing the Activities of States in the Exploration and Use of Outer Space, including the Moon and Other Celestial Bodies—known universally as the Outer Space Treaty—which entered into force on 10 October 1967. Negotiated against the backdrop of the space race and the Vietnam War, the Treaty represented one of the most significant achievements of Cold War diplomacy.

> *"Outer space, including the Moon and other celestial bodies, is not subject to national appropriation by claim of sovereignty, by means of use or occupation, or by any other means."*
>
> – Outer Space Treaty, Article II, 1967

Article I declared that the exploration and use of outer space shall be carried out for the benefit and in the interests of all countries, irrespective of their degree of economic or scientific development, and shall be the province of all mankind. Article II—the Treaty's most consequential provision—prohibited national appropriation of outer space by any means. Article III required that space activities be conducted in accordance with international law, including the United Nations Charter. Article IV prohibited the placement of nuclear weapons or weapons of mass destruction in orbit and required that the Moon and other celestial bodies be used exclusively for peaceful purposes. Article VI imposed state responsibility for national space activities, and Article VII established liability for damage caused by space objects.

The Treaty was opened for signature on 27 January 1967 and entered into force on 10 October of the same year—a remarkably swift timeline reflecting the urgency felt by both superpowers. The United States, the Soviet Union, and the United Kingdom were among the first signatories. As of 2025, over 114 states have ratified the Treaty, and an additional 23 have signed but not ratified it, making it one of the most widely accepted instruments of international law governing any specific domain.

The speed of its adoption was itself a testament to the power of the foundational consensus that had developed since Sputnik. States that disagreed on virtually every other aspect of international relations found common ground in the recognition that outer space required a different legal framework than any domain previously governed by international law. The Treaty's brevity—just seventeen articles—reflects both the urgency of its creation and the deliberate strategy of establishing broad principles while leaving detailed implementation to subsequent instruments and evolving practice.

The Treaty's architects were acutely aware of the contrast with airspace sovereignty. Rather than asserting exclusive control, space law embraced functional openness. Outer space was framed as a domain accessible to all states, governed by shared principles rather than territorial claims. This approach reflected both idealism—in its vision of peaceful cooperation and shared benefit—and pragmatism—in its recognition that outer space could not be governed through fragmented sovereignty.

Importantly, the Outer Space Treaty did not abolish law in space; it reimagined it. States remained responsible for their nationals' activities in space, whether conducted by governmental agencies or private entities. They retained jurisdiction over objects and personnel launched into space under their authority. Law followed the flag rather than the territory. This jurisdictional model preserved accountability without imposing sovereignty over the physical domain of outer space itself—a conceptual innovation of remarkable elegance and practical importance.

The Outer Space Treaty's foundational principles were subsequently elaborated through four additional instruments: the Agreement on the Rescue of Astronauts (1968), which established obligations to assist astronauts in distress and return them to their launching state; the Convention on International Liability for Damage Caused by Space Objects (1972), which created a detailed liability framework; the Convention on Registration of Objects Launched into Outer Space (1976), which required states to maintain registries of space objects; and the Moon Agreement (1979), which attempted—with limited success—to establish a more detailed regime for celestial bodies. Together, these five instruments constitute the core corpus of international space law, providing the legal architecture within which all subsequent governance has developed.

Figure 10: Signing of the Outer Space Treaty, 1967

Source: United Nations (Public Domain).

The Legal Divergence: Air Law and Space Law Compared

The birth of space law thus marked a fundamental shift in international legal thinking. For the first time, humanity created a legal regime for a domain that no state could own, yet all could use. This achievement stands in stark contrast to the history of air law, where sovereignty emerged as the dominant—indeed, unchallenged—organizing principle.

> ■ **Air Law vs. Space Law: The Fundamental Divergence**
>
> Air Law: Sovereignty-based. Every state has complete and exclusive control over its airspace. Access requires consent.
>
> Space Law: Openness-based. Outer space is free for exploration and use by all states. No sovereignty claims permitted.
>
> Air Law: Territorial jurisdiction. Law applies to activities within defined airspace boundaries.
>
> Space Law: Flag-state jurisdiction. Law follows the state of registry, not the physical location of the activity.
>
> Air Law: Security-driven. The framework emerged in response to military threats from above.
>
> Space Law: Cooperation-driven. The framework emerged from a shared interest in preventing conflict in a new domain.

Together, air law and space law form a legal continuum, reflecting fundamentally different solutions to fundamentally different technological realities. Air law territorialized the sky because aircraft operated within the atmosphere, could be controlled and intercepted, and posed direct threats to the territory below. Space law de-territorialized orbit because satellites could not be controlled through traditional means, required continuous global transit, and served functions—communication, navigation, weather observation—that benefited all states.

This divergence was not merely doctrinal; it was architectural. Air law operates through a dense web of bilateral agreements layered atop a multilateral framework, with ICAO providing institutional coordination. Space law operates through a smaller number of multilateral treaties supported by an expanding body of soft law—guidelines, principles, and best practices—developed through COPUOS. Air law governs primarily through permission (states must authorize access to their airspace). Space law governs primarily through obligation (states must ensure their activities conform to shared principles).

The implications of this structural difference extend far beyond formal legal categories. They shape how disputes are resolved, how new technologies are regulated, how commercial interests are balanced against public goods, and how governance adapts to change. Understanding this divergence—its origins, its logic, and its consequences—is essential to navigating the increasingly complex landscape of twenty-first-century aerospace governance.

The Concept of the Global Commons

The legal status of outer space drew on a much older tradition: the concept of the global commons. Domains such as the high seas, Antarctica, and the deep seabed had long posed a common legal challenge—they lay beyond national territory yet were subject to human use. International law had developed frameworks for each, balancing access against conservation, freedom against responsibility.

The law of the sea provided a particularly instructive comparison. Hugo Grotius's mare liberum had established the principle that the seas, being incapable of permanent occupation, should remain open to all nations. Over time, this principle was refined through treaty and practice, resulting in the complex zonal system of the United Nations Convention on the Law of the Sea (UNCLOS), which balances coastal state rights with the freedom of navigation on the high seas.

Outer space inherited this conceptual lineage but adapted it to unique conditions. Unlike the seas, outer space lacks natural boundaries, is three-dimensional, and is inherently indivisible. A satellite in orbit traverses the "airspace" of every state beneath its orbital path. These characteristics strengthened the case for collective governance and weakened arguments for territorial control. The recognition of outer space as a domain beyond sovereignty reflected not idealism alone, but pragmatic legal realism: no state could effectively control outer space without the cooperation of others.

Peaceful Use as a Foundational Norm

The principle of peaceful use occupies a unique position in the architecture of air and space law. In air law, peaceful use coexists with military aviation under the umbrella of regulated sovereignty—military aircraft operate routinely within national and, by agreement, foreign airspace. In space law, peaceful use assumes a far more foundational role, serving as one of the normative pillars of the entire regime.

The origins of this principle lie in the post-war international legal thought of the 1940s and 1950s, shaped by the catastrophic consequences of unrestricted technological competition in two world wars. Outer space, emerging as a new domain at the height of Cold War tension, was deliberately framed as a domain where conflict must be constrained and competition channeled into peaceful pursuits. The Outer Space Treaty reflected this aspiration: Article IV prohibited weapons of mass destruction in orbit and demilitarized celestial bodies.

Peaceful use, however, does not prohibit all military activity in space. The prevailing interpretation treats "peaceful" as meaning "non-aggressive" rather than "non-military." Reconnaissance satellites, military communications, navigation, and early warning systems operate continuously in orbit without legal challenge. What the peaceful use principle establishes is not a ban on military presence, but a normative hierarchy—prioritizing stability, cooperation, and restraint over aggression and uncontrolled competition.

***

Chapter Summary

This chapter has traced the arc of aerospace law from its earliest origins in myth and philosophy to the creation of a comprehensive international legal regime for air and space. The journey encompasses millennia of human aspiration, centuries of scientific progress, decades of legal debate, and the transformative impact of two world wars and a space race that reshaped the international order.

The central narrative is one of divergence. Humanity's first sustained entry into the sky—through balloons and aircraft—reinforced sovereignty, producing a legal regime built on territorial control, state consent, and exclusive jurisdiction. Humanity's second great ascent—into orbit and beyond—deliberately rejected sovereignty, producing a legal regime built on openness, shared access, and collective responsibility. This divergence was not accidental; it was the product of conscious legal choice, shaped by the distinctive characteristics of each domain and the security realities of each era.

> ■ **The Central Thesis**
>
> The story of international air and space law begins not with governments or conventions, but with a deeper transformation: the moment the sky ceased to be unreachable and became a space of human action. From that moment forward, every advance in capability has produced a corresponding legal response—first extending sovereignty upward, then consciously abandoning it at the threshold of outer space.

Looking Ahead: The Foundations and Their Legacy

The foundational choices examined in this chapter—sovereignty for airspace, openness for outer space—were not inevitable. They were the product of specific historical circumstances, technological realities, and political calculations. Different circumstances might have produced different outcomes. Had the Soviet Union launched Sputnik during a period of acute military tension, states might have reacted with protests rather than silence, and the legal status of outer space might look very different today. Had commercial aviation developed without the catalyst of two world wars, airspace sovereignty might have taken a more permissive form.

Understanding the contingency of these choices is essential for appreciating the challenges that lie ahead. The legal frameworks established in the mid-twentieth century were designed for a world of two spacefaring superpowers, limited commercial aviation, and no significant private space activity. That world no longer exists. Today, over eighty nations operate satellites. Private companies launch rockets, build space stations, and plan missions to the Moon and Mars. Thousands of satellites form mega-constellations in low Earth orbit. Hypersonic vehicles blur the boundary between air and space. Artificial intelligence manages increasingly autonomous space operations.

Each of these developments tests the foundations laid in this chapter. Whether those foundations prove adequate—or whether they must be reimagined for a new era—is the question that animates the remainder of this book.

One pattern, however, is clear from the historical record examined in this chapter. At every critical juncture—the first balloon flights, the advent of powered aviation, the militarization of airspace, the launch of Sputnik—the international community has demonstrated a capacity for legal innovation that, while imperfect and often delayed, has ultimately produced governance frameworks capable of managing new domains. This capacity for adaptation is perhaps the most important legacy of the foundational era examined here. It suggests that even as the challenges grow more complex, the tradition of creative legal response established in the twentieth century provides a foundation—if not a guarantee—for the governance challenges of the twenty-first.

The chapters that follow will explore these challenges in detail, examining how the foundational principles of air and space law are being tested, adapted, and in some cases fundamentally questioned by the realities of contemporary space activity. The story of aerospace law is far from complete; indeed, its most consequential chapters may yet be unwritten.

The legal choices made in the wake of Sputnik continue to define humanity's relationship with the cosmos. They determine who may access space, under what conditions, with what responsibilities, and subject to whose oversight. As the chapters that follow will demonstrate, the foundational principles established in this era—non-appropriation, state responsibility, peaceful use, and international cooperation—remain the architecture upon which all subsequent space governance has been built. Whether that architecture can sustain the weight of twenty-first-century ambitions—commercialization, resource extraction, military competition, and human settlement—is the defining question of contemporary space law.

The answer, as with every previous chapter in the history of aerospace law, will depend not merely on the evolution of technology, but on the choices that humanity makes about how to govern its ascent.

***

End of Chapter 1

Chapter 2

AIRSPACE, SOVEREIGNTY, AND THE LIMITS OF THE SKY

From Roman property maxims to the Chicago Convention, the principle of airspace sovereignty was forged through centuries of legal thought, technological disruption, and the crucible of two world wars. This chapter traces how the sky became sovereign territory—and where that sovereignty reaches its limits.

Part 1

Early Theories of Airspace and the Rise of Sovereignty

Before airspace became a defined legal concept, it existed only as an implicit extension of land. For centuries, legal systems were built on horizontal notions of territory, boundaries, and jurisdiction. Land could be measured, borders demarcated, and seas divided into zones of control or freedom. Vertical space, by contrast, remained largely irrelevant to law so long as human activity was confined to the Earth's surface. The emergence of flight forced jurists and states alike to confront a question that had long been ignored: does sovereignty extend upward, and if so, how far?

The question was not merely theoretical. It touched the very foundations of statehood. Territory, population, and government are the constitutive elements of a state under international law. Territory had always been understood horizontally—as the surface area within recognized borders. The notion that territory might also extend vertically was intuitive but, until flight became possible, practically irrelevant. The moment humans entered the sky, the vertical dimension of sovereignty demanded legal attention.

The Roman Maxim and Its Legacy

Early legal thought drew heavily from Roman law, particularly the maxim cuius est solum, eius est usque ad coelum et ad inferos—"he who owns the land owns it up to the heavens and down to the depths." This principle, attributed to the medieval glossator Accursius and later transmitted into English common law through the commentaries of Sir Edward Coke and Sir William Blackstone, reflected an assumption of absolute vertical ownership. The landowner's domain extended indefinitely upward and downward, mirroring the unchallenged dominion of surface possession.

For centuries, this doctrine posed little practical difficulty. No individual could occupy or exploit the airspace above land in any manner that interfered with surface ownership. The maxim served primarily as a logical extension of property concepts—a way of saying that ownership implied exclusivity in all directions. It was embedded in domestic property law rather than public international law, and it governed disputes between neighbors over overhanging branches, protruding structures, and encroaching roots rather than questions of interstate relations.

The first meaningful challenges arose not from aviation but from technological intrusions into vertical space that predated flight by decades. Tall structures cast shadows and obstructed views. Projectiles and artillery shells traversed airspace. Telegraph wires crisscrossed above private land. Mining operations extended property rights deep underground. Each of these developments prompted courts to consider whether the usque ad coelum maxim should be applied literally or functionally.

■ **Coke's Commentary on the Maxim**

Sir Edward Coke, in his First Institute of the Laws of England (1628), affirmed the cuius est solum doctrine as a fundamental principle of English property law: "For he that hath the land, hath it to the sky and to the centre of the earth." This formulation would prove remarkably durable, persisting in Anglo-American property law well into the twentieth century before being qualified by the demands of aviation.

Gradually, courts began to recognize that absolute vertical ownership was impractical in a modernizing world. A distinction emerged between airspace necessary for the ordinary use and enjoyment of land—a zone of practical dominion extending some distance above the surface—and the vast, unoccupied sky above it, which no individual could effectively possess or control. This distinction was pivotal: it introduced the idea that vertical rights were not unlimited but functional, tied to actual use rather than abstract principle.

This development in domestic property law, however, did not immediately translate into an international doctrine. The question of whether a state's sovereignty—as opposed to a landowner's property right—extended into the sky remained unaddressed. It would take the advent of practical flight, and the security anxieties it provoked, to elevate the question of airspace from property law to international relations.

Balloons, Borders, and the First Legal Gaps

The advent of balloon flight in the late eighteenth century forced the issue of vertical sovereignty onto the international stage. As described in Chapter 1, balloons drifted across borders without regard for political boundaries, often landing unpredictably in foreign territory. The implications were immediate: if airspace was sovereign, then a balloon crossing a border without permission constituted a violation; if airspace was free, then no permission was required. In the absence of treaties or established custom, states responded inconsistently, relying on diplomatic discretion rather than legal principle.

These early encounters revealed a fundamental tension that would characterize the entire development of air law: the conflict between the physical nature of the medium and the legal desire for control. The atmosphere is continuous, fluid, and borderless. Political boundaries, drawn on maps and enforced on the ground, do not manifest as visible barriers in the sky. Wind carries balloons and, later, aircraft across frontiers without regard for sovereignty. The challenge for law was to impose order on a medium that inherently resisted it.

Several tentative approaches emerged during the nineteenth century. Some jurists proposed that airspace should be treated as analogous to territorial waters—sovereign up to a certain distance, free beyond. Others argued for complete freedom, on the grounds that the air, like the high seas, could not be permanently occupied. Still others insisted on absolute sovereignty, arguing that the security of the state demanded control over every cubic meter of air above its territory. None of these positions commanded consensus, and the question remained unresolved as the century drew to a close.

■ **Three Early Theories of Airspace**

1. Freedom of the Air: Airspace is analogous to the high seas—open to all, owned by none. Primary advocate: Paul Fauchille (France).
2. Zonal Sovereignty: States control lower airspace (like territorial waters); upper air is free. Proposed by various jurists in the early 1900s.
3. Absolute Sovereignty: Airspace is inseparable from territory below—complete state control extends upward indefinitely. Primary advocate: John Westlake (UK).

State practice ultimately resolved the debate decisively in favor of absolute sovereignty.

The Impact of Powered Flight

As aviation technology advanced from balloons to powered aircraft, the questions became impossible to ignore. Aircraft differed fundamentally from balloons in every legally relevant respect: they were controllable, navigable, and repeatable. A balloon flight was an event; a scheduled airline route was a system. This capability transformed flight from an occasional curiosity into a systematic mode of transportation, commerce, and surveillance, intensifying concerns over security and sovereignty to an unprecedented degree.

States increasingly viewed unauthorized overflight as a potential threat, particularly in an era of intensifying geopolitical rivalry and colonial expansion. The aerial capabilities that had seemed remarkable in 1903 became routine by 1912: aircraft crossed the English Channel, flew over the Alps, and demonstrated ranges that could bridge national borders with ease. Military planners quickly recognized that the airplane would transform warfare as decisively as the railroad and the telegraph had done in the nineteenth century—and perhaps more so.

From Property Law to Public International Law

A crucial but often overlooked transition occurred in the late nineteenth and early twentieth centuries: the elevation of airspace from a concept in domestic property law to a question of public international law. In property law, the vertical dimension concerned relations between private individuals—a landowner and a trespasser, a building owner and a neighbor. In international law, the vertical dimension concerned relations between states—the sovereign prerogatives of territorial control versus the aspirations of international navigation.

This transition was not seamless. Property law concepts, shaped by centuries of settled practice, did not translate easily into the international arena. The usque ad coelum maxim had governed disputes between individuals; adapting it to interstate relations required reconceiving the sky not merely as the space above privately owned land, but as the space above sovereign territory. This reconception was driven primarily by security concerns: the realization that aircraft could observe, photograph, and ultimately attack the territory below transformed airspace from a question of property into a question of survival.

The colonial dimension further complicated matters. European powers maintained vast colonial territories across Africa, Asia, and the Pacific. Airspace above these territories was claimed by the colonizing state, extending the sovereignty principle across continents. This had practical consequences for the development of early aviation routes, many of which followed colonial connections—British routes through Egypt, India, and Malaya; French routes through North and West Africa; Dutch routes through the East Indies. Colonial airspace sovereignty thus intertwined with broader questions of imperial power, making the freedom-versus-sovereignty debate not merely an abstract legal question but a matter of geopolitical strategy.

By the eve of the First World War, airspace was increasingly treated as an extension of territorial sovereignty, even in the absence of comprehensive international agreement. States enacted national legislation asserting control over aerial navigation, establishing prohibited zones around military installations, and requiring advance permission for foreign aircraft. The war itself would accelerate this trend dramatically, converting emerging norms into entrenched doctrine through the harsh logic of survival.

> ■ **State Practice Precedes Legal Certainty**
>
> The early theories of airspace reveal a fundamental characteristic of international law: sovereignty over airspace did not emerge because jurists agreed upon it; it emerged because states acted as though it existed. Law followed power, technology, and security imperatives—a pattern that would repeat throughout the history of aerospace governance.

***

Part II

Freedom of the Air vs. Territorial Control: The Great Legal Debate

As powered flight moved from experimental novelty to practical capability in the early twentieth century, international legal scholarship entered a period of intense debate over the proper legal status of airspace. This debate—often framed as freedom of the air versus territorial sovereignty—was not merely academic. It reflected deeper tensions between globalization and security, commerce and control, and technological optimism and geopolitical realism. The outcome of this debate would shape the structure of international air law for generations and establish precedents that continue to influence governance discussions today.

The Case for Freedom

Advocates of the freedom of the air drew their primary inspiration from maritime law, particularly the doctrine of mare liberum, which had long treated the high seas as a domain open to all states. The most prominent champion of this position was the French jurist Paul Fauchille, who devoted decades of scholarly work to developing a comprehensive legal framework for aerial navigation based on the principle of freedom.

Fauchille first presented his ideas to the Institut de Droit International in 1902, proposing that airspace, like the high seas, should be open to navigation by all states, subject only to limited regulatory powers exercised by the territorial state below. He argued that the atmosphere was, by its physical nature, incapable of permanent occupation or exclusive control. Just as no state could own the wind or the clouds, no state should be permitted to exclude others from the air above its territory.

In Fauchille's view, unrestricted aerial navigation would promote peace, economic integration, and scientific cooperation—benefits that far outweighed any security concerns.

> *"The air is free. States exercise over the atmospheric space above their territory only those rights necessary for their self-preservation."*
>
> – Paul Fauchille, address to the Institut de Droit International, 1910

The freedom-of-the-air position was also grounded in practical and economic considerations. Early aircraft had limited range and reliability, making long-distance flights difficult even without legal barriers. Imposing additional regulatory constraints—requiring permissions, designating corridors, establishing fees—seemed unnecessary and counterproductive at a stage when aviation was struggling to prove its commercial viability. Moreover, proponents argued that technological progress would soon render national control of airspace ineffective. Just as coastal fortifications had failed to prevent maritime navigation, anti-aircraft measures would eventually prove inadequate against advanced aircraft. Law, they argued, should anticipate this reality rather than resist it.

Fauchille was not alone in his advocacy. Other notable supporters of aerial freedom included the Belgian jurist Ernest Nys and several Scandinavian scholars who viewed the air as a natural commons essential for international communication. The freedom position also attracted support from commercial interests, particularly in nations with ambitious aviation industries that stood to benefit from unimpeded access to foreign markets.

The economic dimension of the debate deserves emphasis. By the early 1910s, entrepreneurs and engineers were already envisioning commercial air routes connecting major European cities. The Wrights' patents were being licensed across the continent. Manufacturers in France, Germany, and Britain were competing to build faster, more reliable aircraft. For these nascent industries, sovereignty-based restrictions threatened to impose costly delays, bureaucratic complications, and market fragmentation. An open sky meant open markets; a sovereign sky meant negotiation, permits, and potential exclusion.

Conversely, the sovereignty position had its own economic logic. States that controlled airspace access could extract commercial concessions: landing fees, traffic rights, reciprocal market access. Sovereignty gave smaller states leverage they would not otherwise possess—the ability to bargain for access on favorable terms. This dynamic would later become central to international aviation economics, as the bilateral air service agreement system that emerged after the Chicago Convention turned airspace access into a tradeable commodity.

The Case for Sovereignty

Opponents of the freedom position emphasized the qualitative differences between airspace and the high seas that made the maritime analogy fundamentally misleading. The most influential advocate of absolute airspace sovereignty was the British jurist John Westlake, whose arguments proved far more persuasive to governments than Fauchille's idealistic vision.

Westlake and his intellectual successors stressed several critical distinctions. First, the high seas lie beyond national territory; airspace lies directly above it. A ship on the high seas poses no immediate threat to a coastal state's heartland; an aircraft overhead can observe, photograph, and potentially attack the most sensitive installations. Second, maritime navigation is inherently slow, giving coastal states time to respond to threats; aerial navigation is fast and potentially undetectable, compressing response times to minutes or seconds. Third, the seas had been navigated for millennia under established customary law; aviation was entirely new, with no comparable body of practice to constrain it.

A fourth distinction, often overlooked but equally important, concerned the relationship between medium and territory. Ships navigate on the surface of the sea, a medium physically separate from the territory of any state. Aircraft, however, navigate through a medium—the atmosphere—that is physically continuous with, and inseparable from, the territory below. There is no gap between a state's land and the air above it; the air begins at the surface. This physical continuity made the analogy to the high seas seem not merely unconvincing but fundamentally inapposite. For sovereignty advocates, the air above a state's territory was as much a part of that territory as the soil beneath it.

The security argument was decisive. In an era of escalating geopolitical rivalry, governments were acutely sensitive to the vulnerability that unrestricted overflight would create. Reconnaissance flights during peacetime could reveal military dispositions, fortification plans, and industrial capabilities. In wartime, unrestricted access to airspace would give attackers an insurmountable advantage. For many states, particularly those with extensive land borders and concentrated industrial centers, freedom of the air was not merely undesirable—it was existentially threatening.

■ **Why the Maritime Analogy Failed**

Distance: Ships operate far from national heartlands; aircraft operate directly overhead.

Speed: Maritime approaches take hours or days; aerial intrusion takes minutes.

Observation: Ships cannot easily survey interior territory; aircraft provide comprehensive surveillance.

Attack capability: Naval bombardment is limited to coastal areas; aerial bombing reaches any target.

Historical practice: Freedom of the seas developed over centuries of customary law; aviation had no comparable tradition.

These differences convinced most states that airspace required a fundamentally different legal treatment.

The Institut de Droit International and Early Conferences

The Institut de Droit International considered the airspace question at multiple sessions between 1902 and 1911. These deliberations proved inconclusive, reflecting the fundamental division between French-led advocates of freedom and British-led proponents of sovereignty. The Institut's 1906 session in Ghent produced a draft resolution that attempted a compromise, recognizing state sovereignty over lower airspace while preserving freedom of transit at higher altitudes. However, this zonal approach satisfied neither side and was not adopted.

By 1910, the debate had expanded beyond academic circles to intergovernmental diplomacy. The Paris Conference of 1910 on aerial navigation brought together representatives of nineteen European states to discuss the regulation of international flight. The Conference revealed deep divisions: France, supported by several smaller states, advocated for substantial aerial freedom; Britain, Germany, and Russia insisted on comprehensive sovereignty. The Conference failed to produce a binding agreement, but its proceedings documented the intensity of the debate and the growing urgency of resolution.

Figure 11: Delegates at the Paris Convention for the Regulation of Aerial Navigation, 1919

Source: Public Domain.

The 1910 Conference is historically significant for another reason: it demonstrated the limitations of purely academic approaches to new legal challenges. Fauchille's carefully reasoned arguments, published in leading law journals and presented to learned societies, had little impact on the negotiating positions of governments whose primary concern was not jurisprudential elegance but national security. The gap between academic discourse and state practice—a recurring feature of international law—was particularly wide in the context of airspace, where the security implications of the wrong legal choice were potentially existential.

The failure of pre-war diplomatic efforts to resolve the airspace question had a paradoxical effect: it ensured that the resolution would be imposed by practice rather than negotiation. When states could not agree in conference rooms, they established their positions through unilateral action—enacting domestic legislation, establishing prohibited zones, and asserting control through military and regulatory measures. By the time the First World War broke out in 1914, the debate had been effectively settled on the ground, even if it remained open in legal theory.

Wartime Practice and the Death of Free Air

The First World War (1914–1918) delivered the decisive blow to the freedom-of-the-air position. The wartime experience demonstrated, beyond any theoretical argument, that airspace was a domain of vital strategic importance. Aircraft conducted reconnaissance, directed artillery fire, bombed cities, and fought each other in aerial combat. Airships targeted civilian populations in unprecedented campaigns of strategic terror. Control of the air above the battlefield—and above the homeland—became a matter of national survival.

Neutral states provided particularly compelling evidence for sovereignty. The Netherlands, Switzerland, Sweden, Denmark, and Norway all asserted comprehensive control over their airspace during the war, intercepting or forcing down aircraft that violated their neutrality. These actions were accepted by belligerents as legitimate exercises of sovereign authority, establishing powerful precedents for the post-war legal order.

The experience of neutral states was legally significant precisely because neutrality had been a well-established status in international law long before aviation. The Hague Conventions of 1907 (in particular Convention V on neutral powers in land warfare and Convention XIII on neutrality in naval warfare) had codified the rights and duties of neutral states. By asserting airspace control as an extension of their neutral status, states such as Switzerland and the Netherlands effectively incorporated the new dimension—vertical space—into the existing framework of sovereignty and neutrality. This integration occurred through practice rather than treaty, but it proved no less binding for that.

> ■ **Neutral Airspace in World War I**
>
> Switzerland's experience during the First World War was particularly instructive. Swiss military forces intercepted multiple belligerent aircraft that entered Swiss airspace, sometimes by force. These incidents were resolved through diplomatic channels, with belligerents generally acknowledging Switzerland's right to control its airspace. This practice contributed directly to the codification of airspace sovereignty in the 1919 Paris Convention.

After the war, the devastation caused by aerial bombing left no appetite for legal experiments that might weaken national defenses. Even states that had once supported freedom of the air—including France, whose jurist Fauchille had championed the position most eloquently—accepted that some form of sovereignty-based regime was unavoidable. The focus of legal discussion shifted accordingly: from whether sovereignty should exist to how it could be exercised without obstructing the civil aviation that all states now recognized as essential.

It is worth pausing to consider what was lost when freedom of the air was abandoned. The idealistic vision of an open sky—aircraft moving freely across borders as ships moved freely across seas—would have produced a fundamentally different international order. Commerce would have flowed more freely. Bilateral negotiations over traffic rights would have been unnecessary. The complex web of air service agreements that characterizes modern aviation governance would never have developed. Whether this alternative would have been better or worse is impossible to know; what is certain is that the choice for sovereignty, once made, proved irreversible.

The freedom-of-the-air ideal did not disappear entirely; it survived in attenuated form. Negotiated transit rights—the first and second freedoms of the air—preserved a measure of aerial access that could function within the sovereignty framework. Commercial agreements, initially bilateral and later supplemented by regional open-skies arrangements, created managed zones of freedom within the sovereign system. But these were concessions granted by sovereign states, not inherent rights. The distinction is fundamental: in air law, access is a privilege, not a liberty.

> ■ **The Enduring Legacy of the Sovereignty-Freedom Debate**
>
> The intellectual legacy of this debate extends far beyond aviation. It established a recurring pattern in international law: when new technologies threaten core security interests, states favor control over openness. This pattern would later be deliberately and consciously reversed when humanity ventured into outer space, where the extension of sovereignty was seen as more dangerous than its absence—a remarkable reversal examined in detail in Chapter 4.

> *"When new technologies threaten core security interests, states invariably favor control over openness. This pattern, established in the airspace debate, would later be deliberately and consciously reversed when humanity ventured into outer space."*
>
> – Observation on patterns in aerospace law

***

Part III

Codification and Consolidation: The Paris and Chicago Conventions

The intellectual and political debates of the early twentieth century found their decisive legal expression in a series of international agreements that transformed emerging practice into binding norms. Chief among these were the Paris Convention of 1919 and the Chicago Convention of 1944, which together codified the principle of airspace sovereignty and established the institutional foundations of modern international air law. These instruments did not merely resolve abstract disputes; they reflected the lived experience of war, technological transformation, and the practical demands of an increasingly interconnected world.

The Paris Convention of 1919

The Paris Convention Relating to the Regulation of Aerial Navigation, signed on 13 October 1919 as part of the broader Versailles settlement, represented the first comprehensive multilateral agreement on international aviation. Its significance lay less in technical detail—though its provisions on aircraft nationality, registration, and airworthiness were groundbreaking—than in its unambiguous articulation of the sovereignty principle.

Article 1 of the Convention declared: "The High Contracting Parties recognise that every Power has complete and exclusive sovereignty over the airspace above its territory." This formulation was deliberate, emphatic, and intended to be final. It resolved the long-standing debate between advocates of free air and proponents of sovereignty decisively and permanently in favor of the latter. The language "complete and exclusive" left no room for residual aerial freedom as a general principle of international law.

> *"The High Contracting Parties recognise that every Power has complete and exclusive sovereignty over the airspace above its territory."*
>
> – Paris Convention Relating to the Regulation of Aerial Navigation, Article 1, 1919

The choice of such emphatic language reflected the security environment of the immediate post-war period. The drafters had witnessed the devastating potential of airpower and were determined to place airspace under firm national control. At the same time, they recognized that absolute sovereignty, standing alone, would prevent international aviation entirely. Accordingly, the Convention included provisions for the recognition of foreign certificates, the granting of limited transit rights, and the establishment of international air navigation rules.

The Convention also created the International Commission for Air Navigation (ICAN), based in Paris, to oversee compliance and develop technical standards. ICAN represented the first permanent international institution dedicated to aviation governance—a prototype for the far more ambitious International Civil Aviation Organization that would succeed it. Through ICAN, states could coordinate regulatory requirements without surrendering sovereignty, establishing a pattern of institutionalized cooperation within a sovereignty-based framework.

ICAN's work, though often overlooked in historical accounts, laid essential groundwork for modern aviation governance. The Commission developed standardized rules of the air, established common approaches to aircraft marking and identification, and created early frameworks for accident investigation. It also revealed the challenges of governing a rapidly evolving technology through consensus: decisions required agreement among states with vastly different aviation capabilities, industrial interests, and security concerns. These institutional challenges would inform the design of ICAO two decades later.

Despite its innovations, the Paris Convention suffered from significant limitations. Its membership was incomplete: the United States, which was rapidly emerging as a leading aviation power, did not ratify the Convention, largely due to concerns about European domination of its institutional structure and the Convention's close association with the Versailles Treaty. Several Latin American states also remained outside the regime. The Soviet Union, for ideological and political reasons, maintained its own separate approach to aviation governance. As a result, the Paris system was pan-European rather than truly global.

The Ibero-American Convention and Regional Developments

The incomplete membership of the Paris Convention prompted parallel regional efforts. The most significant was the Ibero-American Convention on Aerial Navigation (Madrid Convention) of 1926, which applied the sovereignty principle to relations among Spanish- and Portuguese-speaking states. The Havana Convention on Commercial Aviation (1928), adopted under Pan-American auspices, similarly affirmed airspace sovereignty while establishing provisions for commercial air services in the Western Hemisphere.

These regional instruments demonstrated that the sovereignty principle had achieved near-universal acceptance, even among states that had not participated in the Paris negotiations. By the late 1920s, no significant state contested the proposition that airspace was subject to complete and exclusive national control. The debate over freedom versus sovereignty was definitively closed; the remaining questions concerned how sovereignty would be exercised and how international aviation would be facilitated within the sovereignty framework.

The regional approach also established a pattern that continues to shape aviation governance today. Regional organizations—including the European Civil Aviation Conference (ECAC), the African Civil Aviation Commission (AFCAC), the Latin American Civil Aviation Commission (LACAC), and the Arab Civil Aviation Organization (ACAO)—supplement the global ICAO framework with regional standards, procedures, and cooperative mechanisms. This layered architecture enables governance at multiple scales, accommodating both the universality of aviation and the diversity of national and regional circumstances.

The Interwar Transformation of Aviation

The period between the two world wars witnessed an extraordinary transformation in aviation capability and commercial significance. In 1919, aircraft were fragile, unreliable, and limited in range. By 1939, they were capable of transatlantic flight, could carry dozens of passengers in reasonable comfort, and operated on regular schedules linking major cities across multiple continents. Airlines such as Pan American, Imperial Airways, Air France, KLM, and Lufthansa built global networks that knit together distant economies and cultures.

This commercial expansion created enormous pressure for legal harmonization. Each airline route crossing an international border required bilateral negotiation: which aircraft could fly, how many passengers could be carried, what fares could be charged, and which airports could be used. The proliferation of bilateral air service agreements—each reflecting the bargaining power and specific interests of the parties—produced a complex, inconsistent, and often inequitable patchwork of rules. The need for a comprehensive multilateral framework became increasingly evident.

A parallel development of lasting significance was the Warsaw Convention of 1929 (formally the Convention for the Unification of Certain Rules Relating to International Carriage by Air). This instrument addressed airline liability to passengers for death, injury, and baggage loss during international flights. By establishing uniform liability rules, the Warsaw Convention created a measure of legal predictability essential for the growth of commercial aviation. Passengers and airlines alike could operate across borders with a shared understanding of their respective rights and obligations—a significant achievement in an era when national laws varied enormously.

The Warsaw system, modified through subsequent protocols and supplementary conventions (notably the Hague Protocol of 1955, the Guadalajara Convention of 1961, and eventually the Montreal Convention of 1999), demonstrated that sovereignty need not prevent harmonization. States retained sovereign control over their airspace while voluntarily adopting common standards for commercial operations within that airspace. This layered approach—sovereignty at the constitutional level, harmonization at the operational level—became a defining characteristic of international air law.

Year	**Development**	**Legal Significance**
1919	Paris Convention signed	First codification of airspace sovereignty
1926	Madrid Convention adopted	Extended sovereignty principle to Latin America
1928	Havana Convention	Affirmed sovereignty for Pan-American states
1929	Warsaw Convention	Established international airline liability framework
1938	ICAO precursor discussions	States recognize need for global aviation institution
1944	Chicago Convention signed	Created ICAO and modern air law framework
1947	ICAO becomes UN agency	Aviation governance integrated into UN system
1955	193 ICAO member states (by 2025)	Near-universal participation achieved

The Chicago Convention of 1944

The Second World War both devastated and transformed international aviation. Strategic bombing campaigns demonstrated the lethal potential of airpower with terrifying clarity. The Blitz, the firebombing of Dresden and Tokyo, and the atomic attacks on Hiroshima and Nagasaki left no doubt that airspace sovereignty was not merely a legal abstraction but a condition of survival. The Battle of Britain—in which the Royal Air Force defended British airspace against the Luftwaffe in the summer and autumn of 1940—became the defining symbol of airspace sovereignty in action: a nation's very existence depended on its ability to control the sky above it.

Yet the war also demonstrated aviation's extraordinary potential for connecting the world. The Allied air transport system—including operations over the Hump (the Himalayas) to supply China, the Berlin Airlift, and transatlantic ferry routes—showed that aircraft could move people and materials across oceans with unprecedented speed. The logistical infrastructure built during the war—airports, navigation systems, air traffic control procedures, meteorological services—would form the foundation of post-war civil aviation. Military necessity had created the physical and organizational infrastructure for the greatest expansion of international connectivity in human history.

Remarkably, even before the war had concluded, the United States convened the International Conference on Civil Aviation in Chicago, from 1 November to 7 December 1944. Fifty-four states participated in what would become one of the most consequential diplomatic conferences of the twentieth century. The resulting Convention on International Civil Aviation—universally known as the Chicago Convention—would become the foundational document of modern air law.

Article 1 of the Chicago Convention reaffirmed the sovereignty principle in language that echoed its Parisian predecessor: "The contracting States recognize that every State has complete and exclusive sovereignty over the airspace above its territory." The continuity was deliberate; the drafters intended to signal that the fundamental legal principle had survived the war unchanged, even as the institutional framework would be dramatically strengthened.

The Convention's transformative achievement was institutional. It established the International Civil Aviation Organization (ICAO) as a permanent specialized agency—initially with its own constitution and governing structure, and from 1947 as a specialized agency of the United Nations. ICAO was given an ambitious mandate: to develop international standards and recommended practices (SARPs) for aviation safety, navigation, security, efficiency, and environmental protection. Through ICAO, states could harmonize technical requirements, share safety information, and coordinate operational procedures—all while retaining sovereignty over their airspace.

■ ICAO: The Architecture of Global Aviation Governance

Assembly: All 193 member states participate; meets every three years to set policy.

Council: 36 elected states; serves as the executive and legislative body.

Standards and Recommended Practices (SARPs): Over 12,000 technical standards in 19 Annexes.

Annexes cover everything from personnel licensing (Annex 1) to environmental protection (Annex 16).

Compliance is monitored through the Universal Safety Oversight Audit Programme (USOAP).

ICAO's SARPs are not directly binding but are implemented through national legislation by member states.

The ICAO Annexes system deserves particular attention, as it represents one of the most effective mechanisms for international technical regulation ever devised. Each Annex addresses a specific aspect of aviation—from personnel licensing (Annex 1) and rules of the air (Annex 2) through aeronautical telecommunications (Annex 10) and aviation security (Annex 17) to environmental protection (Annex 16). Standards within these Annexes are technically binding on member states unless they file differences; Recommended Practices represent best practices that states are encouraged but not required to adopt. This layered approach enables harmonization without imposing uniformity, accommodating the different capabilities and circumstances of states at varying stages of aviation development.

The Convention also introduced critical distinctions that continue to shape international aviation governance. It differentiated between scheduled and non-scheduled international air services, granting states greater regulatory control over the former. Scheduled services—regular commercial flights between designated points—could only operate with the explicit permission of each state along the route. Non-scheduled services, such as charter flights, enjoyed somewhat greater flexibility, though states retained the right to impose conditions.

The contentious question of commercial traffic rights—the so-called "freedoms of the air"—proved too divisive for the main Convention. Instead, they were addressed in separate instruments: the International Air Services Transit Agreement (the "Two Freedoms Agreement") and the International Air Transport Agreement (the "Five Freedoms Agreement"). The Two Freedoms Agreement, which granted the right to overfly and make technical stops, achieved broad acceptance. The Five Freedoms Agreement, which included commercial traffic rights, was adopted by fewer states and eventually fell into disuse as bilateral air service agreements became the preferred mechanism for allocating commercial rights.

■ **The Five Freedoms of the Air**

1st Freedom: The right to fly over a foreign country without landing.

2nd Freedom: The right to make a technical stop (refueling) in a foreign country without embarking or disembarking passengers.

3rd Freedom: The right to carry passengers or cargo from the home country to a foreign country.

4th Freedom: The right to carry passengers or cargo from a foreign country back to the home country.

5th Freedom: The right to carry passengers or cargo between two foreign countries, on a route that originates or terminates in the home country.

Additional 'freedoms' (6th through 9th) were later articulated in practice but have no treaty basis. The allocation of traffic rights remains one of the most commercially significant aspects of international aviation governance.

The Chicago Conference itself was marked by intense negotiations between three competing visions. The United States, with the world's most powerful aviation industry emerging from wartime production, advocated for maximum liberalization—open skies with minimal regulatory constraints. Britain, whose pre-war aviation dominance had been eroded, favored a more regulated approach that would protect weaker airlines from American competition. A third group of states sought a fully internationalized system in which a single international authority would allocate routes and set fares. None of these positions prevailed entirely; the Chicago Convention was a compromise, preserving sovereignty while creating mechanisms for negotiated access.

This compromise had profound and lasting consequences. By placing commercial aviation within a bilateral negotiation framework, the Chicago system created a market for airspace access. States with strategically located territory—geographic gateways, transit corridors, refueling stops—could extract economic value from their position. States with powerful airlines could leverage their market strength. The result was a system that, while far from perfect, distributed benefits more broadly than either pure sovereignty or pure freedom would have achieved.

> ■ **The Chicago Convention's Enduring Legacy**
>
> The genius of the Chicago Convention lies in its combination of legal principle and institutional innovation. It preserved absolute sovereignty while creating mechanisms for cooperative exercise of that sovereignty. This formula—sovereignty in principle, cooperation in practice—has sustained international air law for eight decades and has proven remarkably adaptable to technological change, from propeller aircraft to supersonic jets to unmanned aerial systems.

***

Part IV

The Upper Limits of Sovereignty: Where Does Airspace End?

The principle of complete and exclusive sovereignty over airspace, as codified by the Paris and Chicago Conventions, appears deceptively simple. In practice, however, it rests on an unresolved and deeply complex question: how far upward does airspace extend? While air law presumes the existence of a vertical boundary to sovereignty, international law has never defined where airspace ends and another legal regime—the regime of outer space—begins. This ambiguity lies at the intersection of science, law, and politics, and it continues to shape the relationship between the two primary branches of aerospace governance.

The Scientific Challenge

From a scientific standpoint, the atmosphere does not terminate at a fixed altitude. Earth's atmosphere is a continuum of gases—nitrogen, oxygen, argon, carbon dioxide, and trace elements—that gradually thin with increasing altitude. The troposphere extends to approximately 12 kilometers, giving way to the stratosphere, which reaches about 50 kilometers. Above the stratosphere lie the mesosphere (to approximately 85 kilometers), the thermosphere (to approximately 600 kilometers), and the exosphere, which fades imperceptibly into interplanetary space over thousands of kilometers. There is no clear natural boundary—no wall, no visible transition, no abrupt change—that marks the end of the atmosphere and the beginning of outer space.

Aerodynamic flight becomes progressively more difficult as air density decreases, but there is no altitude at which flight becomes categorically impossible. Some experimental aircraft have flown at altitudes exceeding 100 kilometers, while satellites in low Earth orbit experience atmospheric drag at altitudes below 400 kilometers. The physical reality of a gradual transition complicates any attempt to draw a precise legal boundary. Unlike terrestrial borders, which can be surveyed, mapped, and fenced, the vertical dimension resists demarcation.

The problem is further complicated by the fact that the boundary—if one were to be drawn—is not fixed. The atmosphere expands and contracts in response to solar activity. During periods of high solar activity, increased ultraviolet radiation heats the upper atmosphere, causing it to expand upward. During solar minima, the atmosphere contracts. This means that any altitude-based boundary would correspond to different physical conditions depending on the eleven-year solar cycle—a complication that no proposed delimitation theory has adequately addressed.

Temperature, too, behaves counterintuitively. While the troposphere grows colder with altitude, the stratosphere warms (due to ozone absorption of ultraviolet radiation), the mesosphere cools again, and the thermosphere becomes extremely hot (temperatures can exceed 2,000 degrees Celsius, though the air is so thin that these temperatures have little thermal effect). These complex physical transitions underscore the artificiality of any single-altitude boundary.

■ Atmospheric Layers and the Challenge of Delimitation

Troposphere (0–12 km): Where weather occurs and conventional aircraft operate.

Stratosphere (12–50 km): Home to the ozone layer; reached by high-altitude balloons and reconnaissance aircraft.

Mesosphere (50–85 km): Meteors burn up here; too thin for aircraft, too dense for sustained orbit.

Thermosphere (85–600 km): International Space Station orbits here (400 km); atmospheric drag still present.

Exosphere (600–10,000 km): Gradual transition to interplanetary space.

No natural "edge" exists. The atmosphere simply fades away—a continuum, not a boundary.

Competing Legal Theories of Delimitation

Legal scholars have proposed numerous theories for delimiting airspace from outer space, each reflecting different priorities and different conceptions of what law should achieve. These theories fall into three broad categories: spatial (altitude-based), functional (activity-based), and hybrid approaches. None has achieved consensus, and the resulting ambiguity remains one of the most distinctive features of international aerospace law.

Spatial theories propose that outer space begins at a fixed altitude above the Earth's surface. Proponents argue that a defined boundary would provide legal certainty, enabling states, regulators, and operators to know with confidence which legal regime governs any given activity. Proposals have varied widely, from 80 kilometers (the altitude occasionally used by the United States to award astronaut wings) to 100 kilometers (the Kármán line, widely cited but not legally adopted) to 110 or 120 kilometers.

The appeal of spatial delimitation is clarity. With a fixed boundary, questions of jurisdiction, liability, and regulatory competence would be resolved by altitude alone. Aircraft operating below the line would be subject to air law and national sovereignty; spacecraft operating above it would be governed by space law and the freedom of outer space. Insurance, licensing, and dispute resolution could be tailored accordingly.

However, spatial theories face formidable objections. First, any chosen altitude would be inherently arbitrary, disconnected from the gradual physical transition between atmosphere and space. Second, a fixed boundary would become obsolete as technology evolves. Vehicles that routinely cross the boundary—spaceplanes, reusable launch vehicles, hypersonic aircraft—would transition between legal regimes during a single flight, creating jurisdictional complexity rather than simplicity. Third, and most importantly from a political perspective, spatial delimitation would permanently constrain sovereignty. States would be required to accept that their jurisdiction extends no higher than the agreed altitude, regardless of future capabilities. This prospect has proven unacceptable to most governments.

Figure 12: Manfred Lachs – Judge and President of the International Court of Justice

Source: Public Domain.

Functional theories take a different approach, focusing on the nature and purpose of the activity rather than the altitude at which it occurs. Under this view, aviation activities are governed by air law and space activities are governed by space law, regardless of where they take place.

The key question is not "how high?" but "what kind of activity?" This approach avoids arbitrary altitude thresholds and accommodates technological evolution. It also reflects how states have actually behaved in practice: satellite operations have been treated as space activities from the outset, even during launch and re-entry phases that occur within atmospheric space.

> ■ **The Kármán Line**
>
> Named after Hungarian-American aerospace engineer Theodore von Kármán (1881–1963), the Kármán line at approximately 100 km represents the altitude at which an aircraft would need to travel at orbital velocity to generate sufficient aerodynamic lift. The Fédération Aéronautique Internationale (FAI) recognizes 100 km as the boundary of space for record-keeping purposes, but this has no binding legal status in international law.

Functional theories, however, introduce their own forms of uncertainty. Determining the "nature" of an activity can be contentious, especially for dual-use technologies. A single vehicle may perform multiple functions during different phases of flight—launching as a rocket, operating as a satellite, and re-entering as a glider. Classification becomes a matter of interpretation rather than measurement, introducing subjectivity into what ideally should be an objective determination.

Moreover, the functional approach can produce counterintuitive results. Under strict functional classification, a military reconnaissance satellite operating at 200 kilometers would be governed by space law (freedom of access), while a research balloon at 40 kilometers would be governed by air law (sovereignty). Yet the satellite conducts surveillance activities identical in purpose to those that prompted sovereignty claims in the first place, while the balloon poses no security threat whatsoever. The functional approach thus creates a paradox in which the most security-sensitive activities escape sovereignty precisely because of the altitude at which they occur—an outcome that many states find unsatisfactory.

Hybrid approaches attempt to combine elements of spatial and functional theories, typically by envisioning a transitional zone—sometimes called "near space" or the "mesosphere gap"—where legal classification depends on both altitude and activity. Within this zone, specific rules might apply, reflecting shared jurisdiction or cooperative oversight between air and space regulatory authorities. While intellectually attractive, hybrid approaches multiply rather than reduce complexity, require agreement on zone boundaries that is itself contentious, and have attracted limited political support.

The Politics of Non-Decision

Despite decades of deliberation—particularly within the Legal Subcommittee of COPUOS, which has had delimitation on its agenda since the 1960s—no theory of delimitation has been formally adopted in international law. This outcome reflects not indecision but a deliberate political choice. States have consistently preferred ambiguity to the risks of premature precision.

The reasons are both strategic and practical. Spacefaring states fear that a defined boundary would constrain their operational flexibility, potentially subjecting certain activities to unwanted regulatory oversight. Non-spacefaring states worry that delimitation could be used to legitimize activities they cannot monitor or control. Both groups recognize that the current model—in which the absence of a boundary has not prevented the orderly conduct of air and space activities—functions adequately for the time being.

The U-2 Incident and the Altitude Question

The political sensitivity of the delimitation question was dramatically illustrated by the U-2 incident of 1 May 1960. An American U-2 reconnaissance aircraft, piloted by Francis Gary Powers, was shot down over Soviet territory while flying at an altitude of approximately 21 kilometers. The Soviet Union protested the flight as a violation of its airspace sovereignty; the United States could not deny that the aircraft had been operating above Soviet territory, regardless of its extreme altitude.

The incident revealed a critical gap in the legal framework. The U-2 was clearly an aircraft operating within the atmosphere, subject to air law and sovereignty principles. But what if a future vehicle operated at 80, 100, or 120 kilometers? Would the same sovereignty claims apply? The U-2 shootdown reinforced the association between sovereignty and security at extreme altitudes, making states even more reluctant to commit to a boundary that might compromise their defensive capabilities or their ability to protest foreign intrusions.

The incident also demonstrated the practical difficulties of enforcement at extreme altitude. The Soviet Union required its most advanced surface-to-air missile system—the S-75 Dvina—to reach the U-2's operating altitude. At higher altitudes, enforcement would become progressively more difficult, eventually becoming impossible with any foreseeable technology. This created a paradox at the heart of the sovereignty concept: a state's sovereignty extended upward to an undefined height, but its ability to enforce that sovereignty diminished rapidly with altitude. Sovereignty without enforcement was, in practical terms, theoretical rather than operational.

■ **The U-2 Incident: Key Facts**

Date: 1 May 1960. Pilot: Francis Gary Powers (CIA).

Operating altitude: approximately 21,000 meters (70,000 feet).

Shot down by Soviet S-75 Dvina surface-to-air missile over Sverdlovsk.

Powers survived and was captured; exchanged for Soviet spy Rudolf Abel in February 1962.

The incident derailed a planned Paris summit between Eisenhower and Khrushchev.

Legal significance: Confirmed that sovereignty applies at extreme atmospheric altitudes; raised unresolved questions about the upper limit of sovereign airspace.

Figure 13: The U-2 Incident, 1960

Source: Public Domain.

> *"The refusal to define where outer space begins is not a failure of law but a deliberate strategy of constructive ambiguity—preserving flexibility while avoiding sovereignty disputes that could destabilize space governance."*
>
> – On the pragmatics of non-delimitation

This constructive ambiguity has been remarkably effective. Satellite operations proceed without jurisdictional challenge. Aircraft operate within national airspace under well-established rules. Launch and re-entry phases are managed through national licensing regimes and coordinated through ICAO's NOTAM (Notice to Air Missions) system, which temporarily closes airspace corridors to protect both aviation and launch operations. The boundary question arises only at the margins—and at the margins, pragmatic solutions have thus far prevailed.

The COPUOS Legal Subcommittee continues to include delimitation as an agenda item, and several states—notably Russia, which proposed a formal boundary at 100 kilometers in the 1970s—have periodically renewed calls for resolution. However, the agenda item has remained largely dormant, with discussions reflecting the same positions that have been held for decades. The absence of any operational crisis attributable to the lack of delimitation reduces the urgency that might otherwise drive resolution. As one commentator has observed, the delimitation question is a problem in search of a crisis—and so long as the crisis does not materialize, the problem will remain unresolved.

Emerging Technologies and the Erosion of Ambiguity

However, technological developments are now testing the durability of this arrangement with increasing urgency. Several categories of emerging technology operate precisely in the transitional zone that constructive ambiguity was designed to manage, and their proliferation is making the boundary question harder to avoid.

High-altitude pseudo-satellites (HAPS)—unmanned platforms that loiter at altitudes of 18–25 kilometers for extended periods—provide surveillance, communications, and internet connectivity services that overlap with satellite functions. They operate within airspace technically subject to sovereignty but perform roles traditionally associated with space-based systems. Their regulatory classification varies by jurisdiction, creating inconsistency.

Suborbital vehicles designed for space tourism—such as those operated by Blue Origin and Virgin Galactic—ascend beyond conventional airspace, briefly enter conditions associated with outer space (microgravity, views of Earth's curvature), and return to Earth without completing an orbit. Are these flights governed by air law, space law, or something else entirely? Different states have adopted different answers.

Hypersonic vehicles capable of speeds exceeding Mach 5 operate at extreme altitudes and traverse vast distances in minutes. Their military applications—rapid global strike, intelligence collection, missile defense evasion—raise acute sovereignty and security concerns. If a hypersonic vehicle operates at 80 kilometers altitude, is it in sovereign airspace? Can a state intercept or engage it without violating international law?

Reusable launch vehicles—most notably SpaceX's Starship—launch from terrestrial spaceports, ascend through controlled airspace, enter orbit, and return to Earth, crossing potential jurisdictional boundaries multiple times in a single flight. Regulatory frameworks must somehow accommodate these transitions without imposing impossible compliance burdens on operators or creating gaps in oversight.

National regulatory approaches to these technologies vary significantly, revealing the lack of international consensus. The United States treats commercial space activities—including suborbital flights—under a separate licensing regime administered by the Federal Aviation Administration's Office of Commercial Space Transportation (AST). This regime applies regardless of the altitude reached, focusing on the nature and purpose of the activity. Australia similarly licenses space activities under its Space (Launches and Returns) Act. In contrast, European approaches tend to distinguish more sharply between aviation (regulated by national civil aviation authorities and EASA) and space activities (regulated by national space agencies), creating potential gaps for vehicles that straddle both domains.

The United Arab Emirates offers an instructive example of a state navigating these challenges in real time. The UAE's Space Agency, established in 2014, operates alongside the General Civil Aviation Authority (GCAA), with responsibilities for different aspects of aerospace activity. As the UAE develops its space sector—including the Mars mission Hope, the Rashid lunar rovers, and plans for commercial space activities—the interaction between air law and space law frameworks will require ongoing attention and, likely, innovative regulatory solutions.

■ **Technologies Testing the Air–Space Boundary**

HAPS (High-Altitude Pseudo-Satellites): Stratospheric platforms performing satellite-like functions.

Suborbital Tourism: Vehicles briefly entering space conditions without achieving orbit.

Hypersonic Vehicles: Mach 5+ aircraft operating at extreme altitudes with military applications.

Spaceplanes: Vehicles transitioning between aerodynamic and orbital flight in a single mission.

Reusable Launch Vehicles: Systems crossing jurisdictional boundaries repeatedly.

Each of these technologies challenges the assumption that air and space can be governed as separate domains.

Security, Sovereignty, and the Future

Security considerations further complicate the delimitation question. States remain deeply invested in airspace control as a matter of national defense, and any attempt to limit sovereignty vertically is viewed with suspicion, particularly in an era of hypersonic weapons, orbital reconnaissance, and potential space-to-ground strike capabilities. The collapse of the Open Skies Treaty—from which the United States withdrew in 2020 and Russia followed in 2021—demonstrated how sensitive airspace access remains even among the most capable states, and how quickly cooperative frameworks can unravel when trust erodes.

The development of anti-satellite (ASAT) weapons further blurs the line between airspace defense and space operations. Ground-based ASAT systems launch projectiles through sovereign airspace to strike targets in orbit; co-orbital ASAT systems maneuver from space toward their targets. These capabilities challenge the assumption that air and space operations can be neatly separated into distinct legal domains with distinct rules. A defensive response to an approaching object at 100 kilometers altitude might simultaneously involve air defense systems (governed by sovereignty) and space assets (governed by freedom of access)—creating jurisdictional confusion with potentially catastrophic consequences.

Conversely, extending sovereignty too far upward risks encroaching upon the freedom of outer space, undermining the legal foundations of satellite operations that the entire world depends upon. Global communications, navigation, weather forecasting, financial systems, and military command and control all rely on satellites operating in orbits that transit above every state on Earth. Asserting territorial claims over these orbits would be not merely legally controversial but practically catastrophic.

■ The Pragmatic Coexistence Model

In practice, international law has adopted a pragmatic coexistence model: air law governs activities relying on aerodynamic flight within controlled airspace; space law governs orbital and deep-space activities requiring freedom from territorial interference. Between these domains lies a transitional zone where legal classification depends on context—the nature of the activity, the characteristics of the vehicle, and the intent of the operator—rather than altitude alone.

This model has worked reasonably well, largely because state practice has avoided pushing its limits. Yet as technology continues to blur the line between air and space, and as commercial and military interests intensify in the transitional zone, pressure will mount for greater clarity. Whether this clarity will take the form of formal delimitation, new hybrid regulatory regimes, activity-based licensing frameworks, or continued reliance on functional interpretation remains one of the most important open questions in international aerospace governance.

***

Chapter Summary

Chapter 2 has traced the development of airspace sovereignty from its intellectual origins in Roman property law through its codification in the Paris and Chicago Conventions to its current confrontation with the limits of the atmosphere itself. The narrative reveals a legal regime forged in the crucible of war, shaped by the competing imperatives of security and commerce, and sustained by institutional innovation of remarkable durability.

The sovereignty principle that emerged from this process is among the most firmly established norms in all of international law. No state disputes it. No treaty qualifies it. No court has overturned it. For eighty years, it has provided the legal foundation for a global aviation system that, as of 2025, carries over 4.7 billion passengers annually and generates over three trillion dollars in economic activity. ICAO's 193 member states represent near-universal participation in a governance system that has proven capable of adapting to technological change while preserving its foundational legal principle.

The journey from the Roman maxim to the Chicago Convention illustrates several enduring lessons for aerospace governance. First, law responds to technology, not the other way around; every significant legal development examined in this chapter was triggered by a technological capability that outran existing rules. Second, state practice creates law: the sovereignty principle was established through behavior before it was codified in treaties. Third, institutional innovation can reconcile apparently contradictory imperatives: ICAO demonstrated that absolute sovereignty and international cooperation can coexist, provided that adequate institutional mechanisms exist to manage the tension between them. Finally, the bilateral model that emerged from the Chicago system—exemplified by the 1946 Bermuda Agreement between the United States and the United Kingdom, which became the template for thousands of subsequent bilateral air service agreements—demonstrated that sovereignty could be a platform for managed liberalization rather than an obstacle to international connectivity.

Yet the chapter has also shown how this principle reaches its limits at the edge of the atmosphere. Sovereignty presupposes control; control presupposes a defined domain. Where the atmosphere fades into space, the domain of sovereignty becomes uncertain, and the model that served aviation so well begins to strain under the weight of technologies that were unimaginable when the Chicago Convention was drafted in a wartime conference room in 1944.

The unresolved question of where airspace ends and outer space begins is not merely a technicality. It marks the boundary between two fundamentally different legal philosophies—one built on territorial control, the other on shared access. As emerging technologies—HAPS, suborbital vehicles, hypersonic weapons, spaceplanes—increasingly operate in the transitional zone between these philosophies, the pressure for resolution will grow. The constructive ambiguity that has served the international community for six decades may not survive the technological disruptions of the twenty-first century.

One final observation is warranted. Since the 1990s, a movement toward aviation liberalization—embodied in open skies agreements, regional single aviation markets, and the increasing role of low-cost carriers—has progressively relaxed the constraints that sovereignty once imposed on commercial aviation. The European Union's internal aviation market, created through a series of liberalization packages in the 1990s, effectively established freedom of the air among member states for commercial purposes. Similar arrangements have emerged in ASEAN, Africa, and the Gulf region. These developments do not abolish sovereignty; they demonstrate that sovereignty can be exercised permissively as well as restrictively. The sovereign choice to open markets is itself an exercise of sovereignty. This insight—that sovereignty enables openness as readily as it constrains it—provides a conceptual bridge between the air law tradition and the space law tradition examined in the chapters that follow.

Understanding how and why sovereignty became the organizing principle of air law is essential to understanding why it was deliberately rejected at the threshold of outer space. That rejection—and the domain it created—is the subject of Chapter 3, which examines the most fundamental question in aerospace governance: what, exactly, is outer space?

***

End of Chapter 2

Chapter 3

WHAT IS OUTER SPACE? SCIENCE, LAW, AND THE BOUNDARY PROBLEM

Where does the sky end and the cosmos begin? This deceptively simple question has resisted resolution for over sixty years, defying scientists, lawyers, and diplomats alike. This chapter examines why—and explores whether the answer even matters.

Part 1

Scientific Conceptions of Outer Space and the Problem of Definition

At first glance, the question "What is outer space?" appears deceptively simple. In everyday language, outer space is imagined as the vast, dark expanse beyond Earth's atmosphere—a realm of stars, planets, and cosmic emptiness. For scientists, however, and even more so for lawyers, this intuitive understanding quickly dissolves into complexity. The absence of a clear physical boundary between Earth's atmosphere and the void beyond lies at the heart of one of the most enduring and consequential problems in international aerospace law: the impossibility of defining outer space through purely scientific means.

From a physical perspective, Earth's atmosphere is not a discrete shell surrounding the planet like an eggshell encasing an egg. It is a continuum of gases—predominantly nitrogen and oxygen, with trace amounts of argon, carbon dioxide, water vapor, and other constituents—that gradually thin with increasing altitude. The troposphere, stratosphere, mesosphere, thermosphere, and exosphere merge imperceptibly into one another, each characterized by different temperature profiles, chemical compositions, and physical behaviors, but none separated from its neighbors by a clear dividing line. Even at altitudes exceeding several hundred kilometers, traces of atmospheric particles remain detectable, exerting measurable drag on satellites in low Earth orbit.

The Classical Legacy: Earth and the Heavens

Early astronomical and philosophical thought did little to clarify the issue—though it did, paradoxically, contribute to it. Classical cosmology, particularly the Aristotelian system that dominated Western thought for nearly two millennia, treated the heavens as a fundamentally different realm, governed by distinct physical laws. In Aristotle's universe, the sublunary world—everything below the Moon—was composed of the four classical elements (earth, water, air, fire) and subject to change, decay, and imperfection. The superlunary world—the realm of celestial bodies—was composed of a fifth element (aether or quintessence) and characterized by eternal, perfect, circular motion.

This sharp conceptual division between Earth and the celestial sphere persisted well into the early modern period, reinforcing the intuitive notion that space was "elsewhere"—a categorically different domain separated from the terrestrial world by a fundamental discontinuity. The theological overtones were powerful: the heavens were the abode of the divine, while the Earth was the province of the mortal. Crossing the boundary between them was, in this conceptual framework, not merely a physical challenge but a metaphysical impossibility.

Modern physics dismantled this distinction with revolutionary force. Copernicus removed the Earth from the center of the universe. Kepler demonstrated that planetary orbits were elliptical, not circular. Galileo observed imperfections on the Moon's surface, shattering the notion of celestial perfection. Newton's law of universal gravitation demonstrated that the same physical force governed the fall of an apple and the orbit of the Moon. There was no discontinuity, no boundary, no separate domain of celestial physics. The same laws operated everywhere—on the surface, in the atmosphere, and in the farthest reaches of the cosmos.

> *"The same physical laws govern motion both on Earth and beyond it. In demonstrating this unity, modern physics erased the conceptual boundary that had once separated the terrestrial from the celestial."*
>
> – On the legacy of Newtonian mechanics

For law, this scientific revolution created a paradox. The old cosmology had provided a clear, if mythological, boundary between Earth and the heavens. Modern science, by unifying terrestrial and celestial physics, removed that boundary entirely. In its place, science offered a continuum—a gradual transition from dense atmosphere to tenuous gas to effective vacuum—that resisted the categorical distinctions on which legal systems depend.

The philosophical implications were equally significant. If the same laws of physics governed both terrestrial and celestial motion, then there was no principled basis for treating the sky above a state's territory as fundamentally different from the land below it. The atmosphere was simply an extension of the physical environment, subject to the same forces and amenable to the same methods of investigation. This insight undermined the philosophical basis for any natural boundary between airspace and outer space. Whatever boundary might be drawn would be a human construction, not a discovery of nature.

The practical consequence was that law would have to do what science could not: impose order on a continuum. This is not unique to aerospace law—all legal boundaries are, to some extent, human constructions imposed on physical or social continua. The boundary between territorial waters and the high seas is a measured distance, not a natural feature. The age of majority is a legislative choice, not a biological threshold. What makes the air–space boundary distinctive is the absence of any consensus on where to draw the line and the profound consequences—for sovereignty, security, commerce, and human activity—that flow from the choice.

The Kármán Line: A Convenient Fiction

One of the most frequently cited scientific reference points for the beginning of outer space is the Kármán line, commonly placed at an altitude of approximately 100 kilometers above mean sea level. Named after the Hungarian-American aerospace engineer Theodore von Kármán (1881–1963), this line represents the altitude at which an aircraft would need to travel at orbital velocity to generate sufficient aerodynamic lift to support itself. Below this altitude, aerodynamic flight is theoretically possible; above it, only orbital mechanics can sustain an object in motion. The Kármán line thus marks, in engineering terms, the transition from aeronautics to astronautics.

The Fédération Aéronautique Internationale (FAI), the international body responsible for aeronautical and astronautical records, has adopted 100 kilometers as its definition of the boundary of space for record-keeping purposes. Under this convention, any flight exceeding 100 kilometers is classified as a spaceflight, and its occupants qualify as astronauts. Several national space agencies, including those of Australia and many European states, also use the 100-kilometer threshold.

■ The Kármán Line: Origin and Controversy

Theodore von Kármán calculated that at approximately 83.6 km, an aircraft would need to fly faster than orbital velocity to maintain aerodynamic lift.

The FAI rounded this figure to 100 km for administrative convenience.

The United States uses 80 km (50 miles) as its boundary for awarding astronaut wings.

NASA and the U.S. Air Force have historically applied the 80 km threshold.

Neither the 80 km nor 100 km boundary has any status in international law.

The discrepancy reflects institutional preference rather than scientific consensus.

Despite its widespread use, the Kármán line has no inherent legal authority. It is a functional approximation, not a natural boundary. Moreover, even its precise altitude is contested. Von Kármán's original calculation yielded a figure closer to 83 or 84 kilometers; the 100-kilometer figure is a rounded administrative convention. Some researchers have argued that the effective boundary of aerodynamic flight lies closer to 118 kilometers, while others have proposed values as low as 75 kilometers depending on the assumptions made about vehicle design and atmospheric conditions.

The United States has traditionally used a different threshold entirely. The U.S. Air Force and NASA have historically awarded astronaut wings to individuals who exceed an altitude of 50 miles (approximately 80 kilometers), reflecting an American institutional tradition that predates the FAI's adoption of the 100-kilometer standard. This discrepancy between American and international practice underscores the constructed nature of any chosen boundary and the influence of institutional culture on ostensibly scientific definitions.

The practical consequences of this discrepancy are not trivial. In 2018, the FAI announced that it was reviewing the 100-kilometer boundary in light of new research suggesting that the effective boundary of aerodynamic flight may lie closer to 80 kilometers—aligning with the American standard. The review, which has not yet produced a definitive conclusion, highlighted the sensitivity of the threshold question even among scientific and sporting organizations. If the FAI were to lower its boundary to 80 kilometers, it would retroactively reclassify some flights as spaceflights and some individuals as astronauts—demonstrating the very real consequences that flow from definitional choices.

The Diversity of Space-Related Activities

The advent of aerospace engineering further blurred the distinction between atmospheric and cosmic domains. Aircraft operate by exploiting aerodynamic lift—the pressure differential created when air flows over a wing—which diminishes as air density decreases. At sea level, air density is approximately 1.225 kg/m^3; at 30 kilometers, it has fallen to roughly 0.018 kg/m^3—less than 2 percent of its sea-level value. At 100 kilometers, the density is approximately 0.0000006 kg/m^3—so thin that aerodynamic lift becomes negligible for any practical wing design. Rockets and spacecraft, by contrast, rely on propulsion systems that carry their own oxidizer and are therefore independent of the atmosphere. This functional distinction—aerodynamic flight versus propulsive spaceflight—has often been invoked to differentiate airspace from outer space.

Yet even this seemingly clear distinction proves inadequate upon closer examination. High-altitude aircraft such as the SR-71 Blackbird operated at altitudes exceeding 25 kilometers, at the very limits of aerodynamic flight. Sounding rockets and experimental vehicles such as the X-15—which reached an altitude of 107.8 kilometers in 1963—occupied intermediate regimes where aerodynamic and astronautical principles overlapped. The X-15's pilot, Joseph Walker, was retroactively recognized as an astronaut under the U.S. 80-kilometer standard, though his flight would not have qualified under the FAI's 100-kilometer criterion. Such discrepancies illustrate how the absence of a unified standard creates real inconsistencies in how space is defined and who qualifies as a space traveler.

Scientific ambiguity is further compounded by the extraordinary diversity of activities that occur at different altitudes. Satellites in low Earth orbit—typically between 200 and 2,000 kilometers—may experience measurable atmospheric drag, requiring periodic reboost to maintain their orbits. The International Space Station, orbiting at approximately 400 kilometers, loses several kilometers of altitude each month due to residual atmospheric friction. These facts complicate the notion that orbital activities occur "in space" in any physically clean sense.

At the other end of the spectrum, high-altitude scientific balloons routinely reach altitudes of 35 to 45 kilometers, well above 99 percent of the atmosphere by mass. High-altitude pseudo-satellites (HAPS)—unmanned platforms designed for persistent surveillance and communications—operate at similar altitudes. These platforms perform functions traditionally associated with satellites (communications relay, Earth observation, internet connectivity) while remaining well within the atmosphere. Their existence challenges the assumption that satellite-like functions necessarily imply space-like legal treatment.

Sounding rockets, used for scientific research, traverse the full spectrum from atmospheric to space altitudes in a single flight, collecting data through the mesosphere and lower thermosphere before descending. Suborbital tourism vehicles carry passengers to altitudes of 80 to 110 kilometers for brief periods of microgravity before returning to Earth. Hypersonic glide vehicles may operate at altitudes of 40 to 100 kilometers while traveling at speeds approaching orbital velocity. Each of these activities occupies a different point on the atmospheric continuum, and none fits neatly into either the "airspace" or "outer space" category.

■ **Activities Across the Altitude Spectrum**

0–12 km: Commercial aviation, military aircraft, weather systems.

12–50 km: Stratospheric balloons, HAPS, U-2/SR-71 reconnaissance aircraft.

50–85 km: Sounding rockets, meteors, mesospheric research.

80–100 km: Suborbital tourism, Kármán/U.S. astronaut boundaries.

100–200 km: Suborbital trajectories, very brief orbital passes.

200–2,000 km: Low Earth orbit (ISS, Earth observation, Starlink).

2,000–36,000 km: Medium Earth orbit (navigation satellites).

~36,000 km: Geostationary orbit (communications, weather).

No single altitude separates 'atmosphere' from 'space' in a way that accommodates all these activities.

Science, Law, and the Epistemological Mismatch

From a scientific standpoint, therefore, outer space is best understood not as a place with fixed boundaries, but as a zone characterized by functional conditions: the dominance of orbital mechanics over aerodynamic lift, the practical impossibility of sustained atmospheric flight, the necessity of rocket-based propulsion, and the exposure to the space environment (vacuum, radiation, microgravity). Yet even these criteria evolve as technology advances. Vehicles once thought impossible now operate routinely in regimes that defy earlier assumptions.

This evolving scientific landscape poses a fundamental problem for law. Legal systems rely on definitions that are stable, predictable, and enforceable. Categories must be clear enough to assign jurisdiction, allocate liability, and determine regulatory competence. Scientific continua resist such clarity. Any attempt to define outer space solely by reference to physical properties risks becoming obsolete as technology progresses. What is unreachable today may be accessible tomorrow; what is impractical now may become routine within a decade.

The challenge is thus not merely technical but epistemological. Science describes reality as it is observed and measured, embracing uncertainty, probability, and continua. Law constructs categories to regulate behavior, demanding thresholds, boundaries, and binary determinations. Where scientific observation reveals gradual transitions, law demands clear lines. This mismatch between modes of understanding explains why, more than six decades after the first satellite launch, no universally accepted scientific definition of outer space has been incorporated into international law.

> ■ **The Core Dilemma**
>
> Science cannot provide a natural boundary between atmosphere and space because none exists. Law requires a boundary to determine jurisdiction, liability, and applicable rules. This fundamental mismatch—between the continuous reality of physics and the categorical demands of governance—is the essence of the boundary problem.

This does not mean that science is irrelevant to legal analysis. On the contrary, scientific understanding provides essential context for legal reasoning. It explains why certain regulatory approaches are feasible and others are not. It informs assessments of risk, capability, and environmental impact. What science cannot do, however, is supply a definitive boundary that resolves legal questions once and for all. The problem of defining outer space has therefore migrated from the laboratory to the negotiating table—from a question of physics to a question of politics.

***

Part II

Legal Theories of Delimitation: Spatial, Functional, and Hybrid Approaches

If science exposes the absence of a natural boundary between airspace and outer space, law responds by attempting to construct boundaries where none exist physically. Since the earliest days of spaceflight, jurists have proposed a range of legal theories to delimit outer space from airspace, each reflecting different priorities: certainty, flexibility, sovereignty, and technological realism. These theories—spatial, functional, and hybrid—form the core of a debate that has persisted for over sixty years without resolution.

Spatial (Altitude-Based) Theories

Spatial theories propose that outer space begins at a fixed altitude above the Earth's surface. Under this approach, sovereignty extends upward only to a defined height, beyond which outer space—free from national appropriation and governed by space law—begins. The primary appeal of spatial theories lies in their clarity. A fixed boundary would provide legal certainty, enabling regulators, operators, insurance companies, and courts to determine applicable law with confidence on the basis of a single measurable variable: altitude.

Proponents of spatial delimitation argue that international law routinely relies on legal fictions to achieve order. Maritime zones—territorial seas, contiguous zones, exclusive economic zones, continental shelves—are defined by measured distances from baselines rather than by natural features. These zones are legal constructs, yet they function effectively because states have agreed upon them. Airspace and outer space could, in principle, be separated by a similarly agreed altitude. The result would be a clear jurisdictional map: below the line, sovereignty and air law apply; above it, freedom and space law govern.

The most commonly proposed altitude is 100 kilometers, corresponding to the Kármán line. This proposal has been advanced by several states within COPUOS, most notably by the Soviet Union (later Russia) and a number of developing countries. Colombia notably proposed in the 1970s that geostationary orbit—at approximately 36,000 kilometers above the equator—should be subject to the sovereignty of the equatorial state beneath it, a position known as the Bogotá Declaration of 1976. This claim was rejected by the broader international community but illustrated the potential consequences of spatial reasoning taken to its logical conclusion.

■ **The Bogotá Declaration (1976)**

On 3 December 1976, eight equatorial states (Brazil, Colombia, Congo, Ecuador, Indonesia, Kenya, Uganda, and Zaire) signed the Bogotá Declaration.

The Declaration claimed sovereignty over segments of the geostationary orbit above each signatory's territory.

The signatories argued that the geostationary orbit was a 'limited natural resource' linked to the gravitational field of equatorial states.

The claim was rejected by COPUOS and the broader international community as incompatible with the Outer Space Treaty's prohibition on national appropriation.

The Bogotá Declaration remains legally ineffective but historically significant as an illustration of the sovereignty claims that spatial reasoning can generate.

However, spatial theories face formidable objections. First, any chosen altitude would be inherently arbitrary, disconnected from the gradual physical transition between atmosphere and space. Why 100 kilometers and not 80, 110, or 150? The absence of a scientific justification for any specific figure undermines the perceived objectivity of the approach. Second, a fixed boundary risks technological obsolescence. As vehicles capable of operating across wider altitude ranges emerge—spaceplanes, hypersonic gliders, reusable launch vehicles—a rigid line could constrain innovation or produce anomalous legal outcomes in which a single vehicle transitions between legal regimes during a single flight.

Perhaps most importantly, spatial delimitation raises sovereignty concerns that have proven politically insurmountable. States fear that agreeing to a fixed upper limit would permanently curtail their jurisdiction, potentially exposing them to security risks from activities conducted just above the boundary. For this reason, despite decades of discussion, no spatial boundary has gained sufficient political support to be codified in international law.

The historical record reveals a striking pattern: proposals for spatial delimitation have come predominantly from states that are not themselves major spacefaring powers. The Soviet Union's proposal for a 100–110 kilometer boundary, while supported by its space program's technical capabilities, was also motivated by a desire to constrain U.S. reconnaissance satellite activities. Several developing states have supported spatial delimitation as a means of clarifying and protecting their sovereignty against what they perceive as technological encroachment by more powerful neighbors. The United States, by contrast, has consistently opposed any fixed boundary, viewing it as an unnecessary constraint on operational freedom—a position that has been supported, with varying degrees of enthusiasm, by most other spacefaring states.

The Maritime Analogy Revisited

The debate over spatial delimitation is often enriched—and complicated—by comparison with the law of the sea. Maritime law has successfully employed spatial zones defined by measured distances: the 12-nautical-mile territorial sea, the 24-nautical-mile contiguous zone, the 200-nautical-mile exclusive economic zone, and the continental shelf extending up to 350 nautical miles. If the law of the sea can impose boundaries on a continuous medium, why cannot air and space law do the same?

The analogy is instructive but ultimately limited. Maritime zones were developed over centuries of customary practice, codified through decades of negotiation (culminating in UNCLOS in 1982), and anchored to a physical reference point—the baseline, typically the low-water mark along a coast. They reflect a progressive transition from full sovereignty (territorial sea) through limited functional jurisdiction (contiguous zone, EEZ) to freedom (high seas). This layered approach accommodates competing interests by creating graduated zones of authority rather than a single sharp boundary.

Applying this model to the vertical dimension would require agreement not only on a single boundary but potentially on multiple zones of graduated authority—a territorial atmosphere, a contiguous zone, an exclusive economic atmosphere, and a high space. While some scholars have proposed precisely this, the political obstacles are formidable. The vertical dimension lacks the physical reference points (coastlines, baselines) that anchor maritime zones. The interests at stake—satellite overflight, launch trajectories, military surveillance—are qualitatively different from those at sea. And the institutional framework for negotiation—COPUOS, operating by consensus—is far less conducive to compromise than the UN Conference on the Law of the Sea, which operated by majority vote.

Functional Theories

Functional theories reject altitude as the primary criterion and instead focus on the nature and purpose of the activity being conducted. Under this approach, activities intended for aviation—relying on aerodynamic lift, operating within atmospheric conditions, and serving transportation or observation purposes—fall under air law, while activities intended for space exploration, satellite operations, or orbital mechanics fall under space law, regardless of the altitude at which they occur.

The functional approach has several significant advantages. It avoids arbitrary altitude thresholds and accommodates technological evolution seamlessly. A new vehicle type does not require renegotiation of a boundary; it simply requires classification according to its function. The approach also reflects how states have actually behaved in practice since the dawn of the space age. From the earliest days of spaceflight, states treated orbital activities as distinct from aviation, even though launch and re-entry phases occur within atmospheric space. Rockets passing through sovereign airspace on their way to orbit have never been treated as violations of airspace sovereignty, because their function—reaching orbit—places them within the space law framework.

Yet functional theories also introduce forms of uncertainty that spatial approaches avoid. Determining the "purpose" or "nature" of an activity can be contentious, especially for dual-use technologies. A single vehicle may perform multiple functions during different phases of flight: launching as a rocket, deploying a satellite, de-orbiting as a glider, and landing as an aircraft. Spaceplanes such as the retired Space Shuttle or the planned Dream Chaser combine characteristics of both aircraft and spacecraft. Suborbital tourism vehicles carry passengers to altitudes associated with space but never achieve orbit, placing them in an ambiguous category that functional analysis does not cleanly resolve.

Moreover, functional approaches can undermine the predictability that commercial operators require. An investor, insurer, or regulator needs to know in advance which legal regime applies to a given activity. If classification depends on interpretation rather than measurement, legal uncertainty increases, potentially chilling investment and complicating enforcement.

The insurance dimension is particularly revealing. Space insurance and aviation insurance operate as distinct markets with different risk models, policy structures, and premium calculations. A suborbital tourism flight must be insured against third-party damage, but the applicable liability framework—and therefore the insurance product required—depends on whether the flight is classified as an aviation activity or a space activity. Under the Liability Convention (1972), launching states bear absolute liability for damage caused on the surface of the Earth by space objects. Under aviation liability frameworks (the Montreal Convention of 1999), airlines bear liability subject to different limits and procedures. The functional approach does not automatically resolve this classification, creating practical difficulties for insurers and operators alike.

Hybrid Approaches

Recognizing the limitations of purely spatial or purely functional theories, some scholars have proposed hybrid models that combine elements of both. These approaches typically envision a transitional zone—often referred to as "near space" or the "mesosphere gap"—where legal classification depends on both altitude and function. Within this zone, specific activities might be governed by tailored rules reflecting shared jurisdiction or cooperative oversight between air law and space law authorities.

Hybrid models seek to balance certainty with flexibility. By acknowledging a gray area rather than denying it, they aim to manage overlap rather than eliminate it. A transitional zone could accommodate emerging technologies—HAPS, suborbital vehicles, hypersonic aircraft—that do not fit neatly into either existing regime. It could provide a framework for cooperative regulation, risk management, and dispute resolution in a domain that currently falls between jurisdictional stools.

However, hybrid approaches inherit the political challenges of spatial delimitation (agreement on zone boundaries) and the interpretive challenges of functional theories (classification of activities within the zone). Establishing a transitional regime would require unprecedented international negotiation and would inevitably involve trade-offs that states have thus far been unwilling to make. As a result, hybrid theories remain largely academic proposals, admired for their intellectual elegance but lacking political traction.

The idea of a transitional zone is not without historical precedent, however. The law of the sea's contiguous zone and exclusive economic zone represent precisely this kind of intermediate regime—domains where sovereignty is attenuated and specific functional authorities are exercised without full territorial control. The Antarctic Treaty System establishes a governance framework for a domain where sovereignty claims are "frozen" rather than resolved. These precedents suggest that international law is capable of managing ambiguous domains through creative institutional design—if the political will exists to attempt it.

A particularly innovative hybrid proposal, advanced by several scholars, would combine a spatial threshold (e.g., the lowest perigee of any orbiting object, typically around 100–120 kilometers) with a functional exception for transit through sovereign airspace by objects launched into or returning from outer space. Under this model, sovereignty would extend upward to the defined threshold, but the right of innocent passage—borrowed from the law of the sea—would permit launch vehicles, returning spacecraft, and similar objects to transit sovereign airspace without constituting a violation. This approach would preserve sovereignty while accommodating the operational realities of spaceflight, but it has not yet attracted sufficient state support to advance beyond academic discussion.

Criterion	**Spatial (Altitude)**	**Functional (Activity)**
Basis	Fixed altitude (e.g., 100 km)	Nature/purpose of activity
Strength	Legal certainty and clarity	Flexibility and adaptability
Weakness	Arbitrary and rigid	Subjective and unpredictable
Sovereignty	Constrains sovereignty vertically	Avoids sovereignty questions
Technology	Risks obsolescence	Accommodates evolution
State support	Russia, some developing states	U.S., most spacefaring states
Legal status	Not adopted	Dominant in practice

> ■ **Why No Theory Has Prevailed**
>
> Delimitation is not merely a technical question but a deeply political one. States have consistently prioritized operational freedom and strategic flexibility over legal precision. By avoiding formal delimitation, they have allowed space activities to develop without reopening sovereignty disputes—a pragmatic choice that has sustained the space law regime for six decades.

***

Part III

State Practice, COPUOS Debates, and the Politics of Non-Decision

While scholars debated delimitation in journals and conferences, states quietly answered the question through practice. This practice—more than any theory—has shaped the legal reality of outer space. Rather than defining where outer space begins, states collectively chose not to decide, allowing operational necessity and political consensus to substitute for formal legal boundaries. This pattern of deliberate restraint is one of the most distinctive features of international space law and one of the most important to understand.

Sputnik and the Power of Silence

The first and most decisive act of state practice occurred in 1957 with the launch of Sputnik 1, as examined in detail in Chapter 1. The satellite's orbital path passed repeatedly over the territory of multiple sovereign states. Under any strict interpretation of airspace sovereignty extending indefinitely upward, such overflight would have constituted a violation. Yet no state objected. This absence of protest was not accidental or the result of inattention; it was a calculated convergence of interests among both superpowers and non-spacefaring states, producing a rare moment of tacit consensus during one of the most dangerous periods of the Cold War.

Declassified documents reveal that the Eisenhower administration had anticipated this moment and deliberately prepared for it. The United States had considered launching its own satellite first but chose to allow the Soviet Union to establish the precedent of free overflight. American strategists recognized that if the first satellite were American, Soviet objections to overflight could create a legal precedent restricting U.S. reconnaissance satellite programs—programs that were considered vital to national security. By allowing the Soviet Union to launch first without objection, the United States ensured that the principle of free overflight would be established by Soviet practice, making it politically impossible for the Soviets to later object to American satellites.

This strategic calculation—known informally as the "freedom of space" doctrine—represents one of the most consequential acts of legal engineering in modern diplomatic history. The Eisenhower administration effectively used the absence of objection as a lawmaking tool, creating customary international law through deliberate inaction. The brilliance of the strategy lay in its invisibility: by not protesting, the United States simultaneously protected its own future satellite programs, established a norm of free overflight, and avoided a public confrontation with the Soviet Union during a period of extreme tension.

Through this tacit acceptance, free satellite overflight emerged as customary international law, independent of formal delimitation. The legal significance cannot be overstated. Without a single treaty provision, without a single resolution, and without a single judicial decision, the international community established one of the most consequential norms in modern international law: that activities in orbit are not subject to territorial sovereignty. Silence became consent, consent became practice, and practice became law.

This episode established a powerful and enduring precedent: outer space activities would be governed by functional necessity rather than territorial claims. From that moment onward, the legal distinction between airspace and outer space was drawn implicitly through behavior, not altitude. States did not need to agree on where space begins; they needed only to agree that satellites could operate without territorial interference. This functional consensus proved sufficient for the development of the entire subsequent space law regime.

The Role of COPUOS

The institutional embodiment of this approach emerged within the United Nations Committee on the Peaceful Uses of Outer Space (COPUOS). From its earliest sessions in the late 1950s, COPUOS recognized the delimitation issue as legally significant—but politically volatile. The Committee's membership included both spacefaring and non-spacefaring states, each with divergent interests and different calculations about the risks and benefits of delimitation.

Non-spacefaring states often favored delimitation, viewing a clear boundary as a safeguard against encroachment and inequality. If outer space began at a defined altitude, these states reasoned, the sovereignty of their airspace would be explicitly protected up to that altitude, and the freedom of outer space would be explicitly guaranteed above it. Ambiguity, they argued, benefited powerful states that could exploit uncertainty to their advantage. A defined boundary would level the playing field by providing legal clarity accessible to all.

Spacefaring states, by contrast, consistently resisted formal definition, emphasizing the risks of restricting access or triggering sovereignty disputes. The United States and the Soviet Union—and later Russia, China, and the European spacefaring states—recognized that their space programs required maximum operational flexibility. Any defined boundary could constrain future activities, create liability complications, or provoke demands for overflight fees or sovereignty-based restrictions. Ambiguity served their interests by preserving the freedom of action that their space programs required.

■ COPUOS and the Delimitation Question

The COPUOS Legal Subcommittee has had delimitation on its agenda continuously since the 1960s.

Dozens of working papers have been submitted by member states proposing various approaches.

Russia has repeatedly proposed a formal boundary at 100–110 km; the U.S. has consistently opposed any fixed boundary.

A 2018 COPUOS questionnaire revealed that most states do not consider delimitation urgent.

The Committee operates by consensus, meaning any state can effectively block progress.

As of 2025, no consensus has been reached and no formal action has been taken.

Despite repeated agenda items, working papers, and informal consultations spanning six decades, COPUOS has never reached consensus on delimitation. Reports routinely acknowledge the importance of the issue while deferring substantive action to future sessions. Working groups have been established, disbanded, and re-established without producing binding outcomes. This pattern illustrates a central feature of space governance: consensus is valued over resolution, and stability over precision.

A 2018 COPUOS questionnaire on national approaches to delimitation and characterization of space activities produced illuminating results. Of the states that responded, a clear majority indicated that they did not consider the absence of delimitation to be a significant obstacle to their space activities. Several spacefaring states explicitly stated that they did not support the adoption of a fixed boundary. Non-spacefaring states were more likely to express interest in delimitation, but their positions were diverse, with no single proposal commanding broad support. The questionnaire confirmed what decades of debate had suggested: there is no constituency large or powerful enough to drive delimitation to a conclusion.

The positions of the two largest spacefaring states deserve particular attention, as their sustained opposition has effectively prevented any progress. The United States has consistently maintained that no definition or delimitation of outer space is necessary or desirable at the present time. American delegations have argued that the current functional approach—in which the nature of the activity, rather than the altitude, determines the applicable legal regime—has proven adequate and should not be replaced by a rigid boundary that could constrain future operations. Russia (formerly the

Soviet Union), while historically more sympathetic to delimitation, has not been willing to push the issue against American opposition, recognizing that doing so within the consensus-based COPUOS framework would be futile.

Constructive Ambiguity as Governance Strategy

The refusal to define outer space should not be mistaken for legal paralysis or institutional failure. On the contrary, it reflects a deliberate strategy of constructive ambiguity—a choice to preserve flexibility by declining to commit to a definition that might prove premature, contentious, or constraining. This strategy has deep roots in diplomatic practice; it is employed wherever the costs of precision exceed the benefits of clarity.

Constructive ambiguity in space governance has enabled remarkable achievements. Without resolving the boundary question, the international community has successfully established a regime that permits uninterrupted satellite operations across the globe, supports the rapid expansion of global communications and navigation systems, enables comprehensive Earth observation for weather forecasting, climate monitoring, and disaster response, and avoids sovereignty-based conflict in orbit. These achievements would have been far more difficult—perhaps impossible—if states had insisted on resolving the boundary question before proceeding with space activities.

The economic scale of what constructive ambiguity has enabled is staggering. The global space economy exceeded $470 billion in 2024, encompassing satellite telecommunications, navigation services, Earth observation, launch services, and an expanding commercial space sector. Global positioning systems—GPS, GLONASS, Galileo, BeiDou—provide positioning, navigation, and timing services that underpin financial markets, transportation networks, emergency services, and precision agriculture. All of these capabilities depend on satellite overflight of every state on Earth, conducted without permission and without objection. The economic infrastructure of the modern world thus rests, in a very real sense, on the legal foundation of constructive ambiguity.

> *"The absence of a defined boundary is not a failure of law, but a deliberate strategy that reflects the unique challenges of governing a domain beyond traditional territorial control. Law follows conduct rather than territory."*
>
> – On the pragmatics of non-delimitation

At the same time, ambiguity shifts the regulatory burden from territorial rules to activity-based norms. Rather than asking "where is this activity taking place?" (a question that depends on delimitation), the law asks "what is this activity, who is responsible for it, and what obligations apply?" This shift is embodied in the Outer Space Treaty's framework of state responsibility (Article VI), liability (Article VII), and jurisdiction (Article VIII), which attach legal consequences to conduct and registry rather than to location.

National Legislation and the De Facto Boundary

While international law has avoided delimitation, national legislation offers a revealing window into how states actually treat the boundary question in practice. As of 2025, more than thirty states have enacted national space legislation governing the authorization, supervision, and liability of space activities conducted by their nationals. These laws must, by necessity, define their own jurisdictional scope—and in doing so, they implicitly or explicitly address the boundary question.

Most national space laws avoid specifying an altitude at which space begins. Instead, they define space activities functionally: launch operations, satellite operations, re-entry operations, and related activities are regulated regardless of the altitude at which they occur. The U.S. Commercial Space Launch Act, the UK Space Industry Act 2018, the Australian Space (Launches and Returns) Act 2018, and the UAE Federal Law on Space Affairs (2019) all adopt variations of this functional approach. By regulating activities rather than domains, these laws sidestep the delimitation question while providing practical governance.

A few states, however, have adopted explicit or implicit spatial elements. Australia's legislation applies to launches that reach or exceed 100 kilometers, effectively adopting the Kármán line as a domestic threshold. Denmark's Outer Space Act (2016) similarly references 100 kilometers. These examples demonstrate that states can, when motivated by practical regulatory needs, adopt spatial criteria without waiting for international consensus. The resulting patchwork—some states using functional definitions, others using spatial thresholds—creates potential for regulatory inconsistency in an increasingly global industry.

> ■ **National Space Legislation and the Boundary**
>
> United States: Functional approach. Regulates 'launch' and 'reentry' activities without specifying altitude.
>
> Australia: References 100 km threshold for determining whether a launch is a 'space activity.'
>
> United Kingdom: Functional approach. Space Industry Act 2018 defines 'spaceflight activities' broadly.
>
> UAE: Federal Law No. 12 of 2019 on Space Sector regulates space activities without altitude specification.
>
> Denmark: Outer Space Act (2016) references 100 km as the boundary of outer space.
>
> Russia: Has proposed 100–110 km boundary internationally but does not enshrine it in domestic legislation.
>
> Over 30 states now have national space legislation; the majority use functional definitions.

Customary Delimitation Without Demarcation

Through consistent and largely uncontested practice over more than sixty years, states have created a de facto understanding of outer space that functions independently of formal delimitation. Activities clearly associated with orbital mechanics—satellite operations, space station habitation, interplanetary missions—are universally treated as space activities, governed by space law. Aircraft, even at extreme altitudes, remain subject to air law and national sovereignty. Launch and re-entry operations, though they traverse sovereign airspace, are regulated through national licensing regimes rather than airspace sovereignty claims.

This practice has produced what might be called customary delimitation without demarcation. Outer space is recognized not by where it begins, but by what is done there. The boundary exists functionally, even if it has never been formally drawn. This is not unprecedented in international law—customary law frequently establishes norms that are recognized and followed without being codified—but the persistence and stability of this particular custom, in the absence of any supporting treaty definition, is remarkable.

The strength of this custom should not, however, obscure its fragility. Customary law depends on consistent practice accompanied by opinio juris—the belief that the practice is legally required. If states begin to behave differently—asserting sovereignty at higher altitudes, challenging satellite overflight, or classifying emerging technologies in inconsistent ways—the custom could erode. The question is whether the technological and geopolitical developments of the twenty-first century will maintain the conditions that have sustained this custom since 1957.

Several developments suggest that the consensus may be weakening, even if slowly. The Bogotá Declaration of 1976, though rejected by the international community, represented an early challenge to the customary norm of free access to outer space. More recently, some states have begun to assert expanded claims over near-space activities, including demands for notification or authorization of suborbital flights transiting over their territory. China's 2007 ASAT test and Russia's 2021 ASAT test both demonstrated willingness to conduct destructive military operations in domains that the prevailing custom treats as free from sovereignty claims. While neither test was framed as a sovereignty assertion, both illustrated the capacity and willingness of major powers to act unilaterally in domains where legal rules remain ambiguous.

The proliferation of mega-constellations—SpaceX's Starlink, Amazon's Kuiper, and others—introduces yet another pressure point. These constellations involve thousands of satellites in low Earth orbit, each of which overflies every state on Earth multiple times daily. As the number of satellites grows from thousands to tens of thousands, the physical presence of foreign-registered objects above sovereign territory becomes impossible to ignore. While no state has yet objected to this presence, the scale of the phenomenon is unprecedented, and the assumption that silence will continue indefinitely cannot be taken for granted.

***

Part IV

New Technologies, Near Space, and the Future of Delimitation

The legal tolerance for ambiguity that has characterized international space law since the launch of Sputnik is now being tested by rapid technological change. While traditional satellites and aircraft occupied relatively distinct operational domains—aircraft in the troposphere and lower stratosphere, satellites in orbit above several hundred kilometers—emerging technologies increasingly operate in the transitional region between airspace and outer space, often referred to as near space. These developments challenge the assumptions that have allowed the boundary problem to remain unresolved and raise urgent questions about whether the long-standing strategy of non-decision can continue indefinitely.

The Rise of Near-Space Technologies

Near space is not a formally recognized legal category, but it has gained prominence as a descriptive term for altitudes above conventional aviation (roughly 20 kilometers) and below stable orbital flight (roughly 160 kilometers). Technologies operating in this region include high-altitude pseudo-satellites (HAPS), suborbital launch vehicles, hypersonic aircraft, reusable launch systems, and spaceplanes. These platforms blur traditional distinctions by combining characteristics of both aircraft and spacecraft, operating in regimes where neither air law nor space law provides a comprehensive framework.

Figure 14: Solar-Powered Unmanned Aerial Vehicle (UAV) Operating in the Stratosphere

Source: NASA (Public Domain).

High-altitude solar-powered platforms, such as Airbus's Zephyr and various systems under development by other manufacturers, can loiter at altitudes of 18 to 25 kilometers for weeks or even months at a time, providing persistent surveillance, communications relay, and internet connectivity. They perform functions virtually identical to those performed by satellites, yet they operate within the atmosphere and, theoretically, within sovereign airspace. Their regulatory classification varies by jurisdiction: some states treat them as aircraft, others as novel categories requiring bespoke regulation.

Hypersonic vehicles—both military and civilian—represent another category of challenge. Vehicles capable of sustained flight at speeds exceeding Mach 5 operate at extreme altitudes, traversing vast distances in minutes. Military hypersonic glide vehicles, such as those under development by the United States, Russia, and China, can maneuver at altitudes of 40 to 100 kilometers, evading traditional air defense systems. Their legal status is uncertain: are they aircraft in sovereign airspace, or something else entirely?

The distinction matters enormously for international security law. Under the law of armed conflict, the legality of engaging a target depends, inter alia, on the domain in which it operates and the rules applicable to that domain. If a hypersonic vehicle is classified as an aircraft in sovereign airspace, the overflown state may have the right to intercept it as a violation of sovereignty. If it is classified as a space object—or as operating in an unregulated transitional zone—the legal basis for engagement becomes far less clear. The ambiguity is not merely academic; it could influence split-second decisions during a military crisis, with potentially catastrophic consequences.

The proliferation of reusable launch vehicles adds yet another dimension. SpaceX's Falcon 9 first-stage boosters routinely return to landing pads after delivering payloads to orbit, flying back through the atmosphere and landing vertically. SpaceX's Starship, designed for full reusability, will ascend through sovereign airspace, enter orbit, and return—potentially to a different country than the one from which it launched. Point-to-point Starship flights, if they become commercially viable, would routinely cross the boundary region while carrying passengers and cargo between cities on opposite sides of the globe, creating a new category of transportation that defies existing legal categories entirely.

Suborbital Flight and the Commercial Frontier

Suborbital spaceflight illustrates the boundary problem in particularly sharp commercial relief. Companies such as Blue Origin (New Shepard) and Virgin Galactic (SpaceShipTwo) now offer flights that ascend beyond conventional atmospheric limits—to altitudes of approximately 100 and 85 kilometers respectively—providing passengers with brief exposure to microgravity and views of Earth from space before returning to the surface. These flights do not achieve orbit, yet they clearly differ from conventional aviation in their trajectory, purpose, and passenger experience.

The regulatory treatment of suborbital flights varies significantly across jurisdictions. The United States regulates commercial human spaceflight under 51 U.S.C. Chapter 509 (Commercial Space Launch Activities), administered by the Federal Aviation Administration's Office of Commercial Space Transportation (FAA AST). This framework treats suborbital flights as space activities regardless of the altitude reached. European states, by contrast, have generally not developed comprehensive suborbital regulatory frameworks, creating potential gaps as European operators enter the market.

The commercial stakes are substantial. The suborbital tourism market—currently valued at several hundred million dollars annually—is projected to grow significantly as costs decrease and competition increases. Point-to-point suborbital transport, which would use rocket-powered vehicles to connect distant cities in under an hour, has attracted investment from major aerospace companies. If realized, such services would routinely transit the boundary region, moving passengers from sovereign airspace through near space and back—a journey that current legal frameworks do not seamlessly accommodate.

The passenger safety dimension adds urgency. Aviation passengers are protected by decades of refined safety regulation, mandatory insurance, and established liability frameworks. Space participants (as they are currently classified in U.S. law) enjoy fewer regulatory protections, reflecting the experimental nature of human spaceflight. As suborbital tourism evolves from adventure sport to mainstream travel, the regulatory gap between aviation safety standards and space participant waivers will become increasingly difficult to sustain. The FAA's congressionally mandated "learning period"—during which passenger safety regulations for commercial human spaceflight are limited—has been extended multiple times, most recently to 2025, deferring the inevitable reckoning with this regulatory asymmetry.

■ **Suborbital Tourism: Key Operators and Altitudes**

Blue Origin New Shepard: Apogee ~100+ km (above Kármán line). Vertical launch and landing.

Virgin Galactic SpaceShipTwo: Apogee ~85 km (above U.S. astronaut threshold). Air-launched spaceplane.

SpaceX Starship (point-to-point concept): Suborbital trajectory at ~100+ km connecting global cities.

Regulatory treatment differs: U.S. treats all as space activities; international consensus absent.

Insurance, liability, and passenger safety standards remain fragmented across jurisdictions.

Security and Strategic Dimensions

Beyond commerce, near-space technologies carry profound security implications that intensify the pressure on the boundary question. Hypersonic weapons systems—including both hypersonic cruise missiles and hypersonic glide vehicles—can deliver conventional or nuclear warheads at speeds and trajectories that challenge existing missile defense architectures. Their ability to operate at extreme altitudes within the boundary region complicates detection, tracking, and interception, raising acute concerns about strategic stability.

From a legal perspective, these capabilities challenge existing frameworks governing the use of force, sovereignty, and arms control. If a hypersonic glide vehicle operates at 80 kilometers altitude above a state's territory, does it constitute a violation of airspace sovereignty? If so, does the overflown state have the right to intercept or engage it? If the vehicle is above the undefined boundary, does freedom of outer space protect its passage? The absence of clarity increases the risk of miscalculation and escalation—risks that the boundary question was never designed to manage.

Anti-satellite (ASAT) weapons add another layer of complexity. Ground-based ASAT systems launch kinetic interceptors through sovereign airspace to strike targets in orbit. Co-orbital ASAT systems maneuver within orbital space to approach and potentially disable other satellites. The intersection of air defense, missile defense, and space operations creates a multi-domain challenge that the current bifurcated framework—air law below, space law above, with no defined boundary between them—is ill-equipped to address.

The 2021 Russian ASAT test—in which a direct-ascent missile destroyed the defunct Cosmos 1408 satellite, generating over 1,500 trackable debris fragments in low Earth orbit—crystallized these concerns. The missile was launched from a ground-based facility, transited through sovereign Russian airspace, crossed the undefined boundary into outer space, and struck a target in orbit. The resulting debris field threatened the International Space Station and numerous operational satellites. This single event implicated air law (the launch through airspace), space law (the destruction of a space object and creation of debris), arms control law (the military use of outer space), and environmental law (the pollution of the orbital environment). The absence of a defined boundary made it impossible to determine at which point different legal regimes should have applied.

> ■ **The 2021 Russian ASAT Test**
>
> Date: 15 November 2021. Target: Cosmos 1408 (defunct Soviet-era satellite).
>
> Weapon: Direct-ascent kinetic interceptor (Nudol system).
>
> Result: Over 1,500 trackable debris fragments; thousands more too small to track.
>
> The ISS crew sheltered in evacuation spacecraft as debris passed within threatening proximity.
>
> Condemned by the U.S., UK, EU, Japan, and others; no formal legal consequences under existing treaties.
>
> Highlighted the inadequacy of existing legal frameworks for addressing multi-domain security threats.

Environmental and Sustainability Concerns

The boundary problem also intersects with emerging concerns about environmental sustainability. Near-space operations may affect atmospheric layers—particularly the stratospheric ozone layer—through rocket exhaust emissions, contribute to orbital debris during launch and re-entry phases, or interfere with astronomical observation through light pollution and radio frequency interference. Existing environmental norms were not designed with these activities in mind, and neither air law nor space law provides comprehensive environmental coverage for the transitional zone.

The growing volume of launches—SpaceX alone conducted over 90 orbital missions in 2023—means that the environmental impact of transiting the atmosphere is no longer negligible. Black carbon and alumina particles deposited in the stratosphere by rocket exhaust may contribute to ozone depletion and climate effects. Defining legal responsibility for these impacts requires clarity about which regulatory framework applies—a question that, once again, depends on the unresolved boundary between air and space.

The International Civil Aviation Organization (ICAO), responsible for environmental standards in aviation, has begun to consider the atmospheric impact of launch and re-entry operations. In 2024, ICAO's Committee on Aviation Environmental Protection (CAEP) initiated discussions on the interaction between aviation environmental standards and space launch emissions. These discussions highlight the institutional gap created by the absence of delimitation: ICAO's mandate covers aviation within the atmosphere, while COPUOS addresses activities in outer space. Activities that transit between the two domains—every launch and every re-entry—fall into an institutional no-man's-land.

The debris problem further complicates matters. Fragments from launch vehicle stages, fairings, and spent upper stages re-enter the atmosphere unpredictably, posing risks to aviation and populations below. The liability framework for such incidents depends on whether the object is classified as a "space object" under the Liability Convention—a classification that implicitly assumes the object was operating in outer space. For components that fail and fall back to Earth without ever reaching orbital altitude, the classification is ambiguous. The growing frequency of launches makes these edge cases increasingly likely.

Possible Paths Forward

Several paths lie ahead for the future of delimitation. The first and most likely in the near term is continued reliance on functional interpretation, extending the current model of constructive ambiguity. Under this approach, states would address emerging challenges through incremental national regulation, bilateral agreements, and non-binding guidelines, avoiding the political costs of formal boundary-setting. This path is attractive to spacefaring states and consistent with established practice, but it risks growing regulatory fragmentation as national approaches diverge.

A second possibility is the gradual development of soft-law instruments addressing near-space activities specifically. Guidelines on suborbital flight, high-altitude platforms, or hypersonic operations—developed through ICAO, COPUOS, or other multilateral forums—could provide clarity without the rigidity of treaty law. Over time, such instruments might contribute to the formation of customary norms, creating a practical framework without requiring formal delimitation. This approach has precedent in the space debris mitigation guidelines adopted by COPUOS in 2007, which have influenced national regulation without achieving treaty status.

ICAO has already begun to explore this territory. Its Space Learning Group, established in 2020, has been studying the interaction between aviation operations and space launch and re-entry activities, focusing on safety coordination, air traffic management around launch sites, and the integration of space vehicles into the aviation system. While these efforts are preliminary, they represent a significant institutional acknowledgment that the air–space interface can no longer be managed through informal arrangements alone. If ICAO develops formal guidance on space operations within or transiting through airspace, it would constitute a de facto partial delimitation—defining the boundary through operational rules rather than altitude.

The International Telecommunication Union (ITU) offers another potential avenue. The ITU already governs the allocation of radio frequency spectrum and orbital slots for satellites, functions that implicitly assume a distinction between atmospheric and space-based systems. Expanding ITU's role to address spectrum issues arising from HAPS and other near-space platforms could contribute to the normative framework without requiring explicit delimitation. The convergence of telecommunications, aviation, and space governance in the transitional zone suggests that multiple institutions, each contributing its own area of expertise, may collectively produce the regulatory clarity that no single institution can achieve alone.

A third, more ambitious path would involve formal delimitation or the creation of a new legal regime for near space. This could take the form of a treaty defining a spatial boundary, a functional classification framework, or a hybrid transitional zone with cooperative management provisions. While intellectually appealing and advocated by some developing states, this approach would require unprecedented political consensus and faces formidable obstacles. The experience of COPUOS—sixty years of discussion without resolution—suggests that formal delimitation remains a distant prospect.

> ■ **The Enduring Significance of the Boundary Problem**
>
> The question of where outer space begins is ultimately a question about how law adapts to human expansion. It reflects the tension between territorial thinking and functional necessity, between sovereignty and cooperation, between the desire for certainty and the reality of ambiguity. For more than half a century, international space law has navigated this tension through restraint and pragmatism. Whether this approach remains viable will depend on the pace of technological change, the intensity of geopolitical competition, and the willingness of states to prioritize stability over control.

***

Chapter Summary

Chapter 3 has examined the boundary problem from every angle—scientific, legal, political, and technological—and has found that the question "What is outer space?" resists easy answers. Science reveals a continuum where law demands a threshold. Spatial theories offer clarity at the cost of arbitrariness. Functional theories offer flexibility at the cost of predictability. Hybrid approaches promise the best of both worlds but deliver the complexity of each. The maritime analogy, while suggestive, ultimately proves more misleading than helpful.

The international community's response to this dilemma has been remarkable in its consistency: six decades of deliberate non-decision, sustained by a constructive ambiguity that has proven far more durable and effective than most observers predicted. Satellites orbit freely, aircraft operate within sovereign airspace, and the vast majority of space activities proceed without jurisdictional dispute. The boundary problem, for all its theoretical significance, has not prevented the development of a functional and broadly effective governance regime.

Several factors have sustained this ambiguity. The physical separation between most air activities (conducted well below 20 kilometers) and most space activities (conducted well above 200 kilometers) has meant that the boundary region has, until recently, been sparsely populated. The consensus among spacefaring states that formal delimitation would constrain operational freedom has prevented any state from forcing the issue. The COPUOS consensus rule has ensured that no majority can impose delimitation over the objections of a minority. And the demonstrable success of the current approach—measured by the uninterrupted growth of space activities since 1957—has reduced the urgency of reform.

Yet the chapter has also shown that the conditions sustaining this ambiguity are changing. Near-space technologies—HAPS, suborbital vehicles, hypersonic weapons, reusable launch systems—are increasingly populating the transitional zone that constructive ambiguity was designed to manage. Commercial investment, military planning, and environmental concerns are all creating pressure for greater regulatory clarity. National legislation is diverging, with some states adopting spatial thresholds and others relying on functional definitions, creating potential for regulatory conflict in an increasingly international industry.

The question is no longer whether the boundary problem matters—it clearly does—but whether the political will exists to address it before technology forces the issue. The history examined in this chapter suggests that law responds to capability, not the other way around. If that pattern holds, the boundary question will be resolved not by academic debate or diplomatic negotiation but by the accumulation of state practice in response to new technologies—just as the legal status of outer space itself was established not by treaty but by the tacit acceptance of satellite overflight in 1957.

Understanding the boundary problem is essential to understanding everything that follows in this book. The legal status of outer space—its characterization as res communis, the province of all mankind—depends on a distinction between airspace and outer space that has never been formally drawn. The principles of non-appropriation, freedom of exploration, and state responsibility all assume a domain called "outer space" without defining it. The entire edifice of space law rests on a foundation that, while functionally sound, remains formally unfinished.

This unfinished quality is not necessarily a weakness. Indeed, it may be a strength—a form of built-in adaptability that has allowed space law to evolve without the constraints of premature precision. But it also means that the governance of outer space depends, in the final analysis, on a shared understanding that has never been made explicit. That understanding—rooted in the tacit consensus of 1957, reinforced by six decades of consistent practice, and sustained by the mutual interest of spacefaring and non-spacefaring states alike—is the true foundation of international space law. If it holds, the boundary problem remains manageable. If it fractures, the consequences will extend far beyond the transitional zone.

In the next chapter, we turn from boundaries to philosophy, examining how outer space has been conceptualized as a shared domain through doctrines such as res communis and the common heritage of mankind—and what these concepts mean for the governance of a domain that no one owns but everyone uses.

***

End of Chapter 3

Part II
LEGAL ARCHITECTURE OF SPACE GOVERNANCE

Chapter 4

OUTER SPACE AS A LEGAL DOMAIN: RES COMMUNIS OR COMMON HERITAGE OF MANKIND?

Who owns outer space? No one—and perhaps everyone. This chapter traces the competing legal philosophies that have sought to answer this question, from Roman res communis through the common heritage of mankind to the Artemis Accords, and examines what these answers mean for humanity's future among the stars.

Part 1

Philosophical and Historical Origins of Shared Legal Domains

The question of how outer space should be legally classified did not arise in a vacuum. Long before the first satellite entered orbit, international law had grappled with the governance of domains that lay beyond effective territorial control. Oceans, polar regions, and the deep seabed all forced jurists to confront a fundamental problem: how should law regulate spaces that cannot be owned, yet must be used? The legal concepts that emerged from these debates provided the intellectual foundation for the governance of outer space—and the tensions within those concepts continue to shape space law today.

Res Communis: The Roman Foundation

At the heart of this foundation lies the Roman law concept of res communis—things that are by their nature incapable of private or public ownership and are open to use by all. Classical Roman jurists applied this concept to natural elements such as air, flowing water, the sea, and the seashore. These resources were understood as essential to life and commerce, and therefore inappropriate subjects of exclusive ownership. The Institutes of Justinian, compiled in the sixth century CE, articulated the principle with characteristic clarity: "By the law of nature these things are common to mankind—the air, running water, the sea, and consequently the shores of the sea."

While Roman law was a domestic legal system, its conceptual categories profoundly influenced later European legal thought and, eventually, public international law. The distinction between res communis (things common to all), res nullius (things owned by no one but capable of appropriation), and res publica (things owned by the state) provided a vocabulary for categorizing domains beyond individual ownership. The classification mattered: a res communis domain could be used by all but owned by none, while a res nullius domain was simply unclaimed territory waiting to be appropriated.

The distinction between res communis and res nullius would prove critical for outer space. If outer space were classified as res nullius, it would be open to appropriation by the first state to claim it—a prospect that, in the context of the Cold War space race, was both legally plausible and politically terrifying. The classification as res communis foreclosed this possibility, establishing outer space as permanently open and permanently unowned. The choice between these categories was not merely academic; it was a choice about the future of human civilization beyond Earth.

> *"By the law of nature these things are common to mankind—the air, running water, the sea, and consequently the shores of the sea."*
>
> – Institutes of Justinian, Book II, Title I

Mare Liberum and the Freedom of the Seas

The application of res communis to the high seas represents one of the most enduring and consequential examples of this conceptual tradition. During the early modern period, European powers debated fiercely whether oceans could be claimed as extensions of territorial sovereignty. Spain and Portugal, bolstered by papal decrees, asserted exclusive control over vast oceanic areas. England and the Netherlands challenged these claims, invoking both practical necessity and philosophical principle.

The doctrine of mare liberum, famously articulated by Hugo Grotius in his 1609 treatise of the same name, argued that the seas must remain free for navigation and trade. Grotius's argument was not merely economic; it was philosophical and, in its way, scientific. He contended that the sea's physical characteristics—its vastness, fluidity, and resistance to permanent occupation—rendered exclusive ownership both impractical and unjust. The sea could not be fenced, cultivated, or settled; therefore, it could not be owned. Use was permitted; appropriation was not.

The eventual acceptance of freedom of the seas established a powerful precedent for all subsequent discussions of global commons. It demonstrated that international law could recognize domains as legally open without descending into lawlessness. Freedom did not imply the absence of law; rather, it implied governance through shared norms rather than territorial claims. States could use the seas freely, but they were required to respect the rights of others, to refrain from piracy and interference, and to cooperate on matters of common concern. This distinction—between freedom and anarchy, between openness and lawlessness—would later prove crucial in shaping space law.

It is worth noting that Grotius's position did not go unchallenged. The English jurist John Selden countered with Mare Clausum (1635), arguing that the seas were capable of appropriation and that English sovereignty extended over surrounding waters. The Grotius-Selden debate echoed through the centuries, finding resolution only in the modern law of the sea, which balances coastal state sovereignty (in territorial waters) with freedom of navigation (on the high seas). This compromise—graduated zones of authority from full sovereignty to complete freedom—demonstrated that the choice between openness and control need not be binary. Space law, however, has thus far resisted a comparable graduated approach, maintaining the sharp dichotomy between sovereign airspace and free outer space.

Antarctica: A Modern Precedent

The nineteenth and early twentieth centuries witnessed the extension of these ideas to other global commons, most notably Antarctica. Competing territorial claims by seven states (Argentina, Australia, Chile, France, New Zealand, Norway, and the United Kingdom), harsh environmental conditions, and the growing importance of scientific research converged to produce the Antarctic Treaty of 1959—one of the most innovative governance instruments of the twentieth century.

The Antarctic Treaty did not resolve competing sovereignty claims; it suspended them. Article IV froze the legal positions of all parties, preventing new claims and preserving existing ones without validating or invalidating them. The result was a governance model built on the deliberate avoidance of sovereignty disputes—a model that prioritized peaceful scientific cooperation and environmental protection over territorial competition. The parallels to the later space law regime are striking and not coincidental: several of the diplomats involved in the Antarctic Treaty negotiations were also engaged in early discussions about outer space governance.

The Antarctic model introduced two innovations that would prove influential for space law. First, it demonstrated that suspending sovereignty claims—rather than resolving them—could be a viable governance strategy, providing stability while avoiding the political costs of definitive settlement. The Outer Space Treaty's Article II, which prohibits national appropriation entirely rather than merely suspending claims, went further than the Antarctic model, reflecting the greater urgency of preventing a space-based colonial scramble. Second, the Antarctic Treaty System's subsequent development—including the Madrid Protocol on Environmental Protection (1991), which designated Antarctica as a natural reserve devoted to peace and science—showed that governance frameworks could deepen and evolve over time, moving from foundational principles to detailed regulation as circumstances required.

The Deep Seabed: A Cautionary Tale

The deep seabed offers yet another precedent—and a cautionary one. The mineral resources of the ocean floor, particularly the polymetallic manganese nodules lying on the abyssal plains at depths of 4,000 to 6,000 meters, attracted intense interest in the 1960s and 1970s. These nodules contained nickel, copper, cobalt, and manganese—materials of significant industrial value. Their discovery raised immediate questions about ownership and access: could any state claim the deep seabed and its resources, or were they the common property of humanity?

The resolution of this question through Part XI of the United Nations Convention on the Law of the Sea (UNCLOS) in 1982, and its subsequent modification through the 1994 Implementation Agreement, provides essential context for understanding the space resource debate. Part XI established the International Seabed Authority (ISA) to manage deep seabed mining and mandated the equitable sharing of benefits. However, industrialized states—particularly the United States, which did not ratify UNCLOS until the Implementation Agreement modified its most redistributive provisions—objected to what they viewed as excessive regulation and compulsory technology transfer. The result was a compromise that preserved the common heritage designation while substantially reducing its operational implications.

The deep seabed experience carries two lessons for space governance. First, ambitious redistributive frameworks face formidable political resistance from technologically advanced states that stand to lose the most from mandatory benefit-sharing. Second, institutional design matters: governance structures perceived as bureaucratic, biased, or inefficient will be rejected regardless of their normative appeal. Both lessons shaped—and continue to shape—the debate over space resource governance.

■ **Historical Precedents for Space Governance**

High Seas (Grotius, 1609): Freedom of navigation; no sovereignty; use rights for all states.

Antarctica (Treaty, 1959): Sovereignty claims frozen; dedicated to science and peace.

Deep Seabed (UNCLOS Part XI, 1982): Common heritage of mankind; International Seabed Authority.

International Airspace (Chicago Convention, 1944): Sovereignty-based; access by consent only.

Each precedent offered a different governance model; space law drew selectively from all of them.

The Imperfect Analogy

These historical precedents reveal a recurring pattern: when human activity expands into spaces that resist occupation or enforcement, law evolves toward functional openness combined with cooperative restraint. Ownership gives way to access; exclusion yields to regulation. This pattern shaped early thinking about outer space long before the technology to reach it existed.

However, the analogy between outer space and earlier global commons is imperfect in ways that have profound legal consequences. Unlike the seas or Antarctica, outer space is not merely a natural environment to be traversed or studied; it is a domain of extraordinary strategic and technological significance. Satellites provide communication, navigation, intelligence, weather forecasting, and military command and control. Control of space-based infrastructure translates directly into geopolitical and economic power. This reality complicates the application of res communis principles, which assume relatively equal access and benign use.

The philosophical debate over outer space thus extends beyond legal classification to questions of justice and distribution. If outer space is open to all, who benefits in practice? If access depends on technological capability and financial resources, does formal openness merely entrench inequality—masking the dominance of powerful states behind the rhetoric of universality? These questions echo earlier critiques of freedom of the seas, where European naval powers invoked mare liberum while using their superior fleets to dominate global trade. The parallel is uncomfortable but instructive.

In the mid-twentieth century, as spaceflight transitioned from fiction to reality, these concerns took on renewed urgency. Legal scholars and diplomats recognized that choices made at the outset would shape the future of space activity for generations. The concept of res communis offered a familiar and politically palatable starting point. It aligned with existing international law traditions and avoided the contentious implications of collective ownership or redistribution. At the same time, it left unresolved questions about benefit-sharing and long-term governance—questions that would later give rise to the alternative doctrine of the common heritage of mankind.

The decolonization movement of the 1950s and 1960s added a moral dimension to these debates. Newly independent states—many of them emerging from centuries of colonial exploitation—were deeply skeptical of legal frameworks that proclaimed universal freedom while permitting the powerful to dominate. For these states, the history of mare liberum was not merely a legal precedent but a cautionary tale: the freedom of the seas had enabled European imperial powers to project force, extract resources, and control trade routes across the globe. The rhetoric of openness had served the interests of the strong. A space law regime built on the same principles, without explicit mechanisms for equity, risked reproducing the same patterns in a new domain.

This concern was articulated with particular force by representatives of developing states in the United Nations during the 1960s and 1970s. Their arguments drew on the broader political agenda of the New International Economic Order (NIEO)—a movement that sought to restructure global economic relations in favor of developing countries. The common heritage doctrine, when it emerged, was part of this larger political project: an attempt to ensure that the governance of new domains would serve the interests of all humanity, not merely those states with the technological capacity to exploit them first.

> ■ **Res Communis vs. Res Nullius: The Stakes of Classification**
>
> If outer space were classified as res nullius (ownerless but appropriable), it would be open to sovereignty claims by the first state to assert control—potentially triggering a colonial-style scramble for celestial territory. Classification as res communis (common to all, owned by none) foreclosed this possibility. The Outer Space Treaty's Article II, prohibiting national appropriation, effectively codified the res communis approach.

***

Part II

The Outer Space Treaty and the Res Communis Model

The philosophical foundations of shared domains found their most concrete legal expression in the Outer Space Treaty of 1967, the cornerstone of international space law. Negotiated during the height of the Cold War under the auspices of the United Nations, the Treaty reflects a careful balancing act: it embraces the logic of res communis to prevent conflict and territorial competition, while avoiding the stronger redistributive obligations that might have jeopardized political consensus. The result is a legal regime that is deliberately open-ended—principled rather than prescriptive, stabilizing rather than transformative.

Historical Context and Political Compromise

The Outer Space Treaty emerged from a unique geopolitical moment. The United States and the Soviet Union, despite intense rivalry on nearly every other front, shared a common interest in preventing the extension of terrestrial conflict into outer space. Both powers relied increasingly on satellites for communications, navigation, arms control verification, and strategic early warning. Any attempt to claim sovereignty over orbital regions or celestial bodies risked triggering confrontation and undermining these mutual capabilities.

The 1962 Cuban Missile Crisis had demonstrated how quickly superpower rivalry could escalate to the brink of nuclear war. The Treaty on the Non-Proliferation of Nuclear Weapons was under negotiation. In this context, the Outer Space Treaty served a dual function: it was both a governance instrument for space and a confidence-building measure between adversaries. By declaring outer space open to all and owned by none, the Treaty removed incentives for territorial competition while preserving freedom of access for technologically capable states.

The negotiation process itself was remarkably rapid. Building on the 1963 Declaration of Legal Principles (UN General Assembly Resolution 1962), delegations at COPUOS and the First Committee of the General Assembly hammered out the Treaty's text in approximately eighteen months. The speed reflected both the urgency of the moment and the breadth of the consensus: the foundational principles—non-appropriation, freedom of exploration, peaceful use, state responsibility—had already been articulated in the 1963 Declaration and accepted by all major space powers. The Treaty's task was to codify these principles in binding form.

The Treaty's rapid conclusion also owed much to bilateral diplomatic channels between Washington and Moscow. Both superpowers recognized that a multilateral treaty framework would be more stable and legitimate than bilateral arrangements, but the substantive content was largely pre-negotiated between them before being presented to the broader COPUOS membership. This dynamic—great power consensus ratified through multilateral processes—would characterize space law-making for the next decade, producing the Rescue Agreement (1968), the Liability Convention (1972), and the Registration Convention (1976) in quick succession.

Article IV: The Demilitarization Compromise

Article IV of the Outer Space Treaty addresses the military dimension of space governance and represents one of the Treaty's most important—and most misunderstood—provisions. It prohibits the placement of weapons of mass destruction in orbit, the installation of such weapons on celestial bodies, and the establishment of military bases, installations, and fortifications on celestial bodies. However, it does not prohibit the placement of conventional weapons in orbit, nor does it prohibit military use of outer space generally.

This partial demilitarization reflects a deliberate compromise. Both superpowers relied heavily on military satellites for reconnaissance, early warning, communications, and navigation. A complete prohibition of military activity in space would have been unacceptable to either side and would likely have prevented the Treaty from being concluded at all. The drafters therefore drew a distinction between weapons of mass destruction (prohibited in orbit) and other military activities (permitted), and between celestial bodies (fully demilitarized) and outer space generally (partially regulated). This distinction has been criticized as inadequate by proponents of complete space demilitarization, but it has proven durable precisely because it accommodates the security interests of major space powers.

Article I: Freedom of Exploration and Use

> **■ Outer Space Treaty, Article I**
>
> "The exploration and use of outer space, including the Moon and other celestial bodies, shall be carried out for the benefit and in the interests of all countries, irrespective of their degree of economic or scientific development, and shall be the province of all mankind."
>
> "Outer space, including the Moon and other celestial bodies, shall be free for exploration and use by all States without discrimination of any kind, on a basis of equality and in accordance with international law, and there shall be free access to all areas of celestial bodies."

Article I of the Outer Space Treaty closely mirrors the logic of res communis. Freedom is framed as a legal right, not a privilege, and it applies universally—to all states, regardless of their economic or scientific development. The phrase "province of all mankind" signaled a moral commitment to inclusivity, though its precise legal content remained deliberately vague.

Yet this freedom is not absolute. The Article requires that activities be conducted "in accordance with international law" and with due regard to the interests of other states. These qualifiers introduce normative constraints, signaling that openness does not equate to license. Freedom operates within a framework of mutual restraint and responsibility—a principle that echoes the law of the sea's requirement of "due regard" for the rights and interests of other states.

Importantly, Article I avoids specifying how benefits are to be shared. It affirms that exploration and use "shall be carried out for the benefit and in the interests of all countries," but leaves the meaning of "benefit" undefined. This ambiguity was intentional. It allowed consensus among states with divergent views on redistribution, while preserving a moral commitment to inclusivity that developing states could invoke in future negotiations. The phrase was aspirational rather than operational—a promise without a mechanism.

The phrase "province of all mankind" has generated extensive scholarly debate. Some commentators interpret it as a rhetorical flourish without independent legal content—a decorative affirmation of universality that adds nothing to the operative provisions of the Treaty. Others argue that it creates a substantive legal obligation, requiring states to consider the interests of non-spacefaring nations when conducting space activities. Still others view it as a compromise formulation that falls short of the common heritage of mankind concept (which would be formally introduced in the Moon Agreement a decade later) but gestures in its direction.

The practical significance of this linguistic ambiguity became apparent in the context of space resource utilization. Proponents of commercial extraction argue that "province of all mankind" denotes openness and accessibility—the domain is open to all, and its benefits are realized through use, which is itself open to all states. Opponents argue that "province of all mankind" implies a collective interest that cannot be satisfied by unilateral exploitation—that resources extracted from a domain designated as humanity's province must, in some meaningful sense, benefit all of humanity, not merely the extracting state or company. This interpretive dispute remains unresolved and lies at the heart of contemporary space governance debates.

Article II: Non-Appropriation and the Rejection of Sovereignty

> *"Outer space, including the Moon and other celestial bodies, is not subject to national appropriation by claim of sovereignty, by means of use or occupation, or by any other means."*
>
> – Outer Space Treaty, Article II

Article II is the Treaty's most explicit expression of the res communis model and its single most important provision. It prohibits national appropriation of outer space, the Moon, and other celestial bodies "by claim of sovereignty, by means of use or occupation, or by any other means." The breadth of this prohibition is striking. The drafters included "or by any other means" to foreclose creative circumvention—a lesson learned from the history of colonial acquisition, where sovereignty had been asserted through discovery, occupation, effective control, papal grant, and treaty cession.

The prohibition reflects the drafters' determination to prevent the gradual normalization of territorial claims through practice. In air law and maritime law, sovereignty had expanded incrementally as states asserted control over adjacent zones. Article II was designed to halt this process in space before it could begin. No use, however prolonged or intensive, could ripen into ownership. No occupation, however permanent, could generate sovereignty. The domain would remain forever open.

At the same time, the Article carefully limits its scope to national appropriation. It does not explicitly address private ownership, nor does it define the legal status of extracted resources. This silence—whether intentional or the product of an era when private space activity was unimaginable—would later become a focal point of controversy, as states and scholars debated whether commercial resource extraction could be reconciled with the non-appropriation principle.

The interpretive challenge is subtle but consequential. If a private company, authorized by its home state, extracts water ice from the Moon and claims ownership of that water, has the home state engaged in "national appropriation"? The company is not claiming sovereignty over the extraction site; it is not asserting territorial control or exclusive jurisdiction over the lunar surface. It is claiming ownership only of the material it has physically removed. Proponents of this interpretation draw on the analogy of fishing: no one claims sovereignty over the ocean by catching fish, and the fish become the property of the fisher upon capture, even though the ocean remains a commons.

Opponents counter that the analogy is imperfect. Fish are renewable; minerals are not. The high seas are vast and access is widely distributed; the most valuable lunar resources are concentrated in a small number of locations (permanently shadowed craters near the poles) where first-movers enjoy decisive advantages. Extracting resources from these locations could effectively deny access to latecomers—not through a formal sovereignty claim, but through the practical reality of prior occupation and infrastructure placement. This concern—that resource extraction could produce de facto appropriation through the back door—animates much of the opposition to unilateral resource legislation and the Artemis Accords.

Jurisdiction Without Territory

One of the most innovative features of the Outer Space Treaty is its approach to jurisdiction. Article VIII provides that a state on whose registry a space object is carried retains jurisdiction and control over that object, and over any personnel thereof, while in outer space or on a celestial body. Rather than asserting control over territory, the Treaty links jurisdiction to objects and personnel—a model sometimes described as "quasi-flag state" jurisdiction by analogy with the law of the sea.

This approach aligns with the res communis philosophy by decoupling governance from geography. Law follows the actor, not the place. A space station remains under the jurisdiction of its launching state regardless of where it orbits—whether above the Pacific Ocean, the Sahara, or the polar ice caps. In doing so, the Treaty creates a functional legal order capable of operating in a domain where territorial enforcement is physically impossible and conceptually inappropriate.

The practical implications are far-reaching. Crimes committed aboard a space station are subject to the jurisdiction of the registry state. Property rights in space objects are determined by the law of the launching state. Disputes between personnel of different nationalities on a jointly operated facility require coordination between national legal systems—a challenge that has been addressed, for the International Space Station, through the 1998 Intergovernmental Agreement (IGA), which allocates jurisdiction among partner states based on module registration.

State Responsibility and the Public-Private Interface

Article VI of the Outer Space Treaty introduces a principle with no parallel in any other area of international law: states bear international responsibility for all national activities in outer space, whether carried out by governmental agencies or by non-governmental entities. Moreover, non-governmental activities require the "authorization and continuing supervision" of the appropriate state. This provision effectively makes states the guarantors of private behavior in space—a remarkable extension of sovereign responsibility.

The rationale for this approach was straightforward. In 1967, space activity was exclusively governmental, and the drafters could not have anticipated the explosion of commercial space activity that would follow. Nevertheless, they recognized that private actors might eventually enter the domain and took the precaution of ensuring that states would remain accountable. The result is a legal architecture in which private companies can operate in space, but only under the umbrella of state authorization and supervision.

This architecture has profound implications for the res communis model. It means that the freedom of outer space is mediated through states. Private actors do not have direct standing under the Outer Space Treaty; their rights and obligations flow from the national legislation of their authorizing state. The res communis domain is thus governed not by a single set of international rules directly applicable to all actors, but by a patchwork of national regulatory frameworks unified only by the broad principles of the Treaty itself. This mediated freedom creates both flexibility and inconsistency—flexibility because states can adapt their regulation to national circumstances, inconsistency because different states may interpret the same Treaty principles in divergent ways.

■ The Outer Space Treaty: Key Provisions and Res Communis Logic

Article I: Freedom of exploration and use; province of all mankind; benefit of all countries.

Article II: Non-appropriation by sovereignty, use, occupation, or any other means.

Article III: Activities in accordance with international law and the UN Charter.

Article IV: No weapons of mass destruction in orbit; celestial bodies for peaceful purposes.

Article VI: States bear responsibility for national space activities (governmental and non-governmental).

Article VII: States are liable for damage caused by their space objects.

Article VIII: Registry state retains jurisdiction over objects and personnel.

As of 2025: 114 ratifications and 23 signatures.

■ Strengths and Limits of the Res Communis Model

The res communis framework has maintained stability in outer space for nearly sixty years by preventing sovereignty claims and enabling the growth of global satellite infrastructure. However, its limitations are increasingly apparent: freedom of access does not guarantee equality of opportunity. States with advanced technology reap disproportionate benefits, while others remain largely dependent on shared services. The model's silence on resource exploitation has created uncertainty that contemporary developments are forcing into the open.

***

Part III

The Moon Agreement and the Common Heritage of Mankind

If the Outer Space Treaty represents a cautious embrace of openness through the res communis model, the Moon Agreement of 1979 embodies a far more ambitious—and controversial—vision. By introducing the doctrine of the common heritage of mankind (CHM), the Agreement sought to address concerns about inequality, exploitation, and long-term governance that the res communis framework left unresolved. Its limited acceptance, however, reveals the political and structural challenges of translating moral aspiration into binding international law.

Origins of the Common Heritage Concept

The concept of the common heritage of mankind did not originate in space law. It emerged in the late 1960s in response to technological advances that made previously inaccessible resources—particularly the mineral-rich manganese nodules of the deep seabed—available for exploitation. The Maltese ambassador Arvid Pardo delivered a landmark address to the United Nations General Assembly in 1967, proposing that the deep seabed and its resources be declared the common heritage of mankind—not merely open to all (res communis) but collectively owned and managed for the benefit of all humanity, with particular attention to the needs of developing countries.

Pardo's proposal was revolutionary in its implications. Unlike res communis, which emphasizes freedom of access and the absence of ownership, CHM emphasizes collective ownership, equitable benefit-sharing, management through international institutions, reservation for peaceful purposes, and intergenerational responsibility. Resources designated as the common heritage of mankind are not merely open; they are held in trust for humanity as a whole, including future generations who have not yet been born. The concept thus introduced a temporal dimension absent from res communis—an obligation not only to present users but to posterity.

The common heritage concept, as articulated by Pardo and subsequently elaborated by scholars and diplomats, comprises five essential elements that distinguish it from res communis. First, the domain in question cannot be appropriated by any state or private entity. Second, it must be managed by an international authority acting on behalf of all humanity. Third, the benefits derived from the domain must be shared equitably among all states. Fourth, the domain must be reserved for peaceful purposes. Fifth, the domain must be preserved for future generations. These five elements—non-appropriation, international management, benefit-sharing, peaceful use, and intergenerational equity—constitute the normative core of CHM and differentiate it sharply from the more permissive res communis framework.

■ **Five Elements of the Common Heritage of Mankind**

1. Non-appropriation: The domain cannot be owned by any state or private entity.
2. International management: An international authority manages the domain on behalf of all humanity.
3. Benefit-sharing: Benefits from exploitation must be shared equitably among all states.
4. Peaceful use: The domain is reserved for peaceful purposes.
5. Intergenerational equity: The domain must be preserved for future generations.

These elements go significantly beyond the res communis model, which guarantees only non-appropriation and freedom of access.

> *"The sea-bed and the ocean floor, and the subsoil thereof, beyond the limits of national jurisdiction, as well as the resources of the area, are the common heritage of mankind."*
>
> – Arvid Pardo, address to the UN General Assembly, 1 November 1967

These ideas gained legal traction during the Third United Nations Conference on the Law of the Sea (1973–1982), which ultimately incorporated the CHM concept into Part XI of UNCLOS, establishing the International Seabed Authority (ISA) to manage deep seabed mining. The success of CHM in the law of the sea context—however qualified by the 1994 Implementation Agreement that significantly modified Part XI—inspired its proponents to extend the doctrine to outer space.

The Moon Agreement's Legal Architecture

The Agreement Governing the Activities of States on the Moon and Other Celestial Bodies—commonly known as the Moon Agreement—was adopted by the UN General Assembly in 1979 and entered into force in 1984. It builds upon the Outer Space Treaty but departs from it in crucial respects. Article 11(1) declares that "the Moon and its natural resources are the common heritage of mankind." This declaration carries significant legal implications that go well beyond the non-appropriation principle of the Outer Space Treaty.

Under the Moon Agreement, the CHM designation means that no state or private entity may claim ownership of lunar resources. The exploitation of those resources must be governed by an international regime to be established "as such exploitation is about to become feasible." This future regime would be responsible for the orderly development of lunar resources, the equitable sharing of benefits—with "special consideration" given to developing countries—and the rational management of resources. The Agreement also emphasizes scientific cooperation, environmental protection, and the obligation to inform the UN Secretary-General of any activities on the Moon.

> ■ **Moon Agreement, Article 11 (Key Provisions)**
>
> 11(1): The Moon and its natural resources are the common heritage of mankind.
>
> 11(3): Neither the surface nor subsurface of the Moon shall become the property of any state, international organization, or non-governmental entity.
>
> 11(5): States Parties undertake to establish an international regime to govern exploitation of natural resources of the Moon as such exploitation is about to become feasible.
>
> 11(7)(d): An equitable sharing by all States Parties in the benefits derived from those resources, whereby the interests and needs of the developing countries shall be given special consideration.
>
> The Agreement entered into force in 1984 but has been ratified by only 18 states as of 2025.

Political Resistance and Limited Ratification

Despite its normative ambition, the Moon Agreement has attracted only limited support. As of 2025, it has been ratified by just eighteen states—none of which are major spacefaring nations. The United States, Russia, China, India, Japan, and the European spacefaring states have not ratified it, and several have explicitly indicated that they do not intend to do so. As a result, the Moon Agreement's legal impact on the actual conduct of space activities has been minimal.

Several factors explain this resistance. First, spacefaring states viewed the CHM doctrine as overly restrictive. The requirement to establish an international regime before resource exploitation could proceed was seen as an obstacle to innovation, investment, and national advantage. The precedent of the International Seabed Authority—which had been criticized by industrialized states as bureaucratic and biased toward developing country interests—provided a cautionary example. States feared that a comparable institution for lunar governance would impose burdensome regulatory requirements and mandatory benefit-sharing mechanisms that would deter private actors and slow technological progress.

Second, the Agreement's ambiguity undermined its appeal. While it called for an international regime, it provided minimal detail on how such a regime would function—its decision-making procedures, enforcement mechanisms, membership criteria, or dispute resolution processes. This vagueness was perhaps unavoidable given that lunar exploitation was decades away, but it created uncertainty that states were unwilling to accept as a binding commitment.

Third, the geopolitical climate had shifted decisively between 1967 and 1979. The cooperative spirit that had enabled the Outer Space Treaty—born of post-Cuban Missile Crisis détente and a shared desire to prevent space weaponization—had given way to renewed competition. The United States was developing the Space Shuttle; the Soviet Union was expanding its space station program; both were investing heavily in military space capabilities. In this environment, states prioritized strategic autonomy over collective management.

The fate of the Moon Agreement also illustrates a broader pattern in international law: the timing of legal innovation matters as much as its content. The Outer Space Treaty succeeded in part because it was negotiated at a moment of shared vulnerability—both superpowers recognized the catastrophic potential of space weaponization and were willing to accept mutual constraints. The Moon Agreement, by contrast, was negotiated during a period of renewed assertiveness, when major powers were less inclined to accept obligations that limited their freedom of action. The lesson for contemporary space governance is clear: ambitious multilateral instruments are most likely to succeed when the major actors perceive mutual vulnerability and shared risk—conditions that may or may not obtain in the current era of intensifying space competition.

Normative Influence Despite Legal Weakness

Although the Moon Agreement lacks widespread acceptance as binding law, its normative influence should not be underestimated. It crystallized debates about equity, sustainability, and intergenerational justice that continue to shape discussions of space governance decades later. Concepts first introduced or formalized by the Agreement—benefit-sharing, environmental stewardship, rational resource management, attention to developing country interests—resurface in virtually every contemporary policy debate about lunar and asteroid resource utilization.

The Moon Agreement also serves as a persistent reminder of what the Outer Space Treaty left unresolved. By articulating a more comprehensive vision of space governance—one that addressed not only who may act in space but who benefits from those actions—the Agreement exposed the limitations of the res communis model and challenged the international community to think more seriously about distributive justice in outer space.

Res Communis vs. Common Heritage: A False Dichotomy?

The tension between res communis and CHM is often presented as a binary choice between two incompatible philosophies. In practice, however, the future of space governance may lie somewhere between these models. Absolute freedom (res communis without qualification) risks entrenching inequality, allowing technologically advanced states to monopolize resources while invoking the rhetoric of openness. Rigid collective control (common heritage with mandatory redistribution) risks stifling innovation, deterring investment, and creating institutional bottlenecks that prevent resource utilization from proceeding at all.

A more nuanced analysis reveals that the two concepts share important common ground. Both reject national appropriation of celestial territory. Both affirm that space activities should serve the interests of all humanity. Both presuppose some form of international cooperation, even if they disagree about its institutional expression. The disagreement is less about ultimate values than about mechanisms: how should benefits be shared? Through market access and voluntary cooperation (the res communis approach) or through institutional management and mandatory redistribution (the common heritage approach)?

Contemporary scholarship has increasingly explored hybrid frameworks that draw on both traditions. Proposals include voluntary benefit-sharing agreements linked to licensing conditions, technology transfer programs funded by revenues from space resource activities, common-pool resource management models adapted from Elinor Ostrom's Nobel Prize-winning research on the governance of shared resources, and multilateral investment frameworks that give developing states equity participation in space resource ventures. These approaches seek to capture the dynamism of market-based systems while addressing the equity concerns that animate the common heritage tradition.

Feature	**Res Communis (OST)**	**Common Heritage (Moon Ag.)**
Ownership	No state ownership	No state or private ownership
Access	Free for all states	Free, but subject to international regime
Resources	Silent on extracted resources	Governed by future international regime
Benefit-sharing	Aspirational ('benefit of all')	Mandatory and equitable
Institutions	State responsibility model	International management authority
Developing states	Equal in principle	Special consideration required
Ratification	114 states (2025)	18 states (2025)
Political support	Universal among space powers	Rejected by all space powers

***

Part IV

Contemporary Resource Extraction and the Future of Space Governance

The long-standing debate between res communis and the common heritage of mankind has moved decisively from theory to practice in the twenty-first century. Advances in space technology, coupled with growing scientific understanding of lunar and asteroid geology, have transformed resource extraction from speculative possibility into a realistic near-term objective. These developments are reshaping the legal landscape of outer space and testing the adequacy of both governance models.

The Emergence of Space Resource Utilization

For decades, space resources were discussed primarily in abstract terms. Today, state agencies and private companies actively pursue technologies capable of extracting water ice, rare minerals, helium-3, and other valuable materials from the Moon and near-Earth asteroids. Water, in particular, has extraordinary strategic importance: it can be converted into hydrogen and oxygen—rocket propellant components—enabling in-space refueling that could dramatically reduce the cost of deep space missions. Water is also essential for life support, making it the critical enabler of sustained human presence beyond Earth.

Figure 15: NASA's Space Launch System (SLS) Rocket on the Launch Pad

Source: NASA (Public Domain).

NASA's Artemis program, which aims to return humans to the Moon and establish a sustained presence there, explicitly envisions the utilization of lunar resources—particularly water ice deposits identified in permanently shadowed craters near the lunar south pole. China's Chang'e program has similar objectives. India, Japan, South Korea, and the UAE have all conducted or are planning lunar missions with resource characterization as a primary objective. Private companies including SpaceX, Blue Origin, ispace, and Astrobotic are developing landers, rovers, and extraction technologies with commercial resource utilization in mind.

Beyond water ice, the Moon contains substantial deposits of minerals and metals with potential industrial applications. Helium-3, a rare isotope on Earth but relatively abundant in the lunar regolith due to billions of years of solar wind implantation, has been proposed as a fuel for future nuclear fusion reactors—though this application remains speculative. Rare earth elements, titanium, and iron are present in lunar rocks and soil. Regolith can be processed into construction materials via sintering or 3D printing, enabling the construction of lunar habitats from local materials rather than relying on expensive Earth-to-Moon transport. This concept—known as in-situ resource utilization (ISRU)—is central to the economic case for sustained lunar presence and is a primary driver of the legal debate over resource ownership.

Near-Earth asteroids present even more dramatic resource possibilities. Some asteroids contain concentrations of platinum-group metals (platinum, palladium, rhodium, iridium) that dwarf terrestrial reserves. A single metallic asteroid a few hundred meters in diameter could, in theory, contain more platinum than has ever been mined on Earth. While the technical challenges of asteroid mining are formidable—requiring precise navigation, autonomous extraction in microgravity, and either in-space processing or return of material to Earth or cis-lunar space—several companies have pursued these goals, and NASA's OSIRIS-REx mission demonstrated the feasibility of collecting material from an asteroid's surface.

This shift has profound legal implications. While the Outer Space Treaty prohibits national appropriation of celestial bodies, it does not explicitly address the ownership of extracted resources. States and private actors have seized upon this silence to argue that use does not equate to appropriation—that extracting water from lunar regolith is analogous to catching fish on the high seas, where the resource becomes property upon capture even though the ocean itself remains common.

National Legislation and the Artemis Accords

Several states have enacted national legislation recognizing the rights of their nationals to own and commercialize space resources. The United States led this movement with the Commercial Space Launch Competitiveness Act of 2015 (particularly Section 51303), which affirmed that U.S. citizens engaged in commercial recovery of space resources are entitled to own, transport, use, and sell such resources in accordance with applicable law. Luxembourg followed in 2017 with its own Space Resources Act, explicitly designed to attract space mining companies to establish European headquarters there. The UAE's Federal Law No. 12 of 2019 on the Regulation of the Space Sector includes provisions addressing space resource activities. Japan enacted similar legislation in 2021.

■ National Space Resource Legislation

United States (2015): Commercial Space Launch Competitiveness Act, §51303. Citizens may own extracted space resources.

Luxembourg (2017): Space Resources Act. First European law recognizing space resource property rights.

UAE (2019): Federal Law No. 12 on Space Sector. Includes provisions for space resource activities.

Japan (2021): Act on Promotion of Business Activities Related to Exploration and Development of Space Resources.

India (proposed): Draft Space Activities Bill includes resource utilization provisions.

Critics argue these laws constitute 'creeping appropriation' that undermines the Outer Space Treaty.

The most significant multilateral development has been the Artemis Accords, a series of bilateral agreements between the United States and partner states establishing principles for civil space exploration and use. Launched in 2020, the Accords are not a treaty; they are non-binding political commitments implemented through individual bilateral agreements between NASA and partner space agencies. As of early 2025, over forty states have signed the Accords, making them the most widely endorsed framework for lunar governance outside the Outer Space Treaty itself.

The Artemis Accords address a range of governance issues beyond resource extraction. They include provisions on transparency (publicly releasing scientific data), interoperability (using common standards for systems that may need to interact), emergency assistance (helping astronauts in distress regardless of nationality), registration of space objects, preservation of outer space heritage (protecting historic sites such as Apollo landing areas), prevention of harmful interference, and orbital debris mitigation. These provisions draw heavily on existing Outer Space Treaty obligations while adding specificity that the Treaty itself lacks.

Section 10 of the Artemis Accords addresses space resources directly, affirming that the extraction of space resources "does not inherently constitute national appropriation under the Outer Space Treaty." The Accords draw a distinction between resource extraction (permissible) and sovereignty over celestial territory (prohibited), arguing that the two are legally separable. Signatories commit to informing the Secretary-General of the United Nations and the scientific community about their resource utilization activities and to operating in a manner consistent with the Outer Space Treaty.

> *"The Signatories affirm that the extraction of space resources does not inherently constitute national appropriation under the Outer Space Treaty, and that contracts and other legal instruments relating to space resources should be consistent with that Treaty."*
>
> – Artemis Accords, Section 10, 2020

Critics of the Artemis Accords raise several concerns. First, the Accords were negotiated bilaterally by the United States rather than through the multilateral COPUOS process, raising questions about inclusivity and legitimacy. Second, the resource extraction provisions effectively interpret the Outer Space Treaty in a manner favorable to spacefaring states, without the consent of the broader treaty community. Third, the Accords' provisions on "safety zones"—areas around operations where states would coordinate to avoid harmful interference—could, critics argue, function as de facto territorial claims, creating zones of exclusive control that Article II was designed to prevent.

Defenders of the Accords counter that they represent a practical and transparent approach to space governance in the absence of a comprehensive multilateral framework. They note that the Accords expressly reaffirm the Outer Space Treaty, that safety zones are temporary and activity-based rather than territorial, and that the alternative—waiting for COPUOS consensus that may never materialize—risks leaving space activities entirely unregulated. The debate remains vigorous and unresolved.

The China-Russia Alternative: ILRS

The emergence of a parallel framework starkly illustrates the geopolitical dimension of the governance debate. In 2021, China and Russia announced plans for the International Lunar Research Station (ILRS), a joint initiative to establish a long-term robotic and eventually crewed research base at the lunar south pole. The ILRS framework operates outside the Artemis Accords system, with its own set of participating states and its own governance principles. As of early 2025, several states—including Pakistan, Venezuela, South Africa, Egypt, Thailand, and Belarus—have signed cooperation agreements with the ILRS initiative.

The coexistence of two competing lunar governance frameworks—one led by the United States (Artemis Accords), the other by China and Russia (ILRS)—raises the specter of fragmented space governance. Different rules for resource extraction, safety zones, environmental protection, and heritage site preservation could apply depending on which framework a given operator subscribes to. This fragmentation would undermine the universality that both res communis and common heritage presuppose and could create zones of competing jurisdiction on the lunar surface—precisely the outcome that the Outer Space Treaty was designed to prevent.

The fragmentation risk lends urgency to multilateral efforts within COPUOS. A comprehensive, universally accepted framework for space resource governance—even one that begins with modest, non-binding guidelines—would provide common ground between competing blocs and reduce the risk of conflicting claims. The COPUOS Working Group on the Legal Aspects of Space Resource Activities, established in 2022, represents the most promising venue for such efforts, though progress has been slow and expectations remain modest.

Environmental and Ethical Dimensions

Resource extraction also raises environmental and ethical concerns that neither res communis nor the Artemis Accords adequately address. Celestial bodies possess scientific value that could be irreversibly damaged by unregulated exploitation. The permanently shadowed craters near the lunar south pole, which contain the water ice deposits most attractive for extraction, are also among the most scientifically valuable sites in the solar system—pristine records of billions of years of solar system history. Extracting water from these craters would alter them permanently, potentially destroying scientific data that can never be recovered.

The Apollo landing sites represent another category of concern. These locations—where human footprints, equipment, and flags have remained undisturbed for over fifty years—possess cultural and historical significance that transcends national boundaries. While no international instrument formally protects them, the United States has proposed "safety zones" around Apollo sites under the Artemis Accords framework, and in 2020 NASA issued voluntary guidelines for the protection of historic lunar sites. Whether these measures are sufficient to protect heritage sites from the pressures of commercial activity remains an open question.

The common heritage doctrine offers a conceptual framework for addressing these concerns by emphasizing stewardship and intergenerational equity. Even if the Moon Agreement itself remains marginal, its principles continue to inform debates about sustainable space development and provide a moral vocabulary for those who argue that the commercial exploitation of celestial bodies must be accompanied by obligations to preserve, protect, and share.

The concept of planetary protection—historically focused on preventing biological contamination between Earth and other celestial bodies—is also evolving to encompass broader environmental stewardship. The Committee on Space Research (COSPAR) maintains planetary protection guidelines that all spacefaring nations have historically observed. As commercial lunar and Mars missions multiply, however, the voluntary nature of these guidelines may prove insufficient. The intersection of environmental protection, resource governance, and heritage preservation in the space domain represents one of the most complex and underexplored challenges in contemporary international law.

The Role of Developing States

A persistent and legitimate concern underlying the entire res communis versus common heritage debate is the position of developing states. The Outer Space Treaty's promise that exploration and use shall be conducted "for the benefit and in the interests of all countries" has not been accompanied by effective mechanisms for translating this aspiration into reality. As of 2025, the overwhelming majority of space activities—launch services, satellite operations, crewed spaceflight, resource exploration—are conducted by a small number of technologically advanced states and their commercial entities.

Developing states have legitimate interests in space governance that extend beyond abstract participation. Satellite communications and Earth observation data are essential for development, disaster management, climate adaptation, and food security. Access to orbital slots and radio frequency spectrum is increasingly competitive. The benefits of space resource utilization—if they materialize—could either widen or narrow the global development gap, depending on the governance framework that is adopted.

The Group of 77 and China—the largest intergovernmental organization of developing countries within the United Nations—has consistently advocated for governance frameworks that include explicit benefit-sharing provisions, capacity-building commitments, and institutional mechanisms that give developing states a meaningful voice. While these positions have not prevailed in the Artemis Accords framework, they continue to influence COPUOS deliberations and will shape any future multilateral instrument on space resource governance.

Toward a New Governance Paradigm

The future of space governance is unlikely to be defined by a single doctrine. Neither pure res communis (which permits extraction without regulation) nor pure common heritage (which subordinates extraction to international management) commands sufficient political support to serve as the exclusive framework. Instead, governance is likely to evolve through incremental adaptation, blending elements of both models with pragmatic regulatory innovations.

Several trends are already visible. The Artemis Accords represent a move toward activity-based governance—regulation of specific operations rather than comprehensive domain management. COPUOS has established a Working Group on the Legal Aspects of Space Resource Activities, signaling that the multilateral system is beginning to engage with the issue, albeit slowly. Academic proposals for "adaptive governance" frameworks envision regimes that evolve as technology and activity levels change, beginning with voluntary guidelines and escalating to binding rules as extraction becomes commercially significant.

The Hague International Space Resources Governance Working Group, an independent initiative involving academics, industry representatives, and government officials from multiple countries, produced a set of Building Blocks for the Development of an International Framework on Space Resource Activities in 2019. These Building Blocks propose a set of principles—including priority rights based on prior use, international information-sharing requirements, environmental protection obligations, and benefit-sharing mechanisms—that could form the basis of a future multilateral instrument. While not binding, the Building Blocks represent the most detailed attempt to date to bridge the gap between res communis and common heritage approaches, and they have influenced discussions within COPUOS.

The trajectory of space resource governance thus appears to be one of incremental norm-building rather than grand institutional design. Rather than a single comprehensive treaty—which the experience of the Moon Agreement suggests would be politically impossible—governance is likely to emerge through the accumulation of national legislation, bilateral and plurilateral agreements, soft-law guidelines, and institutional practices that gradually converge on shared standards. This process is messy, fragmented, and uncertain, but it is also adaptive and resilient—qualities that may prove more valuable than elegance in a domain characterized by rapid technological change and intense geopolitical competition.

The role of private actors adds a dimension absent from earlier commons governance. When the Outer Space Treaty was negotiated, space activity was exclusively governmental. Today, private companies are the primary drivers of innovation, investment, and operational capability. SpaceX has reduced launch costs by an order of magnitude. Blue Origin, Rocket Lab, and dozens of other companies are expanding access to orbit. Private companies are designing lunar landers, developing asteroid mining technologies, and building commercial space stations. Any governance framework must accommodate private interests while preserving the public character of outer space—a balance that neither res communis nor common heritage was designed to achieve.

The emerging model appears to be one of state authorization and continuing supervision (as required by Article VI of the Outer Space Treaty), with states serving as intermediaries between private actors and the international community. Under this model, private companies operate in outer space under licenses granted by their home states. The home state sets conditions that reflect both national policy and international obligations. The international community establishes principles and guidelines that states are expected to implement through national legislation. This layered architecture—international principles, national implementation, private operation—represents a pragmatic adaptation of the res communis framework to the commercial space age.

Whether this model is adequate for the challenges ahead remains to be seen. As private capabilities grow and state oversight becomes more complex, the risk of regulatory arbitrage increases—companies may register in states with the weakest regulatory requirements, much as shipping companies flag vessels in states with minimal maritime oversight. The analogy to "flags of convenience" in maritime law is direct and concerning. Preventing a race to the bottom in space regulation will require either harmonized international standards or mutual recognition agreements that establish minimum regulatory floors—mechanisms that do not yet exist in the space domain.

> ■ **The Central Question**
>
> The debate between res communis and common heritage is ultimately a debate about the relationship between freedom and justice in outer space. Res communis prioritizes freedom—openness, access, and the absence of territorial claims. Common heritage prioritizes justice—equity, benefit-sharing, and collective stewardship. The challenge for the twenty-first century is to construct a governance framework that honors both values, recognizing that freedom without justice produces inequality, while justice without freedom produces paralysis.

***

Chapter Summary

Chapter 4 has traced the philosophical, legal, and political dimensions of a question that lies at the heart of space governance: what kind of domain is outer space? The answer matters enormously, because it determines who may act in space, who benefits from space activities, and what obligations accompany the extraordinary freedoms that the space law regime provides.

The res communis model, embodied in the Outer Space Treaty, has proven remarkably successful in preventing territorial conflict and enabling the growth of a global space economy. Its emphasis on freedom, non-appropriation, and state responsibility provided a stable foundation during a period when space activity was dominated by two superpowers and the primary concern was preventing militarized competition. For nearly sixty years, this framework has sustained an unprecedented era of cooperative space exploration and commercial development.

The common heritage model, articulated in the Moon Agreement, offered a more comprehensive vision—one that addressed not only access but equity, not only freedom but responsibility, not only present use but future stewardship. Its failure to achieve widespread acceptance reflects not the invalidity of its concerns but the political obstacles to implementing redistributive norms in a domain dominated by a small number of technologically advanced states. The questions it raised—about who benefits, who decides, and who is accountable—remain as urgent as ever.

The contemporary landscape is defined by the tension between these models. National resource legislation, the Artemis Accords, the ILRS framework, and the nascent COPUOS working group represent different attempts to manage this tension, each with its own combination of freedom and regulation, unilateralism and multilateralism, pragmatism and principle. No single approach has yet emerged as dominant, and the governance framework that will ultimately govern space resource utilization remains under construction.

The stakes of this construction project are immense. The Moon's water ice deposits, if commercially exploitable, could enable a permanent human presence beyond Earth—one of the most transformative developments in the history of civilization. Asteroid resources, if accessible, could provide materials worth trillions of dollars and fundamentally alter terrestrial economics. The governance choices made in the coming decades will determine not only who extracts these resources and on what terms, but whether the expansion of human activity into the solar system replicates the extractive patterns of terrestrial colonialism or pioneers more equitable models of shared development.

The historical record provides both cautionary and encouraging precedents. The exploitation of the Americas, Africa, and Asia by European colonial powers demonstrated the devastation that occurs when powerful actors exploit new domains without regard for the rights of others. The Antarctic Treaty System and the International Space Station partnership demonstrate that cooperative governance of shared domains is possible, even among strategic rivals, when the political will exists and the institutional design is sound.

What is clear is that the choices made in the coming decades will have consequences that extend far beyond legal doctrine. They will determine whether humanity's expansion into space replicates the inequalities and conflicts of terrestrial history or charts a different course—one in which the extraordinary promise of space is shared more broadly and managed more wisely than the commons of the past.

In the next chapter, we turn from legal philosophy to institutional structure, examining the role of the United Nations and international organizations in governing outer space activities—the architecture through which these competing visions are debated, negotiated, and translated into the norms that shape humanity's future among the stars.

***

End of Chapter 4

Chapter 5

THE UNITED NATIONS AND THE ARCHITECTURE OF SPACE GOVERNANCE

From the first emergency resolutions following Sputnik to the sprawling committee system of today, the United Nations has served as the primary forum for space governance. This chapter traces how an ad hoc response to the space age became the institutional backbone of international space law—and examines whether that architecture can endure the pressures of the twenty-first century.

Part 1

Origins of United Nations Involvement in Outer Space

The governance of outer space is inseparable from the institutional framework of the United Nations, whose involvement predates the formal development of space law itself. Unlike many areas of international regulation that evolved gradually through state practice and bilateral agreements, space governance emerged almost immediately as a multilateral concern. This early institutionalization reflects both the unprecedented nature of space technology and the acute geopolitical anxieties of the mid-twentieth century.

The United Nations was founded in the aftermath of the Second World War with the express purpose of maintaining international peace and security. Its Charter emphasized collective responsibility, peaceful cooperation, and the prevention of armed conflict. When the prospect of spaceflight became reality, it was natural that the UN would be called upon to address its implications. Outer space represented not merely a new physical domain, but a potential extension of military rivalry into an environment where escalation could have catastrophic consequences. The fear that the space race could become a weapons race—that nuclear warheads might be placed in orbit, that satellites might be used for first-strike targeting, that the heavens might become another theater of Cold War confrontation—gave the governance of outer space an urgency that few other emerging issues could match.

Figure 16: United Nations Committee on the Peaceful Uses of Outer Space (COPUOS)

Source: United Nations (Public Domain).

Sputnik and the Institutional Response

The launch of Sputnik 1 on 4 October 1957 served as the catalyst for formal UN engagement. The satellite's success demonstrated that space technology was no longer speculative and that its strategic implications were immediate. States recognized that unregulated competition in space could destabilize global security, particularly if weapons of mass destruction were deployed beyond Earth. The UN General Assembly quickly became the primary forum for articulating collective concern and exploring legal responses.

In 1958, the General Assembly adopted Resolution 1348 (XIII), its first substantive resolution addressing outer space. The resolution called for the peaceful use of space, the avoidance of national appropriation, and the establishment of a committee to study legal, scientific, and technical problems arising from space exploration. This resolution did not create binding law, but it established a normative direction that would prove remarkably durable. It signaled that space activities would be subject to international scrutiny and that unilateral action would be politically constrained by collective expectation.

Later that same year, the General Assembly established the Ad Hoc Committee on the Peaceful Uses of Outer Space, reflecting a recognition that sustained institutional engagement was necessary.

The Committee's initial mandate was broad: to study the legal, scientific, and technical problems arising from space exploration and to propose appropriate measures. Crucially, the Committee included both spacefaring and non-spacefaring states, ensuring from the outset that governance would not be monopolized by those with technological advantage.

The Ad Hoc Committee's early sessions were complicated by Cold War tensions. The Soviet Union initially boycotted the Committee, arguing that its composition was biased toward Western states. This boycott was resolved through the expansion of membership and the adoption of informal working methods that accommodated both blocs. The resolution of this early crisis established an important precedent: COPUOS would operate through inclusion and accommodation rather than exclusion and confrontation. The willingness of both superpowers to participate in—and ultimately support—the Committee, despite their profound ideological differences, reflected the shared recognition that space governance was too important to be held hostage to Cold War politics.

■ **Key Early UN Resolutions on Outer Space**

Resolution 1348 (XIII), 1958: Recognized the common interest of mankind in outer space; established the Ad Hoc Committee.

Resolution 1472 (XIV), 1959: Made COPUOS a permanent committee of the General Assembly.

Resolution 1721 (XVI), 1961: Commended the peaceful use of outer space; called for registration of launches.

Resolution 1802 (XVII), 1962: Called for international cooperation and the development of legal principles.

Resolution 1962 (XVIII), 1963: Declaration of Legal Principles Governing the Activities of States in the Exploration and Use of Outer Space.

These resolutions established the normative foundation that the Outer Space Treaty (1967) would later codify.

From Ad Hoc Committee to Permanent Institution

The transition from an ad hoc body to a permanent committee in 1959 marked a critical step in the architecture of space governance. Resolution 1472 (XIV) established the Committee on the Peaceful Uses of Outer Space (COPUOS) as a standing committee of the General Assembly, with an initial membership of twenty-four states. COPUOS was tasked not only with preventing conflict, but with facilitating cooperation, information exchange, and capacity-building. Its creation embedded space governance permanently within the UN system and signaled that the international community regarded outer space as a matter of long-term collective concern, not a temporary emergency.

The early work of COPUOS unfolded against the backdrop of intense Cold War rivalry. Yet paradoxically, this rivalry fostered cooperation in legal matters. Both superpowers had an interest in stabilizing expectations and avoiding misunderstandings that could escalate into nuclear confrontation. The United Nations provided a neutral platform where ideological adversaries could negotiate shared principles without conceding strategic advantage. The resulting norms—enshrined first in General Assembly resolutions and later in binding treaties—bore the imprint of this dual motivation: genuine commitment to peaceful cooperation, tempered by hard-headed strategic calculation.

During its formative years, COPUOS focused on identifying foundational principles rather than detailed regulation. This approach reflected both political necessity and legal prudence. Attempting to regulate every aspect of space activity at an early stage would have risked deadlock. Instead, the Committee sought to articulate broad norms capable of guiding future development—an approach that proved remarkably effective. The 1963 Declaration of Legal Principles, adopted by consensus, distilled agreement on non-appropriation, freedom of exploration, state responsibility, and international cooperation. These principles formed the backbone of the Outer Space Treaty, negotiated just four years later.

The 1963 Declaration deserves particular attention as a case study in effective norm development. Resolution 1962 (XVIII) articulated nine principles that would govern state behavior in outer space. These included the freedom of exploration and use, the applicability of international law, the prohibition of national appropriation, the obligation to conduct activities in the interest of all countries, state responsibility for national activities, the duty to avoid harmful contamination, the obligation to assist astronauts in distress, and the retention of jurisdiction over space objects. Each of these principles was later incorporated into binding treaty law—a remarkable demonstration of the pathway from political declaration to legal obligation.

The speed of this transition—from General Assembly resolution in 1963 to binding treaty in 1967—reflected the extraordinary political urgency of the moment. The Limited Test Ban Treaty had been signed in August 1963, establishing a precedent for arms control cooperation between the superpowers. The assassination of President Kennedy in November 1963 and the subsequent escalation of the Vietnam War created pressures for diplomatic achievements that could demonstrate the continuing viability of superpower détente. The Outer Space Treaty served this purpose admirably: it was a genuine governance achievement with real strategic significance, yet it required neither side to make painful concessions.

Beyond the superpower dynamic, the early COPUOS years also witnessed the emergence of a distinctive diplomatic culture centered on technical expertise and patient dialogue. Unlike the General Assembly or the Security Council, where political grandstanding and bloc voting dominated, COPUOS fostered a more collegial atmosphere. Delegates included scientists, engineers, and legal scholars as well as diplomats, and the technical subcommittee's work provided a shared empirical foundation that grounded legal discussions in operational reality. This culture of technical cooperation, while sometimes tested by political disagreements, has proven remarkably durable and continues to distinguish COPUOS from more politicized UN bodies.

The Preventive Character of Space Governance

The UN's early involvement in space governance thus reflects a distinctive model of international regulation. Rather than reacting to conflict after it occurred—the pattern that had characterized the development of the laws of war, maritime law, and most other branches of international law—the UN sought to anticipate and prevent conflict through normative guidance. This preventive orientation distinguishes space law from many other areas of international law and helps explain its unusual success: by establishing rules before disputes arose, the framers avoided the political bitterness and institutional dysfunction that often accompany post-conflict regulation.

Another defining feature of UN involvement was its emphasis on universality. From the outset, space governance was framed as a matter of concern to all humanity, not merely to technologically advanced states. The language of the earliest resolutions—"common interest of mankind," "benefit of all peoples"—was deliberately inclusive, legitimizing the participation of developing countries and reinforcing the idea that outer space should not become an exclusive domain. This universalist framing served multiple purposes: it built broad political support for the governance framework, it constrained the most aggressive ambitions of the superpowers, and it created a normative baseline against which future actions could be evaluated.

The universalist framing also had practical institutional consequences. When COPUOS expanded its membership from twenty-four to over one hundred states, it was responding to the demand of newly independent and developing countries to participate in space governance—a demand that the universalist language of the founding resolutions made politically impossible to refuse. This expansion has been criticized for complicating decision-making, but it has also ensured that space governance retains a legitimacy that narrower, club-based arrangements—such as the Artemis Accords—cannot easily match.

The UN's role in space governance was therefore both symbolic and practical. Symbolically, it affirmed that outer space belonged within the realm of international cooperation rather than unilateral control. Practically, it created institutional mechanisms capable of sustaining dialogue, developing norms, and adapting—however slowly—to technological change. These mechanisms have not always worked perfectly, and the gaps in the governance framework are real. But the alternative—a world in which outer space was governed, if at all, by bilateral agreements between the superpowers—would almost certainly have been less stable, less inclusive, and less responsive to the interests of the broader international community.

"The exploration and use of outer space shall be carried on for the benefit and in the interests of all mankind."

– UN General Assembly Resolution 1962 (XVIII), 1963

> ■ **The UN's Unique Role in Space Governance**
>
> The United Nations did not merely respond to the space age; it shaped the legal and institutional framework within which the space age unfolded. By establishing COPUOS before the first human spaceflight, the UN ensured that governance preceded exploitation—a rare achievement in the history of international regulation that prevented outer space from becoming a domain of unregulated competition.

***

Part 11

COPUOS: Structure, Mandate, and Working Methods

The United Nations Committee on the Peaceful Uses of Outer Space (COPUOS) occupies a unique position within the international legal system. Unlike many UN bodies that address existing conflicts or established domains, COPUOS was created to govern a realm that humanity had only just begun to enter. Its structure, mandate, and working methods reflect this forward-looking purpose, emphasizing inclusivity, consensus, and gradual norm development over coercive regulation.

Institutional Structure

COPUOS operates as a subsidiary body of the UN General Assembly and is supported administratively by the United Nations Office for Outer Space Affairs (UNOOSA), headquartered in Vienna. UNOOSA serves as the secretariat for the Committee, preparing documentation, facilitating meetings, coordinating technical assistance programs, and maintaining the Register of Objects Launched into Outer Space. The Office also administers capacity-building programs, including the UN Programme on Space Applications, which assists developing countries in using space technology for sustainable development.

The Committee's membership has expanded steadily since its inception, reflecting the growing number of space-interested nations. From twenty-four members in 1959, COPUOS has grown to one hundred and two member states as of 2025—making it one of the largest committees in the UN system. This expansion underscores the Committee's commitment to universality, though it also complicates decision-making by increasing the diversity of interests and perspectives that must be accommodated.

The membership trajectory tells a story of space governance's evolution. The original twenty-four members included the major spacefaring states, their allies, and a small number of non-aligned countries. Subsequent expansions in the 1970s and 1980s added many newly independent developing states, reflecting the decolonization movement's impact on international institutions. The most recent expansions have included Gulf states (the UAE became a member in 2014), African states (Nigeria, South Africa, Kenya), and small island developing states, whose interests in satellite-based disaster management and climate monitoring have driven their engagement with space governance. Each expansion has brought new perspectives and priorities to the Committee, enriching its discussions while making consensus more challenging to achieve.

The Committee's work is carried out primarily through two permanent subcommittees: the Scientific and Technical Subcommittee (STSC) and the Legal Subcommittee (LSC). This bifurcated structure is one of COPUOS's defining features. It recognizes that space governance requires both technical understanding and legal interpretation, and that effective regulation depends on continuous dialogue between these domains.

■ **COPUOS at a Glance (2025)**

Established: 1959 (permanent committee under UN General Assembly).

Membership: 102 states (expanded from 24 in 1959).

Secretariat: United Nations Office for Outer Space Affairs (UNOOSA), Vienna.

Subcommittees: Scientific and Technical Subcommittee (STSC); Legal Subcommittee (LSC).

Decision-making: Consensus (no formal voting).

Outputs: Treaties, guidelines, principles, technical reports, and General Assembly resolutions.

Annual sessions: Plenary (June), STSC (February), LSC (March/April).

Observers: Over 40 international and non-governmental organizations.

The Scientific and Technical Subcommittee

The STSC addresses the empirical and engineering dimensions of space activity. Its agenda covers space debris, space weather, near-Earth objects, nuclear power sources in outer space, the use of space technology for disaster management, remote sensing, global navigation satellite systems, and capacity-building. The Subcommittee's work provides the evidentiary and technical foundation upon which legal norms are built. Without reliable scientific information about orbital debris density, collision probabilities, or the environmental effects of launch emissions, the Legal Subcommittee cannot develop meaningful regulatory guidance.

The STSC also serves as a conduit for information-sharing among states with different levels of space capability. Technical presentations, expert workshops, and the Inter-Agency Space Debris Coordination Committee (IADC)'s reports to the Subcommittee ensure that the latest scientific findings are available to all delegations, not merely those with their own research capabilities. This democratization of technical knowledge is one of COPUOS's most important—if least visible—functions.

The IADC, while not formally a UN body, illustrates the institutional ecosystem that supports COPUOS. Founded in 1993, the IADC comprises the space agencies of thirteen states and ESA, and serves as the primary technical forum for coordinating debris mitigation research and policy. The IADC's Space Debris Mitigation Guidelines, first adopted in 2002 and revised in 2007, provided the technical foundation for the COPUOS guidelines endorsed by the General Assembly. This relationship—technical body produces evidence, COPUOS translates evidence into norms, General Assembly endorses norms—exemplifies the layered governance model that characterizes contemporary space regulation.

In recent years, the STSC has expanded its agenda to address emerging challenges including space weather (solar storms that can damage satellites and disrupt communications), near-Earth objects (asteroids and comets that pose impact risks), the use of nuclear power sources in outer space, and the environmental sustainability of launch operations. Each of these topics requires close integration of scientific analysis and legal policy—precisely the kind of interdisciplinary work that COPUOS's bifurcated structure was designed to facilitate.

The Legal Subcommittee

The Legal Subcommittee focuses on the development and interpretation of legal principles governing space activities. Its agenda includes the status and application of the five UN space treaties, the definition and delimitation of outer space, the legal aspects of space resource activities, the regulation of space traffic, national space legislation, and the legal framework for space debris remediation. The LSC has been responsible for drafting all five space treaties and for developing the major soft-law instruments that now supplement the treaty regime.

The LSC's agenda has expanded considerably in recent years, reflecting the growing complexity of space activities. Current agenda items include the legal aspects of space resource activities (addressed through a dedicated working group), the potential legal models for activities in the exploration, exploitation, and utilization of space resources, and general exchange of views on the legal aspects of space traffic management. The Subcommittee also maintains standing items on the status of the five UN space treaties, national legislation relevant to the peaceful exploration and use of outer space, and capacity-building in space law—the last reflecting a recognition that many states lack the legal expertise needed to implement their international obligations effectively.

Working methods within the LSC have evolved considerably since its early years. During the treaty-making era (1966–1979), the Subcommittee functioned primarily as a negotiating forum, producing binding instruments through intensive diplomatic engagement. Since the end of the treaty-making era, the LSC has shifted toward the development of non-binding guidelines and principles, reflecting the political difficulty of negotiating new treaties in an increasingly multipolar environment. Working groups—typically established for specific topics such as space debris, space resource activities, or the long-term sustainability of outer space—have become the primary vehicles for substantive progress.

The working group mechanism deserves close attention, as it is the engine of contemporary COPUOS law-making. Working groups typically operate with a limited mandate and a defined time horizon, though extensions are common. They meet during LSC sessions and sometimes intersessionally. Their chairs—usually experienced diplomats or legal scholars drawn from the COPUOS membership—play a critical role in managing negotiations, drafting compromise texts, and maintaining momentum. The quality and diplomatic skill of working group chairs has often determined whether a particular initiative succeeds or stalls.

One of the most contentious issues within COPUOS—and one that illustrates the limits of the consensus model—is the relationship between civilian and military space activities. The Outer Space Treaty provides that outer space shall be used exclusively for peaceful purposes in relation to celestial bodies (Article IV), but it does not prohibit military activities in space generally. The interpretation of "peaceful purposes" has been debated for decades: does it mean "non-aggressive" (the predominant view, which permits military support functions such as reconnaissance and communications) or "non-military" (a stricter reading that would prohibit all military activities)?

This ambiguity has allowed military space activities to expand without clear international regulation. The Conference on Disarmament in Geneva has jurisdiction over space weapons issues, but it has made no substantive progress on space security for decades, blocked by disagreements between major powers over verification, scope, and definitions. COPUOS, for its part, has generally avoided military issues, maintaining its focus on peaceful uses and deferring security questions to the disarmament bodies. This institutional division—peaceful uses in Vienna, security issues in Geneva—reflects a political compromise that has enabled COPUOS to function effectively but has left military space activities in a governance vacuum.

Consensus as a Governing Principle

Perhaps the most distinctive feature of COPUOS is its reliance on consensus decision-making. Unlike many UN bodies that operate by majority vote, COPUOS seeks agreement among all participating states before adopting any substantive outcome. This practice has profound implications for the character and pace of space law development.

Consensus fosters legitimacy. When norms emerge from unanimous agreement, they carry greater moral and political weight than those imposed by majority over the objections of a significant minority. This legitimacy is particularly important in a domain where enforcement mechanisms are weak or nonexistent. A guideline adopted by consensus is more likely to be implemented by all states than one adopted over objections, because it reflects a genuine shared commitment rather than an externally imposed obligation.

At the same time, consensus imposes formidable constraints. Controversial issues—such as delimitation, resource exploitation, military uses of space, and binding environmental obligations—are frequently deferred because they threaten to break agreement. A single state can effectively block progress on any topic it regards as contrary to its interests. The result is that COPUOS tends to favor incremental progress over bold legal innovation, producing outcomes that represent the lowest common denominator rather than the highest aspiration. This dynamic has led critics to characterize COPUOS as reactive and slow—charges that have some validity but overlook the genuine achievements that consensus has produced.

The consensus principle also shapes the language and ambition of COPUOS outputs. Guidelines and recommendations are typically worded in hortatory rather than mandatory language—"states should" rather than "states shall," "are encouraged to" rather than "are required to." Qualifications, exceptions, and escape clauses are built into texts to accommodate dissenting views. The resulting documents are sometimes criticized as toothless, but they serve a different function than binding legislation: they articulate shared expectations, establish benchmarks for responsible behavior, and create reputational costs for non-compliance.

Observer Organizations and External Engagement

COPUOS has granted permanent observer status to more than forty international and non-governmental organizations, reflecting a recognition that space governance involves a wide range of stakeholders beyond national governments. Observers include the International Astronautical Federation (IAF), the Committee on Space Research (COSPAR), the International Institute of Space Law (IISL), the Secure World Foundation, the Space Generation Advisory Council, and various industry associations and academic bodies.

Observers may attend sessions, submit written statements, and participate in discussions, but they have no decision-making authority. Their influence operates through persuasion, expertise, and agenda-setting rather than formal power. Despite these limitations, observer organizations play an important role in the COPUOS ecosystem: they inject technical knowledge, represent perspectives that national delegations may overlook, and provide continuity of expertise across sessions. The Secure World Foundation and the European Space Policy Institute, for example, publish annual assessments of space sustainability that inform COPUOS discussions and shape the broader policy debate.

The question of whether COPUOS should formalize industry participation—going beyond observer status to establish structured consultation mechanisms or advisory bodies—is increasingly debated. Proponents argue that the commercial space sector's growing dominance makes formal engagement essential for effective governance. Opponents worry that industry influence could skew norms toward commercial interests at the expense of broader public concerns, including equity, environmental protection, and developing country access.

> *"COPUOS embodies a paradox: its greatest strength—consensus—is also its most significant constraint. The same mechanism that produces legitimacy also produces delay."*
>
> – On the dynamics of consensus governance

The Role of UNOOSA and Capacity-Building

The United Nations Office for Outer Space Affairs plays a role that extends well beyond secretariat functions. UNOOSA administers the Space Applications Programme, which provides technical assistance to developing countries seeking to use space technology for development. It coordinates the International Committee on Global Navigation Satellite Systems (ICG), facilitates the Space Mission Planning Advisory Group (SMPAG) for planetary defense, and manages the UN Platform for Space-based Information for Disaster Management and Emergency Response (UN-SPIDER).

These programs are significant because they help realize the universalist aspiration embedded in space governance from the outset. By building technical capacity in developing countries, UNOOSA ensures that the governance framework is not merely formally inclusive but substantively so—that all states, not merely the technologically advanced, can participate meaningfully in space activities and space governance. The practical impact of these programs—training hundreds of professionals, supporting disaster response coordination, and enabling satellite data access for developing countries—represents one of the most tangible benefits of the UN's space governance architecture.

UN-SPIDER deserves particular mention as an illustration of how space governance translates into practical benefit. Established by the General Assembly in 2006, UN-SPIDER provides developing countries with access to space-based information for disaster management and emergency response. During natural disasters—earthquakes, floods, hurricanes, volcanic eruptions—UN-SPIDER facilitates the activation of the International Charter on Space and Major Disasters, through which space agencies provide satellite imagery to disaster-affected countries free of charge. This mechanism has been activated hundreds of times since its establishment in 2000, providing critical information for disaster response operations around the world.

UNOOSA also maintains the Space4SDGs initiative, which promotes the use of space technology for achieving the United Nations Sustainable Development Goals. Applications include satellite-based precision agriculture for food security, remote sensing for environmental monitoring, telecommunications for education and healthcare in remote areas, and navigation services for transportation efficiency. These programs demonstrate that the benefits of space activity—the "benefit of all countries" that Article I of the Outer Space Treaty envisions—can be made concrete through institutional effort, even in the absence of mandatory benefit-sharing mechanisms.

***

Part III

Law-Making Through Consensus: Treaties, Soft Law, and State Practice

The development of international space law under the auspices of the United Nations illustrates a distinctive model of law-making—one that relies less on coercive authority and more on consensus, persuasion, and gradual norm internalization. In a domain where enforcement is inherently limited and technological change is rapid, this model has proven both resilient and adaptive. Understanding how law is made through COPUOS requires attention not only to treaties, but also to the increasingly important interplay between soft law, state practice, and institutional dialogue.

The Five Space Treaties: Foundational Law

The most visible products of UN space governance are the five multilateral space treaties negotiated between 1967 and 1979. These treaties form the core of binding international space law and represent the most intensive period of space law-making in history.

Treaty	Year	Key Provisions	Ratifications (2025)
Outer Space Treaty	1967	Non-appropriation, freedom of exploration, state responsibility, peaceful use	114
Rescue Agreement	1968	Obligation to rescue and return astronauts; return of space objects	99
Liability Convention	1972	Absolute liability on Earth; fault-based liability in space	98
Registration Convention	1976	Mandatory registration of space objects; creation of UN Register	72
Moon Agreement	1979	Common heritage of mankind; international resource regime	18

Treaty-making within COPUOS followed a careful and deliberate process. Draft provisions were debated extensively within the Legal Subcommittee, refined through working groups, and ultimately submitted to the General Assembly for adoption. This process prioritized clarity and political acceptability over regulatory detail. As a result, the treaties articulate broad principles rather than exhaustive operational rules—a strategic choice that has contributed to their remarkable durability.

The principle-based character of the space treaties stands in sharp contrast to many other international legal instruments. The United Nations Convention on the Law of the Sea, for example, runs to over 300 articles and nine annexes, providing detailed rules on virtually every aspect of ocean governance. The five space treaties, collectively, contain fewer than 70 articles. This brevity was deliberate: detailed regulation risked rapid obsolescence in a domain where technology was advancing at unprecedented speed, and it risked political deadlock in an environment where consensus was essential. By articulating principles rather than prescriptions, the treaties created a framework flexible enough to accommodate developments their drafters could not have foreseen—including the rise of commercial space activity, the deployment of satellite mega-constellations, and the emergence of space resource utilization as a practical possibility.

The five treaties were negotiated during a unique geopolitical window: the Cold War period when U.S.-Soviet competition in space paradoxically fostered cooperation on legal frameworks. Both superpowers had powerful incentives to establish rules that would stabilize expectations and prevent misunderstandings. The resulting treaties bear the imprint of this bilateral dynamic, reflecting compromises between American and Soviet positions that were subsequently endorsed by the broader international community.

Each treaty built upon its predecessors, creating a layered architecture of increasing specificity. The Outer Space Treaty (1967) established foundational principles. The Rescue Agreement (1968) elaborated the obligation to assist astronauts in distress and return space objects, reflecting the humanitarian concerns raised by the early crewed missions—concerns made vivid by the near-disaster of Apollo 13 in 1970. The Liability Convention (1972) addressed the practical question of who pays when space objects cause damage, establishing the dual standard of absolute liability on Earth and fault-based liability in space that will be examined in detail in Chapter 6. The Registration Convention (1976) created a transparency mechanism by requiring states to register space objects and provide orbital parameters—essential for attribution, conjunction assessment, and accountability.

The Moon Agreement (1979), as discussed in Chapter 4, represented the most ambitious attempt to extend governance to celestial bodies but failed to achieve widespread acceptance. Its limited ratification effectively marked the end of the treaty-making era in space law, demonstrating that the political consensus required for binding instruments had exhausted itself by the late 1970s.

After 1979, the treaty-making process effectively ceased. No new multilateral space treaty has been concluded in over four decades. This hiatus reflects several factors: the end of superpower bilateralism as the driver of space law, the increasing complexity and diversity of space activities, the entry of new space actors with different priorities, and the political difficulty of achieving consensus on contentious issues such as resource exploitation, space traffic management, and military activities. The era of foundational treaty-making is over; what has emerged in its place is a more diffuse and incremental model of norm development.

The Rise of Soft Law

As space activities diversified and intensified, the limitations of treaty-making became increasingly apparent. Negotiating new binding agreements proved politically difficult in a more multipolar and commercially driven environment. In response, COPUOS turned increasingly to soft-law instruments—non-binding guidelines, principles, and best practices that shape behavior without creating formal legal obligations.

Soft law now occupies a central place in contemporary space governance. The most significant instruments include the Principles Relating to Remote Sensing of the Earth from Outer Space (1986), the Principles Relevant to the Use of Nuclear Power Sources in Outer Space (1992), the Space Debris Mitigation Guidelines (2007), and the Guidelines for the Long-term Sustainability of Outer Space Activities (LTS Guidelines, 2019). Each of these instruments was adopted by COPUOS consensus and endorsed by the General Assembly, lending them significant political—if not strictly legal—weight.

■ **Major Soft-Law Instruments in Space Governance**

Remote Sensing Principles (1986): Norms for Earth observation from space.

Nuclear Power Sources Principles (1992): Safety framework for nuclear-powered spacecraft.

Space Debris Mitigation Guidelines (2007): 25-year deorbit rule; passivation; collision avoidance.

LTS Guidelines (2019): 21 guidelines covering sustainability, transparency, and cooperation.

COPUOS Working Group on Space Resource Activities (2022–): Developing norms for resource extraction.

All adopted by consensus; all non-binding; all influential in national regulation.

Soft law offers several advantages over treaty law in the contemporary space governance environment. It can be developed more quickly, updated more easily, and tailored to technical realities. It allows states to experiment with norms before committing to binding obligations. It accommodates the participation of non-state actors—industry, academia, civil society—more readily than formal treaty processes. And it avoids the all-or-nothing dynamic of treaty ratification, where states must accept an entire package or reject it entirely.

The evolution of COPUOS's approach to norm development can also be traced through the three UNISPACE conferences convened by the United Nations. UNISPACE I (1968, Vienna) focused on the benefits of space technology for developing countries. UNISPACE II (1982, Vienna) addressed the practical applications of space technology and called for greater international cooperation. UNISPACE+50 (2018, Vienna)—commemorating the fiftieth anniversary of the first conference—adopted the "Space2030" Agenda, which articulated a vision for the future of space governance organized around four pillars: space economy, space society, space accessibility, and space diplomacy. The Space2030 Agenda, endorsed by the General Assembly in 2021, represents the most comprehensive attempt to articulate a forward-looking governance vision within the UN system, even though its provisions remain aspirational rather than binding.

The UNISPACE process illustrates both the strengths and limitations of the UN's approach. The conferences have been effective at building political consensus, raising awareness, and establishing normative directions. They have been less effective at producing specific regulatory outcomes or binding commitments. The gap between aspiration and implementation—between the visionary language of conference declarations and the practical realities of space governance—is one of the persistent challenges of the UN-centered approach.

The Space Debris Mitigation Guidelines illustrate the soft-law model at its best. Developed through years of technical analysis within the STSC, informed by the work of the Inter-Agency Space Debris Coordination Committee (IADC), and refined through extensive negotiation in the LSC, the Guidelines established norms that have been widely incorporated into national regulation. The 25-year post-mission disposal guideline, for example, has been adopted as a regulatory requirement by the United States, Europe, Japan, and many other spacefaring states. Without ever becoming binding international law, the Guidelines have effectively changed behavior across the space industry.

The Guidelines for the Long-term Sustainability of Outer Space Activities (LTS Guidelines), adopted by COPUOS in 2019 after nearly a decade of negotiation, represent the most comprehensive soft-law instrument in space governance to date. The twenty-one guidelines address a sweeping range of issues: policy and regulatory frameworks for space activities, safety of space operations, international cooperation and information-sharing, scientific and technical research, and awareness of the space environment. They encourage states to develop national regulatory frameworks, share orbital data, coordinate conjunction assessments, and adopt practices that reduce the creation of space debris.

The negotiation of the LTS Guidelines was itself instructive. The process was marked by protracted disagreement on several issues, including the legal status of the guidelines (some states sought binding language while others insisted on voluntariness), the treatment of military space activities (many states argued that military activities should be included, while others resisted any mention), and the question of whether the guidelines should address space resource activities. The final text represents a carefully negotiated compromise that advances governance without resolving the most contentious issues—a pattern entirely consistent with COPUOS's consensus methodology.

A second working group, known informally as "LTS 2.0," has been established to develop additional guidelines addressing topics not covered by the original twenty-one—including space traffic management, active debris removal, and the environmental impact of mega-constellations. Whether this follow-on process can maintain the momentum established by the first set of guidelines remains to be seen, but its existence demonstrates that the soft-law approach has not been exhausted.

From Soft Law to Customary Law

Although soft-law instruments are formally non-binding, they can influence the development of customary international law. When states consistently follow guidelines out of a sense of legal or normative obligation—the subjective element known as opinio juris—practice may crystallize into binding custom. This process is gradual, often contested, and difficult to pinpoint in time, but it underscores the normative power of consensus-based outcomes.

In space governance, the line between soft law and custom is particularly fluid. Many states have incorporated COPUOS guidelines directly into national legislation or regulatory practice, blurring the distinction between voluntary guidance and legal requirement. When a sufficient number of states treat a guideline as legally binding—whether through formal legislation, administrative regulation, or consistent operational practice—the guideline may acquire the status of customary international law, binding even on states that did not participate in its development.

The debate over whether specific space governance norms have achieved customary status is ongoing. The prohibition on deliberately creating long-lived space debris, for example, may be approaching customary status given the near-universal condemnation of destructive ASAT tests and the widespread adoption of debris mitigation measures. In April 2022, the United States announced a unilateral moratorium on destructive direct-ascent ASAT testing, and several other states subsequently endorsed this position—a development that may accelerate the crystallization of a customary norm. The principle of free satellite overflight, discussed in Chapters 2 and 3, has almost certainly achieved customary status through more than six decades of uncontested practice. Other norms—such as the 25-year post-mission disposal guideline—remain more clearly in the soft-law category, though their trajectory toward custom is visible.

The process of customary law formation in the space domain is complicated by the relatively small number of states that conduct space activities. Traditional customary international law theory requires widespread and consistent state practice, but in space governance, the practice of the dozen or so most active spacefaring states may carry disproportionate weight. The question of whether a norm adopted primarily by spacefaring states can bind non-spacefaring states—through the persistent objector doctrine or otherwise—is theoretically significant and may become practically important as more states develop space capabilities.

The Role of State Practice and National Legislation

State practice plays a critical role in filling gaps left by treaties and soft law. As of 2025, more than thirty states have enacted national space legislation governing the authorization, supervision, and liability of space activities conducted by their nationals. These laws translate international obligations into domestic requirements, adapting broad treaty principles to specific national contexts. The growth of national space legislation has been particularly rapid since 2010, driven by the commercialization of space activity and the recognition that states bear international responsibility for all national space activities—including those of private companies—under Article VI of the Outer Space Treaty. States that fail to enact adequate supervisory legislation risk international liability for the activities of their nationals without having the regulatory tools to manage that risk.

National space legislation also serves as a testing ground for legal innovation. Concepts that prove workable at the national level—such as licensing conditions for debris mitigation, insurance requirements for launch activities, or authorization frameworks for space resource utilization—may later be harmonized through multilateral dialogue within COPUOS. Conversely, divergent national practices may signal the need for international clarification or coordination, prompting the development of new soft-law instruments.

The diversity of national approaches is itself instructive. The United States, with the longest history of commercial space regulation, has developed a complex multi-agency framework: the Federal Aviation Administration (FAA) licenses launches and re-entries, the Federal Communications Commission (FCC) licenses satellite communications, the National Oceanic and Atmospheric Administration (NOAA) licenses remote sensing, and the Department of Commerce is developing a regulatory framework for space situational awareness. The United Kingdom's Space Industry Act 2018, by contrast, establishes a single licensing regime administered by the Civil Aviation Authority, reflecting a more streamlined approach. France's Loi relative aux opérations spatiales (2008) was one of the first national space laws to incorporate detailed debris mitigation requirements into licensing conditions. The UAE's Federal Law No. 12 of 2019 on the Regulation of the Space Sector represents one of the most recent national frameworks, designed specifically to attract international investment to a state with ambitious but relatively young space ambitions.

These national frameworks collectively constitute a laboratory of governance innovation. When multiple states adopt similar regulatory approaches—for example, requiring licensees to comply with debris mitigation guidelines—their converging practice strengthens the normative force of the underlying international guidelines and may contribute to the formation of customary international law. When national approaches diverge—for example, on the regulation of space resource extraction—the divergence highlights areas where international coordination is needed and may catalyze multilateral discussion within COPUOS.

The relationship between national and international law in the space domain is thus reciprocal and dynamic. International norms shape national legislation; national legislation, in turn, influences the evolution of international norms through the accumulation of consistent practice. This feedback loop is one of the most important—and least visible—mechanisms of space law development.

■ The Treaty-to-Practice Pipeline

Step 1: Scientific evidence identifies a problem (e.g., orbital debris growth models).

Step 2: STSC and expert bodies (e.g., IADC) develop technical recommendations.

Step 3: Legal Subcommittee translates recommendations into guidelines or principles.

Step 4: COPUOS adopts the instrument by consensus.

Step 5: General Assembly endorses the instrument through a resolution.

Step 6: States incorporate the instrument into national legislation and licensing conditions.

Step 7: Consistent national implementation may contribute to customary international law.

This pipeline—from science to custom—is the primary mechanism of space law development in the post-treaty era.

■ The Three Pillars of Space Law-Making

International space law rests on three mutually reinforcing pillars: binding treaties that establish foundational principles; soft-law instruments that provide operational guidance; and national legislation that translates both into enforceable domestic rules. The interaction among these pillars—rather than any single instrument—constitutes the living body of space law.

***

Part IV

Institutional Limits and the Future of Space Governance Reform

The institutional architecture of space governance built around the United Nations and COPUOS has proven remarkably durable. For more than six decades, it has facilitated cooperation, prevented overt conflict, and guided the peaceful development of outer space. Yet durability should not be mistaken for sufficiency. As space activities expand in scale, diversity, and strategic importance, the limits of the existing governance framework are becoming increasingly visible. These limits raise difficult questions about whether incremental adaptation will suffice, or whether more substantial reform is required.

The Pace Problem: Technology vs. Governance

Technological innovation in space now proceeds at a speed that far outpaces traditional multilateral processes. Commercial launch systems evolve on timelines measured in months. Satellite mega-constellations are deployed in years. On-orbit servicing, active debris removal, and space-based manufacturing are transitioning from concept to operation. By contrast, consensus-based norm development within COPUOS often requires years or even decades of deliberation.

The mismatch is stark. SpaceX's Starlink constellation grew from zero to over 6,000 satellites in approximately four years (2019–2023). The COPUOS Long-term Sustainability Guidelines took over a decade to negotiate (2010–2019). By the time multilateral norms are established, the technological landscape they were designed to address may have changed beyond recognition. This pace problem is structural: consensus governance is inherently deliberate, while commercial space development is inherently urgent.

The resulting regulatory gaps create real risks. Emerging activities—on-orbit servicing, active debris removal, in-space manufacturing, point-to-point suborbital transport—may operate for extended periods without clear international guidance, relying instead on national regulation, industry self-regulation, or informal norms. While this flexibility can encourage innovation, it also increases the risk of fragmentation, conflict, and environmental harm.

On-orbit servicing (OOS) provides a vivid example. Companies and agencies are developing technologies to approach, dock with, inspect, refuel, repair, or relocate satellites already in orbit. These capabilities have enormous commercial and strategic value—extending the life of multi-billion-dollar satellites, repositioning assets for optimal coverage, or removing malfunctioning objects from valuable orbits. Yet the same technologies that enable beneficial servicing could also be used for hostile purposes: inspecting adversary satellites, interfering with their operations, or physically disabling them. The governance framework for OOS—distinguishing between benign and hostile approaches, establishing notification protocols, defining rights and responsibilities—does not yet exist at the international level. National regulations are developing on a fragmented, case-by-case basis, without the coordinating influence of multilateral norms.

Private Actors and the Representation Gap

One of the most profound shifts in space activity is the rise of private actors as central—and in some sectors, dominant—participants. Commercial companies now design, launch, and operate systems that rival or exceed those of many states. SpaceX, through its Falcon 9 and Starship programs, has fundamentally altered the economics of space access. Amazon's Project Kuiper, OneWeb, and other constellation operators are reshaping satellite communications. Private companies are developing lunar landers, space stations, and asteroid mining capabilities.

Yet these actors participate in international governance only indirectly, through national delegations. COPUOS has over forty observer organizations, including some industry associations and non-governmental organizations, but these observers have no decision-making authority and limited influence on outcomes. The result is a representation gap: the entities most directly affected by space governance norms—and most responsible for implementing them—have the least voice in shaping those norms.

This gap has practical consequences. National interests do not always align with commercial realities. A state may support ambitious debris mitigation requirements within COPUOS while its domestic licensing regime exempts favored companies from compliance. Regulatory frameworks developed without meaningful industry input may be technically impractical, economically burdensome, or simply irrelevant to the operations they are intended to govern. Conversely, the absence of industry accountability in multilateral processes may allow commercial actors to evade responsibilities that they would bear if they participated directly.

The challenge is particularly acute for mega-constellation operators. A single company—SpaceX—operates more satellites than any government in history. Its decisions about orbital altitude, deorbit procedures, conjunction avoidance, and spectrum use have consequences for every other user of the orbital environment. Yet SpaceX's interests are represented in COPUOS only through the U.S. delegation, which must balance the company's commercial priorities against broader national security, diplomatic, and scientific objectives. This mediated representation is neither efficient nor fully adequate for the governance challenges that mega-constellations present.

Finding mechanisms to incorporate private-sector perspectives without undermining the state-centric character of international law is one of the most important governance challenges of the coming decades. The tension is real: international law is made by and between states, and allowing private actors to participate directly in law-making would fundamentally alter the character of the international legal system. Yet ignoring the operational realities of commercial space activity produces governance norms that are disconnected from the activities they are intended to regulate.

> ■ **The Governance Gap: Space in 2025 vs. Space in 1967**
>
> 1967: Two spacefaring states; exclusively governmental activity; fewer than 200 objects in orbit.
>
> 2025: Over 90 spacefaring states; thousands of private operators; 13,000+ active satellites.
>
> 1967: One launch per month. 2025: Multiple launches per week (SpaceX alone: 90+ per year).
>
> 1967: COPUOS membership: 28 states. 2025: COPUOS membership: 102 states.
>
> 1967: No commercial space economy. 2025: Global space economy exceeds $470 billion.
>
> The governance architecture designed for the 1967 environment must now accommodate the 2025 reality.

Institutional Fragmentation Beyond COPUOS

Space governance increasingly extends beyond COPUOS alone. The International Telecommunication Union (ITU) governs the allocation of radio frequency spectrum and orbital slots for satellites—resources of enormous economic value that are subject to increasing demand and competition. The ITU's Radio Regulations, updated through World Radiocommunication Conferences (WRCs) held every three to four years, constitute a binding legal framework for spectrum management that is functionally separate from the COPUOS-centered space law regime.

Other institutions play complementary roles. The International Civil Aviation Organization (ICAO) is increasingly involved in managing the intersection of aviation and space launch activities, particularly the coordination of airspace closures during launches and the integration of suborbital vehicles into the air traffic management system. The International Organization for Standardization (ISO) develops technical standards for space operations, including the ISO 24113 standard on space debris mitigation, which translates COPUOS guidelines into engineering specifications. The World Meteorological Organization (WMO) coordinates the use of weather satellites. The Committee on Space Research (COSPAR), a scientific body under the International Science Council, maintains planetary protection guidelines that inform both national regulation and international practice.

Regional organizations add another layer of institutional complexity. The European Space Agency (ESA), with twenty-two member states and a budget exceeding €7 billion (2024), is both a space agency and a governance institution, developing common European positions on space policy and coordinating member state activities within COPUOS. The African Union Commission has established a Space Strategy and an African Space Agency (AfSA), reflecting the continent's growing space ambitions. APSCO, the Asia-Pacific Space Cooperation Organization, coordinates space cooperation among its member states. These regional bodies develop governance norms that complement—and sometimes diverge from—the universal frameworks established through COPUOS.

Ad hoc plurilateral arrangements—most notably the Artemis Accords—operate entirely outside the UN system, establishing governance norms through bilateral agreements among willing partners. The coexistence of UN-centered governance, ITU spectrum management, ICAO aviation coordination, ISO technical standards, regional frameworks, and plurilateral accords creates a polycentric governance landscape that is rich in normative output but challenging in coordination. Ensuring coherence across these structures—preventing contradictory norms, minimizing regulatory gaps, and avoiding forum-shopping—will be essential to managing the increasingly complex space environment.

Lessons from Past Crises

The space governance system has been tested by several incidents that illustrate both its strengths and its weaknesses. The Cosmos 954 incident of January 1978, in which a Soviet nuclear-powered radar satellite re-entered the atmosphere and scattered radioactive debris across northern Canada, tested the liability framework established by the 1972 Liability Convention. Canada presented a claim against the Soviet Union for damages; the two states ultimately settled for CAD 3 million—a fraction of Canada's actual cleanup costs. The settlement was negotiated diplomatically rather than through the Convention's Claims Commission, establishing a precedent of bilateral negotiation that has characterized space liability disputes ever since.

More recently, the 2009 collision between the active Iridium 33 communications satellite and the defunct Russian Cosmos 2251 satellite—the first accidental collision between two intact satellites—generated over 2,000 trackable debris fragments and highlighted the inadequacy of existing debris mitigation norms for dealing with legacy objects already in orbit. The collision demonstrated that debris mitigation (preventing the creation of new debris) must be complemented by active debris remediation (removing existing debris)—a topic that has since moved to the forefront of COPUOS discussions but remains without a comprehensive governance framework.

The 2021 Russian ASAT test, discussed in Chapter 3, tested the governance system's capacity to respond to deliberate debris creation. The test was widely condemned but produced no formal legal consequences, illustrating the enforcement gap that characterizes the current framework. These incidents collectively demonstrate that while the governance architecture has maintained broad stability, its ability to prevent harm, assign accountability, and adapt to new threats remains limited.

Paths Toward Reform

Reform of the space governance architecture need not imply abandonment of existing institutions. COPUOS and the UN system retain irreplaceable advantages: universality, legitimacy, accumulated expertise, and a track record of successful norm development. The question is how to adapt these institutions to a faster, more complex, and more commercially driven environment.

Several reform pathways are under discussion. First, strengthening coordination between COPUOS and other relevant bodies—particularly the ITU, ICAO, and regional space agencies—could reduce fragmentation and ensure that governance norms are consistent across domains. Joint working groups, cross-institutional consultations, and harmonized reporting requirements could improve coherence without requiring institutional merger or reorganization. The precedent of the UN Inter-Agency Meeting on Outer Space Activities (UN-Space), which brings together over thirty UN entities with space-related activities for annual coordination, suggests that improved institutional coherence is achievable through existing mechanisms.

Second, enhancing the participation of non-state actors in COPUOS processes could address the representation gap. This might take the form of expanded observer status, structured consultation mechanisms, public-private dialogue forums, or the establishment of an industry advisory committee. Models exist in other governance domains—the International Maritime Organization, for example, grants consultative status to industry associations that participate actively in regulatory development.

Third, developing modular soft-law instruments tailored to specific activities—rather than comprehensive frameworks covering all of outer space—could increase the pace and relevance of governance. Activity-specific guidelines for on-orbit servicing, active debris removal, mega-constellation management, or suborbital transport could be developed more quickly than universal instruments and could be updated as technology evolves.

More ambitious reforms—such as granting COPUOS binding regulatory authority, creating a World Space Organization analogous to the World Trade Organization, or establishing an international space court—remain unlikely in the near term. The political conditions that would make such reforms possible—a major space incident, a debris cascade, or a sovereignty crisis—may eventually arise, but they have not yet materialized. In the meantime, incremental adaptation remains the most politically feasible—and probably the most effective—approach.

The prospect of a Kessler syndrome—a cascading chain reaction of collisions in low Earth orbit that could render certain orbital bands unusable for generations—represents perhaps the most significant potential catalyst for governance reform. First described by NASA scientist Donald Kessler in 1978, the syndrome envisions a scenario in which the density of objects in orbit reaches a tipping point beyond which collisions generate debris faster than it can be removed by natural orbital decay. Recent modeling suggests that certain orbital bands may already be near or at this tipping point. A major cascading event could destroy billions of dollars of space infrastructure, disrupt critical satellite services, and threaten the viability of human spaceflight—consequences severe enough to galvanize the political will for fundamental governance reform.

Short of such a crisis, the most promising reform pathway lies in strengthening the connections between existing institutions rather than creating new ones. A coordinated governance ecosystem—in which COPUOS establishes principles, the ITU manages spectrum, ICAO coordinates airspace, ISO develops technical standards, and national regulators implement and enforce—may prove more effective than a centralized authority. This polycentric model sacrifices the elegance of unified governance for the resilience of distributed decision-making, relying on coordination mechanisms rather than hierarchical authority to maintain coherence.

The experience of internet governance offers an instructive parallel. The internet is governed not by a single international authority but by a network of institutions—ICANN, the IETF, regional internet registries, national regulators—that operate at different scales and with different mandates. This polycentric model has proven remarkably effective at managing a complex global infrastructure, even as it has struggled with issues of legitimacy, representation, and coordination. Space governance may evolve toward a similar model, with COPUOS serving as the overarching normative authority while specialized institutions manage specific operational domains.

> *"The architecture of space governance was designed for a world of two spacefaring superpowers. It must now serve a world of ninety spacefaring states, thousands of private operators, and an orbital environment of unprecedented complexity."*
>
> – On the need for institutional adaptation

■ Continuity and Change

The future of space governance will be shaped by a tension between continuity and change. The principles articulated in the early years of space law—peaceful use, non-appropriation, cooperation, responsibility—retain broad support and continuing relevance. Their implementation, however, must adapt to a more crowded, competitive, and commercialized space environment. The challenge is to preserve the core values that have sustained six decades of peaceful space activity while developing the institutional capacity to address the challenges of the next six.

***

Chapter Summary

Chapter 5 has examined the institutional foundations of international space governance, tracing the arc from the UN's first emergency responses to Sputnik through the creation of COPUOS, the development of the five space treaties, the rise of soft-law governance, and the contemporary challenges that threaten to outpace the system's capacity to adapt.

The architecture is impressive in its achievements. No other domain of international law has been governed as successfully with so few enforcement mechanisms. The prevention of sovereignty claims in outer space, the establishment of free satellite overflight, the development of liability and registration frameworks, and the emergence of debris mitigation norms all testify to the effectiveness of the consensus-based model pioneered by COPUOS. These achievements are not merely legal abstractions; they underpin the $470 billion global space economy and the satellite-dependent infrastructure—communications, navigation, weather forecasting, financial services—on which modern civilization depends.

The architecture's success is also evident in what has not happened. No state has asserted sovereignty over any part of outer space. No conflict over space resources has occurred. No major dispute over satellite overflight has disrupted space operations. The absence of conflict in a domain of intense strategic competition is itself a remarkable achievement—one that reflects the stabilizing effect of the norms, institutions, and practices examined in this chapter.

Yet the architecture is also showing its age. The pace problem, the representation gap, the challenge of institutional fragmentation, and the enforcement deficit are not merely theoretical concerns; they are operational realities that affect the safety, sustainability, and equity of space activities today. The incidents examined in this chapter—Cosmos 954, Iridium-Cosmos, the 2021 ASAT test—illustrate the costs of governance gaps that the existing framework cannot close.

The question for the coming decades is whether the political will exists to adapt the governance framework before a crisis forces the issue—or whether, as has happened so often in human history, reform will wait until the costs of inaction become impossible to ignore. The historical pattern examined in this chapter suggests grounds for cautious optimism: the space governance system has demonstrated a capacity for incremental adaptation, developing new soft-law instruments in response to emerging challenges while preserving the foundational principles established in the 1960s. Whether this incremental approach can keep pace with the exponential growth of space activity is the central governance question of our time.

What this chapter has also shown, however, is that the UN-centered governance architecture—for all its limitations—remains indispensable. No alternative framework offers the same combination of universality, legitimacy, accumulated expertise, and normative authority. The Artemis Accords, for all their practical value, cannot substitute for multilateral norms developed through inclusive processes. Regional arrangements, while valuable, cannot address global challenges. Bilateral agreements, while essential for operational coordination, cannot establish the universal standards that a global domain requires. The United Nations, and COPUOS in particular, will remain at the center of space governance for the foreseeable future—not because the architecture is perfect, but because no better alternative exists.

In the next chapter, we turn from institutions to accountability, examining how international law allocates responsibility and liability for damage caused by space activities—the legal mechanisms through which the principles explored in this chapter acquire practical force.

***

End of Chapter 5

Chapter 6

STATE RESPONSIBILITY AND LIABILITY FOR SPACE ACTIVITIES

When a satellite falls from the sky or debris strikes a spacecraft, who is accountable? This chapter examines the legal mechanisms that assign responsibility and liability for space activities—from Cold War treaty negotiations to the contemporary challenges of mega-constellations, orbital debris, and cyber interference.

Part 1

Foundations of State Responsibility in Space Law

The rapid expansion of human activity into outer space has made questions of responsibility and liability unavoidable. Satellites provide indispensable services to billions of people. Launch activities carry inherent risks. Orbital congestion increases the likelihood of collision and harm. In a domain where enforcement mechanisms are limited and jurisdiction is fragmented, international law relies heavily on the attribution of responsibility to states. This reliance reflects both practical necessity and a deeper principle: states remain the primary subjects of international law, even when activities are conducted by private actors, multinational consortia, or international organizations.

Responsibility as a Cornerstone of International Law

State responsibility is a foundational doctrine of international law. It establishes that when a state commits an internationally wrongful act—a breach of an international obligation attributable to that state—it bears responsibility for the consequences. The doctrine serves multiple functions: it affirms accountability, deters unlawful conduct, and provides a framework for reparation. The International Law Commission's Articles on Responsibility of States for Internationally Wrongful Acts (2001) codified the general principles governing state responsibility, and these principles apply to space activities just as they apply to any other domain of state conduct.

In the context of space activities, responsibility plays an especially critical role, compensating for the absence of territorial jurisdiction and centralized enforcement. Unlike terrestrial domains, outer space lacks permanent human presence, physical borders, or international policing.

Law must therefore operate through indirect control, linking actions in space to actors on Earth. The attribution of responsibility to states provides this essential link, ensuring that space activities remain subject to legal oversight regardless of where they occur.

The doctrine of state responsibility in space law operates alongside—but is conceptually distinct from—the specialized liability regime established by the Liability Convention. While state responsibility addresses breaches of international obligations (wrongful acts), the liability regime addresses compensation for damage (which may or may not involve wrongful acts). Understanding this distinction is essential for navigating the legal framework that governs accountability in outer space.

Article VI of the Outer Space Treaty: The Keystone Provision

> ■ **Outer Space Treaty, Article VI**
>
> "States Parties to the Treaty shall bear international responsibility for national activities in outer space, including the Moon and other celestial bodies, whether such activities are carried on by governmental agencies or by non-governmental entities, and for assuring that national activities are carried out in conformity with the provisions set forth in the present Treaty."
>
> "The activities of non-governmental entities in outer space, including the Moon and other celestial bodies, shall require authorization and continuing supervision by the appropriate State Party to the Treaty."

Article VI of the Outer Space Treaty is the keystone of the responsibility framework in space law. It declares that states bear international responsibility for all national activities in outer space, whether conducted by governmental agencies or non-governmental entities. This provision reflects a deliberate and radical policy choice: private participation in space does not dilute state responsibility. On the contrary, states are made the guarantors of private behavior in a domain where no international authority exercises direct oversight.

Article VI imposes two core obligations. First, states must authorize and continually supervise the space activities of non-governmental entities operating under their jurisdiction. This requirement ensures that private actors do not operate in a regulatory vacuum; their activities must be reviewed, approved, and monitored by a responsible state. Second, states remain internationally responsible for those activities regardless of domestic arrangements. A state cannot escape responsibility by delegating space operations to private companies or by structuring its domestic law to insulate itself from liability.

The emphasis on "authorization and continuing supervision" highlights the preventive dimension of responsibility. States are expected not merely to react to harm after it occurs, but to regulate space activities proactively through licensing regimes, technical standards, insurance requirements, and compliance mechanisms. This preventive function is critical in a domain where the consequences of failure—orbital debris, collision cascades, damage to other states' assets—may be irreversible and disproportionate to the original activity.

The practical implementation of authorization and continuing supervision varies considerably among states. The most developed licensing regimes—those of the United States, France, the United Kingdom, and Australia—require operators to submit detailed applications demonstrating technical competence, financial responsibility, insurance coverage, and compliance with debris mitigation guidelines. The licensing authority evaluates the application, imposes conditions, and monitors compliance throughout the mission's lifetime. Less developed regimes may authorize activities with minimal oversight, creating potential gaps in the global supervisory framework.

The concept of "continuing supervision" is particularly demanding. It requires states not merely to approve activities at the outset but to monitor them throughout their operational life—including the end-of-life phase, when debris mitigation obligations (such as post-mission disposal) must be fulfilled. For a satellite designed to operate for fifteen years, continuing supervision may require tracking license compliance over a period longer than many government administrations. The bureaucratic and technical demands of this obligation are significant, and not all states possess the institutional capacity to fulfill them adequately.

The scope of Article VI is notably broad. It applies to "national activities," a term that encompasses activities conducted by a state's nationals, from its territory, or under its jurisdiction—potentially extending to activities by foreign companies that launch from a state's spaceport or operate under its licensing regime. The precise boundaries of "national activities" remain debated, but the prevailing interpretation favors a functional approach that captures all activities over which a state exercises effective authority.

The 'Appropriate State' Question

Article VI raises a question that has grown increasingly pressing in the commercial era: which state is the "appropriate" state for authorizing and supervising a particular space activity? When a company incorporated in Luxembourg launches a satellite from a site in French Guiana operated by a European launch provider, using a platform manufactured in the United States and serving customers in Asia, multiple states have plausible claims to regulatory authority. Each of these states might be considered an "appropriate State Party" under Article VI, yet none may have a comprehensive picture of the activity as a whole.

This fragmentation of regulatory authority creates practical challenges. If no state assumes responsibility, the activity may proceed without adequate oversight—a "responsibility gap" that undermines the Treaty's fundamental architecture. If multiple states assert jurisdiction simultaneously, the operator faces conflicting regulatory requirements—a "jurisdictional overlap" that increases compliance costs and may deter investment. The proliferation of commercial space activities has made these challenges routine rather than exceptional.

National space legislation addresses the "appropriate state" question in divergent ways. Some states, like the United States, assert jurisdiction based on the nationality of the operator. Others, like France, assert jurisdiction based on launch from national territory. Still others, like Luxembourg, assert jurisdiction based on corporate registration. No international mechanism exists to coordinate these overlapping jurisdictional claims, and COPUOS has not yet developed guidelines on the topic. The result is a patchwork of national approaches that, collectively, may leave gaps in coverage or impose redundant requirements.

International Organizations and Space Activities

The Outer Space Treaty also addresses the responsibility of international intergovernmental organizations that conduct space activities. Article VI provides that when activities are carried out by an international organization, responsibility is borne jointly by the organization and by its member states that are parties to the Treaty. Article XIII further provides that the Treaty's provisions apply to international organizations, provided that the majority of member states are parties to the Treaty and the organization accepts the rights and obligations thereunder.

This framework was designed primarily with the European Space Agency (ESA) in mind, though it also applies to other international space organizations such as EUMETSAT, the European Organisation for the Exploitation of Meteorological Satellites. In practice, the allocation of responsibility between an international organization and its member states raises complex questions about which entity exercises "authorization and continuing supervision" and how liability is distributed in the event of damage. The 1972 Liability Convention addresses this through a separate Convention provision (Article XXII) allowing international organizations to declare acceptance of the Convention's obligations—a mechanism that ESA has invoked.

Article VII: Liability for Damage

While Article VI addresses responsibility for ensuring compliance with international obligations, Article VII introduces the concept of liability for damage caused by space objects. It provides that a launching state is internationally liable for damage caused by its space object on the surface of the Earth, to aircraft in flight, or to space objects of another state or its nationals. This provision establishes the principle of state liability and provides the conceptual foundation for the more detailed regime developed in the Liability Convention of 1972.

The relationship between Articles VI and VII illustrates the dual architecture of accountability in space law. Article VI creates a general obligation of oversight and compliance—a continuing duty that exists regardless of whether any harm occurs. Article VII creates a specific obligation to compensate for damage—a duty triggered only when harm materializes. Together, they ensure that states cannot launch objects into space without accepting both the regulatory burden of supervision and the financial burden of potential harm. This dual architecture has no exact parallel in other domains of international law and represents one of the space law regime's most distinctive contributions to international legal theory.

The Registration Convention and Attribution

The Convention on Registration of Objects Launched into Outer Space (1975) complements the responsibility and liability framework by establishing a transparency mechanism essential for attribution. Under the Registration Convention, the launching state must register space objects in a national registry and provide information to the UN Secretary-General, including the launching state's identity, the satellite's designator, the date and location of launch, and basic orbital parameters (inclination, nodal period, apogee, perigee).

Registration serves multiple functions within the accountability framework. It identifies the state with jurisdiction and control over a space object (under Article VIII of the Outer Space Treaty), it facilitates attribution when damage occurs, and it provides a public record that supports space situational awareness and conjunction assessment. Without registration, it would be far more difficult to determine which state is responsible for a particular space object and therefore liable for damage it causes.

However, compliance with the Registration Convention is imperfect. Some states fail to register space objects promptly or accurately. The information provided is often insufficient for precise identification—general orbital parameters do not uniquely identify objects in increasingly crowded orbital bands. Objects may change orbits after registration without updated filings. And the Convention applies only to objects "launched into Earth orbit or beyond," potentially excluding suborbital objects that do not complete a full orbit. These compliance gaps weaken the attribution infrastructure on which both the responsibility and liability frameworks depend.

The ILC Articles and General International Law

The space law regime of state responsibility does not operate in isolation from general international law. The International Law Commission's Articles on State Responsibility (2001) provide the framework for attributing conduct to states, determining the consequences of internationally wrongful acts, and establishing obligations of cessation and reparation. These principles supplement the Outer Space Treaty's specific provisions, filling gaps in areas such as countermeasures, force majeure, necessity, and the responsibility of international organizations.

The ILC Articles establish that a state is responsible for an internationally wrongful act when conduct attributable to it constitutes a breach of an international obligation. In the space context, this means that a state that fails to authorize and supervise its nationals' space activities—in breach of Article VI of the Outer Space Treaty—commits an internationally wrongful act and must cease the breach and provide reparation. The available forms of reparation include restitution (restoring the situation to what it was before the breach), compensation (for financially assessable damage), and satisfaction (for non-material harm, such as an acknowledgment of the breach).

The interaction between the specialized space law regime and general international law is particularly important in cases involving multiple responsible states, international organizations (such as ESA or EUMETSAT), or activities that straddle the boundary between space law and other legal domains (such as telecommunications law, environmental law, or the law of armed conflict). General principles of state responsibility provide the connective tissue that links these domains and ensures analytical coherence. A state's responsibility for space activities is not limited to the specific provisions of the five space treaties; it extends to all applicable international obligations, including customary international law, other treaty commitments, and general principles of law.

■ **Responsibility vs. Liability: A Critical Distinction**

Responsibility concerns the breach of an international obligation and the resulting duty to cease the wrongful act and provide reparation. Liability focuses on compensation for damage, regardless of whether a wrongful act occurred. In space law, certain activities may cause damage even when conducted lawfully and with due care—the Liability Convention addresses this by imposing absolute liability for surface damage. The two concepts are complementary: responsibility ensures compliance; liability ensures compensation.

***

Part 11

The Liability Convention: Scope, Structure, and Operation

While Article VI of the Outer Space Treaty establishes the principle of state responsibility, it does not by itself resolve the practical problem of compensation for damage caused by space activities. That task is undertaken by the Convention on International Liability for Damage Caused by Space Objects (1972), commonly known as the Liability Convention. Adopted at a time when space activity was expanding rapidly and the risks of harm were becoming tangible, the Convention represents one of the most concrete and operational instruments of international space law.

Rationale and Historical Context

The Liability Convention was negotiated against the backdrop of increasing satellite launches, growing international cooperation, and early incidents that highlighted the potential for harm. The 1960s had witnessed several re-entries of space objects, including uncontrolled descents of rocket stages and satellite components. While no major disaster had yet occurred, the prospect of a space object striking a populated area—or damaging another state's satellite—generated sufficient concern to motivate the negotiation of a compensation framework.

The Convention draws inspiration from analogous liability regimes in aviation and nuclear law. The 1952 Rome Convention on Damage Caused by Foreign Aircraft to Third Parties on the Surface established the precedent of absolute liability for damage caused by aircraft to persons and property on the ground—a principle directly transposed into space law. Nuclear liability conventions, including the 1963 Vienna Convention on Civil Liability for Nuclear Damage, provided models for channeling liability to operators and establishing compensation mechanisms for ultra-hazardous activities. In space law, however, the absence of territorial jurisdiction and the transboundary nature of harm required a novel approach that preserved state-level liability rather than delegating it to operators.

The choice to locate liability at the state level rather than the operator level was consequential. In aviation and nuclear law, liability typically attaches to the operator (airline or nuclear plant operator) rather than the state. In space law, by contrast, the state is the liable party under international law, even when the activity is conducted by a private company. This reflects the reality of the 1970s, when space activity was almost entirely governmental, and the Article VI principle that states bear responsibility for all national space activities. The practical implication is that injured parties must channel their claims through diplomatic processes rather than suing operators directly in national courts—a requirement that significantly affects the accessibility and efficiency of the compensation mechanism.

The distinction has become increasingly problematic in the commercial era. When a private company's satellite causes damage, the injured party cannot bring a claim directly against the company under the Liability Convention; it must persuade its own government to present a diplomatic claim against the launching state. The launching state, in turn, may seek reimbursement from the operator under domestic law or contractual arrangements. This layered process—victim to victim's government to launching government to operator—introduces delay, political discretion, and potential loss of information at each stage. Proposals to allow direct claims by private parties or to establish an international tribunal for space liability disputes have been discussed academically but have not gained political traction.

Definition of Key Terms

The Convention adopts deliberately broad definitions of its core terms. "Damage" encompasses loss of life, personal injury, and loss of or damage to property of states, persons (natural or juridical), or international intergovernmental organizations. This expansive definition ensures comprehensive protection, though it does not explicitly address purely economic loss—an omission of growing significance in an era when satellite service disruptions can cause billions of dollars in economic harm without physical destruction.

> ■ **Liability Convention: Key Definitions**
>
> Damage: Loss of life, personal injury, or loss of or damage to property of states, persons, or international organizations.
>
> Launching state: (a) A state which launches or procures the launching of a space object; (b) A state from whose territory or facility a space object is launched.
>
> Space object: Includes component parts and its launch vehicle and parts thereof.
>
> Multiple launching states: Jointly and severally liable for damage under absolute liability.
>
> Claims period: One year from the date of damage or identification of the liable launching state.
>
> As of 2025: 98 ratifications, 19 signatures.

The definition of "launching state" is deliberately expansive, capturing multiple points of involvement in a single launch. A state may qualify as a launching state because it conducted the launch, procured the launch (contracted for it), or provided its territory or facility for the launch. Where multiple states qualify, they are jointly and severally liable, ensuring that victims can seek full compensation from any responsible state. This multi-pronged definition was designed for an era of government-dominated launch activity, but it has proven remarkably adaptable to the commercial era, where launches frequently involve multiple states in different capacities.

Absolute Liability on the Surface of the Earth

The Convention's most distinctive feature is its adoption of absolute liability for damage caused on the surface of the Earth or to aircraft in flight. Under Article II, a launching state is liable regardless of fault. The victim need only establish that damage occurred and that it was caused by a space object. No proof of negligence, recklessness, or intent is required.

This strict standard reflects the heightened risk posed to uninvolved third parties. Individuals and states on the ground have no ability to influence, predict, or control the trajectory of space objects. They cannot consent to the risk, take precautionary measures, or apportion responsibility through contract. It would be unjust to require such involuntary risk-bearers to prove that the launching state was at fault. Absolute liability shifts the burden of risk to those who create it—and who are best positioned to manage it through insurance, engineering standards, and operational safeguards.

The practical significance of absolute liability has grown as launch frequency has increased. In 2023, more than 200 orbital launches were conducted worldwide, depositing thousands of objects into orbit—each of which will eventually re-enter the atmosphere, with larger objects potentially surviving to reach the surface. While most debris burns up during re-entry, larger components—engine bells, pressure vessels, fuel tanks—can survive and strike the ground with lethal force. In 2022, debris from a SpaceX Falcon 9 upper stage landed on a farm in New South Wales, Australia. In 2024, a piece of ISS hardware survived re-entry and struck a home in Naples, Florida. Neither incident caused personal injury, but both demonstrated the continuing reality of surface risk from space activities.

The analogy to aviation and nuclear liability is instructive. Just as airlines are held strictly liable for damage caused by their aircraft to persons on the ground, launching states are held strictly liable for damage caused by their space objects on the surface. The principle is the same: those who engage in ultra-hazardous activities that create unilateral risks for bystanders must bear the costs when those risks materialize.

Fault-Based Liability in Outer Space

By contrast, damage occurring elsewhere than on the surface of the Earth—most notably, damage to another state's satellite in orbit—is subject to a fault-based liability regime under Article III. The launching state is liable only if the damage is due to its fault or the fault of persons for whom it is responsible.

This distinction reflects the different risk profiles of terrestrial and orbital environments. In outer space, actors are typically sophisticated operators with comparable technological capabilities and shared situational awareness. Both parties to an orbital collision are, in principle, capable of tracking objects, calculating conjunction probabilities, and executing avoidance maneuvers. Requiring proof of fault in this context encourages responsible conduct—collision avoidance, debris mitigation, information-sharing—while avoiding the imposition of automatic liability that could discourage cooperation and innovation.

The fault-based standard raises significant practical challenges, however. As discussed in Part III, proving fault in orbital incidents requires access to detailed technical data that may be classified, proprietary, or controlled by the party alleged to be at fault. The standard of care against which conduct is measured is not defined by the Convention and must be inferred from evolving norms, industry standards, and soft-law instruments. These ambiguities create uncertainty that the Convention's drafters could not have fully anticipated.

> *"The absolute liability standard for surface damage reflects a fundamental principle of justice: those who create risks for involuntary bystanders must bear the costs when those risks materialize."*
>
> – On the rationale for strict liability in space law

Claims Procedure and Diplomatic Settlement

The Convention establishes a claims procedure rooted in diplomatic channels. Claims must be presented by states on behalf of their nationals or themselves through diplomatic means. If the claimant state and the launching state cannot reach agreement within one year of the claim's presentation, either party may request the establishment of a Claims Commission, composed of three members: one appointed by each party and a third chosen jointly or, failing agreement, by the UN Secretary-General.

The Claims Commission's decision is binding only if the parties have so agreed; otherwise, it is recommendatory. This structure reflects the political sensitivity of international claims and the reluctance of states to submit to binding adjudication without consent. The practical effect is that most disputes are resolved through diplomatic negotiation rather than formal proceedings—a pattern exemplified by the Cosmos 954 settlement, discussed below.

The Convention also includes an exoneration provision (Article VI) that has attracted significant scholarly attention. A launching state is exonerated from absolute liability if it establishes that the damage resulted wholly or partially from "gross negligence or from an act or omission done with intent to cause damage" on the part of the claimant state or its nationals. This provision prevents states or their nationals from deliberately creating situations in which damage occurs and then claiming compensation—a form of moral hazard defense. However, the exoneration defense has never been invoked in practice, and its precise scope remains untested.

The Convention's one-year statute of limitations for claims (Article X) creates an additional practical constraint. Damage must be identified and attributed, diplomatic channels must be engaged, and a formal claim must be presented—all within twelve months. For incidents involving small debris objects that may not be detected or attributed for months, this time frame may be insufficient. The Registration Convention's requirement that claims may be presented within one year of identification of the liable launching state provides some flexibility, but the overall timeline remains tight for complex incidents.

> **■ Cosmos 954: The Only Claim Under the Liability Convention**
>
> On 24 January 1978, the Soviet nuclear-powered radar satellite Cosmos 954 re-entered the atmosphere and scattered radioactive debris across a vast area of Canada's Northwest Territories.
>
> Canada presented a claim to the Soviet Union for CAD 6 million in cleanup costs, invoking the Liability Convention.
>
> The claim was settled diplomatically in 1981 for CAD 3 million—approximately half of Canada's claimed costs.
>
> The settlement avoided the Claims Commission mechanism and left many legal questions unresolved.
>
> Cosmos 954 remains the only instance in which the Liability Convention has been formally invoked between states.

Joint and Several Liability

Where two or more states qualify as launching states for the same space object, they are jointly and severally liable for damage caused on the surface of the Earth (Article IV). This means that the injured party may seek full compensation from any one of the launching states, leaving it to those states to apportion costs among themselves through separate agreements. This rule protects victims from the complexities of multi-state launch arrangements and ensures that compensation is not delayed or diminished by disputes among responsible parties.

Joint and several liability has become increasingly important as commercial launch arrangements have grown more complex. A single launch may involve a launch provider from one state, a satellite operator from another, a customer from a third, and a launch facility in a fourth. Under the Convention, all four states could potentially qualify as launching states, each bearing the full weight of joint liability. This reality has driven the development of elaborate indemnification and cross-waiver agreements at the national level, through which participating states allocate risk among themselves without affecting the rights of injured third parties.

National Implementation and Insurance Requirements

The Liability Convention establishes state liability at the international level, but national legislation determines how that liability is managed domestically. Most spacefaring states have enacted laws that require operators to obtain third-party liability insurance as a condition of licensing, creating a financial safety net that supplements the international framework. The United States requires commercial launch licensees to obtain insurance covering the maximum probable loss from third-party damage, with the government providing an additional layer of indemnification above the insured amount—a structure sometimes described as a "financial responsibility pyramid."

The French Space Operations Act (2008) requires operators to demonstrate financial capacity to cover third-party liability up to €60 million, with the French government assuming liability beyond this threshold. The United Kingdom's Space Industry Act 2018 establishes a similar tiered structure with mandatory insurance and government indemnification. These national frameworks translate the Convention's state-level liability into operational financial requirements, ensuring that funds are available for compensation without requiring the cumbersome diplomatic processes envisioned by the Convention.

Cross-waiver agreements represent another important development. In the commercial launch industry, all parties to a launch—the launch provider, the satellite operator, their respective contractors, and their governments—typically agree to waive claims against each other for damage arising from the launch, regardless of fault. These waivers do not affect the rights of uninvolved third parties under the Liability Convention, but they significantly simplify the allocation of risk among participants. The International Space Station partnership employs a similar cross-waiver mechanism through the 1998 Intergovernmental Agreement, under which each partner state waives claims against the others for damage arising from ISS operations.

The Convention in Practice: Limited Invocation

Despite its careful architecture, the Liability Convention has been formally invoked only once in over fifty years—the Cosmos 954 incident of 1978. Several subsequent incidents could have given rise to claims but did not. The 2009 collision between Iridium 33 and Cosmos 2251—the first accidental hypervelocity collision between two intact satellites, generating over 2,000 trackable debris fragments—did not result in a claim under the Convention. Iridium LLC, a private U.S. company, had no standing to bring a claim directly; only the United States government could present a claim on its behalf. The U.S. government chose not to do so, reportedly because it did not wish to establish a precedent that might expose the United States to reciprocal claims for its own orbital debris.

This pattern of non-invocation reveals a fundamental tension in the Convention's design. States are both potential claimants and potential respondents. A state that aggressively pursues claims against others sets a precedent that may be used against it in future incidents. This mutual deterrence effect—analogous to the strategic logic of nuclear deterrence—explains why states prefer diplomatic settlement, insurance mechanisms, and cross-waiver agreements to formal legal proceedings. The Convention functions less as a litigation framework and more as a background norm that shapes behavior by establishing the threat of liability without routinely actualizing it.

> ■ **The Dual Standard of Liability**
> The Liability Convention establishes two distinct liability standards: absolute liability for damage on the surface of the Earth (Article II), reflecting the involuntary risk borne by ground-based populations, and fault-based liability for damage in outer space (Article III), reflecting the shared agency and capability of orbital operators. This dual standard balances the interests of victims, operators, and the broader international community.

***

Part III

Fault, Causation, and Evidentiary Challenges

While the Liability Convention establishes the basic architecture of compensation for space-related damage, its practical operation—particularly for damage occurring in outer space—raises complex questions of fault, causation, and proof. These questions are not merely technical; they go to the heart of whether the liability regime can function effectively in an increasingly congested and contested orbital environment.

The Meaning of Fault in Outer Space

The Convention does not define "fault," leaving its interpretation to general principles of international law. In practice, fault has been understood to encompass negligence, lack of due care, and failure to comply with applicable norms. Determining fault in space activities, however, is inherently challenging. Space operations involve sophisticated technology, automated decision-making systems, and complex chains of command that blur the line between human error and technical malfunction. A satellite collision may result from inaccurate tracking data, delayed maneuver decisions, software glitches, communication failures, or a combination of all four.

Moreover, the standard of care expected of space actors is not static. What constitutes due diligence evolves with technology, practice, and normative development. As collision avoidance systems, space situational awareness capabilities, and debris mitigation guidelines become more widespread and sophisticated, expectations of responsible behavior increase correspondingly. A failure to adhere to widely accepted guidelines—such as the COPUOS Space Debris Mitigation Guidelines or the Inter-Agency Space Debris Coordination Committee (IADC) guidelines—may increasingly be viewed as evidence of fault, even though those guidelines are formally non-binding.

The evolution of soft-law standards thus creates a dynamic relationship between normative development and liability assessment. As guidelines become more specific and widely adopted, they raise the bar for due diligence. An operator that ignores conjunction warnings, fails to execute a collision avoidance maneuver, or neglects to passivate an end-of-life satellite may find that its conduct is judged not against the minimal standards of the 1972 Convention era, but against the significantly higher expectations of the twenty-first century. This dynamic illustrates how soft law and liability regimes interact to shape behavior—each reinforcing the other in a virtuous cycle of rising standards.

Causation in a Congested Orbital Environment

Establishing causation presents an equally formidable challenge. Orbital incidents often involve multiple contributing factors, including prior debris, inaccurate tracking data, unpredictable space weather, and the cumulative effects of decades of space activity. Isolating a single cause—or attributing responsibility among multiple actors—can be extraordinarily difficult.

The problem is exacerbated by the Kessler syndrome risk, where collisions generate debris that increases the probability of further collisions in a self-reinforcing cascade. In such scenarios, damage may result from a chain of events spanning years or decades and involving numerous actors. A piece of debris that damages a satellite in 2025 may have originated from a fragmentation event in 2007 (such as the Chinese ASAT test), which struck a rocket body launched in 1995, which was manufactured by a company no longer in existence. Traditional causation analysis, which seeks a direct and proximate link between act and harm, is ill-suited to this reality.

International law offers limited guidance on how to address cumulative and cascading harm. Principles of joint and several liability, proportionate responsibility, and market-share liability—developed in domestic tort law to address analogous problems of indeterminate causation—have not yet been incorporated into the international space liability framework. In the absence of clear rules, disputes may hinge on technical assessments and expert testimony, increasing uncertainty, cost, and the time required for resolution.

The environmental law domain offers potentially useful precedents for addressing cumulative harm in outer space. The "polluter pays" principle, widely accepted in international environmental law, assigns the costs of pollution to those who cause it. The concept of "common but differentiated responsibilities," developed in the climate change context, acknowledges that states have contributed to a common problem in differing degrees and should bear proportionate obligations. These principles could inform the development of a space debris liability framework that addresses cumulative environmental degradation rather than individual incidents of damage.

Proposals for a "debris remediation fund"—financed by contributions from launching states proportionate to the amount of debris they have generated—would apply the polluter pays principle to the space domain. Such a fund could finance active debris removal operations without requiring the identification of a specific liable party for each individual piece of debris. While politically ambitious, this approach addresses the systemic character of the debris problem more effectively than the existing incident-based liability framework.

> ■ **Evidentiary Challenges in Space Liability Claims**
>
> Tracking limitations: Current systems can track objects >10 cm in LEO; smaller fragments (1–10 cm) are largely untracked but lethal.
>
> Attribution gaps: Fragmentation debris may be untraceable to its original space object.
>
> Data asymmetry: Precise orbital data may be classified (military) or proprietary (commercial).
>
> Temporal disconnect: Debris-causing events may precede damage by years or decades.
>
> Maneuver ambiguity: Whether an operator 'should have' maneuvered depends on probabilistic conjunction assessments, not certainties.
>
> These challenges make fault-based claims under Article III of the Liability Convention exceptionally difficult to prosecute.

Information Asymmetry and Space Situational Awareness

Proving fault and causation in space incidents requires access to detailed technical data, including precise orbital parameters, conjunction assessment reports, maneuver logs, system performance records, and telemetry data. Such information is often classified, commercially sensitive, or otherwise restricted. States and private operators may be reluctant to disclose data that could expose military capabilities, competitive advantages, or operational vulnerabilities.

This information asymmetry disadvantages potential claimants, particularly smaller states and private actors without independent space situational awareness (SSA) capabilities. The United States, through its Space Surveillance Network operated by the U.S. Space Command, provides conjunction warnings to satellite operators worldwide—a vital public service known as the Conjunction Data Messages (CDMs). However, the data shared through CDMs is often insufficient for legal proceedings, which may require higher-precision measurements, historical tracking records, covariance matrices, and maneuver data that the warning service does not provide.

The Iridium 33–Cosmos 2251 collision of 10 February 2009 illustrates these evidentiary challenges vividly. The collision occurred at an altitude of approximately 790 kilometers at a relative velocity of 11.7 kilometers per second, generating over 2,000 trackable debris fragments. Determining whether either operator was at fault required answering questions that the available evidence could not definitively resolve: Was a conjunction warning issued? If so, was it sufficiently precise to trigger a maneuver decision? Could Cosmos 2251, a defunct satellite, have been maneuvered at all? Did Iridium LLC have the capability and the time to execute an avoidance maneuver? These questions implicate classified U.S. military tracking data, Russian orbital information, and proprietary operational procedures—none of which was publicly available in the detail required for legal adjudication.

The development of improved SSA capabilities—including commercial tracking networks such as LeoLabs and ExoAnalytic Solutions, the European Space Agency's Space Safety Programme, Japan's space debris monitoring system, and India's Network for Space Objects Tracking and Analysis (NETRA)—is gradually reducing information asymmetry. However, these capabilities remain unevenly distributed, and no international mechanism exists to compel the disclosure of SSA data for liability proceedings. Proposals for an international data-sharing agreement—perhaps modeled on the International Civil Aviation Organization's Accident Investigation framework, which requires states to share safety-related information—have gained traction in academic and policy circles but have not yet achieved political support within COPUOS.

The Role of Standards and Best Practices as Evidence

In the absence of binding technical standards, soft-law instruments play a crucial evidentiary role in liability proceedings. The COPUOS Space Debris Mitigation Guidelines, the Long-term Sustainability Guidelines, ISO 24113 on space debris mitigation, and industry best practices provide benchmarks against which conduct can be assessed. Compliance with such guidelines supports a defense against allegations of fault; deviation suggests negligence or recklessness.

This evidentiary function gives soft-law instruments a practical significance that extends well beyond their formal legal status. An operator that demonstrates compliance with internationally recognized guidelines strengthens its position in any liability dispute. An operator that ignores those guidelines does so at its legal peril, even though the guidelines impose no binding obligation. Over time, consistent reference to these standards in claims and negotiations could contribute to their elevation from voluntary guidance to de facto legal obligations—a process that would effectively transform soft law into hard law through the mechanism of liability adjudication.

Several specific examples illustrate the growing significance of soft-law standards in liability assessment. The 25-year post-mission disposal guideline—originally developed by the IADC, adopted by COPUOS in 2007, and endorsed by the General Assembly—has become the de facto minimum standard of care for end-of-life management. An operator that fails to deorbit a satellite within 25 years (or the increasingly common 5-year standard) would face strong presumptions of fault if its defunct satellite caused a collision. Similarly, the COPUOS Long-term Sustainability Guidelines' provisions on conjunction assessment and collision avoidance establish expectations that, if unmet, could support findings of negligence.

The interaction between soft law and liability thus creates a powerful incentive structure. Operators comply with guidelines not merely because compliance is "good practice" but because non-compliance creates legal exposure. This incentive structure operates regardless of whether the guidelines are formally binding, demonstrating that the legal significance of a norm depends not only on its formal status but on its practical consequences. In the space domain, those consequences are shaped by the liability framework, the insurance market, and the licensing requirements that collectively define the operational environment.

> *"In space law, soft-law guidelines and liability standards exist in a symbiotic relationship: guidelines define the standard of care, while liability enforcement gives guidelines their teeth."*
>
> – On the interaction between soft law and liability

***

Part IV

Contemporary Risks: Debris, Mega-Constellations, and Cyber Interference

The liability framework established in the early decades of space exploration now operates in an environment radically different from that which its drafters envisioned. The orbital domain of the 1970s was sparsely populated, state-dominated, and characterized by large, expensive satellites operated with military discipline. Today's environment is congested, commercialized, and increasingly contested. Space debris, satellite mega-constellations, and cyber interference represent interconnected risks that challenge existing legal concepts of responsibility and liability, exposing gaps that demand renewed attention.

Space Debris as a Systemic Risk

Space debris has emerged as the most visible and persistent threat to the safety and sustainability of outer space activities. As of 2025, tracking systems monitor approximately 36,000 objects larger than ten centimeters in low Earth orbit, but modeling estimates suggest there are over one million fragments between one and ten centimeters and more than one hundred million fragments smaller than one centimeter. Each of these objects, traveling at orbital velocities of seven to eight kilometers per second, carries kinetic energy sufficient to cause catastrophic damage. A one-centimeter fragment striking a satellite delivers the impact energy of a hand grenade.

From a liability perspective, debris complicates every element of the analytical framework. Attribution is the first challenge: when debris causes damage, identifying the originating space object—and by extension the responsible launching state—can be difficult or impossible. Fragmentation events may occur years or decades after launch, and debris may be altered by subsequent collisions, atmospheric drag, or orbital perturbations. The Liability Convention presupposes traceability, an assumption that is increasingly strained by orbital reality.

Even when attribution is possible, the Convention's framework raises difficult questions. If a defunct satellite launched by State A fragments spontaneously due to residual propellant, generating debris that damages a satellite operated by State B, is State A liable under the absolute liability standard (for surface damage) or the fault-based standard (for damage in space)? Does the failure to passivate the satellite—a now-standard practice recommended by the IADC and COPUOS guidelines—constitute fault? The answers depend on interpretive choices that the Convention's text does not resolve.

The temporal dimension of debris liability adds further complexity. Most of the 36,000 tracked objects in orbit were launched decades ago, under regulatory regimes far less rigorous than those in force today. The upper stages of rockets launched in the 1960s and 1970s—many of which were never passivated and remain laden with residual propellant—constitute a significant fraction of the most dangerous debris objects. If one of these legacy objects fragments and causes damage, the launching state bears liability under the Convention. But the standard of care applicable to activities conducted fifty years ago—when debris mitigation was not yet a recognized concern—may differ substantially from the standard applicable today. Whether fault can be retroactively assessed against standards that did not exist at the time of launch is a question with profound implications for the liability framework.

Scenario	Liability Standard	Key Challenges
Re-entering debris hits building	Absolute (Art. II)	Attribution if debris is untracked
Active satellite strikes another	Fault-based (Art. III)	Proving failure to maneuver; data access
Debris from old satellite hits active one	Fault-based (Art. III)	Attribution across decades; passivation standard
Cascade debris from prior collision	Uncertain	Indeterminate causation; multiple actors
Cyber attack disables satellite	Outside Convention scope	No physical damage; attribution of cyber attack
Jamming causes service disruption	Outside Convention scope	Economic loss only; no 'damage' as defined

Mega-Constellations and Aggregate Risk

The deployment of satellite mega-constellations numbering in the thousands represents a qualitative shift in space activity. SpaceX's Starlink constellation exceeded 6,000 satellites by late 2023, with regulatory approval for up to 12,000. Amazon's Project Kuiper plans over 3,200 satellites. OneWeb operates approximately 600. China has announced plans for its own mega-constellation of 13,000 satellites. If all proposed constellations are deployed, the number of active satellites in orbit could exceed 100,000 within the coming decade—a tenfold increase from today's levels.

This scale transforms the liability calculus in several ways. First, mega-constellations create aggregate risk that transcends individual operator behavior. Even if each operator complies with best practices, the cumulative density of objects in popular orbital bands increases collision probability for everyone. Traditional fault-based analysis, focused on discrete incidents and individual negligence, is ill-equipped to address this systemic dimension.

Second, mega-constellations challenge notions of due diligence. What level of collision avoidance capability is sufficient when a constellation operator must manage thousands of conjunction warnings per day? SpaceX's Starlink satellites execute autonomous collision avoidance maneuvers using onboard AI, but the frequency of these maneuvers—and their impact on other operators who must adjust their own activities in response—raises questions about the allocation of responsibility for a shared orbital environment. The concept of "right of way" in space—which operator must maneuver when two satellites are on a potential collision course—has no established legal framework, leaving coordination to ad hoc arrangements and voluntary practices.

The absence of formal traffic management rules in orbit stands in stark contrast to the sophisticated frameworks governing aviation (managed by ICAO through standardized air traffic control procedures) and maritime navigation (governed by the International Regulations for Preventing Collisions at Sea, or COLREGs). In both domains, clear rules of the road—right of way, speed limitations, separation standards—reduce collision risk and assign responsibility when incidents occur. The absence of comparable rules in space means that liability for orbital collisions must be determined ex post through fault analysis, rather than by reference to pre-established operational obligations. Developing space traffic management norms—potentially through COPUOS, ICAO, or a new specialized body—is widely recognized as one of the most urgent governance priorities in the space domain.

Third, mega-constellations raise concerns about orbital carrying capacity. Like a highway with a finite number of lanes, orbital bands have a finite capacity for satellites before collision risk becomes unmanageable. If that capacity is consumed by a small number of early-mover constellation operators, latecomers—including developing states seeking to deploy their own satellite systems—may be effectively excluded. This raises questions of equity and access that the existing liability framework, focused on compensation for specific incidents of damage, was not designed to address.

Regulatory responses to mega-constellation risks are beginning to emerge, but they remain fragmented and inadequate. In September 2022, the U.S. Federal Communications Commission adopted a new rule requiring satellite operators in LEO to deorbit their satellites within five years of end of mission—significantly tightening the previous 25-year guideline. The European Space Agency has endorsed a "zero debris" policy for future missions. However, these regulatory actions are national or regional in scope and do not address the fundamental coordination challenge: in the absence of international rules, each state regulates its own operators according to its own standards, and no mechanism exists to manage the aggregate impact of multiple constellations on the shared orbital environment.

The environmental dimension of mega-constellations adds another layer of concern. Studies have shown that the re-entry of large numbers of aluminum-bodied satellites deposits alumina particles in the upper atmosphere, potentially affecting ozone chemistry and contributing to stratospheric warming. The long-term environmental effects of deorbiting thousands of satellites per year—as mega-constellation operators plan to do through regular fleet replacement—are not yet fully understood. Nor is it clear which legal framework governs these atmospheric effects: space law addresses activities in outer space, while environmental law addresses pollution of the atmosphere. Re-entering satellites—transitioning from one domain to the other—fall into a regulatory gap that neither framework adequately covers.

Cyber Interference and Intangible Harm

Cyber interference introduces a fundamentally different category of risk that exposes the most significant gap in the current liability framework. Satellites rely on software, data links, command-and-control systems, and ground infrastructure that are vulnerable to cyberattack. Interference may disrupt services, corrupt data, degrade performance, or compromise operational control without causing any physical damage to the satellite itself.

The Liability Convention's definition of "damage" is limited to physical harm: loss of life, personal injury, and loss of or damage to property. Purely economic loss or service disruption falls outside its scope, leaving victims of cyber interference without clear remedies under the specialized space liability regime. A cyberattack that disables a navigation satellite—disrupting aviation, maritime shipping, financial transactions, and emergency services worldwide—could cause billions of dollars in economic damage without triggering the Liability Convention.

Attribution presents an additional obstacle. Identifying the perpetrator of a cyberattack is notoriously difficult, even with advanced forensic capabilities. State-sponsored cyber operations are frequently conducted through proxies, cut-outs, and deniable infrastructure designed to obscure origin. Even when attribution is technically possible, political considerations may prevent states from publicly identifying responsible parties. The result is a compound accountability gap: the liability framework does not cover the harm, and even if it did, the responsible party may be unidentifiable.

The cyberattack on Viasat's KA-SAT network on 24 February 2022—timed to coincide with the Russian invasion of Ukraine—illustrates these challenges concretely. The attack disabled satellite internet terminals across Ukraine and beyond, affecting tens of thousands of users including German wind turbine remote monitoring systems. The European Union, the United Kingdom, and the United States attributed the attack to Russia, but Russia denied responsibility. The damage was primarily economic and operational rather than physical: no satellite was physically destroyed, but the service disruption was severe and widespread. Under the Liability Convention, this attack would not have generated a compensable claim, because no "damage" as defined by the Convention occurred. The victims had to seek remedies through national law, insurance, and diplomatic channels rather than the international space liability regime.

These challenges underscore the need to integrate space law with broader international legal regimes addressing cyber operations and information security. The Tallinn Manual on the International Law Applicable to Cyber Operations provides interpretive guidance on how existing international law applies to cyber activities, including those affecting space infrastructure. Rule 80 of the Tallinn Manual 2.0 addresses attacks on objects indispensable to the survival of the civilian population, which could encompass attacks on satellites providing essential communications, navigation, or weather services. However, the application of these rules to space-based systems remains underexplored, and the Manual itself is a scholarly work without binding legal authority. Absent a comprehensive legal framework linking space law, cyber law, and the law of armed conflict, liability gaps will continue to undermine confidence in the space-based infrastructure on which modern civilization increasingly depends.

Toward an Adapted Liability Framework

Addressing contemporary risks requires a combination of legal, technical, and institutional responses that go beyond the existing treaty framework. Enhanced transparency through mandatory data-sharing and space traffic coordination can reduce collision risk and improve attribution. Clearer norms of responsible behavior—whether through strengthened soft-law instruments, industry standards, or eventual treaty amendment—can raise the standard of care and provide more determinate benchmarks for liability assessment.

Active Debris Removal: New Liability Questions

The emergence of active debris removal (ADR) as a realistic technological capability raises novel liability questions that the existing framework is poorly equipped to address. ADR involves physically approaching, capturing, and deorbiting defunct satellites or large debris objects—operations that require close proximity to and physical contact with objects belonging to other states. Under the Liability Convention, a launching state retains jurisdiction and control over its space objects indefinitely, even after they cease functioning. An ADR operator that removes another state's defunct satellite without authorization could, paradoxically, be liable for "damage" to that object under the Convention's fault-based standard.

This legal anomaly creates a perverse disincentive: the states and companies most capable of removing dangerous debris face potential liability for doing so. Resolving this problem requires either treaty interpretation that exempts consensual ADR operations from the liability framework, bilateral agreements between the ADR operator's state and the state of registry for the target object, or new international guidelines establishing a right of removal under specified conditions. COPUOS has begun discussing these issues, but no consensus has yet emerged on the legal framework for ADR—even as the technical capabilities mature and the operational need grows more urgent.

The Space Insurance Market

Insurance mechanisms, which have developed significantly since the 1970s, play an increasingly important role in managing space-related risk. The space insurance market, concentrated in London, Paris, and the Bermuda markets, provides coverage for launch failure, in-orbit anomalies, third-party liability, and loss of revenue. Annual premiums range between two and three billion dollars, covering a total insured value in the tens of billions. Major underwriters include Lloyd's of London syndicates, AXA XL, Allianz, and a network of specialist reinsurers.

Insurance requirements, imposed through national licensing regimes, effectively create a private-sector supplement to the international liability framework. When a licensed operator causes damage to third parties, the insurance policy provides the initial layer of compensation—often hundreds of millions of dollars—without requiring diplomatic claims between states. Government indemnification above the insured amount provides a second layer. The international liability framework provides a third layer, applicable when damage exceeds both insurance and indemnification.

The space insurance market also functions as a de facto regulatory mechanism. Insurers impose conditions on coverage that effectively require operators to comply with best practices in debris mitigation, collision avoidance, and operational safety. An operator that cannot obtain insurance at reasonable rates—because its practices are deemed too risky by underwriters—may find it practically impossible to obtain a launch license. This market-based discipline operates alongside government regulation, creating a dual enforcement mechanism that is more effective than either component alone.

Proposals for reform include extending the Liability Convention's definition of damage to encompass economic loss and service disruption, establishing presumptions of fault for certain categories of conduct (such as failure to comply with debris mitigation guidelines), creating international data-sharing mechanisms for liability proceedings, and developing collective risk management frameworks that address systemic risks such as orbital congestion. Whether these reforms are pursued through treaty amendment, soft-law evolution, or technological innovation remains an open question—but the need for adaptation is increasingly clear.

The most politically feasible path forward may be a combination of soft-law interpretation and national legislative harmonization rather than formal treaty amendment. Amending the Liability Convention would require consensus among its nearly one hundred parties—a daunting political challenge. By contrast, COPUOS could develop interpretive guidelines that clarify how the Convention's provisions apply to contemporary scenarios, while national legislatures could update their domestic space laws to address gaps in areas such as cyber liability, debris remediation, and commercial operator accountability. This dual-track approach—multilateral guidance combined with national implementation—has proven effective in other areas of space governance and is likely the most realistic strategy for adapting the liability framework to twenty-first-century realities.

■ **The Evolving Challenge**

The Liability Convention was designed for an era of sparse orbital activity, state-dominated operations, and physical damage. It must now contend with a congested orbital environment, thousands of commercial operators, cascading debris risks, and cyber threats that cause harm without physical impact. The framework's foundational principles—accountability, compensation, prevention—remain sound. Its operational mechanisms require adaptation to remain effective.

***

Chapter Summary

Chapter 6 has explored how international law assigns responsibility and liability for space activities, tracing the doctrinal foundations from the Outer Space Treaty's Article VI through the Liability Convention's dual standard and into the contemporary challenges that test the framework's adequacy.

The responsibility framework established in Article VI remains one of the most distinctive features of international space law. By making states the guarantors of all national space activities—governmental and private alike—the Treaty ensures that no space activity occurs without a responsible state standing behind it. This principle has served as the foundation for the development of national licensing regimes, insurance requirements, and compliance mechanisms that translate international obligations into domestic reality.

The Liability Convention's dual standard—absolute liability on the surface, fault-based liability in space—represents an elegant but increasingly strained balancing of competing interests. On the surface, involuntary risk-bearers are protected by strict liability. In orbit, sophisticated operators are held to a fault standard that encourages responsible conduct while preserving freedom of action. The limited invocation of the Convention—only Cosmos 954 has generated a formal claim—reflects both its success as a deterrent and the preference of states for diplomatic rather than legal settlement of disputes.

The evidentiary challenges examined in Part III reveal the operational limitations of the existing framework. Proving fault in orbital incidents requires access to data that is often classified or proprietary. Establishing causation in a congested orbital environment requires attribution capabilities that remain unevenly distributed. The evolving standard of care, shaped by soft-law instruments that are formally non-binding but practically influential, creates a dynamic but uncertain legal landscape.

The contemporary risks examined in Part IV—debris, mega-constellations, and cyber interference—represent the most serious challenges to the liability framework's continuing effectiveness. Each exposes gaps in the Convention's coverage: attribution gaps for debris, systemic risk gaps for mega-constellations, and definitional gaps for cyber harm. The emergence of active debris removal adds a further dimension, creating novel liability questions that the existing framework is poorly equipped to resolve.

Yet the framework's foundational principles—state accountability, prevention through authorization and supervision, compensation for damage, and the dual standard of absolute and fault-based liability—remain sound and continue to shape behavior in ways that are often invisible but enormously consequential. The licensing regimes, insurance requirements, and operational standards that have developed under the umbrella of Articles VI and VII of the Outer Space Treaty, together with the Liability Convention, constitute a functioning system of accountability that, for all its limitations, has prevented any space-related harm from escalating into an international crisis.

The path forward lies not in discarding this framework but in adapting it—extending its concepts to cover new forms of harm, strengthening its evidentiary infrastructure through improved SSA and data-sharing, and supplementing its state-level architecture with mechanisms that can accommodate the growing role of private actors. The space insurance market, national licensing regimes, and emerging soft-law instruments are already performing this adaptive function. Whether these incremental developments will prove sufficient in the face of exponentially growing space activity is the central question of contemporary space liability law.

In the next chapter, we turn from accountability to conflict, examining how international law seeks to regulate military uses of outer space and prevent the extension of armed conflict into a domain on which all of humanity depends.

***

End of Chapter 6

Chapter 7

MILITARY USES OF OUTER SPACE AND THE LAW OF ARMED CONFLICT

Outer space was never a purely civilian domain. From the first reconnaissance satellites to today's anti-satellite weapons and cyber operations, military activity has shaped the trajectory of space law. This chapter examines the legal frameworks that seek to prevent conflict in orbit while accommodating the strategic realities that make space indispensable to modern warfare.

Part 1

'Peaceful Purposes,' Militarization, and Early Legal Debates

From the earliest days of space exploration, the relationship between military activity and legal restraint has shaped the development of international space law. Outer space was never a purely civilian domain; its strategic value was evident from the moment satellites demonstrated their potential for reconnaissance, communication, and early warning. The challenge facing the international community was not whether the military would use space, but how such use could be regulated to prevent conflict and escalation.

The Meaning of 'Peaceful Purposes'

The concept of "peaceful purposes" occupies a central yet contested place in space law. Article IV of the Outer Space Treaty provides that the Moon and other celestial bodies shall be used "exclusively for peaceful purposes," but the Treaty's treatment of outer space more broadly is less restrictive. The Preamble refers to the "peaceful exploration and use of outer space"; Article I declares that space shall be "free for exploration and use by all States." The omission of the word "exclusively" from the general provisions on outer space—in contrast to its inclusion for celestial bodies—was deliberate, reflecting divergent views among negotiating states during the Cold War.

Two interpretations have competed since the Treaty's negotiation. The first, supported primarily by developing states and some Western scholars, equates "peaceful" with "non-military." Under this view, any military activity in outer space would be inconsistent with the Treaty's objectives, and only scientific and civilian activities would be permitted. This interpretation finds support in the Antarctic Treaty (1959), which uses the phrase "for peaceful purposes only" and has been understood to prohibit all military activity on the continent.

Figure 17: Emerging Legal Challenges in Military Activities in Outer Space

Source: Generated using OpenAI Sora.

The second and dominant interpretation, adopted by both superpowers during the Cold War and upheld by subsequent state practice, understands "peaceful" as "non-aggressive" rather than non-military. According to this view, military uses of space are permissible so long as they do not involve the threat or use of force in violation of the UN Charter. Military support functions—

reconnaissance, communications, navigation, early warning, meteorological observation, arms control verification—are lawful because they support national security without constituting acts of aggression. This interpretation aligns with the broader principle of international law that prohibits the use of force (Article 2(4) of the UN Charter) but does not prohibit military preparedness or support activities per se.

State practice has overwhelmingly favored the non-aggressive interpretation. From the earliest satellite programs, military involvement in space has been extensive and continuous, with virtually no protest from other states. The United States, the Soviet Union, and subsequently China, India, France, Japan, and many other states have operated military satellites openly. This consistent, unchallenged practice has effectively determined the legal meaning of "peaceful purposes" in the context of outer space, anchoring it in restraint against aggression rather than in demilitarization.

The non-aggressive interpretation also aligns with the UN Charter's framework on the use of force. Article 2(4) of the Charter prohibits the threat or use of force against the territorial integrity or political independence of any state, while Article 51 preserves the inherent right of self-defense. Article III of the Outer Space Treaty provides that activities in space shall be carried on "in accordance with international law, including the Charter of the United Nations." Read together, these provisions permit military activities in space that do not involve the use or threat of force—a reading that accommodates military support functions while constraining acts of aggression. The practical effect is a legal framework that permits the vast majority of current military space activities while prohibiting only their most destabilizing manifestations.

■ **Outer Space Treaty, Article IV**

"States Parties to the Treaty undertake not to place in orbit around the Earth any objects carrying nuclear weapons or any other kinds of weapons of mass destruction, install such weapons on celestial bodies, or station such weapons in outer space in any other manner."

"The Moon and other celestial bodies shall be used by all States Parties to the Treaty exclusively for peaceful purposes. The establishment of military bases, installations and fortifications, the testing of any type of weapons and the conduct of military manoeuvres on celestial bodies shall be forbidden."

Early Militarization of Space

The militarization of space occurred rapidly and almost inevitably. Within months of Sputnik's launch in 1957, both superpowers were developing reconnaissance satellites that would fundamentally transform intelligence gathering. The United States' CORONA program (operational 1960–1972) provided photographic coverage of denied areas of the Soviet Union that no human agent could match. The Soviet Zenit program served analogous purposes. These reconnaissance systems were among the most closely guarded secrets of the Cold War, yet their existence was widely known—and tacitly accepted—by both sides.

The early legal treatment of military satellites was shaped by the Partial Nuclear Test Ban Treaty of 1963, which prohibited nuclear explosions in outer space. This prohibition was prompted not by abstract principle but by the concrete consequences of the Starfish Prime nuclear test of July 1962, in which a 1.4-megaton warhead detonated at approximately 400 kilometers altitude. The test produced an electromagnetic pulse that disrupted radio communications across the Pacific, created an artificial radiation belt that persisted for years, and damaged or destroyed at least six satellites—including both American and Soviet assets. The indiscriminate, transboundary consequences of the test demonstrated that nuclear weapons in the space environment posed risks qualitatively different from those on Earth. The resulting prohibition, codified first in the PTBT and later reinforced by the Outer Space Treaty's Article IV, represents one of the clearest and most consequential achievements of space arms control.

The tacit acceptance of reconnaissance satellites is one of the most consequential early developments in space law. The Soviet Union, which had initially protested overhead satellite flights as violations of sovereignty—consistent with its earlier objections to U-2 overflights—quietly abandoned its objections as its own reconnaissance capabilities matured. Neither superpower challenged the legality of the other's reconnaissance satellites. This mutual restraint established a de facto norm of freedom of observation from orbit that has never been seriously contested, even though no treaty explicitly authorizes military reconnaissance from space. The norm's acceptance illustrates how state practice can generate customary law: consistent, unopposed behavior, accompanied by an implicit acceptance of its legality, crystallizes into a legal rule without formal treaty codification.

Communication satellites enabled secure, global military command and control. Navigation satellites—beginning with the U.S. Transit system in the 1960s and culminating in the Global Positioning System (GPS)—revolutionized military operations by providing precise positioning, navigation, and timing (PNT) services. Early warning satellites, such as the U.S. Defense Support Program (DSP), detected missile launches by their infrared signatures, providing minutes of advance warning that became an integral component of nuclear deterrence. Weather satellites provided battlefield intelligence. Signal intelligence satellites intercepted communications and electronic emissions.

These capabilities were widely viewed as stabilizing rather than destabilizing, particularly during the Cold War. By reducing the risk of surprise attack, verifying arms control compliance, and enhancing deterrence credibility, space-based systems contributed to strategic stability. As a result, their deployment was generally tolerated—even implicitly encouraged—within the international community. Legal debates focused less on whether such activities were lawful and more on how to prevent their escalation into the weaponization of space.

The role of reconnaissance satellites in arms control verification deserves particular emphasis. The SALT I agreements (1972), the ABM Treaty (1972), the INF Treaty (1987), and subsequent arms control instruments relied on "national technical means of verification"—a diplomatic euphemism for reconnaissance satellites—to monitor compliance. The ABM Treaty explicitly prohibited interference with national technical means, effectively creating a legal protection for reconnaissance satellites that reinforced their legitimacy. This self-reinforcing dynamic—military satellites enabling arms control, arms control legitimizing military satellites—illustrates the complex relationship between military space activity and international legal restraint.

The Strategic Defense Initiative (SDI), announced by President Reagan in 1983, represented the most ambitious proposal for the weaponization of space during the Cold War. SDI envisioned a multi-layered missile defense system incorporating space-based interceptors, directed-energy weapons, and kinetic kill vehicles designed to destroy Soviet ballistic missiles in their boost phase. The initiative provoked intense legal debate: critics argued that space-based weapons would violate the ABM Treaty's restrictions on space-based components, while supporters contended that defensive systems did not constitute "weapons" within the Treaty's meaning. SDI was never fully implemented, but it demonstrated that the legal constraints of Article IV—limited to WMD and celestial body prohibitions—provided no barrier to conventional weapons concepts in orbital space.

Militarization vs. Weaponization

A crucial distinction in space law discourse separates militarization from weaponization. Militarization refers to the use of space systems for military support functions: surveillance, communications, navigation, early warning, and meteorological observation. Weaponization refers to the placement or development of weapons designed to damage, degrade, or destroy targets in, from, or through space.

International space law permits militarization while restricting weaponization—though the restriction is partial, not comprehensive. Article IV of the Outer Space Treaty prohibits nuclear weapons and other weapons of mass destruction in orbit, but it does not prohibit conventional weapons in orbital space. On celestial bodies, the prohibition is broader: all military activities (bases, fortifications, weapons testing, maneuvers) are forbidden. This asymmetry creates a legal landscape in which military support from orbit is lawful, WMD in orbit is prohibited, conventional weapons in orbit are not explicitly prohibited, and all military activity on the Moon and other celestial bodies is prohibited.

■ **The Legal Spectrum of Military Activities in Space**

PERMITTED: Military reconnaissance, communications, navigation, early warning, meteorological satellites.

PROHIBITED: Nuclear weapons or other WMD in orbit or on celestial bodies.

PROHIBITED: Military bases, installations, fortifications, weapons testing, or maneuvers on celestial bodies.

NOT EXPLICITLY PROHIBITED: Conventional weapons in Earth orbit (gap in treaty coverage).

NOT EXPLICITLY PROHIBITED: Ground-based weapons targeting satellites (ASAT systems).

NOT EXPLICITLY ADDRESSED: Cyber operations against space systems.

The Outer Space Treaty restricts the most destabilizing capabilities but leaves significant gaps in the regulation of conventional military space activities.

This distinction—between what the law prohibits and what it merely does not authorize—is critical. The gaps in Article IV's coverage have become increasingly consequential as technology has evolved. Kinetic anti-satellite weapons, directed-energy systems, co-orbital interceptors, and electronic warfare capabilities all exploit the space between the Treaty's specific prohibitions and its general aspiration toward peaceful use.

> *"Space has been militarized since the first reconnaissance satellite was placed in orbit. The legal challenge has never been to demilitarize space, but to prevent its weaponization."*
>
> – On the distinction between militarization and weaponization

■ **Early Arms Control: The Pattern of Incrementalism**

Early attempts to ban all military activity in space failed because both superpowers depended on military satellites for strategic stability. The resulting legal framework reflects capability-specific constraints—prohibiting the most destabilizing weapons while permitting stabilizing support functions. This incremental approach, driven by strategic calculation rather than idealism, established the pattern that continues to characterize arms control in space.

***

Part II

Weapons in Space and Arms Control Efforts

As space-based capabilities became integral to national security, the question of weapons in outer space moved from theoretical concern to practical policy challenge. International law has long sought to prevent the extension of armed conflict into new domains, yet space presents unique verification, definitional, and strategic difficulties. Arms control efforts in this domain reveal a persistent tension between normative ambition and military necessity—a tension that remains unresolved.

Treaty Constraints and Their Gaps

The principal binding constraints on weapons in space are found in Article IV of the Outer Space Treaty. As discussed in Part I, these constraints prohibit WMD in orbit and demilitarize celestial bodies, but they leave conventional weapons in orbital space unregulated. The Partial Test Ban Treaty (1963) prohibits nuclear explosions in outer space, reinforcing the OST's WMD ban. The ABM Treaty (1972)—abrogated by the United States in 2002—limited space-based missile defense components. No subsequent treaty has addressed conventional weapons in space.

Several additional treaty gaps deserve attention. The Outer Space Treaty does not prohibit ground-based anti-satellite weapons, which can target satellites from terrestrial launch sites without placing any weapon in orbit. It does not address electronic warfare (jamming, spoofing, dazzling) directed against satellites. It does not regulate cyber operations against space systems. And it does not prohibit dual-use technologies—such as on-orbit servicing platforms or debris removal systems—that could be repurposed for hostile applications. These gaps reflect the limits of a treaty negotiated in the 1960s for a technological landscape that has since transformed beyond recognition.

The abrogation of the Anti-Ballistic Missile Treaty by the United States in 2002 removed one of the few binding constraints that indirectly limited space weaponization. The ABM Treaty, signed in 1972, prohibited the development, testing, and deployment of space-based missile defense systems and their components. While its primary purpose was strategic stability between the United States and the Soviet Union, the Treaty had the secondary effect of constraining the development of space-based interceptors and directed-energy weapons. Its abrogation opened the door to programs such as the U.S. Missile Defense Agency's research into space-based interceptors and removed a restraint that, however imperfect, had limited certain categories of space weaponization for three decades.

The Comprehensive Nuclear-Test-Ban Treaty (CTBT), though not yet in force, would reinforce the PTBT's prohibition on nuclear explosions in outer space if it were to enter into force. The CTBT's

International Monitoring System includes provisions relevant to space—including detection of nuclear explosions in any environment—but the Treaty's non-entry into force limits its practical contribution to space security governance.

The Dual-Use Problem

The dual-use character of space technology represents perhaps the most fundamental obstacle to arms control in space. Many capabilities that serve legitimate civilian or commercial purposes—rendezvous and proximity operations, robotic manipulation, active debris removal, on-orbit inspection, space situational awareness—are technically indistinguishable from capabilities that could be used to interfere with, disable, or destroy another state's satellites. A spacecraft designed to service a malfunctioning satellite could, with trivial modification of intent, disable an adversary's asset.

This dual-use problem defeats object-based arms control approaches. Unlike nuclear warheads, which are physically distinctive and whose production can be monitored through observable indicators (centrifuge facilities, reactor operations, test explosions), space weapons cannot be identified by their physical characteristics alone. A "weapon" in space is defined not by its design but by its intended use—and intent is precisely what cannot be verified by remote observation. Any arms control regime that attempts to prohibit "space weapons" must therefore confront the question of what constitutes a weapon in the absence of objective physical criteria.

The verification challenge is compounded by the proliferation of rendezvous and proximity operations (RPO) in orbit. Both the United States and Russia have conducted RPO missions in which satellites have approached other space objects at close range—sometimes within a few hundred meters. Russia's Luch/Olymp satellite, for example, has been observed maneuvering between Western communications satellites in geostationary orbit, conducting what appeared to be signal intelligence collection. The United States' Geosynchronous Space Situational Awareness Program (GSSAP) satellites conduct similar proximity operations for space domain awareness. These activities are conducted without formal notification and without clear legal constraints, occupying a gray zone between legitimate space operations and potentially hostile behavior.

The absence of agreed norms of behavior for proximity operations creates significant escalation risk. When a satellite approaches another state's satellite at close range, the target state cannot determine whether the approach is for intelligence gathering, testing of ASAT capabilities, or preparation for a future attack. This ambiguity may trigger defensive responses—maneuvering the target satellite away, repositioning other assets, or escalating political or military tensions. Developing norms or rules of the road for proximity operations—minimum approach distances, notification requirements, exclusion zones around sensitive assets—has been identified by the OEWG on space threats as a priority, but no consensus has emerged on specific measures.

The PPWT and PAROS Debates

Two major multilateral initiatives have sought to address the weaponization of space. The first is the draft Treaty on the Prevention of the Placement of Weapons in Outer Space (PPWT), introduced jointly by Russia and China at the Conference on Disarmament in 2008 and revised in 2014. The PPWT would prohibit the placement of weapons in outer space and the threat or use of force against space objects. The second is the broader concept of Prevention of an Arms Race in Outer Space (PAROS), which has been on the Conference on Disarmament's agenda since 1985 but has never produced a negotiating mandate.

The PPWT has been criticized on several grounds. The United States and its allies have objected that the draft does not address ground-based ASAT weapons—a significant gap given that Russia, China, and India have all demonstrated kinetic ASAT capabilities launched from the ground. Critics also argue that the PPWT's definitional framework is inadequate, failing to resolve the dual-use problem, and that its verification provisions are insufficient to detect non-compliance. Supporters, primarily Russia and China along with many developing states, argue that the PPWT represents a pragmatic starting point and that perfect should not be the enemy of good.

The definitional problems of the PPWT illustrate the broader challenge. The draft defines a "weapon in outer space" as any device placed in outer space that is designed to eliminate, damage, or disrupt normal functioning of objects in outer space, on the Earth's surface, or in its atmosphere. Critics note that this definition would not cover ground-based ASAT weapons (which are not "placed in outer space"), co-orbital systems that approach targets without being specifically "designed" as weapons, or cyber operations against satellite ground stations. The definition also raises the question of whether a satellite designed for debris removal—but capable of deorbiting an adversary's satellite—would qualify as a "weapon." These definitional difficulties are not merely technical; they reflect the fundamental challenge of regulating dual-use technology through object-based prohibitions.

The impasse at the Conference on Disarmament reflects deeper structural problems. The CD operates by consensus, and any single member can block the adoption of a negotiating mandate. The United States has consistently opposed negotiations on a space weapons ban, arguing that existing international law is adequate and that verification challenges make a new treaty impractical. Russia and China have pressed for negotiations while simultaneously developing their own counter-space capabilities—Russia through its Nudol direct-ascent system and co-orbital programs, China through both kinetic and electronic counter-space capabilities. This combination of diplomatic advocacy for arms control and parallel weapons development has generated mutual distrust that makes genuine negotiation difficult.

The CD's inability to produce results has prompted calls for alternative negotiating venues. The OEWG on space threats, discussed below, represents one such alternative—operating under the General Assembly rather than the CD and using a broader, more inclusive format. Whether norm-setting through the General Assembly process can eventually generate the political momentum for binding instruments remains uncertain, but the shift away from the CD reflects a growing recognition that the traditional arms control architecture is inadequate for the space domain.

Confidence-Building Measures and Transparency

In the absence of binding arms control, states have increasingly focused on transparency and confidence-building measures (TCBMs) as intermediate steps. In 2013, the UN General Assembly endorsed the report of the Group of Governmental Experts (GGE) on Transparency and Confidence-Building Measures in Outer Space Activities, which recommended voluntary measures including notification of launches, exchange of orbital data, risk reduction consultations, and visits to space facilities.

TCBMs do not prohibit any capability or constrain any activity. They aim instead to reduce the risk of misperception and miscalculation by increasing the predictability and transparency of space operations. In a domain where the difference between a benign proximity operation and a hostile approach may be indistinguishable from a distance, improved communication can reduce the likelihood that a routine activity is mistaken for an attack—a miscalculation that could trigger escalation.

The European Union attempted a more structured approach with its proposed International Code of Conduct for Outer Space Activities, developed between 2008 and 2015. The Code sought to establish voluntary commitments regarding debris mitigation, notification of maneuvers, and the avoidance of harmful interference. However, the initiative failed to achieve broad multilateral support, with many developing states objecting to what they perceived as a Western-led process that lacked inclusive negotiation. The EU Code's failure illustrates the importance of procedural legitimacy in multilateral norm development: even substantively reasonable proposals may be rejected if they are perceived as imposing norms rather than negotiating them.

More recently, the UN General Assembly established an Open-Ended Working Group (OEWG) on Reducing Space Threats Through Norms, Rules, and Principles of Responsible Behaviour, which met from 2022 to 2023. The OEWG adopted a report identifying responsible and irresponsible behaviors in space, including the deliberate creation of long-lived debris, testing of destructive ASAT weapons, and dangerous proximity operations. While the report did not produce binding norms, it represented the first broadly inclusive multilateral process to address space security issues outside the Conference on Disarmament—a significant procedural breakthrough that may lay the groundwork for future normative development.

The practical implementation of TCBMs has been uneven. While some states have embraced greater transparency—the United States publishes detailed orbital data through its space catalog and provides conjunction warnings globally through the 18th Space Defense Squadron—others maintain strict secrecy about their military space programs. Russia's military satellite operations are largely opaque. China provides limited orbital data and does not participate in multilateral data-sharing arrangements. The asymmetry of transparency creates its own risks: a transparent actor may inadvertently reveal vulnerabilities, while an opaque actor preserves strategic ambiguity. Achieving balanced transparency—sufficient to reduce miscalculation without compromising legitimate security interests—remains a significant challenge.

Space as a Warfighting Domain

The legal landscape has been further complicated by the explicit recognition of space as a warfighting domain by major military powers. The United States established the United States Space Force as an independent military branch in December 2019—the first new branch of the U.S. armed forces since the Air Force was created in 1947. France restructured its Air Force as the Air and Space Force (Armée de l'Air et de l'Espace) in 2020 and established a Space Command. The United Kingdom established a Space Command in 2021. China's Strategic Support Force, established in 2015, integrates space, cyber, and electronic warfare capabilities. Russia's Aerospace Forces (Vozdushno-kosmicheskiye sily) combine air and space operations under a unified command.

These institutional developments signal that major powers regard space not merely as a supporting domain for terrestrial military operations, but as a domain in which military advantage must be contested and defended. The establishment of dedicated space military commands has implications for deterrence, escalation management, and the development of military doctrine. From a legal perspective, the creation of space-focused military organizations does not in itself violate international law—military space activity is permitted under the non-aggressive interpretation of "peaceful purposes." However, it reflects a strategic posture that increases the salience of the legal gaps identified in this chapter and intensifies the urgency of developing norms to manage military competition in space.

Initiative	Forum	Status	Key Limitation
PPWT (2008/2014)	Conference on Disarmament	No negotiating mandate	Does not address ground-based ASAT
PAROS	Conference on Disarmament	Agenda item since 1985; no progress	No consensus on scope or mandate
GGE on TCBMs (2013)	UN General Assembly	Report endorsed; voluntary measures	Non-binding; uneven implementation
EU Code of Conduct (2008–2015)	European Union initiative	Failed to achieve multilateral support	Perceived as Western-led; non-inclusive process
UNGA Res. on No First Placement	UN General Assembly	Annual resolution (Russia-led)	Non-binding; does not address ASAT
OEWG on Space Threats (2022–2023)	UN General Assembly	Report adopted 2023	Non-binding; disagreement on binding norms

> *"Arms control in space has produced more proposals than agreements. The combination of dual-use technology, verification difficulties, and strategic distrust has proven extraordinarily resistant to diplomatic resolution."*
>
> – On the arms control impasse in space

***

Part III

Anti-Satellite Activities and State Practice

Among the various military capabilities associated with outer space, anti-satellite (ASAT) activities present the most direct and visible challenge to the legal framework governing peaceful use. Unlike abstract debates over weaponization, ASAT tests and operations have produced tangible, observable consequences—most notably the creation of long-lived space debris. State practice in this area provides critical insight into how international law is interpreted, contested, and potentially reshaped under strategic pressure.

The Spectrum of ASAT Capabilities

ASAT capabilities span a wide spectrum of technologies, from kinetic destruction to reversible electronic interference. Direct-ascent kinetic interceptors, launched from the ground on ballistic trajectories, physically collide with satellites at closing velocities that can exceed ten kilometers per second, destroying the target and generating thousands of debris fragments. Co-orbital ASAT systems are placed in orbit and maneuvered to approach a target satellite, potentially using kinetic impact, directed energy, or robotic manipulation to disable or destroy it. Directed-energy weapons—ground-based or space-based lasers—can damage satellite sensors or structural components at the speed of light. Electronic warfare capabilities—jamming, spoofing, dazzling—can degrade or disrupt satellite operations without physical contact. Cyber operations can compromise satellite command-and-control systems, corrupt data, or seize operational control.

Each category presents different legal challenges. Kinetic ASAT tests produce the most visible and legally significant consequences through debris creation. Non-kinetic methods—electronic warfare, cyber operations, directed energy below the damage threshold—may leave no physical trace, creating formidable attribution and evidence challenges. The legal framework, developed primarily with physical destruction in mind, is poorly adapted to reversible interference that degrades satellite performance without destroying hardware.

Electronic warfare against satellites is already a routine feature of modern military operations, though rarely acknowledged publicly. GPS jamming and spoofing have been documented in conflict zones including Syria, Ukraine, and the Baltic region. Russia has deployed mobile GPS jamming systems that create denial-of-service zones extending hundreds of kilometers. The Viasat/KA-SAT cyberattack of February 2022, discussed in Chapter 6, demonstrated the vulnerability of satellite ground infrastructure to cyber operations. These activities occupy an ambiguous legal space: they interfere with space systems without physically destroying them, they may affect civilian and military users indiscriminately, and they are extraordinarily difficult to attribute with the certainty required for legal accountability.

A History of ASAT Testing

The history of ASAT testing spans six decades and four states. The United States conducted the first ASAT tests in the early 1960s, using modified nuclear-armed missiles (Programs 505 and 437) to demonstrate the ability to destroy satellites. The high-altitude nuclear tests of 1962—including the Starfish Prime test, which detonated a 1.4-megaton warhead at 400 kilometers altitude—destroyed or damaged multiple satellites through electromagnetic pulse effects and enhanced radiation belts. These tests contributed directly to the Partial Test Ban Treaty's prohibition on nuclear explosions in outer space.

The Soviet Union developed and tested co-orbital ASAT systems from the 1960s through the 1980s, placing interceptor satellites in orbits that could approach and destroy targets through fragmentation warheads. The United States resumed kinetic ASAT testing in 1985 with the ASM-135 missile, which destroyed a defunct U.S. satellite (Solwind P78-1) at 555 kilometers altitude. A bilateral moratorium on ASAT testing was subsequently discussed but never formalized.

> **■ Major ASAT Tests and Their Consequences**
>
> 1962: U.S. Starfish Prime nuclear test (400 km altitude)—destroyed/damaged multiple satellites; led to Partial Test Ban Treaty.
>
> 1968–1982: Soviet co-orbital ASAT program—multiple tests; fragmentation warhead approach.
>
> 1985: U.S. ASM-135 destroys Solwind P78-1 (555 km)—relatively low debris impact due to altitude.
>
> 2007: China destroys Fengyun-1C weather satellite (865 km)—3,500+ trackable fragments; most debris-generating event in history.
>
> 2008: U.S. Operation Burnt Frost destroys USA-193 (247 km)—low orbit ensured rapid debris decay.
>
> 2019: India Mission Shakti destroys Microsat-R (283 km)—400+ fragments; most decayed rapidly.
>
> 2021: Russia destroys Cosmos 1408 (480 km)—1,500+ trackable fragments; forced ISS crew to shelter.

The 2007 Chinese Test: A Turning Point

The most consequential ASAT test in history occurred on 11 January 2007, when China destroyed its own defunct Fengyun-1C weather satellite at an altitude of approximately 865 kilometers using a direct-ascent kinetic interceptor. The test generated over 3,500 trackable debris fragments—the single largest debris-creating event in the history of spaceflight—along with an estimated 150,000 fragments too small to track but large enough to damage or destroy operational satellites.

The test's consequences were extraordinary in both physical and normative terms. Physically, the debris cloud contaminated orbits used by hundreds of active satellites, including remote sensing, weather observation, and communications systems operated by dozens of states. Because the test occurred at a relatively high altitude, much of the debris will remain in orbit for decades or centuries, posing a long-term collision risk. As of 2025, over 3,000 of the original tracked fragments remain in orbit—a persistent hazard that has already necessitated hundreds of collision avoidance maneuvers by operational satellites.

Normatively, the test provoked widespread international condemnation. The United States, Japan, Australia, Canada, the United Kingdom, and many other states issued formal protests. The test was cited as evidence of the inadequacy of existing arms control frameworks and contributed to renewed calls for debris mitigation, transparency measures, and ASAT restraint. China's response—initially muted, then characterized as a routine test not directed against any state—satisfied few observers. The episode demonstrated that ASAT testing, even against a state's own satellite, imposes costs on the entire international community through debris creation.

Operation Burnt Frost and India's Mission Shakti

The United States responded to the Chinese test with Operation Burnt Frost in February 2008, in which a modified SM-3 missile destroyed the malfunctioning U.S. reconnaissance satellite USA-193 at approximately 247 kilometers altitude. The U.S. government characterized the operation as a safety measure, arguing that the satellite's hydrazine fuel tank posed a hazard to populations on the ground if it survived re-entry intact. Critics viewed the operation as a thinly disguised ASAT demonstration designed to signal U.S. counter-space capability. The low altitude of the intercept ensured that virtually all debris re-entered the atmosphere within weeks—a contrast with the long-lived debris produced by the Chinese test—but the operation nonetheless illustrated the tension between stated rationale and perceived intent that characterizes much of military space activity.

Figure 18: Launch of a Modern Space Launch Vehicle

Source: Public Domain.

India conducted its own kinetic ASAT test, Mission Shakti, on 27 March 2019, destroying the Microsat-R target satellite at approximately 283 kilometers altitude. The test generated some 400 trackable fragments, most of which decayed within months due to the low altitude. India characterized the test as a demonstration of technological capability necessary for national security, while emphasizing the low-altitude profile as a responsible approach that minimized long-term debris. The test provoked criticism from NASA and several states but less condemnation than the Chinese or Russian tests, in part because of the lower debris consequence and India's diplomatic framing.

The progression from the Chinese test (high altitude, massive long-lived debris) through the U.S. test (low altitude, minimal debris, safety rationale) to the Indian test (low altitude, moderate debris, capability demonstration) to the Russian test (medium altitude, significant long-lived debris) illustrates how states have attempted to balance ASAT capability demonstration with debris management—and how the normative environment has shifted to make debris creation increasingly unacceptable regardless of the testing state's intent.

Legal Analysis: Are ASAT Tests Prohibited?

Whether ASAT tests violate existing international law remains formally contested, though the normative balance has shifted significantly. Several legal arguments bear on the question. First, Article IX of the Outer Space Treaty requires states to conduct space activities with "due regard to the corresponding interests of all other States Parties." Deliberately creating thousands of debris fragments that endanger other states' satellites arguably violates this obligation of due regard, particularly when the debris persists for decades and no operational necessity compels the test.

Second, the growing body of soft law—including the COPUOS Space Debris Mitigation Guidelines, the Long-term Sustainability Guidelines, and the 2022 General Assembly resolution on destructive ASAT testing—creates an increasingly dense normative environment that conditions the legal assessment of ASAT activities. While individually non-binding, these instruments collectively establish expectations of responsible behavior that make debris-generating ASAT tests increasingly difficult to justify.

Third, the unilateral moratoria declared by the United States and over thirty other states, combined with the General Assembly resolution, may contribute to the emergence of a customary norm prohibiting destructive direct-ascent ASAT testing. Customary international law requires both consistent state practice and a sense of legal obligation (opinio juris). The moratoria provide evidence of practice; the General Assembly resolution—and the legal arguments advanced in its support—provide evidence of opinio juris. Whether a customary norm has crystallized remains debatable, but the trajectory is clearly toward prohibition.

The persistent objector doctrine complicates this analysis. Russia and China voted against the General Assembly resolution and have not joined the moratorium. Under customary international law, a state that consistently objects to an emerging norm during its formation may claim exemption from the norm once it crystallizes. If Russia and China maintain their opposition throughout the norm's development, they could argue that they are not bound by a customary prohibition on destructive ASAT testing—a result that would undermine the norm's effectiveness precisely with respect to the states whose behavior it most needs to constrain.

The 2021 Russian Test and the ASAT Moratorium Movement

On 15 November 2021, Russia destroyed the defunct Cosmos 1408 satellite at approximately 480 kilometers altitude using a Nudol direct-ascent missile. The test generated over 1,500 trackable debris fragments and forced the crew of the International Space Station—which orbits at approximately 420 kilometers—to take shelter in their return vehicles as debris fragments passed nearby. The juxtaposition was striking: a Russian missile test endangered Russian cosmonauts aboard a jointly operated space station.

International condemnation was swift and strong. The United States described the test as "reckless and irresponsible." The United Kingdom, France, Germany, Japan, and many other states issued similar statements. The test catalyzed a political movement toward a moratorium on destructive ASAT testing. In April 2022, Vice President Kamala Harris announced that the United States would commit to not conducting destructive direct-ascent ASAT missile tests and called on other states to follow suit. Canada, New Zealand, Japan, Germany, France, the United Kingdom, Switzerland, South Korea, and over thirty other states subsequently endorsed the moratorium.

In December 2022, the UN General Assembly adopted Resolution 77/41, calling on all states to commit to not conducting destructive direct-ascent ASAT missile tests. The resolution passed with 155 votes in favor, 9 against (including Russia and China), and 9 abstentions. While non-binding, the resolution represents the strongest multilateral expression of normative opposition to destructive ASAT testing and may contribute to the emergence of a customary prohibition over time.

The moratorium movement represents a significant shift in the approach to space security governance. Rather than attempting to negotiate comprehensive arms control agreements through the Conference on Disarmament—a process that has produced no results in four decades—the moratorium approach targets a specific, well-defined behavior (destructive direct-ascent ASAT testing) and builds normative pressure through unilateral commitments and multilateral endorsement. This incremental, behavior-based approach has proven more politically viable than comprehensive treaty proposals, precisely because it does not require states to accept constraints on their broader military space capabilities.

The moratorium's limitations should also be acknowledged. It addresses only destructive direct-ascent testing—one specific ASAT methodology—and does not constrain co-orbital ASAT capabilities, directed-energy weapons, electronic warfare, or cyber operations. A state that commits to the moratorium retains the full range of non-kinetic counter-space capabilities, which are increasingly the preferred methods for space warfare precisely because they avoid the politically costly debris consequences of kinetic testing. The moratorium may therefore redirect rather than eliminate the development of counter-space capabilities—a shift that is environmentally positive but strategically ambiguous.

> ■ **From Silence to Condemnation: The Normative Arc of ASAT Practice**
>
> Early ASAT tests were conducted without legal challenge; states treated them as legitimate exercises of military capability. By 2022, destructive ASAT testing had become the subject of near-universal condemnation, a unilateral moratorium endorsed by over thirty states, and a General Assembly resolution. This normative trajectory—from acceptance to condemnation over six decades—illustrates how state practice, accumulated consequences, and changing expectations can reshape legal norms even in the absence of binding treaty law.

***

Part IV

International Humanitarian Law in Outer Space

As military reliance on space systems deepens, a fundamental legal question acquires increasing urgency: does international humanitarian law (IHL)—the body of law governing the conduct of hostilities during armed conflict—apply to military operations in outer space, and if so, how? While no armed conflict has yet been conducted primarily in space, the deep integration of space assets into terrestrial warfare makes this question practically immediate rather than merely theoretical.

The Applicability of IHL to Space

The prevailing view among legal scholars, military lawyers, and states is that IHL applies to space activities during armed conflict. IHL is not geographically limited; its principles apply wherever hostilities occur. The Geneva Conventions and their Additional Protocols do not exclude outer space from their scope, and the fundamental principles of IHL—distinction, proportionality, military necessity, humanity—are of general application. The Outer Space Treaty itself provides (Article III) that states shall carry on activities in outer space "in accordance with international law, including the Charter of the United Nations." This reference to international law is generally understood to encompass IHL.

However, the application of IHL to space presents novel challenges that existing rules were not designed to address. IHL was developed for terrestrial and, later, aerial and naval warfare. Its concepts of combatants and civilians, military objectives and civilian objects, proportionality and precaution, were articulated with physical battlefields in mind. Translating these concepts to the orbital environment requires careful adaptation—not least because the orbital environment lacks the geographic boundaries that typically define theaters of war, and because damage caused in orbit inevitably affects the global commons.

A threshold question is whether interference with a satellite constitutes an "attack" within the meaning of IHL. Additional Protocol I defines attacks as "acts of violence against the adversary, whether in offence or in defence." Kinetic destruction of a satellite clearly qualifies. But what about electronic jamming that temporarily disrupts a satellite's communications without causing physical damage? Or a cyber operation that corrupts a satellite's software, altering its orbital trajectory? The characterization of these activities as "attacks" determines whether the full panoply of IHL protections—distinction, proportionality, precaution—applies to them. If non-kinetic interference does not qualify as an attack, IHL's protective framework may not be triggered, even when the humanitarian consequences of interference are severe.

Escalation Management and Strategic Stability

The application of IHL to space operations cannot be separated from broader questions of escalation management and strategic stability. Space systems are deeply integrated into nuclear command, control, and communications (NC3) architecture. Early warning satellites detect missile launches. Communications satellites relay launch orders. Navigation satellites guide delivery systems. An attack on these systems—even if intended as a limited, proportionate military action—could be interpreted by the adversary as preparation for a nuclear first strike, triggering catastrophic escalation.

This escalation risk imposes a unique constraint on military space operations that IHL doctrine has not fully addressed. The principle of proportionality requires assessment of military advantage against incidental harm, but it does not account for the risk that a proportionate attack on a space object could trigger an escalatory spiral leading to nuclear use. Some scholars have argued that the escalation risk associated with attacks on strategic space assets is so severe that it effectively renders such attacks disproportionate under any realistic assessment. Others contend that IHL's existing framework is flexible enough to accommodate escalation risk within proportionality analysis. The debate remains unresolved, but its practical importance is enormous.

Distinction: Military Objectives vs. Civilian Objects

The principle of distinction—the obligation to distinguish between military objectives and civilian objects, and to direct attacks only against the former—is the cornerstone of IHL. In the space domain, this principle confronts the pervasive dual-use character of satellite systems. Many satellites serve both civilian and military functions simultaneously. GPS provides navigation for civilian aviation, maritime shipping, financial transactions, and emergency services, while simultaneously providing precision targeting for military operations. Communications satellites carry civilian and military traffic on the same platforms. Earth observation satellites serve agricultural monitoring, disaster response, and military intelligence.

When a satellite serves both civilian and military purposes, how is it classified under IHL? Additional Protocol I defines a military objective as an object which "by its nature, location, purpose or use makes an effective contribution to military action and whose total or partial destruction, capture or neutralization, in the circumstances ruling at the time, offers a definite military advantage." A dual-use satellite that provides military communications during armed conflict may qualify as a military objective, but attacking it would also destroy its civilian functions—potentially affecting civilian populations far from the battlefield.

The scale of civilian dependence on dual-use satellite systems compounds the problem. GPS, for example, serves an estimated four billion civilian users worldwide. Its military applications—precision targeting, battlefield navigation, logistics coordination—represent a small fraction of its total use. Destroying a GPS satellite to deny military precision navigation to an adversary would simultaneously degrade navigation services for civilian aviation, maritime shipping, emergency services, agriculture, financial transactions, and telecommunications across large portions of the globe. The ratio of civilian harm to military advantage in such a scenario would be extraordinarily difficult to justify under proportionality analysis.

The dual-use problem in space is thus more acute than in terrestrial warfare, where military and civilian infrastructure tend to be physically separable. In orbit, a single satellite may serve millions of civilian users and a military command simultaneously. The principle of distinction does not prohibit attacks on dual-use objects, but it requires that the collateral damage to civilian functions be considered in the proportionality assessment.

Proportionality and Cascading Effects

The principle of proportionality prohibits attacks that may be expected to cause incidental loss of civilian life, injury to civilians, or damage to civilian objects that would be excessive in relation to the concrete and direct military advantage anticipated. In the space domain, proportionality analysis must account for cascading effects that have no terrestrial parallel.

Destroying a military communications satellite may generate debris that damages unrelated civilian satellites, disrupting services relied upon by populations in countries not party to the conflict. A kinetic attack on a satellite at 800 kilometers altitude could contaminate an entire orbital shell for decades, affecting hundreds of satellites operated by dozens of states. The incidental harm caused by such an attack—measured not only in immediate damage but in long-term orbital contamination—may vastly exceed the military advantage gained, raising serious proportionality concerns.

The temporal dimension of proportionality in space is particularly challenging. In terrestrial warfare, collateral damage is typically immediate and geographically bounded. In space, the debris generated by a single attack can persist for decades, causing harm long after the conflict that produced it has ended. Whether proportionality analysis should account for such long-term, distributed consequences is a question that existing IHL doctrine does not clearly answer. The precedent of environmental damage in armed conflict—where long-term consequences are increasingly considered relevant to proportionality assessment—suggests that a forward-looking approach is legally warranted, but the precise methodology for incorporating decades-long orbital contamination into a proportionality calculus remains undeveloped.

A concrete scenario illustrates the difficulty. Consider a belligerent state that decides to destroy an adversary's military communications satellite at 850 kilometers altitude. The attack would provide a definite military advantage by disrupting enemy command and control. However, the kinetic intercept would generate an estimated 2,000 debris fragments, some of which would persist in orbit for over a century. These fragments would threaten weather satellites serving civilian populations, scientific missions operated by neutral states, and the International Space Station. The military advantage is concrete and immediate; the collateral damage is diffuse, probabilistic, and extends over decades. How should a commander weigh these factors? IHL provides the conceptual framework—proportionality analysis—but not the operational methodology for making such assessments in the space domain.

■ **Applying IHL Principles to Space Operations**

DISTINCTION: Complicated by pervasive dual-use character of satellites serving both civilian and military functions simultaneously.

PROPORTIONALITY: Must account for cascading debris effects, long-term orbital contamination, and harm to non-party states.

MILITARY NECESSITY: Attacks on space objects must offer a definite military advantage; speculative or marginal advantages may be insufficient.

PRECAUTION: Obligation to choose means and methods that minimize collateral damage; non-kinetic methods (jamming, cyber) may be required if feasible.

ENVIRONMENT: IHL prohibits widespread, long-term, and severe damage to the natural environment; debris cascades may trigger this prohibition.

NEUTRALITY: Global satellite infrastructure means attacks inevitably affect neutral states; heightened due diligence obligations.

Environmental Protection and the Outer Space Environment

IHL includes obligations to protect the natural environment during armed conflict. Additional Protocol I (Article 35(3)) prohibits methods or means of warfare that are "intended, or may be expected, to cause widespread, long-term and severe damage to the natural environment." The ENMOD Convention (1976) prohibits the military use of environmental modification techniques. Whether these provisions apply to the orbital environment—and whether debris constitutes "environmental damage" within their meaning—is debated.

If the orbital environment is understood as part of the natural environment protected by IHL, then kinetic attacks on satellites that generate long-lived debris fields could violate the prohibition on widespread, long-term, and severe environmental damage. The 2007 Chinese ASAT test generated debris expected to persist for centuries, affecting orbital regions used by the entire international community. A wartime attack producing similar consequences would raise serious questions under this standard. The growing recognition of orbital sustainability as an environmental concern—reflected in the COPUOS Long-term Sustainability Guidelines, the debris mitigation frameworks, and the emerging norm against destructive ASAT testing—strengthens the argument that IHL's environmental protections extend to outer space.

The cumulative environmental dimension adds further complexity. A single kinetic attack on one satellite may produce manageable debris. But a sustained campaign of kinetic attacks on multiple satellites could generate debris sufficient to trigger a Kessler cascade—a self-sustaining chain reaction of collisions that renders entire orbital bands unusable for generations. Such a consequence would constitute environmental damage of extraordinary scale and duration, affecting not only the belligerents but all of humanity's future access to orbital space. Whether IHL's environmental protection provisions are sufficient to prohibit actions that risk triggering a Kessler cascade is among the most consequential legal questions in contemporary space security.

Neutrality and Third-State Interests

Space operations during armed conflict inevitably affect neutral states. The global character of space infrastructure—satellites orbiting the Earth provide services to all states beneath their ground track—means that attacks on space objects cannot be geographically contained. Debris generated by an attack on a satellite over one region will eventually distribute across the entire orbital shell, threatening satellites operated by neutral states. Service disruptions caused by attacks on communications or navigation satellites may affect civilian populations in countries that have no involvement in the conflict.

The traditional law of neutrality, which presumes relatively clear geographic separation between belligerents and non-belligerents, is poorly adapted to this reality. Belligerents have an obligation to respect the rights of neutral states, including the inviolability of their territory and property. In space, this obligation requires heightened due diligence and transparency—ensuring that military operations do not disproportionately harm neutral interests. Failure to respect these obligations risks drawing neutral states into the conflict or undermining the cooperative foundations of the space governance regime.

A particularly complex problem arises when belligerents rely on satellite services provided by neutral states or commercial operators registered in neutral states. If a neutral state's communications satellite carries military traffic for a belligerent—either knowingly, through commercial contracts, or unknowingly, because encrypted military data is routed through civilian channels—the satellite's status becomes ambiguous. Is it a protected civilian object? Does the carriage of military traffic transform it into a military objective? The answer depends on whether the satellite's military use is sufficiently significant to constitute an "effective contribution to military action" under IHL. In practice, the interconnected nature of modern communications infrastructure means that virtually any commercial satellite system may carry some military-related traffic, making clean distinctions between military and civilian infrastructure impossible.

These challenges suggest that armed conflict in or through outer space would create unprecedented complications for the law of neutrality. The global character of space infrastructure makes it functionally impossible to conduct hostilities in orbit without affecting neutral states. This reality strengthens the argument for preventive norms—rules that constrain military behavior before conflict erupts—rather than relying solely on IHL to regulate conduct during hostilities. The ASAT moratorium, transparency measures, and norms of responsible behavior discussed in Parts II and III represent steps in this direction.

The Woomera and McGill Manuals

Recognizing the need for interpretive guidance, two major academic projects have sought to clarify how international law applies to military activities in outer space. The McGill Manual on International Law Applicable to Military Uses of Outer Space (MILAMOS), initiated by McGill University's Institute of Air and Space Law, focuses on the peacetime legal framework governing military space activities. It addresses questions of jurisdiction, sovereignty, responsibility, and the permissible scope of military operations in space during periods short of armed conflict. The Woomera Manual on the International Law of Military Space Operations, led by the University of Adelaide and the University of Exeter, addresses the application of international law—including IHL—to military operations in space during armed conflict.

These manuals, while not legally binding, represent the most comprehensive scholarly efforts to apply existing international law to space military operations. They identify areas of consensus among international law scholars, highlight contested interpretations where state practice and legal doctrine diverge, and propose frameworks for resolving legal ambiguities. Their methodology follows the precedent of the San Remo Manual on International Law Applicable to Armed Conflicts at Sea (1994) and the Tallinn Manual on the International Law Applicable to Cyber Operations (2013)—both of which have significantly influenced state practice and military doctrine in their respective domains.

Precautionary Obligations and Non-Kinetic Alternatives

The IHL obligation to take precautions in attack (Additional Protocol I, Article 57) requires parties to an armed conflict to take all feasible precautions to minimize incidental loss of civilian life and damage to civilian objects. In the space domain, this obligation takes on particular significance because of the availability of non-kinetic alternatives to physical destruction.

If a satellite providing military communications can be neutralized through electronic jamming—a reversible measure that does not generate debris and does not destroy the satellite's civilian functions permanently—then the precautionary obligation may require the use of jamming rather than kinetic destruction. Similarly, if a satellite can be disabled through cyber operations rather than physical attack, the principle of precaution may favor the less destructive approach. This reasoning would effectively create a hierarchy of methods: non-kinetic and reversible methods should be preferred over kinetic and irreversible methods when both are feasible and effective.

The practical implications of this analysis are significant. It suggests that the development and deployment of non-kinetic counter-space capabilities—electronic warfare, cyber operations, directed energy below the damage threshold—may not only be strategically attractive but may be legally required under IHL when kinetic alternatives would produce excessive collateral damage. This interpretation would push military space operations toward less destructive methods, potentially reducing the debris consequences of space warfare—though it would also incentivize the development of capabilities that are harder to detect, attribute, and deter.

The Martens Clause and the Dictates of Public Conscience

The Martens Clause, a foundational principle of IHL incorporated into the Preamble of the 1907 Hague Convention IV and reaffirmed in Additional Protocol I, provides that in cases not covered by specific treaty provisions, the protection of the principles of international law "as they result from the usages established among civilized peoples, from the laws of humanity and the dictates of the public conscience" applies. The Clause serves as a residual protection, ensuring that conduct is not rendered lawful merely because no specific prohibition exists.

In the space domain, the Martens Clause may provide a basis for challenging military activities that are technically permitted under existing treaty law but that the international community increasingly regards as irresponsible. Destructive ASAT tests, for example, may not be prohibited by any specific treaty provision, but the growing consensus that such tests are irresponsible—as evidenced by the 2022 General Assembly resolution, the moratoria, and widespread diplomatic condemnation—may bring them within the scope of the Martens Clause's reference to "the dictates of the public conscience." This argument is novel and untested, but it illustrates how general principles of IHL can be deployed to address gaps in space-specific treaty law.

> *"The law of armed conflict applies wherever conflict occurs—including outer space. The challenge is not whether IHL applies to space, but how its principles can be meaningfully implemented in a domain where every attack has global consequences."*
>
> – On the application of IHL to space operations

***

Chapter Summary

Chapter 7 has explored how international law seeks to manage military uses of outer space, tracing the arc from early Cold War debates over "peaceful purposes" through the arms control impasse, the normative evolution of ASAT practice, and the emerging application of international humanitarian law to space operations.

The legal framework that has governed military space activity for over six decades rests on a series of strategic compromises. The Outer Space Treaty's Article IV prohibits the most destabilizing weapons—nuclear weapons and WMD in orbit—while permitting military support functions that both superpowers regarded as essential for strategic stability. This compromise has proven remarkably durable: no nuclear weapon has been placed in orbit, and military reconnaissance from space has become a universally accepted and stabilizing practice.

Yet the framework's gaps have become increasingly consequential. The absence of restrictions on conventional weapons in orbit, ground-based ASAT systems, electronic warfare, and cyber operations leaves broad categories of military activity in a legal gray zone. The dual-use character of space technology defeats traditional object-based arms control approaches. The Conference on Disarmament's inability to negotiate new binding instruments has left normative development to soft law, state practice, scholarly interpretation, and the incremental formation of customary norms through General Assembly resolutions and unilateral commitments.

The most significant normative development in recent years has been the movement toward a moratorium on destructive direct-ascent ASAT testing. The trajectory from tacit acceptance of ASAT tests in the 1960s to near-universal condemnation and a General Assembly resolution in 2022 illustrates how customary norms can evolve through accumulated practice, changed expectations, and the visible consequences of irresponsible behavior. Whether this norm crystallizes into binding custom remains to be seen, but the direction of travel is clear.

The application of IHL to space operations represents the next frontier of legal development. As military space activities become more sophisticated and space assets become more deeply integrated into warfighting, the questions of distinction, proportionality, environmental protection, and neutrality examined in Part IV will move from academic speculation to operational necessity. The Woomera and McGill Manuals provide essential groundwork, but the real test will come when states must apply these principles in practice—under the pressure of armed conflict, where the stakes are highest and the margin for error is smallest.

The overarching lesson of this chapter is that the law governing military uses of outer space has developed not through grand design but through incremental accumulation: treaty prohibitions negotiated under Cold War pressure, state practice that shaped customary understandings, soft-law instruments that filled gaps in the treaty framework, and scholarly interpretation that clarified legal principles for domains the drafters of the Outer Space Treaty could not have fully anticipated. This incremental process has produced a framework that is neither comprehensive nor entirely coherent, but that has nonetheless succeeded in preventing the extension of armed conflict into outer space for over six decades. Whether this success can be sustained in an era of intensifying space competition, proliferating counter-space capabilities, and the explicit recognition of space as a warfighting domain is the central security challenge of contemporary space governance.

In the next chapter, we turn from conflict to cooperation, examining how international law addresses the participation gap between spacefaring and developing states, and the mechanisms—including capacity-building, technology transfer, and institutional support—through which equitable access to space is pursued.

***

End of Chapter 7

Part III
ACCESS, EQUITY, AND COMMERCE

Chapter 8

DEVELOPING STATES, ACCESS TO SPACE, AND CAPACITY-BUILDING

International space law promises that outer space shall be explored and used for the benefit of all countries. Yet the reality of space activity has long been shaped by profound disparities in capability, resources, and participation. This chapter examines how the law addresses the gap between aspiration and reality—through technology transfer debates, capacity-building programs, and the rise of emerging space nations that are reshaping the architecture of space governance.

Part 1

Equity, Access to Space, and the Participation Gap

From its earliest articulation, international space law has been framed in universal terms. The Outer Space Treaty declares that the exploration and use of outer space shall be carried out "for the benefit and in the interests of all countries, irrespective of their degree of economic or scientific development." Article I further provides that outer space shall be "free for exploration and use by all States without discrimination of any kind, on a basis of equality." These provisions establish a normative commitment to inclusivity and shared benefit that is, at least rhetorically, among the strongest in international law.

Yet the practical reality of space activity has long diverged from this aspiration. For most of the space age, a small group of technologically advanced states—the United States, Russia, China, members of the European Space Agency, Japan, and India—has dominated access to space. These states designed and built launch vehicles, operated satellite constellations, conducted scientific missions, and shaped the legal frameworks that govern space activities. The vast majority of the world's states have participated in space only as consumers of services provided by others: satellite television delivered by Western and Asian operators, GPS navigation provided by the United States, weather data generated by satellites operated by a handful of space agencies. This asymmetry gives rise to what may be described as the participation gap—a central equity challenge in contemporary space governance.

Figure 19: The Growing Global Space Industry and Technological Innovation

Source: Generated using OpenAI Sora.

Formal Equality and Substantive Inequality

International law traditionally operates on the principle of sovereign equality: each state possesses equal legal personality and capacity, regardless of material power. In space law, this principle is reflected in the universal language of access and benefit-sharing. Every state, from the United States to Tuvalu, has the legal right to explore and use outer space freely. No state can be excluded from the benefits of space activity, and no state can claim sovereignty over outer space or celestial bodies.

However, formal equality does not translate automatically into substantive equality of opportunity. Space activities require extraordinary financial investment, sophisticated technical expertise, industrial infrastructure, scientific capacity, and regulatory frameworks. A single satellite launch can cost tens or hundreds of millions of dollars. Developing and maintaining a space program requires thousands of trained engineers, scientists, and technicians. The prerequisites of meaningful space participation place it beyond the immediate reach of most developing states, particularly the least developed countries, small island developing states, and landlocked developing countries that face the most acute resource constraints.

The structural nature of the participation gap is evident in the distribution of global space expenditure. In 2024, global government space budgets totaled approximately 103 billion dollars, of which the United States alone accounted for roughly 62 billion. The combined space budgets of all African countries were estimated at less than 500 million dollars—less than one percent of the global total. This financial asymmetry translates directly into asymmetric participation: the states that invest most in space capability have the greatest influence over space governance, while the states that invest least have the least voice in decisions that affect them.

As a result, the benefits of space—while theoretically shared—are often mediated through services provided by spacefaring nations or by commercial companies based in those states. Developing countries receive satellite imagery for disaster management, but they do not control the satellites. They benefit from satellite communications, but they do not set the terms of service. They rely on GPS for navigation and timing, but they have no influence over the system's operation or availability. This dependent relationship creates both opportunity and vulnerability—a dynamic that raises fundamental questions about the meaning of "benefit and in the interests of all countries" in practice.

The participation gap has also generated legal and political challenges that reflect developing states' frustration with perceived structural inequities. The Bogotá Declaration of 1976, in which eight equatorial states (Brazil, Colombia, Congo, Ecuador, Indonesia, Kenya, Uganda, and Zaire) asserted sovereign rights over segments of the geostationary orbit above their territories, was the most dramatic expression of this frustration. The Declaration argued that the geostationary orbit, as a "physical fact linked to the reality of our planet," was subject to the sovereignty of subjacent equatorial states rather than to the non-appropriation principle of the Outer Space Treaty. Although the Declaration was rejected by the broader international community and has not generated lasting legal effects, it illustrated the depth of developing country concern about equitable access to space resources and the perception that existing governance frameworks served the interests of technologically advanced states at the expense of others.

> *"The exploration and use of outer space, including the Moon and other celestial bodies, shall be carried out for the benefit and in the interests of all countries, irrespective of their degree of economic or scientific development, and shall be the province of all mankind."*
>
> – Outer Space Treaty, Article I

Historical Roots of the Participation Gap

The participation gap has deep historical roots in the geopolitical circumstances of the space age's origins. Early space activity was driven by Cold War competition between the United States and the Soviet Union, with enormous state resources devoted to strategic and prestige objectives. The space programs of both superpowers consumed billions of dollars annually—expenditures that dwarfed the entire government budgets of most developing countries. Meanwhile, many developing states were simultaneously navigating the challenges of decolonization, institution-building, and economic development. Space capability was not merely expensive; it was irrelevant to the immediate survival priorities of newly independent nations.

This historical context shaped the rhetorical commitments of early space law. Developing states, many of which participated actively in UN debates on outer space through the Non-Aligned Movement and the Group of 77, insisted that treaty language reflect principles of equity, shared benefit, and cooperation. The Outer Space Treaty's universalist provisions were, in significant part, the product of developing country advocacy. However, the Treaty did not include binding mechanisms for redistribution, technology transfer, or financial assistance. The gap between aspirational language and operational reality was present from the beginning.

The UNISPACE conferences attempted to address this gap through institutional means. UNISPACE I (1968) focused on the practical benefits of space technology for developing countries, emphasizing applications in communications, meteorology, and education. UNISPACE II (1982) expanded the agenda to include remote sensing, disaster management, and the role of the private sector. UNISPACE III (1999) adopted the Vienna Declaration, which set out a comprehensive agenda for space-based development assistance. UNISPACE+50 (2018) adopted the Space2030 Agenda, with its four pillars of space economy, space society, space accessibility, and space diplomacy. Each conference reaffirmed the principle of inclusive benefit and produced programmatic recommendations—but none created enforceable obligations or dedicated funding mechanisms sufficient to close the participation gap.

The equity debates in space law during the 1970s were shaped by the broader movement for a New International Economic Order (NIEO), through which developing states sought to restructure global economic relations to address colonial-era inequalities. The NIEO's influence is most visible in the Moon Agreement's "common heritage of mankind" principle (Article 11), which envisions an international regime for the equitable sharing of benefits derived from lunar resource exploitation. The common heritage concept was also applied to deep seabed resources under the UN Convention on the Law of the Sea (1982), creating the International Seabed Authority as the institutional expression of collective governance over shared resources.

The Moon Agreement's failure to attract major spacefaring states' ratification is often attributed to the common heritage provision's perceived threat to commercial incentives. Yet the principle's influence extends beyond the Agreement itself. It has shaped the normative vocabulary of space governance, informing debates over space resource utilization, orbital slot allocation at the International Telecommunication Union (ITU), and the distribution of benefits from satellite data. The tension between common heritage and commercial exploitation remains one of the defining fault lines of space equity discourse.

The ITU's management of the geostationary orbit illustrates the equity challenge in a particularly concrete way. The geostationary orbit—the ring at approximately 35,786 kilometers altitude where satellites appear stationary relative to the Earth's surface—is a finite natural resource of extraordinary commercial and strategic value. Orbital slots in the geostationary arc, combined with associated radio frequency spectrum, are the foundation of the global satellite communications industry. The ITU allocates these slots through a system that attempts to ensure equitable access for all states, but the practical reality favors states and companies with the technical and financial capacity to file, coordinate, and occupy orbital positions. Several developing states have filed for orbital slots as "paper satellites"—reserving positions without the immediate capacity to use them—as a strategy to protect future access rights, a practice that has generated controversy within the ITU but underscores the urgency with which developing states view the access question.

Dependence, Vulnerability, and the Digital Divide in Space

For developing states, reliance on externally provided space services creates both transformative opportunity and strategic vulnerability. Satellite communications have connected remote communities in Africa, Asia, and the Pacific that terrestrial infrastructure cannot reach. Earth observation data supports agricultural planning, water resource management, and environmental monitoring in countries that lack the resources for extensive ground-based monitoring networks. Weather satellites provide forecasting data that saves lives in regions prone to cyclones, floods, and droughts. Space-derived data is, by any measure, a powerful development tool.

Yet dependence on foreign systems raises fundamental concerns about access, control, resilience, and sovereignty. Interruptions to service—whether due to technical failure, commercial decisions, sanctions, or geopolitical tension—can have disproportionate impacts on states with limited alternatives. When a commercial satellite operator repositions a satellite to serve a more profitable market, the developing country that relied on its coverage may lose access without recourse. When geopolitical tensions lead to restrictions on technology exports or data sharing, developing countries may find themselves cut off from services they had come to depend upon.

The concept of a "digital divide"—widely discussed in the context of internet access and information technology—has a direct analogue in the space domain. States that can operate their own satellites, process their own data, and develop their own applications extract far greater value from space technology than states that merely consume services provided by others. The divide is not merely economic; it is epistemic and strategic. States that control their own space assets can prioritize their own development needs, respond to their own emergencies, and participate in international governance as informed contributors rather than passive beneficiaries.

Recent events have demonstrated the practical consequences of space dependency. When commercial satellite communications providers have restructured their coverage areas for commercial reasons, Pacific island nations and remote communities in Africa and Southeast Asia have experienced service disruptions with no alternative connectivity. The February 2022 cyberattack on Viasat's KA-SAT network—discussed in Chapter 6—disabled satellite internet terminals across Ukraine and affected wind turbine monitoring in Germany, demonstrating how attacks on commercial space infrastructure can cascade across borders and sectors. For developing states dependent on a single foreign provider for critical communications, weather data, or navigation services, such disruptions can be catastrophic.

Climate vulnerability adds urgency to the space access question. Small island developing states (SIDS)—many of which face existential threats from sea-level rise, intensifying cyclones, and ocean acidification—have the greatest need for satellite-derived environmental monitoring, early warning systems, and climate data. Yet these states typically have the least capacity to develop, operate, or even access space systems independently. The paradox is stark: the states most vulnerable to climate change are least equipped to use the space-based tools that could help them adapt. Addressing this paradox requires targeted capacity-building, preferential data access, and institutional support that recognizes the unique circumstances of SIDS and other climate-vulnerable states.

■ **The Space Participation Gap: Key Dimensions**

Financial: A single satellite launch costs $50–500 million; annual budgets of many developing states' entire science sectors are smaller.

Technical: Space programs require thousands of specialized engineers, scientists, and technicians that many states lack.

Industrial: Satellite manufacturing, integration, and testing require facilities and supply chains concentrated in a few states.

Regulatory: Effective space governance requires national space legislation, licensing capacity, and spectrum coordination expertise.

Data: The ability to process, analyze, and apply satellite data requires computing infrastructure and trained analysts.

Diplomatic: Meaningful participation in COPUOS and ITU requires legal and technical delegations that smaller states struggle to field.

Equity as a Dynamic Concept

Equity in space governance is not static. As technology becomes more accessible and costs decline, new opportunities emerge for participation that were unimaginable a generation ago. The small satellite revolution—driven by CubeSat technology, commercial off-the-shelf components, and standardized interfaces—has reduced the cost of an operational satellite from hundreds of millions of dollars to as little as a few hundred thousand. A 3U CubeSat (approximately 30 × 10 × 10 centimeters) can carry imaging, communications, or scientific payloads and can be built by a university team for under one million dollars. Shared launch services, such as SpaceX's Transporter rideshare missions, have reduced the cost of reaching orbit to as little as five thousand dollars per kilogram—a fraction of the fifty thousand dollars per kilogram that was standard a decade ago. Cloud-based data processing platforms such as Google Earth Engine and Amazon Web Services have reduced the infrastructure required to analyze satellite imagery. International partnerships have created pathways for participation that do not require indigenous launch capability.

The proliferation of small satellite programs in developing countries reflects these declining barriers. Between 2010 and 2024, over sixty developing countries launched their first satellite—a pace of entry that would have been inconceivable in the era when space programs required billions of dollars in government investment. Many of these satellites were CubeSats built through international partnerships, university programs, or commercial contracts with companies specializing in small satellite solutions. The question is no longer whether developing countries can access space, but whether that access translates into sustained capability development, industrial competence, and governance influence.

Yet these developments do not eliminate structural disparities; they reshape them. The cost of a CubeSat may be affordable, but the cost of ground stations, mission control, data processing, and a trained workforce is not trivial. Access to shared launch services requires regulatory capacity to obtain frequency coordination and launch licensing. Even as entry barriers decline for basic capabilities, the frontier of advanced space activity—reusable launch vehicles, large constellation operations, human spaceflight, deep space exploration—continues to recede beyond the reach of all but the most technically advanced states. Equity must therefore be understood as a dynamic process requiring continuous adaptation of legal and institutional frameworks, not a static achievement that can be declared complete.

> ■ **The Equity Paradox in Space Law**
>
> International space law establishes the strongest possible normative commitment to inclusive benefit: outer space is the 'province of all mankind.' Yet the same legal framework imposes no binding obligations for technology transfer, financial assistance, or capacity-building. The result is a paradox: the law declares that space benefits belong to everyone, while the practical means to access those benefits remain concentrated in a few states. Bridging this gap requires not merely legal reform but sustained institutional effort, political commitment, and creative partnership.

***

Part 11

Technology Transfer: Legal Frameworks and Political Tensions

Among the mechanisms proposed to bridge the participation gap in space activities, technology transfer has been the most contentious. For developing states, access to space-related technology represents a pathway to autonomy, resilience, and meaningful participation in the governance of a domain that increasingly shapes their economic and strategic futures. For technologically advanced states and private actors, however, technology transfer raises concerns about intellectual property protection, national security, commercial competitiveness, and the risk of proliferation. The legal treatment of technology transfer in space law reflects these competing interests, resulting in a framework that is aspirational rather than compulsory.

Technology Transfer in International Law

Technology transfer is not unique to space law. It has long featured in international economic, environmental, and development law as a tool for promoting equitable participation and addressing global challenges. The United Nations Framework Convention on Climate Change (1992) commits developed country parties to promote and facilitate the transfer of environmentally sound technologies to developing countries. The Convention on Biological Diversity (1992) includes provisions on access to and transfer of technology. The WTO's TRIPS Agreement, while primarily concerned with intellectual property protection, includes provisions acknowledging the need for technology transfer to least developed countries.

These provisions, however, are typically framed in hortatory language, emphasizing cooperation, facilitation, and mutual benefit rather than legal obligation. Technology transfer commitments in international environmental law have been described as "soft obligations"—recognized in principle, difficult to enforce in practice. Space law follows this pattern, reflecting the fundamental difficulty of reconciling redistributive aspirations with the protection of proprietary interests and the imperatives of national security.

Technology Transfer in Space Treaties

The Outer Space Treaty does not explicitly mandate technology transfer. Article I declares that space exploration shall be carried out for the benefit of all countries and that there shall be freedom of scientific investigation. Article III requires activities to be conducted in accordance with international law. Article XI requires states to inform the Secretary-General, the public, and the international scientific community of the nature, conduct, locations, and results of their activities. These provisions create expectations of information-sharing and cooperation but fall short of technology transfer obligations.

The Moon Agreement (1979) goes further, envisaging an international regime to govern the exploitation of natural resources on the Moon and other celestial bodies and to ensure "an equitable sharing by all States Parties in the benefits derived from those resources." Article 11 provides that such a regime should include "an equitable sharing of benefits derived from the exploitation of the natural resources of the moon." While not explicitly framed as technology transfer, the Agreement's emphasis on collective management and equitable benefit-sharing implies a greater role for shared knowledge and capability. However, the Moon Agreement's limited ratification—only eighteen states as of 2025, none of them major spacefaring powers—has curtailed its practical influence.

The 1986 Principles Relating to Remote Sensing of the Earth from Outer Space declare that remote sensing shall be carried out for the benefit of all countries and that sensed states shall have access to data concerning their own territories on a non-discriminatory basis and at reasonable cost. These principles represent one of the most concrete expressions of benefit-sharing in space law, though they remain non-binding and their implementation depends on the policies of sensing states and commercial operators. In practice, the principle of "access at reasonable cost" has been interpreted differently by different stakeholders: some argue it requires near-free access for developing countries, while commercial operators contend that "reasonable cost" includes recovery of development and operational expenses.

The remote sensing debate illustrates a broader structural tension. Developing countries generate much of the data that remote sensing satellites collect—their territories, natural resources, and environmental conditions constitute the very subject matter of Earth observation. Yet they exercise little control over the collection, processing, distribution, and monetization of that data. The argument that states should have privileged access to data about their own territories has intuitive appeal but conflicts with the free-market model of data commercialization that has come to dominate the remote sensing industry. This tension between data sovereignty and commercial freedom is likely to intensify as the volume and value of satellite-derived data continue to grow.

National Export Controls and the ITAR Regime

Technology transfer debates in the space domain cannot be separated from national export control regimes that significantly constrain the practical scope of cooperation. Many space-related technologies are classified as dual-use, with potential military applications that make governments reluctant to share them. The most consequential export control regime affecting space technology transfer is the United States' International Traffic in Arms Regulations (ITAR), administered by the Department of State's Directorate of Defense Trade Controls.

ITAR treats most spacecraft, launch vehicles, and their components as defense articles subject to stringent export licensing requirements. The practical effect is sweeping: a satellite manufactured in Europe that contains a single ITAR-controlled component may be subject to U.S. export restrictions, limiting where it can be launched, who can access it, and how technical information about it can be shared. These restrictions have had a chilling effect on international space cooperation, particularly with developing countries that lack the diplomatic leverage or security clearances needed to navigate the ITAR licensing process.

The ITAR regime's extraterritorial reach has prompted European and other manufacturers to develop "ITAR-free" satellite components—products designed specifically to exclude any U.S.-origin parts or technology, thereby avoiding U.S. export control jurisdiction. This phenomenon illustrates the tension between security-driven restrictions and the commercial and cooperative imperatives of the space sector. For developing countries, ITAR and similar export control regimes represent a significant barrier to technology access, even when cooperation would serve legitimate development objectives.

The Missile Technology Control Regime (MTCR), established in 1987, presents an additional constraint with particular significance for developing states seeking independent launch capability. The MTCR controls the export of complete rocket systems capable of delivering a 500-kilogram payload to a range of at least 300 kilometers (Category I), as well as related subsystems, components, and technology (Category II). Because space launch vehicles use fundamentally the same propulsion technology as ballistic missiles, the MTCR effectively restricts transfers of launch vehicle technology to developing countries—even when the intended application is purely civilian. States seeking to develop indigenous launch programs must therefore rely primarily on domestic R&D, a path that is both longer and more expensive than cooperative development would be.

The MTCR's impact on developing country space programs has been significant. Brazil's VLS launch vehicle program, South Korea's KSLV development, and India's cryogenic engine procurement from

Russia were all affected by MTCR-related restrictions. While the MTCR's non-proliferation objectives are widely acknowledged as legitimate, developing states argue that the regime's application to space launch vehicles—which by definition are designed to reach orbit rather than deliver weapons—conflates peaceful and military technology in ways that unfairly restrict space access. The regime's critics note that MTCR members include all major launch service providers, creating a structural incentive for members to restrict competitors' access to launch technology while maintaining their own commercial dominance in the global launch market.

■ **Key Export Control Regimes Affecting Space Technology**

ITAR (United States): Treats most spacecraft and launch vehicles as defense articles; extraterritorial reach through component-level controls.

EAR (United States): Covers dual-use space technologies; administered by Bureau of Industry and Security.

Wassenaar Arrangement: 42 participating states; voluntary export control coordination for conventional arms and dual-use goods, including space technologies.

MTCR (Missile Technology Control Regime): 35 members; controls transfers of missiles and related technology, including space launch vehicles (Category I systems).

EU Dual-Use Regulation: Controls exports of dual-use items, including certain space technologies; implemented through national licensing authorities.

Intellectual Property and Commercialization

The commercialization of space activity has further complicated technology transfer dynamics. Private companies invest billions of dollars in research and development—reusable launch vehicles, satellite manufacturing techniques, proprietary software, ground system architectures—relying on intellectual property protection to recoup costs and generate returns for investors. From the perspective of commercial space companies, mandatory technology transfer threatens the incentive structure that drives innovation. If the fruits of expensive R&D must be shared with competitors or foreign governments, the investment case for space technology development weakens.

International space law largely defers to national intellectual property regimes, offering little guidance on how proprietary interests should be balanced against equitable access. The 1998 ISS Intergovernmental Agreement includes provisions protecting intellectual property generated on the Space Station, assigning rights based on the nationality of the inventor and the contributing partner. However, this model applies to a specific cooperative project among technologically advanced states and provides limited precedent for broader technology transfer frameworks involving developing countries.

Open innovation and open-source approaches have emerged as potential alternatives to traditional proprietary models. The Libre Space Foundation, for example, develops open-source satellite technology and ground station networks that any organization can use and modify. NASA's open data policy makes vast quantities of scientific data freely available to researchers worldwide. ESA's Copernicus programme provides free and open access to Earth observation data that would cost millions of dollars if procured commercially. These initiatives demonstrate that innovation can coexist with openness—and that open approaches may actually accelerate innovation by expanding the community of contributors and users.

The tension between intellectual property protection and equitable access is not unique to space—it pervades international debates on pharmaceuticals, agriculture, and digital technology. In each domain, the fundamental question is the same: how can innovation incentives be preserved while ensuring that the benefits of technological progress are shared broadly? In the space domain, the answer has increasingly involved alternative pathways that circumvent direct technology transfer while building indigenous capability.

Alternative Pathways: From Transfer to Empowerment

Given the political resistance to mandatory technology transfer and the practical constraints imposed by export controls and intellectual property regimes, capacity-building efforts have increasingly focused on alternative pathways that build capability without requiring the transfer of sensitive technology. These alternatives include training programs at space agencies and universities, joint research projects in which developing country scientists participate as co-investigators, data-sharing initiatives that provide access to satellite-derived information without requiring access to satellite technology itself, and collaborative satellite programs in which developing countries contribute to specific subsystems while international partners supply the platform.

The most successful examples of technology empowerment involve structured partnerships in which the advanced partner commits to progressively transferring design and manufacturing capability to the developing country partner. Algeria's satellite program exemplifies this approach: Alsat-1 (2002) was designed and built largely by SSTL with Algerian participation; Alsat-1B and Alsat-2A (2010) involved substantially more Algerian engineering; and Alsat-2B was built by Algerian engineers at the Centre National des Techniques Spatiales (CNTS) with Airbus Defence and Space guidance. This progressive approach builds genuine indigenous capability while managing technology security concerns.

South Korea's space program demonstrates how a determined middle-income state can achieve advanced capabilities through strategic international partnerships combined with sustained domestic investment. Korea's KSLV-II (Nuri) launch vehicle, which achieved successful orbital insertion in 2022, was developed domestically after decades of cooperative programs with Russia (which supplied the first stage of the earlier KSLV-I) and extensive investment in domestic rocket propulsion research. The trajectory from technology consumer to technology producer took approximately twenty-five years and required sustained government commitment through multiple political administrations.

These examples suggest that the most effective path from technology dependence to technology autonomy is not a single act of transfer but a sustained process of partnership, investment, education, and institutional development. International space law provides the normative framework for such partnerships—emphasizing cooperation, mutual benefit, and shared access—but the practical realization depends on bilateral arrangements, commercial contracts, and domestic policy choices that operate largely outside the international legal framework.

> *"Technology transfer in space law occupies the uncomfortable middle ground between what developing states need and what spacefaring states are willing to provide. The gap between aspiration and obligation defines the politics of space equity."*
>
> – On the technology transfer debate

***

Part III

United Nations Mechanisms: UNOOSA and Cooperative Programs

As binding obligations for technology transfer have remained politically elusive, the international community—particularly through the United Nations—has turned to institutional capacity-building as the primary mechanism for promoting inclusive access to space. At the center of this effort is the United Nations Office for Outer Space Affairs (UNOOSA), based in Vienna, which serves as both a facilitator of cooperation and a conduit through which developing states engage meaningfully with space governance and space activity.

UNOOSA: Mandate and Evolution

UNOOSA was established in 1958 to support the work of COPUOS and to promote international cooperation in the peaceful uses of outer space. Originally a small secretariat function, it has grown into an operational body with programs spanning legal advisory services, technical assistance, space applications, disaster management, and sustainable development. As of 2025, UNOOSA operates with a staff of approximately 50 professionals and a modest budget supplemented by voluntary contributions from member states, space agencies, and private sector partners.

UNOOSA's mandate has evolved significantly over six decades. Its original focus on servicing COPUOS meetings and maintaining the Register of Objects Launched into Outer Space has expanded to encompass direct capacity-building, educational outreach, technical advisory missions, and the coordination of space-based support for sustainable development. This evolution reflects recognition that legal openness alone is insufficient to ensure meaningful participation: states need practical capabilities—trained personnel, institutional frameworks, data access, regulatory expertise—to benefit from the rights that international space law provides.

UNOOSA has also pioneered innovative institutional arrangements to maximize its impact within constrained resources. The "Space for Women" project addresses gender disparities in the space sector through mentoring, networking, and advocacy. The Space Economy Initiative explores how developing countries can participate in the growing commercial space economy. The Office's fellowship programs—jointly administered with ESA, JAXA, CNSA, and other space agencies—provide immersive training experiences that would otherwise be unavailable to professionals from developing countries. These programs demonstrate institutional creativity in the face of resource limitations, leveraging partnerships to deliver capabilities that UNOOSA's own budget could not support.

The Office's approach is grounded in the principle that access to space should be capability-based rather than power-based. Rather than redistributing technology from spacefaring states to others, UNOOSA seeks to empower states by strengthening human capital, institutional frameworks, and regulatory capacity. This approach avoids the political sensitivities associated with direct technology transfer while building the foundations for indigenous space capability.

Flagship Programs

UNOOSA administers several flagship programs aimed at reducing the participation gap. The United Nations Programme on Space Applications (PSA), established in 1971, is the longest-running capacity-building initiative in the space domain. It organizes workshops, training courses, expert meetings, and pilot projects in areas including remote sensing, satellite communications, satellite navigation, space law, and basic space science. The PSA has trained thousands of professionals from over one hundred developing countries, creating networks of expertise that extend well beyond formal program activities.

The Access to Space for All initiative, launched in 2018, represents a qualitative shift in UNOOSA's approach. Rather than focusing exclusively on training and information-sharing, the initiative facilitates direct participation in space missions through partnerships with space agencies and commercial providers. Programs include the KiboCUBE initiative, which offers developing countries the opportunity to deploy CubeSats from the Japanese Experiment Module (Kibo) on the International Space Station; the Drop Tower Experiment Series (DropTES), providing access to microgravity research; and the HyperGravity Experiment Series (HyperGE). These programs lower entry barriers by providing flight opportunities that developing countries could not independently afford, creating hands-on experience that catalyzes further capability development.

Program	Focus	Key Mechanism	Impact
Programme on Space Applications	Training and education	Workshops, courses, pilot projects	Thousands trained from 100+ countries since 1971
KiboCUBE	Satellite deployment	Free CubeSat deployment from ISS/Kibo	Multiple developing country satellites deployed
UN-SPIDER	Disaster management	Technical advisory, access to satellite data	Operational in 70+ countries
Space4SDGs	Sustainable development	Integrating space data into SDG monitoring	Partnerships across UN system
Space Law Advisory	Legal capacity	Model legislation, technical assistance	30+ states assisted with national space law
Regional Centres for Space Science	Education	Affiliated to UN; degree programs	10 centres across Africa, Asia, Latin America

UN-SPIDER and Disaster Management

The United Nations Platform for Space-based Information for Disaster Management and Emergency Response (UN-SPIDER), established by the General Assembly in 2006, provides one of the most concrete examples of how space capabilities can be made accessible to developing countries. UN-SPIDER offers technical advisory support to help states use space-based data for disaster preparedness, early warning, and emergency response. It maintains a network of Regional Support Offices that provide localized expertise and coordinates with the International Charter on Space and Major Disasters, which provides free satellite imagery to disaster-affected states within hours of activation.

UN-SPIDER's operational model illustrates several principles that inform effective capacity-building. First, it addresses a concrete, urgent need—disaster management—that motivates sustained political and institutional support. Second, it provides both data access and the training needed to use that data effectively, recognizing that raw satellite imagery is of limited value without analytical capability. Third, it leverages partnerships with space agencies, commercial operators, and regional organizations to deliver services that UNOOSA could not provide independently. As of 2025, UN-SPIDER has conducted technical advisory missions in over seventy countries and supported disaster response operations affecting millions of people.

Space for Sustainable Development

The Space2030 Agenda, adopted by the General Assembly in 2021, represents the most comprehensive attempt to integrate space applications into the broader sustainable development framework. Its four pillars—space economy, space soci ety, space accessibility, and space diplomacy—provide a structured framework for aligning space activities with the Sustainable Development Goals (SDGs). The Space4SDGs initiative translates this framework into operational projects that demonstrate how satellite data can support specific development objectives: monitoring deforestation (SDG 15), tracking ocean health (SDG 14), improving urban planning (SDG 11), supporting food security (SDG 2), and enhancing climate monitoring (SDG 13).

The integration of space capabilities into SDG implementation has had a significant institutional effect. It has brought space agencies into dialogue with development agencies, health ministries, agricultural authorities, and environmental regulators that had previously seen space as irrelevant to their mandates. This cross-sectoral engagement has broadened the constituency for space investment in developing countries and created new pathways for international cooperation. When a health ministry in sub-Saharan Africa uses satellite data to map malaria risk, or a Pacific island nation uses remote sensing to monitor coastal erosion, the abstract promise of "benefit for all countries" becomes tangible and immediate.

UNOOSA has increasingly engaged the private sector as a partner in capacity-building, reflecting the reality that commercial companies now provide many of the services and capabilities that developing countries need. The Space Solutions Compendium, maintained by UNOOSA, catalogues commercially available space applications relevant to sustainable development. The Office has partnered with companies including Airbus, Planet Labs, and Google to provide satellite data, cloud computing resources, and training to developing countries. The UNOOSA-CNES Space4Water initiative connects water resource managers in developing countries with satellite-derived hydrological data. These public-private partnerships extend UNOOSA's reach and capabilities beyond what its modest budget would otherwise permit.

The relationship between UNOOSA and the private sector raises governance questions, however. As commercial companies become integral to capacity-building delivery, the boundary between public and private interests in space governance blurs. Commercial partners may prioritize markets with revenue potential over countries with the greatest developmental need. Data provided free of charge during capacity-building programs may be monetized once states develop dependency on the services. UNOOSA must navigate these dynamics carefully, ensuring that partnerships serve developmental objectives without creating new forms of commercial dependency that replicate the structural inequalities they seek to address.

Legal Capacity-Building

One of the most significant barriers to meaningful space participation is the absence of robust national space legislation in developing states. Without clear legal frameworks, states may be unable to authorize, supervise, or attract space activities. They may fail to comply with international obligations under Article VI of the Outer Space Treaty, exposing themselves to responsibility for inadequately supervised activities. They may lack the regulatory capacity to license commercial operators, manage spectrum allocations, or enforce debris mitigation requirements.

UNOOSA addresses this gap through legal advisory services, model legislation, and direct technical assistance. The Office has assisted over thirty states in developing or revising national space legislation, providing templates, comparative analysis, and expert consultations. The UN/COPUOS model framework for national space legislation, developed through the Legal Subcommittee, provides guidance on essential elements including authorization and supervision procedures, registration requirements, liability allocation, insurance obligations, and debris mitigation provisions.

Legal capacity-building serves both developmental and compliance objectives. By strengthening domestic legal frameworks, these efforts enable developing states to participate in space activities as responsible actors—authorizing missions, supervising operators, and meeting international obligations. They also create the regulatory environment needed to attract commercial investment, launch service agreements, and partnership opportunities. A state with a well-designed space law sends a signal to the international community that it is a reliable partner for cooperative space activities.

Regional Centres for Space Science and Technology Education

The network of Regional Centres for Space Science and Technology Education, affiliated to the United Nations, represents a sustained investment in human capital development for the space sector. Established beginning in the early 1990s, these centres operate in Africa (Morocco, Nigeria, and Kenya), Asia and the Pacific (India and China), Latin America and the Caribbean (Brazil and Mexico), and Western Asia (Jordan). Each centre offers postgraduate-level education in remote sensing and geographic information systems, satellite communications, satellite meteorology and global climate, space and atmospheric science, and space law and policy.

The Regional Centres have trained thousands of professionals from developing countries, many of whom have gone on to lead national space programs, advise governments on space policy, or establish university-level space education programs in their home countries. The centres' impact extends beyond individual training: they create networks of professionals across regions, facilitate south-south cooperation, and build institutional capacity that outlasts individual program cycles. The Indian-hosted Centre for Space Science and Technology Education in Asia and the Pacific (CSSTEAP), for example, has trained over 3,700 professionals from more than 60 countries since its establishment in 1995.

Limits and Structural Challenges

Despite their value, capacity-building programs face significant limitations. UNOOSA's annual budget—approximately USD 10 million in assessed contributions, supplemented by voluntary funding—is modest by any standard, particularly when measured against the scale of the participation gap it seeks to address. The total annual investment in UN space capacity-building is roughly equivalent to the cost of a single small satellite mission. Voluntary contributions, while essential, are unpredictable and may be directed toward donor priorities rather than recipient needs.

Participation in programs is uneven: states with existing institutional capacity and proactive space agencies tend to benefit most, while the least developed countries—which arguably need support most urgently—may lack the institutional infrastructure to identify opportunities, prepare applications, and absorb assistance effectively. The "absorptive capacity" problem is well-known in development assistance: providing training and equipment is of limited value if the recipient institution lacks the organizational structures to sustain and build upon the initial investment.

Moreover, capacity-building programs, by their nature, address symptoms rather than structural causes of the participation gap. They can train individuals, provide data, and offer flight opportunities, but they cannot compensate for decades of underinvestment in scientific education, industrial development, and research infrastructure. The most effective capacity-building occurs when external assistance catalyzes domestic investment—when a KiboCUBE mission inspires a government to establish a national space agency, or when a UN-SPIDER advisory mission leads to sustained investment in disaster management infrastructure. When external assistance substitutes for rather than catalyzes domestic commitment, its long-term impact is diminished.

> ■ **Capacity-Building as a Legal Strategy**
>
> Capacity-building is not merely a developmental objective; it is a legal strategy for operationalizing international space law. Article VI of the Outer Space Treaty requires states to authorize and supervise space activities, but many states lack the institutional capacity to do so. Legal and technical assistance programs address this gap, enabling states to fulfill treaty obligations while participating meaningfully in space governance. Capacity-building thus serves the dual function of promoting equity and strengthening the international legal order.

***

Part IV

Emerging Space Nations and Future Pathways

The last two decades have witnessed a significant transformation in the global space landscape. A growing number of states—often described as emerging space nations—have moved from passive consumption of space services to active engagement in space activities. This shift has important legal, political, and institutional implications, both for international space law and for the broader architecture of space governance.

Characteristics of Emerging Space Programs

Emerging space nations are not defined solely by economic status. They include developing states, middle-income countries, and technologically ambitious nations that have invested strategically in space capabilities aligned with national development priorities. Common characteristics include incremental development of indigenous satellite programs (often beginning with CubeSats or small satellites before progressing to larger platforms), reliance on international partnerships and shared launch services, focus on application-driven missions rather than prestige projects, and gradual development of domestic legal and regulatory frameworks.

The diversity of emerging space programs is striking. The United Arab Emirates—a middle-income state with no space heritage before 2000—launched the Hope Mars orbiter in 2020, becoming only the fifth entity to reach Mars orbit. The UAE's space program illustrates how strategic investment, institutional design, and international partnerships can compress decades of capability development into years. The Mohammed bin Rashid Space Centre (MBRSC), established in 2006, built its capabilities through a deliberate progression: purchasing satellite imagery, then procuring satellites with technology transfer (DubaiSat-1 with South Korean assistance), then manufacturing satellites domestically (KhalifaSat, built primarily by Emirati engineers), then leading an interplanetary mission. Federal Law No. 12 of 2019 on the Regulation of the Space Sector provided the legal framework to attract international partnerships and commercial investment. The UAE's experience demonstrates that with sufficient political commitment and strategic investment, an emerging space nation can achieve world-class capabilities within a single generation.

Nigeria has operated a succession of Earth observation satellites since NigeriaSat-1 in 2003, built by SSTL with Nigerian engineering participation. Ethiopia launched its first satellite (ETRSS-1) in 2019 with Chinese technical assistance. Rwanda, Kenya, Uganda, Zimbabwe, and Tunisia have all deployed CubeSats or microsatellites. In Asia, Bangladesh, Nepal, Bhutan, and Myanmar have joined the space community through small satellite programs. In Latin America, Costa Rica, Guatemala, and Paraguay have initiated space programs in recent years. The Philippines established its national space agency (PhilSA) in 2019 and enacted comprehensive space legislation. Each of these programs reflects national priorities—agricultural monitoring, disaster management, communications, education, national prestige—and each contributes to the diversification of the global space community.

> ■ **Emerging Space Nations: Selected Milestones**
>
> UAE: Mohammed bin Rashid Space Centre established 2006; KhalifaSat (2018); Hope Mars Mission (2020); announced National Space Fund.
>
> Nigeria: NigeriaSat-1 (2003); NASRDA established; NigComSat-1R communications satellite (2011).
>
> Ethiopia: ETRSS-1 remote sensing satellite (2019); Ethiopian Space Science and Technology Institute.
>
> South Africa: SANSA established 2010; operates ground stations; space weather monitoring.
>
> Philippines: PhilSA established 2019; Diwata microsatellite program; national space legislation enacted.
>
> Costa Rica: First Central American country to establish space agency (AEC, 2021); Irazú satellite project.
>
> Luxembourg: Space resources law (2017); SpaceResources.lu initiative; regulatory framework for commercial space.

Regional Cooperation as a Pathway

Regional cooperation has emerged as a key pathway for states that lack the resources to develop comprehensive space programs independently. By pooling resources, sharing infrastructure, and coordinating policy, regional groupings can achieve capabilities that individual member states could not attain alone. Several regional space organizations and cooperative frameworks have developed in recent decades, each reflecting the specific priorities and political dynamics of its region.

The African Union's African Space Strategy and Policy, adopted in 2017, envisions a coordinated continental approach to space development. The African Space Agency (AfSA), headquartered in Cairo, was formally established in 2023 to coordinate space activities across the continent. AfSA's mandate includes harmonizing regulatory frameworks, coordinating satellite procurement, facilitating data-sharing, and representing African interests in international forums. The establishment of AfSA reflects recognition that individual African states—even those with relatively advanced programs like South Africa, Nigeria, and Egypt—cannot individually match the scale and sophistication of established space powers. A coordinated continental approach, pooling resources and expertise across 55 member states, offers a pathway to capabilities that no single African state could achieve alone.

The Asia-Pacific Space Cooperation Organization (APSCO), established in 2005 and headquartered in Beijing, promotes space cooperation among its member states—including Bangladesh, Iran, Mongolia, Pakistan, Peru, Thailand, and Turkey—through joint satellite programs, training, and data-sharing. APSCO's Student Small Satellite (SSS) program and its Data-Sharing Service Platform illustrate how regional organizations can provide practical capabilities alongside political solidarity. The Latin American and Caribbean Space Agency (ALCE), established in 2021, is the newest regional space organization, reflecting growing interest in space cooperation across the Americas.

Regional cooperation serves multiple functions within the space equity framework. It achieves economies of scale that reduce per-state costs. It enables specialization, with different member states contributing different capabilities to shared programs. It builds political solidarity for advocacy in international forums such as COPUOS and the ITU, where regional blocs can negotiate more effectively than individual states. And it creates regional regulatory frameworks that can attract investment and facilitate commercial partnerships. The European Space Agency, while not a developing-country institution, provides a successful precedent: by pooling the resources of twenty-two member states, ESA has achieved capabilities in launch, Earth observation, navigation, and scientific research that no individual European state—with the possible exception of France or Germany—could have developed independently.

The Role of the Private Sector in Emerging Space Nations

Private actors increasingly serve as enablers for emerging space nations, offering launch services, satellite platforms, data analytics, training, and turnkey solutions at costs significantly below those of traditional government-to-government programs. Companies such as Surrey Satellite Technology Limited (SSTL), which has built satellites for countries including Nigeria, Algeria, and Kazakhstan, and the South African company Dragonfly Aerospace demonstrate that commercial partnerships can accelerate space capability development far faster than indigenous programs alone.

The CubeSat ecosystem has been particularly transformative. Companies such as Nanoracks, Innovative Solutions in Space (ISIS), and Gomspace provide standardized satellite buses, launch integration services, and mission support that enable developing countries to deploy operational satellites within two to three years and at a fraction of traditional costs. University-led CubeSat programs have served as incubators for national space programs in countries including Kenya (1KUNS-PF), Ghana (GhanaSat-1), and Guatemala (Quetzal-1).

The "NewSpace" ecosystem's impact on developing country access extends beyond satellite technology. Commercial satellite imagery providers such as Planet Labs, which operates a constellation of over 200 Dove satellites providing daily global imagery, offer data products at prices accessible to developing country agencies and researchers. Satellite communications providers such as OneWeb and Starlink offer connectivity in regions where terrestrial infrastructure is absent or unreliable. Geospatial analytics platforms such as Descartes Labs and Orbital Insight provide AI-powered analysis of satellite data that was previously available only to well-resourced government agencies or major corporations. These commercial services create a "space applications layer" that developing countries can access without building or operating their own satellites, complementing rather than substituting for indigenous capability development.

However, commercial partnerships also introduce dependencies and risks. A state that relies on foreign companies for satellite manufacturing, launch, and ground operations may develop familiarity with space technology without developing indigenous capability. The distinction between capability acquisition and capability development is critical: purchasing a satellite is not the same as being able to design and build one. Effective technology partnerships balance immediate operational needs with long-term capacity development, incorporating technology transfer, training, and local manufacturing components that build indigenous expertise. The most successful partnerships—such as Algeria's collaboration with Airbus to build Alsat-2B, which included substantial Algerian engineering participation—demonstrate that commercial relationships can serve capacity-building objectives when structured appropriately.

Governance Implications: From Participation to Co-Ownership

The rise of emerging space nations has profound implications for the governance of outer space. As more states acquire operational experience and invest in space capabilities, the dynamics of norm development within COPUOS and other forums shift. Debates that were once dominated by a handful of spacefaring states now incorporate a wider range of perspectives, priorities, and interests. Developing countries increasingly insist that issues of equity, access, and capacity-building receive equal attention alongside traditional agenda items such as debris mitigation, space traffic management, and resource utilization.

The Artemis Accords, initiated by the United States in 2020, illustrate both the opportunities and the equity concerns associated with new governance frameworks. The Accords establish principles for civil exploration of the Moon and other celestial bodies, including commitments to transparency, interoperability, emergency assistance, registration, scientific data release, and resource extraction. As of 2025, over forty states have signed the Accords, including several developing countries. However, the Accords were negotiated outside the UN system as a series of bilateral agreements between the United States and individual signatories, bypassing the multilateral, consensus-based process of COPUOS. Critics argue that this approach allows a single state to set the norms for lunar exploration and resource utilization, potentially marginalizing the interests of non-signatories. Supporters counter that the Accords implement and build upon existing treaty obligations and that their open architecture allows any state to join.

The equity dimension of the Artemis Accords debate reflects a broader tension in space governance between efficiency and inclusivity. Multilateral, consensus-based processes like COPUOS are inclusive but slow; bilateral and plurilateral approaches are faster but risk excluding states that lack diplomatic leverage. For developing countries, the question is not merely whether they can sign the Accords but whether the norms established through such processes will reflect their interests—including interests in equitable benefit-sharing, technology access, and protection against the entrenchment of first-mover advantages by technologically dominant states.

This diversification has both strengthened and complicated space governance. It has strengthened governance by expanding the legitimacy of norms developed through broader participation. A space debris guideline endorsed by 102 COPUOS member states, including dozens of developing countries, carries greater normative weight than one negotiated among a handful of spacefaring powers. It has complicated governance by increasing the number of interests that must be reconciled, the range of priorities that must be balanced, and the time required to achieve consensus in a forum that operates on the unanimity principle.

The most significant governance implication of the emerging space nation phenomenon is the shift from participation to co-ownership. For most of the space age, developing countries participated in space governance primarily as advocates for their interests—pressing for equity provisions, technology transfer commitments, and capacity-building programs. As these states develop their own space capabilities, they become stakeholders with operational experience, technical expertise, and institutional capacity to contribute to norm development as equals. This transition—from beneficiaries of the space regime to co-architects of its future—represents perhaps the most important structural change in space governance since the end of the Cold War.

Future Pathways for Inclusive Space Governance

Looking ahead, several pathways offer the potential to accelerate inclusive participation in space activities and governance. Enhanced data-sharing and open science initiatives—including the Copernicus programme's free and open data policy and the Group on Earth Observations' Global Earth Observation System of Systems (GEOSS)—demonstrate that space-derived data can be made globally accessible without undermining the commercial interests of data providers. The Copernicus model is particularly instructive: by making satellite imagery freely available to all users worldwide, the European Union has created an ecosystem of value-added services, applications, and analytics that benefits developing countries directly while stimulating commercial innovation in Europe. The contrast with proprietary data models—where access is restricted by cost or licensing—illustrates the transformative potential of open data policies for space equity.

Expanded cooperative missions, in which developing countries contribute instruments, ground stations, or data processing to international missions, build capability while producing scientifically valuable results. The AfriCube project, which involves multiple African universities in CubeSat development and deployment, exemplifies this approach. Integration of sustainability and equity considerations into regulatory design—including at the ITU, where orbital slot and spectrum allocation affect developing country access—can prevent the early-mover advantages of technologically advanced states from permanently excluding newcomers. The ITU's World Radiocommunication Conference (WRC) process, which revises the Radio Regulations every three to four years, provides a regular opportunity to address equity concerns in spectrum and orbit allocation, but developing countries must have the technical expertise and diplomatic capacity to participate effectively in these complex negotiations.

Capacity-building for governance participation—not just for technical capabilities—is essential. A developing state that lacks the expertise to participate effectively in COPUOS deliberations, ITU coordination procedures, or Artemis Accords negotiations will be unable to shape the norms that govern its access to and use of outer space. Programs that train diplomats, regulators, and legal advisors alongside engineers and scientists build the comprehensive human capital needed for meaningful governance participation. The Manfred Lachs Space Law Moot Court Competition, the International Space University's Space Studies Program, and UNOOSA's workshops on space law and policy all contribute to this broader form of capacity-building.

These pathways do not require abandoning existing legal principles. They call for renewed commitment to the cooperative ethos embedded in space law and for creative institutional mechanisms that translate legal commitments into practical capabilities. The participation gap in space governance is narrowing, but it has not closed. Whether the next generation of space law and governance will reflect the voices and interests of the entire international community—rather than only its most technologically advanced members—will depend on the political choices, institutional investments, and legal innovations of the coming decades.

> *"True inclusion in space governance goes beyond access to technology or services. It requires participation in the decisions that shape the rules, norms, and priorities governing outer space—the transition from beneficiaries of the regime to co-architects of its future."*
>
> – On the meaning of inclusive space governance

***

Chapter Summary

Chapter 8 has explored how international law and institutions address the persistent disparities in access to space, tracing the tension between formal equality and substantive inequality that has characterized space governance since the Outer Space Treaty's adoption in 1967.

The participation gap—rooted in historical circumstance, sustained by financial and technical barriers, and shaped by the geopolitics of the Cold War and its aftermath—remains a defining challenge. International space law provides a powerful normative foundation for inclusive access, but it has relied on aspiration rather than obligation to achieve equity goals. Treaty provisions declaring that space shall be explored for the benefit of all countries have not been accompanied by binding mechanisms for technology transfer, financial assistance, or capacity redistribution.

Technology transfer, examined in Part II, illustrates the tension between developmental aspiration and strategic reality. Export control regimes, intellectual property protections, and commercial interests constrain the practical scope of technology sharing, even as the normative case for equitable access grows stronger. The political resistance to binding transfer obligations has redirected equity efforts toward alternative mechanisms—capacity-building, data-sharing, partnerships, and institutional support—that are more politically feasible and, in many cases, more effective at building sustained indigenous capability.

The United Nations mechanisms examined in Part III—UNOOSA's flagship programs, UN-SPIDER, the Space2030 Agenda, legal advisory services—represent the international community's most sustained effort to translate equity principles into operational results. These programs have trained thousands of professionals, supported dozens of satellite missions, assisted over thirty states with national space legislation, and connected space technology to sustainable development objectives. Their limitations—modest funding, uneven participation, and the inability to address structural inequalities—are real but should not obscure their substantial achievements.

The rise of emerging space nations, examined in Part IV, represents the most transformative development in the equity landscape. As dozens of states move from passive consumption to active participation in space activities, the dynamics of governance shift. The UAE's Mars mission, Nigeria's satellite program, Kenya's CubeSat deployments, and the Philippines' space agency establishment all signal that the era of exclusive space activity by a handful of states is ending. Regional organizations—AfSA, APSCO, ALCE—amplify this shift by pooling resources and coordinating policy across borders. The Artemis Accords, whatever their merits and limitations, have demonstrated that emerging space nations are sought-after partners whose participation is valued and pursued.

The transition from beneficiary to co-architect—from receiving space services to shaping space rules—promises a more pluralistic, representative, and ultimately more legitimate governance architecture. Whether this promise is fulfilled will depend on sustained investment in capacity-building, continued reduction in access barriers, and the willingness of established spacefaring powers to share governance authority as well as technical knowledge.

In the next chapter, we turn to one of the most transformative forces shaping space activity today: the commercialization of outer space and the legal challenges posed by private actors operating in a domain governed by state-centric international law.

***

End of Chapter 8

Chapter 9

COMMERCIALIZATION OF OUTER SPACE AND THE ROLE OF PRIVATE ACTORS

For most of the space age, governments designed, launched, and operated space systems. Today, private companies build rockets, deploy constellations of thousands of satellites, and plan missions to the Moon and Mars. This chapter examines how the commercialization of outer space has transformed the legal landscape—challenging state-centric frameworks, reshaping regulatory models, and raising fundamental questions about the governance of a domain where private ambition increasingly outpaces public authority.

Part 1

The Rise of Private Space Activity and Legal Transformation

For much of the twentieth century, space activity was the exclusive domain of states. Governments designed, launched, operated, and regulated space systems, viewing them as strategic assets closely tied to national security and scientific prestige. This state-centric model shaped the foundational treaties of international space law, which assume states as the primary—and often sole—actors in outer space. Over the past three decades, however, this model has undergone a profound transformation. Private actors have emerged not merely as contractors or service providers, but as central drivers of innovation, investment, and operational activity in space.

From State Monopoly to Commercial Ecosystem

The commercialization of space did not occur overnight. Early private involvement was largely limited to manufacturing satellites and launch vehicles under government contracts. Companies such as Hughes Aircraft, Lockheed Martin, and Boeing built hardware to government specifications and delivered it for government operation. The commercial role was subordinate: companies executed government-defined missions with government-provided funding, and risk—financial, technical, and legal—was borne overwhelmingly by the state.

The gradual liberalization of telecommunications markets in the 1970s and 1980s opened the first sustained commercial pathway into space. Satellite broadcasting, pioneered by companies such as Intelsat (initially an intergovernmental organization, later privatized) and SES, demonstrated that space could support viable commercial enterprises. Intelsat's transformation is particularly instructive: founded in 1964 as an intergovernmental consortium of over 140 countries, it was privatized in 2001 under pressure from the United States and commercial competitors who argued that its governmental status gave it unfair advantages. The privatization of Intelsat symbolized the broader transition from government-led to market-driven space activity, and it raised legal questions about the succession of international obligations from intergovernmental to private entities that remain relevant today. SES, originally established by the Luxembourg government, became Europe's leading commercial satellite operator and demonstrated that small states could leverage space activities for outsized economic impact.

Figure 20: Future Human Settlements and Commercial Activities in Outer Space

Source: Generated using OpenAI Sora.

Satellite communications became a multi-billion-dollar industry, creating the economic foundation for private investment in space infrastructure. By the early 2000s, commercial satellite services—television broadcasting, internet connectivity, maritime and aviation communications—generated annual revenues exceeding fifty billion dollars. Remote sensing followed a similar trajectory: initially a government monopoly through programs like Landsat (United States, 1972) and SPOT (France, 1986), commercial licensing of satellite imagery gradually created a market for private operators. The passage of the U.S. Land Remote Sensing Policy Act of 1992 authorized private companies to operate remote sensing satellites, leading to the emergence of companies such as DigitalGlobe (now Maxar), GeoEye, and eventually Planet Labs, which operates a constellation of over 200 small satellites providing daily global imagery at resolutions that were classified military capability a generation ago.

The commercialization of navigation services represents a third major pathway. While GPS remains a U.S. government system and its European (Galileo), Russian (GLONASS), and Chinese (BeiDou) counterparts are similarly government-operated, the downstream applications of satellite navigation—precision agriculture, autonomous vehicles, financial transaction timing, logistics optimization, location-based services—have created a commercial ecosystem worth hundreds of billions of dollars annually. This ecosystem depends on freely available government-provided signals, illustrating a distinctive model in which public investment creates the infrastructure for private value creation.

The twenty-first century accelerated this trend dramatically. The convergence of declining launch costs, miniaturization of satellite technology, advances in software and automation, and the entry of venture capital investment enabled new actors to pursue business models that governments and legacy aerospace companies had considered impractical. SpaceX's development of reusable launch vehicles—beginning with the Falcon 9's first stage landing in 2015—reduced launch costs by an order of magnitude and transformed the economic assumptions underlying the entire space industry. Today's space economy encompasses launch providers, satellite operators, data analytics firms, in-orbit service companies, space tourism operators, and prospective resource extraction ventures, with the global space economy valued at approximately 570 billion dollars in 2024.

SpaceX's trajectory illustrates the broader transformation. Founded in 2002 with the stated goal of reducing the cost of space transportation, the company progressed from a startup with three consecutive launch failures to the world's dominant commercial launch provider within two decades. By 2025, SpaceX was conducting over one hundred launches annually—more than all other launch providers combined—while simultaneously deploying the Starlink mega-constellation, developing the Starship super-heavy launch vehicle for lunar and Mars missions, and providing commercial crew transportation to the International Space Station. The company's vertically integrated model—designing, manufacturing, launching, and operating its own systems—broke the traditional division between launch providers and satellite operators, creating a new industrial paradigm that has forced competitors to restructure.

The NewSpace ecosystem extends far beyond launch services. Rocket Lab, founded in New Zealand and now publicly listed in the United States, provides dedicated small satellite launch services with its Electron rocket and has expanded into satellite manufacturing. Planet Labs operates a constellation of over 200 Earth observation satellites providing daily global imagery at a resolution that was classified military capability a generation ago. Spire Global operates a constellation of CubeSats providing weather data, maritime tracking, and aviation surveillance. Relativity Space and Impulse Space are developing next-generation launch vehicles using additive manufacturing. Axiom Space is building the world's first commercial space station. Astroscale is pioneering commercial debris removal services.

Space tourism—once dismissed as science fiction—has become a commercial reality, though still at an early stage. Blue Origin's New Shepard and Virgin Galactic's SpaceShipTwo have conducted suborbital flights carrying paying customers, while SpaceX has launched private orbital missions (Inspiration4 in 2021, Polaris Dawn in 2024). These activities raise novel regulatory questions about passenger safety, informed consent, liability for personal injury, and the applicability of consumer protection law to an activity conducted in outer space. Existing regulatory frameworks—designed for unmanned satellites and government astronauts—must be adapted to accommodate commercial passengers who are neither trained professionals nor government employees.

The financial architecture supporting commercial space activity has itself undergone transformation. Between 2019 and 2022, a wave of space companies—including Virgin Galactic, Rocket Lab, Planet Labs, Spire Global, BlackSky, and AST SpaceMobile—went public through Special Purpose Acquisition Companies (SPACs), raising billions of dollars from public markets. While many of these companies subsequently saw significant share price declines as market conditions changed and growth projections proved optimistic, the SPAC wave demonstrated that space companies could access public capital markets at a scale previously unavailable. Venture capital investment in space companies has averaged eight to ten billion dollars annually since 2020, supporting hundreds of startups across launch, satellite manufacturing, data analytics, and space infrastructure. This capital ecosystem—absent during the government-dominated era—has become a fundamental driver of commercial space innovation, enabling companies to take technological risks that traditional aerospace procurement models would not support.

> ■ **The Global Space Economy: Key Figures (2024)**
>
> Total global space economy: ~$570 billion (satellite services, ground equipment, manufacturing, launch).
>
> Government space budgets: ~$103 billion (of which US ~$62 billion).
>
> Commercial revenue: ~$400 billion (satellite TV, broadband, Earth observation, launch services).
>
> Active satellites in orbit: ~10,000 (up from ~1,000 in 2010).
>
> Annual orbital launches: ~200+ (up from ~70 in 2010).
>
> SpaceX market share: ~65% of global commercial launches by mass to orbit.
>
> Private investment in space companies: ~$8–10 billion annually (venture capital, private equity).

Legal Assumptions Under Strain

International space law was not designed with this level of private participation in mind. The Outer Space Treaty and related instruments assign responsibility and liability to states, even when activities are conducted by non-governmental entities. Article VI requires states to authorize and continually supervise private space activities; Article VII holds launching states liable for damage caused by space objects. These provisions remain legally sound—they have not been amended or superseded—but they place increasing pressure on domestic regulatory systems tasked with implementing international obligations in an environment of rapid commercial growth.

The strain is visible in multiple dimensions. First, the pace of commercial activity outstrips the pace of regulatory development. SpaceX deployed over 6,000 Starlink satellites in approximately four years; the regulatory frameworks governing constellation operations, spectrum coordination, debris mitigation, and orbital traffic management have not evolved at comparable speed. The FCC approved SpaceX's original 12,000-satellite constellation in 2018 and a modification for an additional 7,500 satellites in 2022, but the environmental review process, conjunction assessment procedures, and spectrum coordination mechanisms were designed for an era of dozens of satellites, not thousands. Second, the scale of private activity challenges state supervisory capacity. A licensing authority that once processed a handful of satellite applications per year may now face hundreds, each involving complex technical assessments and international coordination requirements. The FAA's Office of Commercial Space Transportation, responsible for licensing all U.S. commercial launches, has seen its caseload increase from fewer than twenty launches per year in 2015 to over a hundred by 2024, with staffing growth that has not kept pace.

Third, the diversity of commercial activities—from suborbital tourism to on-orbit servicing to in-space manufacturing to commercial space stations—exceeds the categories contemplated by existing regulatory frameworks, creating gaps that regulators must fill through interpretation, guidance, or new legislation. When Axiom Space proposed building a commercial module attached to the International Space Station as a precursor to a free-flying commercial station, no existing regulatory framework specifically addressed the authorization and supervision of commercial habitable structures in orbit. When Varda Space Industries launched a manufacturing capsule to produce pharmaceuticals in microgravity, the regulatory pathway for re-entering a capsule containing manufactured products required novel interpretation of existing reentry licensing requirements.

The fundamental question is not whether the state-centric framework remains valid—it does—but whether states can implement it effectively in a commercial environment that is larger, faster, more diverse, and more technically complex than anything the Treaty's drafters envisioned. The answer varies significantly by jurisdiction, depending on regulatory capacity, political priority, and the balance each state strikes between promoting commercial activity and fulfilling international obligations.

The Changing Role of the State

Commercialization has not diminished the role of the state in space governance; it has redefined it. States remain the indispensable actors in international space law: they authorize and supervise activities, they bear international responsibility and liability, they represent national interests in international forums, and they enforce compliance with treaty obligations. But their operational role has shifted from direct execution to regulation and facilitation. States increasingly function as enablers of private activity rather than as the primary operators of space systems.

The enabling function takes many forms. States invest in basic research that reduces technological risk for commercial ventures. They provide infrastructure—launch ranges, tracking networks, space situational awareness data—that private operators use but could not independently build. They serve as anchor customers, providing guaranteed demand that de-risks commercial investment (as NASA does through the Commercial Crew and CLPS programs). They negotiate international agreements—spectrum allocations, liability arrangements, launch safety standards—that create the legal environment within which commercial activity can occur. And they provide the regulatory framework that gives investors, insurers, and international partners confidence that private space activities are conducted safely and in compliance with international obligations. The state's role has thus evolved from operator to orchestrator—less visible but no less essential.

This shift has profound implications for governance capacity. When a state operates its own satellites, it possesses direct knowledge of mission parameters, operational status, and compliance with international obligations. When a state regulates thousands of private missions, it must rely on operators to provide information, comply with license conditions, and report anomalies—creating an inherent information asymmetry between regulator and regulated entity. The development of effective regulatory capacity—technical expertise, institutional resources, enforcement mechanisms—becomes critical to the functioning of the entire international legal framework.

Normative Implications of Commercialization

The rise of private actors challenges the normative foundations of space law in ways that extend beyond regulatory mechanics. The principle of non-appropriation—Article II's prohibition on national appropriation of outer space—was drafted to prevent Cold War sovereignty claims, but its application to commercial resource extraction and exclusive orbital utilization by private companies raises questions that the Treaty's drafters did not anticipate. The principle of benefit-sharing—Article I's declaration that space exploration shall be carried out for the benefit of all countries—sits uneasily with commercial models in which profits accrue to shareholders rather than to the international community. The principle of due regard—Article IX's obligation to avoid harmful interference with other states' activities—must be operationalized in an environment where thousands of commercial satellites create aggregate congestion risks that no individual operator intended or controls.

These normative tensions are not abstract. When a commercial mega-constellation operator deploys thousands of satellites into orbital bands shared with other states' assets, is the operator demonstrating "due regard" for other users? When a commercial remote sensing company sells high-resolution imagery of a developing country's territory to foreign intelligence services, is the activity conducted "for the benefit and in the interests of all countries"? When a space tourism company launches paying customers who accept personal risk, does the launching state's liability under the Liability Convention adequately protect involuntary risk-bearers on the ground? These questions illustrate how commercialization forces reinterpretation of principles that were drafted for a government-dominated space environment.

> *"The Outer Space Treaty's genius lies in making states permanently responsible for private space activities. Its challenge lies in making that responsibility operational when private activity exceeds what states can effectively supervise."*
>
> – On the regulatory challenge of commercialization

■ **Drivers of Space Commercialization**

Four reinforcing drivers have transformed space from a government domain to a commercial ecosystem: (1) Technological innovation, particularly reusable launch vehicles and satellite miniaturization, which reduced costs by orders of magnitude; (2) Market demand for connectivity, data, and services that created revenue streams to support private investment; (3) Policy shifts in which governments embraced private actors as partners rather than contractors; and (4) Capital markets that recognized space as a growth sector and provided the financing for entrepreneurial ventures. Together, these drivers have created a self-sustaining commercial ecosystem that now generates more economic value than government space programs.

***

Part 11

State Authorization, Supervision, and Regulatory Models

The rapid growth of private space activity has placed state authorization and supervision at the center of contemporary space governance. While international space law remains fundamentally state-centric, it accommodates private participation through a system in which states act as gatekeepers, regulators, and guarantors of compliance. How states design and implement domestic regulatory frameworks has therefore become one of the most consequential determinants of the commercial space environment—shaping not only the competitiveness of national industries but also the effectiveness of international legal obligations.

The Legal Foundation: Article VI in Practice

The legal foundation for state regulation of private space activities lies primarily in Article VI of the Outer Space Treaty, which provides that states bear international responsibility for national activities in outer space, including those carried out by non-governmental entities. As discussed in Chapter 6, this provision imposes two core obligations: authorization (approving activities before they occur) and continuing supervision (monitoring activities throughout their lifecycle). Article VI does not prescribe how these obligations must be fulfilled, granting states considerable discretion in designing domestic regulatory frameworks.

This discretion has produced remarkable diversity. As of 2025, over thirty states have enacted national space legislation, each reflecting different legal traditions, institutional structures, economic priorities, and levels of regulatory ambition. Some states have adopted comprehensive frameworks that consolidate all space-related regulation under a single authority. Others have distributed regulatory responsibility across multiple agencies, each addressing different aspects of space activity. Still others have adopted minimalist frameworks designed to attract commercial investment with the lightest possible regulatory burden.

The question of which state bears authorization and supervision responsibility for a given commercial activity is itself a matter of complexity. Article VI refers to "national activities" but does not define the concept. A satellite may be manufactured in one state, launched from the territory of a second, operated by a company incorporated in a third, and serving customers in dozens of others. Each of these states may have a jurisdictional claim under Article VI, creating potential for overlapping or—more problematically—insufficient regulatory coverage. The concept of the "appropriate state" for authorization and supervision has been the subject of extensive discussion within COPUOS, resulting in a set of recommendations (2013 General Assembly resolution) that encourage states to exercise jurisdiction based on their connection to the activity, but the recommendations are non-binding and leave the fundamental question unresolved.

Corporate structures further complicate jurisdictional determination. Commercial space companies frequently operate through subsidiaries, holding companies, and joint ventures that span multiple jurisdictions. A satellite operator may be incorporated in Luxembourg, managed from the United States, with ground stations in multiple countries and customers worldwide. Determining which state's regulatory authority should license and supervise such an activity requires analysis of corporate structure, operational control, and effective jurisdiction that may yield different answers depending on which state applies its own criteria. The absence of an international coordination mechanism for determining the "appropriate state" creates a risk that some activities may escape effective regulation entirely—falling between jurisdictions rather than being captured by any single national framework.

Jurisdiction	Primary Law	Regulatory Authority	Distinctive Features
United States	Commercial Space Launch Act (1984, amended)	FAA (launch), FCC (comms), NOAA (remote sensing), Commerce (SSA)	Multi-agency model; separate licensing for each activity type
United Kingdom	Space Industry Act 2018	Civil Aviation Authority (CAA)	Single licensing authority; horizontal regulation
France	Space Operations Act 2008 (Loi 2008-518)	CNES (technical), Ministry (licensing)	Mandatory debris mitigation; mandatory insurance; technical expertise

(contd.)

Luxembourg	Law on Space Resources 2017; Space Activities Act 2020	Luxembourg Space Agency	First European space resources law; investment-focused
UAE	Federal Law No. 12 of 2019	UAE Space Agency	Comprehensive; designed to attract international partnerships
New Zealand	Outer Space and High-altitude Activities Act 2017	Ministry of Business, Innovation & Employment	Permits foreign operators; includes environmental provisions
Australia	Space (Launches and Returns) Act 2018	Australian Space Agency	Risk-based approach; facilitates commercial launches from Australian territory

Models of National Regulation

Three broad regulatory models can be identified across jurisdictions. The comprehensive model consolidates space regulation under a single legislative framework and, ideally, a single regulatory authority. The United Kingdom's Space Industry Act 2018 exemplifies this approach, establishing the Civil Aviation Authority as the single licensing body for all space activities from UK territory or by UK nationals. The Act covers launch, orbital activities, suborbital operations, and spaceport licensing under a unified framework, creating regulatory clarity for operators and streamlining international coordination. The comprehensive model prioritizes regulatory coherence and simplicity, reducing compliance costs for operators while creating a clear point of contact for international coordination. The UK's choice to assign space regulation to the CAA—an established aviation regulator with decades of safety oversight experience—reflects a deliberate strategy of leveraging existing institutional capacity rather than building a new regulatory body from scratch.

The sector-specific model distributes regulatory responsibility across multiple agencies, each specializing in a particular aspect of space activity. The United States epitomizes this approach: the Federal Aviation Administration (FAA) licenses launches and reentries, the Federal Communications Commission (FCC) licenses satellite communications, the National Oceanic and Atmospheric Administration (NOAA) licenses commercial remote sensing, and the Department of Commerce is developing a role in space situational awareness and traffic management. This model leverages specialized expertise but creates coordination challenges, potential jurisdictional gaps, and compliance complexity for operators who must navigate multiple regulatory processes.

The U.S. model's jurisdictional gaps have generated significant regulatory debate. Activities that do not fit neatly into existing agency mandates—such as on-orbit servicing, in-space manufacturing, satellite refueling, and commercial space stations—may fall between regulatory jurisdictions. The "Mission Authorization" challenge—determining which agency has authority to license novel activities that are not launches, communications, or remote sensing—has been a recurring policy issue. The American Space Commerce Free Enterprise Act and subsequent legislative proposals have sought to address this gap by establishing the Department of Commerce as a catch-all licensing authority for activities not covered by existing agencies, but comprehensive legislation has not yet been enacted.

France's Space Operations Act of 2008 (Loi relative aux opérations spatiales) represents one of the most technically sophisticated national space laws, reflecting CNES's (Centre National d'Études Spatiales) deep engineering expertise. The Act requires operators to comply with detailed technical regulations covering launch safety, in-orbit operations, debris mitigation, and end-of-life disposal. Notably, the French framework mandates specific debris mitigation measures—including passivation of upper stages and post-mission disposal within twenty-five years—with the force of law, going beyond the voluntary character of international guidelines. France's approach demonstrates that national legislation can convert soft-law standards into binding legal requirements, potentially establishing precedents that influence international practice. The Act also includes a mandatory insurance requirement of sixty million euros and a government liability guarantee above the insured amount, creating a clear financial responsibility framework.

The facilitative or light-touch model minimizes regulatory burden to attract commercial investment. Luxembourg's approach—combining a space resources law (2017) with a general space activities act (2020)—is designed to position the country as a hub for commercial space enterprise, particularly in the emerging field of space resource utilization. New Zealand's framework, which permits foreign operators to launch from New Zealand territory under streamlined licensing procedures, similarly prioritizes market facilitation. These models raise questions about whether light-touch regulation provides sufficient oversight to meet Article VI's requirement of "continuing supervision"—particularly for novel activities where the risks are not yet fully understood.

Continuing Supervision in Practice

If authorization is the gateway to space activity, continuing supervision is the sustained obligation that gives Article VI its real force. Once a satellite is in orbit, its operational life may span fifteen to twenty-five years, during which circumstances change: the operator may be acquired, the mission may evolve, the orbital environment may become more congested, and new risks may emerge. Effective supervision requires regulators to monitor compliance throughout this lifecycle—a task that demands sustained technical expertise, access to operational data, and institutional continuity.

In practice, continuing supervision presents formidable challenges. Most licensing authorities have limited capacity for ongoing monitoring and rely heavily on operator self-reporting. License conditions may require periodic compliance certifications, notification of anomalies, and submission of operational data, but verification of these reports depends on technical capabilities that many regulators lack. The asymmetry of expertise between specialized commercial operators and generalist government regulators creates an inherent oversight gap—particularly for novel activities such as on-orbit servicing, in-space manufacturing, or autonomous collision avoidance where the regulator may have less technical knowledge than the regulated entity.

The challenge is compounded by the growing number and diversity of licensed activities. A regulator that effectively supervised a handful of government satellite missions may struggle to maintain equivalent oversight of hundreds of commercial missions with diverse orbital parameters, mission profiles, and operational practices. The United States' experience illustrates the scaling problem: the FCC's Satellite Division processes thousands of satellite applications and must coordinate spectrum assignments with international bodies, while the FAA's Office of Commercial Space Transportation must evaluate an increasing volume and variety of launch and reentry license applications with limited staffing growth.

Liability, Insurance, and Risk Internalization

Domestic regulatory frameworks play a crucial role in managing liability exposure arising from the Liability Convention's state-level liability architecture. Since international claims are directed at states rather than at private operators, domestic law must ensure that operators bear the financial consequences of damage they cause—internalizing risk that would otherwise fall on taxpayers. States typically accomplish this through mandatory insurance requirements, indemnification obligations, and financial responsibility provisions embedded in licensing conditions.

Insurance requirements vary significantly across jurisdictions. France's Space Operations Act requires operators to maintain insurance of at least sixty million euros—a fixed threshold that applies regardless of mission risk profile. The United States requires insurance covering the "maximum probable loss" as determined by the FAA for each specific launch—a risk-adjusted approach that calibrates requirements to actual hazards. The United Kingdom's framework requires operators to indemnify the government against liabilities arising from their activities, with insurance requirements determined on a case-by-case basis. These differences create inconsistent financial responsibility standards that contribute to the broader problem of regulatory fragmentation.

The space insurance market—concentrated in London, Paris, and Bermuda—provides the financial infrastructure that enables commercial space activity. Approximately thirty to forty specialist underwriters provide coverage for launch, in-orbit operations, and third-party liability, with annual premiums of roughly two to three billion dollars insuring tens of billions in total value. The market functions as a private-sector risk assessment and management mechanism: insurers evaluate mission parameters, operator track record, spacecraft design, and operational procedures before offering coverage, effectively creating a due diligence layer that supplements government licensing decisions.

Regulatory Arbitrage and the Race to the Bottom

The diversity of national regulatory approaches creates incentives for regulatory arbitrage—the practice of selecting jurisdictions with the most favorable regulatory conditions. A satellite operator seeking to minimize insurance costs, debris mitigation obligations, or licensing timeline may choose to register its activity in a jurisdiction with lower standards, even if its operational presence is elsewhere. This dynamic parallels flag-of-convenience practices in maritime law, where shipowners register vessels in states with lower safety and labor standards.

The analogy to maritime flag states is instructive but imperfect. In space law, the concept of "launching state" ties liability to the state from whose territory or facility a launch occurs and to the state that procures the launch—creating multiple jurisdictional hooks that are harder to evade than in maritime law. Nevertheless, the risk of regulatory arbitrage is real. If states compete for commercial business by reducing safety, insurance, or environmental standards below internationally accepted levels, the result could be a race to the bottom that undermines the collective safety and sustainability of the orbital environment.

Recent regulatory developments illustrate both the benefits and risks of national divergence. The FCC's September 2022 rule requiring LEO satellites to deorbit within five years of mission completion—replacing the earlier twenty-five-year guideline—represented a unilateral tightening of standards by the world's largest satellite licensing authority. This action raised the bar for operators licensed in the United States but had no direct effect on operators licensed elsewhere, potentially creating competitive disadvantages for U.S.-licensed operators who must invest in more capable propulsion systems to meet the shorter timeline. Conversely, states that have not adopted comparable requirements may attract operators seeking to avoid the cost of compliance—a dynamic that could undermine the FCC's environmental objectives.

Counteracting this risk requires establishing baseline international expectations—minimum standards for debris mitigation, insurance coverage, collision avoidance, and end-of-life disposal that all licensing states are expected to meet. The COPUOS Space Debris Mitigation Guidelines and Long-term Sustainability Guidelines provide the foundation for such baselines, but their voluntary character limits their effectiveness as constraints on regulatory competition. Converting these soft-law standards into universally observed regulatory minimums—whether through formal adoption, mutual recognition agreements, or market mechanisms such as insurance underwriting standards—remains an urgent governance priority.

"Regulatory competition between states can drive efficiency and innovation, but in a domain where one state's lax standards can create debris that threatens every other state's satellites, competition must be bounded by common baselines of safety and sustainability."

– On the limits of regulatory competition in space

***

Part III

Public–Private Partnerships and Risk Allocation

As private actors have become central to space activity, the relationship between governments and industry has evolved from traditional procurement contracting to sophisticated public–private partnerships (PPPs) characterized by shared objectives, distributed risk, and blurred boundaries between public and private roles. These partnerships now underpin many of the most ambitious space initiatives—from commercial crew transportation to lunar exploration—and they are fundamentally reshaping how responsibility, liability, and control are allocated within the existing legal framework.

Evolution of Government-Industry Relationships

The transformation of government-industry relationships in space can be traced through distinct phases. In the first phase (1950s–1980s), the relationship was hierarchical: governments defined missions, designed systems, and contracted with industry to build hardware to government specifications under cost-plus contracts that placed virtually all financial risk on the state. The Apollo program exemplified this model: NASA managed over 400,000 workers at twenty thousand companies, maintaining detailed control over every aspect of spacecraft design and manufacturing. Innovation occurred within government-defined parameters, and private industry served as an implementing agent rather than an independent strategic actor.

In the second phase (1980s–2000s), commercialization introduced market dynamics. The U.S. Commercial Space Launch Act of 1984 established the first regulatory framework for private launch services, signaling a policy shift toward enabling private activity alongside government programs. The privatization of Intelsat and Eutelsat transferred satellite communications from intergovernmental management to commercial operation. Governments began purchasing satellite communications, remote sensing data, and launch services from commercial providers rather than building systems themselves, shifting operational and financial risk to the private sector. This period also saw the first attempts at private launch ventures—including Orbital Sciences' Pegasus air-launched rocket—that demonstrated the viability of entrepreneurial approaches to space access.

In the third and current phase (2000s–present), the relationship has become genuinely collaborative: governments and private actors co-invest in capabilities, share technical risk, and jointly pursue objectives that neither could achieve independently. This phase is distinguished by a fundamental shift in design authority—from government-specified requirements to government-defined objectives with industry-led design solutions—and by the use of fixed-price contracts that create powerful incentives for cost discipline and innovation. The results have been transformative: capabilities that would have cost tens of billions under traditional procurement have been delivered for fractions of that amount, at faster timescales, and with technical innovations that government programs would not have pursued.

NASA's Commercial Orbital Transportation Services (COTS) program, initiated in 2006, represents the paradigmatic example of this third phase. Rather than contracting for a spacecraft designed to government specifications, NASA provided funded Space Act Agreements to SpaceX and Orbital Sciences (now Northrop Grumman Innovation Systems) to develop commercial cargo transportation to the International Space Station. NASA contributed funding and technical expertise; the companies contributed private capital, design authority, and operational responsibility. The program produced the Falcon 9/Dragon system and the Antares/Cygnus system at a fraction of the cost of traditional government procurement—NASA estimated that the COTS approach cost approximately one-tenth of what a traditional cost-plus contract would have required.

The Commercial Crew Program extended this model to human spaceflight. SpaceX's Crew Dragon and Boeing's Starliner were developed under fixed-price contracts with milestone-based payments, creating strong incentives for cost control and schedule discipline. NASA retained oversight authority and certification requirements—ensuring that safety standards were met—but delegated design decisions and operational responsibility to the private partners. This model demonstrated that public-private partnerships could deliver capabilities as demanding as human spaceflight while reducing costs and accelerating development timelines.

The Artemis program represents the most ambitious application of the PPP model to date. SpaceX's selection in 2021 to develop the Starship Human Landing System under a fixed-price contract of 2.89 billion dollars—subsequently supplemented by additional awards—delegates the development of a lunar landing vehicle to a private company, with NASA providing requirements, oversight, and astronaut crew. The Commercial Lunar Payload Services (CLPS) program contracts multiple small companies to deliver scientific instruments and technology demonstrations to the lunar surface at costs far below traditional government missions. These arrangements extend the PPP model beyond Earth orbit to deep space exploration, testing whether the efficiency gains demonstrated in low Earth orbit can be replicated in more demanding operational environments.

Cross-waiver agreements represent another critical mechanism for risk allocation in commercial space partnerships. Under a cross-waiver, each party to a space activity agrees to bear its own losses and waive claims against other parties, regardless of fault. This approach simplifies risk allocation by eliminating the need for complex fault determination and litigation. The ISS Intergovernmental Agreement's cross-waiver provision has served as a model for commercial launch agreements, public-private partnerships, and multi-party space missions. However, cross-waivers only operate among the contracting parties and do not affect the rights of third parties who suffer damage from a space activity—preserving the Liability Convention's protections for involuntary risk-bearers.

■ NASA's Public-Private Partnership Model

COTS Program (2006–2013): $800 million NASA investment leveraged $1.2 billion in private capital to develop two commercial cargo systems.

Commercial Crew (2014–2020): $6.8 billion total investment to develop two commercial crew vehicles, vs. estimated $25–40 billion under traditional procurement.

Artemis Human Landing System: SpaceX selected in 2021 to develop Starship lunar lander under fixed-price contract of $2.89 billion.

Commercial Lunar Payload Services (CLPS): Multiple small companies contracted to deliver payloads to the lunar surface at costs far below traditional government missions.

Model: NASA provides requirements, funding, technical expertise, and oversight; companies provide design authority, private capital, and operational responsibility.

Risk Allocation in Space PPPs

Risk allocation is the central design challenge in space PPPs. Excessive risk placed on private actors can deter investment, increase costs through risk premiums, and concentrate activity among only the largest and most financially robust companies. Excessive public assumption of risk undermines accountability, creates moral hazard, and may result in taxpayer exposure to losses that private actors should bear. Successful partnerships calibrate risk in line with each party's capacity to manage it.

Technical risk—the risk of hardware failure, software errors, or mission anomalies—is typically allocated to the private partner with specialized engineering expertise. Financial risk may be shared through milestone-based payments that release public funds only upon demonstrated performance, reducing government exposure to cost overruns while providing operators with cash flow tied to achievement. Political and regulatory risk—changes in government policy, budget priorities, or international obligations—remains with the state, which controls these variables. Legal risk, particularly international liability exposure under the Liability Convention, is addressed through insurance requirements and indemnification provisions in the partnership agreement.

European PPP models differ from the American approach in important respects. ESA's public-private partnerships have traditionally involved closer government control and larger public co-investment. The Copernicus Earth observation program, for example, is publicly funded but relies on private companies (primarily Airbus Defence and Space and Thales Alenia Space) for satellite design and manufacturing, with ESA retaining system architecture authority and operational control. The Galileo navigation system was originally conceived as a PPP with a private consortium responsible for deployment and operation, but the model was restructured after the private partners withdrew due to concerns about financial viability—a cautionary example of the limits of private risk appetite for infrastructure-scale space programs with uncertain revenue profiles.

The U.S. government's indemnification framework for commercial launches illustrates a specific risk-sharing arrangement that has enabled the commercial launch industry's growth. Under the Commercial Space Launch Act, as amended, the FAA requires licensed operators to obtain insurance covering the maximum probable loss from third-party damage, as calculated by the FAA for each specific launch. Above this insured amount—which typically ranges from tens of millions to several hundred million dollars depending on mission parameters—the U.S. government provides an additional layer of indemnification (currently up to approximately 3.2 billion dollars, adjusted for inflation). Above the government indemnification layer, the operator bears remaining liability. This three-tier structure—operator insurance, government indemnification, residual operator liability—distributes risk across multiple parties, ensuring that catastrophic losses do not fall entirely on any single actor while preserving private accountability. France, the United Kingdom, and other spacefaring states have adopted analogous tiered frameworks, though with different insurance thresholds and indemnification ceilings.

Accountability and Transparency

The growing reliance on PPPs raises important questions about accountability and transparency. When private actors perform functions traditionally associated with government—providing transportation to the International Space Station, developing lunar landing systems, operating national security launch services—public oversight becomes essential. The public interest in safety, sustainability, and compliance with international obligations does not diminish because a private company rather than a government agency executes the mission.

However, commercial confidentiality may limit transparency. Companies protect proprietary technical information, financial data, and business strategies from public disclosure. Government agencies may defer to these commercial interests, particularly when maintaining a cooperative relationship with a private partner is essential to achieving mission objectives. The result can be a transparency deficit that complicates public scrutiny, congressional oversight, and international confidence in compliance with treaty obligations. When SpaceX's Starlink constellation generates thousands of conjunction warnings per week, the conjunction assessment data, maneuver decisions, and collision avoidance algorithms are proprietary—creating a situation in which the world's largest satellite operator makes decisions affecting the orbital safety of all other operators based on information that is not publicly available or independently verifiable.

The concentration of commercial space activity among a small number of dominant companies creates additional governance challenges. SpaceX's market position—operating the majority of active satellites, conducting the majority of commercial launches, and developing the world's most powerful launch vehicle—gives it an influence over the space environment that exceeds that of most national space agencies. The dependence of governments—including the U.S. government, which relies on SpaceX for national security launches, crew transportation, and cargo delivery—creates leverage that can complicate regulatory enforcement. This concentration of capability and influence in a single private company is unprecedented in the history of space activity and raises questions about the adequacy of regulatory frameworks designed for a more competitive and diversified commercial landscape.

Ensuring accountability in PPP structures requires clear regulatory standards, mandatory reporting requirements, independent safety oversight, and mechanisms for public access to information about compliance and performance. The NASA Aerospace Safety Advisory Panel, which provides independent safety oversight of human spaceflight programs including commercial crew, exemplifies one approach. Regulatory frameworks that require operators to publish debris mitigation plans, conjunction assessment data, and end-of-life disposal strategies provide another mechanism for ensuring that private activity remains subject to public accountability.

■ **The PPP Paradox**

Public-private partnerships in space achieve extraordinary efficiencies—delivering capabilities faster and cheaper than traditional government procurement. But they also redistribute authority in ways that can weaken public oversight, complicate international accountability, and create dependencies that make governments vulnerable to the commercial decisions of their private partners. The challenge is to capture the benefits of partnership while preserving the public accountability that international space law demands.

***

Part IV

Regulatory Fragmentation, Harmonization, and Future Regulation

The commercialization of outer space has introduced unprecedented dynamism into space activities, but it has also exposed a structural weakness in the existing governance framework: regulatory fragmentation. As private actors operate across jurisdictions and states compete to attract investment, the absence of harmonized rules risks undermining safety, sustainability, and legal certainty. This final part examines the causes and consequences of fragmentation, assesses ongoing harmonization efforts, and considers future regulatory pathways.

Sources and Consequences of Fragmentation

Regulatory fragmentation arises primarily from the discretion granted to states under international space law. Article VI of the Outer Space Treaty requires authorization and supervision, but it does not prescribe uniform standards. States have therefore developed domestic regimes reflecting their own policy priorities, legal traditions, economic strategies, and institutional capacities. The resulting diversity—visible in licensing requirements, insurance thresholds, debris mitigation standards, spectrum coordination practices, and enforcement mechanisms—creates an uneven regulatory landscape across which commercial operators must navigate.

For commercial operators, these disparities create incentives for forum shopping: selecting jurisdictions with the most favorable regulatory conditions for a particular activity. While regulatory competition can drive efficiency and innovation, it also risks producing a race to the bottom in which states weaken safety and sustainability standards to attract business. The consequences extend beyond any single jurisdiction: space activities are inherently transboundary, and a satellite licensed under lax standards in one state can create debris that threatens satellites operated by every other state. The tragedy of the commons—in which individually rational behavior produces collectively harmful outcomes—is a persistent risk in an unharmonized regulatory environment.

Mega-constellations illustrate these challenges vividly. A constellation of 12,000 satellites licensed by the United States operates in orbital bands shared with satellites licensed by dozens of other states, each with different collision avoidance procedures, debris mitigation requirements, and frequency coordination practices. Without common standards, coordination becomes ad hoc, collision risk increases, and the collective sustainability of the orbital environment depends on the voluntary cooperation of operators who may have conflicting commercial interests.

Novel Activities and Regulatory Gaps

The rapid diversification of commercial space activities has created categories of activity that existing regulatory frameworks do not adequately address. On-orbit servicing—in which one spacecraft approaches, inspects, repairs, refuels, or repositions another—involves proximity operations that could be benign or hostile, collaborative or unilateral. No international framework distinguishes between a servicing mission and an ASAT approach, and most national licensing regimes lack specific provisions for authorizing and supervising close-approach operations. Northrop Grumman's Mission Extension Vehicle (MEV), which docked with Intelsat satellites to extend their operational lives, was licensed under existing frameworks through creative regulatory interpretation rather than purpose-built regulation.

In-space manufacturing—using microgravity conditions to produce materials, pharmaceuticals, or optical fibers that cannot be efficiently manufactured on Earth—raises questions about product liability, intellectual property jurisdiction, and the application of manufacturing safety standards in a domain governed by space law rather than domestic industrial regulation. Space-based solar power, though still developmental, would involve enormous orbital structures that affect other operators and ground-based populations. Satellite broadband mega-constellations raise questions about astronomical interference, light pollution, atmospheric effects of satellite re-entry, and the concentration of orbital capacity in the hands of a few commercial operators.

Each of these activities falls within the scope of Article VI's authorization and supervision requirements, but regulators must develop new expertise, new procedures, and often new legislation to address them effectively. The regulatory lag—the gap between the emergence of a new commercial activity and the development of an adequate regulatory framework—is a persistent feature of the commercial space environment. States must balance the need to regulate with the risk that premature or overly prescriptive regulation will stifle innovation, drive commercial activity to less regulated jurisdictions, or impose requirements that prove technically inappropriate as activities evolve.

Harmonization Through Soft Law

Recognizing the risks of fragmentation, the international community has pursued harmonization through soft-law instruments, industry standards, and institutional coordination. The COPUOS Space Debris Mitigation Guidelines (2007), the Long-term Sustainability Guidelines (2019), and the evolving discussions on space traffic management provide common reference points that states can incorporate into domestic regulation. While non-binding, these instruments promote convergence by articulating shared expectations of responsible behavior that inform national licensing decisions.

Industry-led standards play an increasingly important role. The International Organization for Standardization (ISO) has developed space-specific standards including ISO 24113 on space debris mitigation, which provides detailed technical guidance on passivation, post-mission disposal, and collision avoidance. The Consultative Committee for Space Data Systems (CCSDS) develops interoperability standards for space communications. Industry associations such as the Space Data Association coordinate conjunction assessment and spectrum management among commercial operators. These private-sector standards complement public regulation by providing the technical specificity that international soft-law instruments typically lack.

The environmental dimension of commercial space activity represents a growing harmonization challenge that existing frameworks have not fully addressed. The re-entry of thousands of mega-constellation satellites at the end of their operational lives—currently five to seven years for Starlink satellites—deposits aluminum oxide and other particulates into the upper atmosphere. Recent research suggests that the accumulated deposition from fleet replacement cycles—replacing thousands of satellites every five to seven years—could affect stratospheric chemistry, ozone concentrations, and Earth's albedo in ways that are not yet fully understood. No regulatory framework—national or international—currently requires environmental impact assessment for the atmospheric effects of satellite re-entry, and the intersection of space law (governing activities in outer space) with environmental law (governing atmospheric pollution) remains a governance gap that commercial activity is rapidly widening.

Astronomical interference from mega-constellations presents another regulatory challenge. The brightness of Starlink satellites in reflected sunlight has disrupted ground-based astronomical observations, particularly at twilight and dawn. The International Astronomical Union, professional astronomy organizations, and national observatories have raised concerns about the cumulative impact of tens of thousands of commercial satellites on scientific research. SpaceX has responded with design modifications (VisorSat, DarkSat) to reduce satellite brightness, and the ITU and COPUOS have begun discussing the issue, but no binding framework exists to require commercial operators to mitigate astronomical interference. The Dark and Quiet Skies initiative, supported by UNOOSA and the IAU, represents the most significant international effort to address this issue, but its recommendations remain voluntary.

The insurance market also functions as a harmonizing mechanism. Space insurers assess risk based on mission parameters, operator track record, and compliance with industry best practices. Operators that fail to meet widely accepted standards—such as the 25-year (or increasingly, 5-year) disposal guideline—may face higher premiums, restrictive coverage terms, or inability to obtain insurance at all. Since insurance is required by most licensing regimes, the insurance market effectively creates a private-sector enforcement mechanism for international standards—a market-based complement to public regulation. The London-based space insurance market, which underwrites the majority of global space risks, has developed sophisticated underwriting criteria that evaluate debris mitigation compliance, collision avoidance capability, and operational track record. These criteria effectively establish a market-defined standard of care that operators must meet to access affordable insurance—regardless of the regulatory requirements of their licensing jurisdiction.

> ■ **Harmonization Mechanisms for Commercial Space Activity**
>
> International soft law: COPUOS Debris Mitigation Guidelines, LTS Guidelines, UN General Assembly resolutions.
>
> ISO standards: ISO 24113 (debris mitigation), ISO 23312 (collision avoidance), ISO 16126 (disposal of satellites).
>
> Industry coordination: Space Data Association, CCSDS, Inter-Agency Space Debris Coordination Committee (IADC).
>
> Insurance market: Risk-based pricing creates market incentives for compliance with best practices.
>
> Mutual recognition: Bilateral/multilateral arrangements recognizing equivalent regulatory standards.
>
> Model legislation: COPUOS/UNOOSA guidance on essential elements of national space legislation.
>
> These mechanisms operate in parallel, creating a multi-layered harmonization framework that compensates for the absence of binding international regulation.

Limits of Voluntary Harmonization

Despite their value, voluntary harmonization efforts face significant limitations. Adoption is uneven: states with developed regulatory capacity and strong engagement with COPUOS are more likely to incorporate international guidelines into domestic law than states with minimal regulatory infrastructure. Compliance depends on national political will, which may fluctuate with changes in government, economic conditions, or competitive pressures. Soft law lacks formal enforcement mechanisms, and its influence may wane when compliance conflicts with commercial or strategic interests.

The absence of mandatory baselines means that the regulatory floor is set by the least demanding jurisdiction rather than by international consensus. An operator that finds one state's debris mitigation requirements too burdensome can seek licensing from a state with weaker standards—

and there is no international mechanism to prevent this. The result is a system in which the highest standards are voluntarily adopted by responsible actors, while the lowest standards are available to those who prioritize cost minimization over sustainability. This asymmetry rewards irresponsible behavior and penalizes responsible operators who invest in compliance.

The enforcement dimension adds further complexity. Even states with well-designed regulatory frameworks may lack the capacity or political will to enforce license conditions effectively. Sanctions for non-compliance—license revocation, financial penalties, denial of future licenses—exist in most national laws but are rarely applied in practice. The space industry's small size and close relationships between regulators and operators create incentives for accommodation rather than adversarial enforcement. Moreover, once a satellite is in orbit, the practical options for enforcement are limited: a licensing authority cannot physically retrieve a satellite that fails to comply with debris mitigation requirements, and financial penalties imposed after mission completion may be inadequate to change behavior during the mission.

The competitive dynamics of the commercial space market intensify these challenges. When states compete for launch business, satellite manufacturing contracts, and technology investment, regulatory standards become competitive instruments. A state that imposes strict debris mitigation requirements may lose business to a state with weaker standards, creating political pressure to relax regulations. This dynamic is analogous to corporate tax competition, in which states reduce tax rates to attract investment—but in the space domain, the externalities of weak regulation fall on the global commons rather than on national budgets. International coordination to establish minimum regulatory standards would address this problem, but it requires collective action among states with divergent interests and unequal regulatory capacities.

Future Regulatory Pathways

The future regulation of commercial space activity is likely to evolve incrementally rather than through comprehensive new treaties. Several pathways offer promise. Model laws and regulatory templates, developed through COPUOS and UNOOSA with input from states, industry, and academia, can guide national implementation and promote convergence without requiring states to accept binding international obligations. The COPUOS Legal Subcommittee's work on national legislation has already produced recommendations on essential elements that national space laws should include—authorization, supervision, registration, liability, insurance, and debris mitigation—that provide a common reference point even though adoption remains voluntary.

Mutual recognition arrangements, in which states with comparable regulatory standards agree to accept each other's licensing decisions, can reduce duplication while maintaining oversight quality. Such arrangements are common in aviation (bilateral aviation safety agreements) and telecommunications (mutual recognition of equipment certification) and could be adapted for space activities. Issue-specific agreements addressing space traffic management, active debris removal, or on-orbit servicing can develop detailed rules for specific activities without requiring comprehensive treaty negotiation—an approach that targets the areas of greatest urgency while avoiding the political obstacles that have stalled broader treaty-making efforts.

The most ambitious proposals envision an international space traffic management framework analogous to the international aviation system managed by ICAO. Such a framework would establish common rules for orbital operations—right of way, conjunction assessment, collision avoidance maneuvers, spectrum coordination, and end-of-life disposal—that all operators would be required to follow. The ICAO model is instructive: over decades, the aviation community developed Standards and Recommended Practices (SARPs) that states adopt into national law, creating a harmonized global regulatory environment that enables safe and efficient international air transport despite different national legal systems. A comparable framework for space traffic management would require agreement on orbital "rules of the road," a common data-sharing infrastructure for space situational awareness, and institutional capacity to coordinate operations among thousands of operators in real time.

The technical and political challenges of such a framework are enormous. Unlike aviation, where aircraft operate in defined airspace under active air traffic control, satellites operate in a three-dimensional orbital environment where physics determines trajectories and where there is no centralized authority directing traffic. Conjunction assessments are probabilistic rather than deterministic: they identify the likelihood of a close approach but cannot predict with certainty whether a collision will occur. Operators must make maneuver decisions based on incomplete information, under time pressure, with commercial costs associated with every propellant-expending maneuver. Politically, space traffic management touches on national security equities—military satellites, classified orbits, dual-use tracking data—that make states reluctant to accept international oversight of their space operations.

Intermediate steps toward space traffic management are already underway. The United States has designated the Department of Commerce as the lead agency for providing civil space situational awareness services, separating this function from the military's space surveillance mission. The European Union is developing its own Space Surveillance and Tracking (EU SST) capability. Japan's JAXA operates a Space Situational Awareness system. Commercial SSA providers—including LeoLabs, ExoAnalytic Solutions, and Slingshot Aerospace—provide tracking data and conjunction assessment services to operators worldwide. These distributed capabilities, if coordinated through appropriate institutional arrangements, could form the foundation for a global space traffic management framework even in the absence of a centralized international authority.

Whatever pathway is pursued, the fundamental principle will remain unchanged: states bear responsibility for the activities of their nationals in outer space. Effective governance depends not on replacing this principle but on strengthening its implementation through coordination, shared standards, and institutional support. Commercialization has transformed the operational landscape of space activity, but it has not—and cannot—transform the legal landscape's foundational architecture. The state remains the indispensable actor, the necessary intermediary between international obligation and private behavior, and the ultimate guarantor of safe and sustainable space activity.

The relationship between international obligation and domestic regulation will determine whether the state-centric framework succeeds in the commercial era. International space law imposes obligations on states; domestic law translates those obligations into requirements for private operators. If domestic law is well-designed, adequately resourced, and effectively enforced, the international framework functions as intended: private activity is conducted safely, sustainability is maintained, and liability for damage is appropriately allocated. If domestic law is weak, poorly enforced, or deliberately permissive, the international framework is undermined—not because its principles are flawed, but because its implementation fails. Strengthening domestic regulatory capacity is therefore not merely a national governance priority; it is an international legal imperative on which the entire architecture of space governance depends.

The commercial space revolution has generated extraordinary benefits: declining costs, expanding access, technological innovation, and new services that improve lives on Earth. It has also generated risks—orbital congestion, debris accumulation, regulatory fragmentation, concentration of market power, and environmental impacts—that require governance responses commensurate with the scale and pace of change. The legal frameworks examined in this chapter provide the tools for that governance, but their effectiveness depends on the political will, institutional capacity, and international cooperation that states bring to the task of implementing them.

> *"The challenge of governing commercial space is not to choose between freedom and regulation, but to design regulatory frameworks that enable innovation while preventing the irreversible degradation of the orbital environment on which all space activity depends."*
>
> – On the regulatory future of commercial space

***

Chapter Summary

Chapter 9 has traced the legal transformation driven by the commercialization of outer space, examining how the rise of private actors has reshaped the operational, regulatory, and institutional landscape of space governance.

The transformation documented in Part I is profound in both scale and kind. The space economy has grown from a government monopoly to a 570-billion-dollar commercial ecosystem in which private companies operate more satellites, conduct more launches, and generate more revenue than government programs. This transformation has strained—but not broken—the state-centric framework of international space law. Article VI's requirement that states authorize and supervise private activities remains the essential bridge between international obligation and commercial reality, but the bridge is under increasing load.

The regulatory models examined in Part II reveal the diversity of approaches that states have adopted to implement their international obligations. Comprehensive models prioritize coherence; sector-specific models leverage specialized expertise; facilitative models prioritize market attraction. Each involves trade-offs between safety, competitiveness, and legal certainty. The risk of regulatory arbitrage—operators selecting jurisdictions with the weakest standards—highlights the need for international baselines that prevent competition from undermining collective safety and sustainability.

The public-private partnerships examined in Part III demonstrate that commercialization has produced extraordinary efficiencies in space activity, delivering capabilities faster and cheaper than traditional government procurement. But PPPs also redistribute authority in ways that can complicate public oversight, create transparency deficits, and challenge the accountability mechanisms that international space law presupposes. Effective partnership requires clear regulatory standards, independent safety oversight, and mechanisms for ensuring that private activity serves public interests as well as commercial objectives.

The regulatory fragmentation examined in Part IV represents the most significant governance challenge arising from commercialization. In the absence of harmonized international standards, the safety and sustainability of the orbital environment depend on voluntary coordination among states with divergent regulatory approaches and competing economic interests. Soft law, industry standards, insurance mechanisms, and institutional coordination provide the tools for convergence, but their voluntary character limits their effectiveness. The environmental dimensions of commercial activity—atmospheric effects of satellite re-entry, astronomical interference, cumulative orbital congestion—add urgency to the harmonization imperative by demonstrating that the externalities of commercial space activity extend beyond the space domain into the terrestrial environment.

The development of internationally recognized regulatory baselines—through whatever combination of soft law, mutual recognition, model legislation, and institutional innovation proves politically feasible—is the central regulatory imperative of the commercial space era. The alternative is not a stable status quo but a progressively degrading orbital environment in which the cumulative effects of uncoordinated commercial activity undermine the sustainability of space operations for all actors. The commercial space industry's extraordinary dynamism has expanded humanity's access to space in ways that were unimaginable a generation ago; the governance challenge is to ensure that this expansion is sustainable, equitable, and consistent with the principles of international cooperation and shared benefit that have defined space law since its inception.

In the next chapter, we turn to a domain where commercialization intersects with some of the most fundamental principles of space law: space resources and utilization, and the contentious question of property rights beyond Earth.

***

End of Chapter 9

Chapter 10

SPACE RESOURCES, UTILIZATION, AND THE FUTURE OF PROPERTY RIGHTS IN OUTER SPACE

Who owns the resources of outer space? This question—once the province of science fiction—has become one of the most consequential legal debates of our time. As states and private companies develop the capability to extract water, minerals, and metals from the Moon, asteroids, and Mars, the ambiguities at the heart of international space law are being tested as never before. This chapter examines the legal status of space resources, the rise of national resource legislation, the Artemis Accords' approach to emerging norms, and the equity and sustainability challenges that will shape the governance of extraterrestrial resources for generations to come.

Part 1

Legal Status of Space Resources Under International Law

The question of who may use, own, or profit from resources found beyond Earth lies at the heart of contemporary space law. As technological advances transform space resource utilization from theoretical possibility to near-term reality, long-standing legal principles are being tested in ways their drafters could scarcely have anticipated. International space law offers foundational guidance, but it does so through principles marked by deliberate ambiguity—reflecting political compromise rather than detailed regulation.

From Exploration to Utilization

Early space law was shaped by exploration rather than exploitation. During the 1960s and 1970s, the focus lay on preventing sovereignty claims, militarization, and conflict in a domain that the superpowers were entering with extraordinary speed and minimal precedent. Resource extraction was discussed primarily in speculative terms, often framed as a distant future concern requiring no immediate legal attention. As a result, the foundational treaties addressed access, non-appropriation, and peaceful use, but they did not address the ownership of extracted materials in any detail.

This historical context explains why the Outer Space Treaty remains largely silent on many issues central to today's debates. The law was designed to keep space open and peaceful—to prevent the Cold War from extending into orbit and to ensure that no state could claim celestial territory as its sovereign domain. It was not designed to regulate commercial mining, industrial processing, or the commercial sale of extraterrestrial materials. The transition from exploration to utilization therefore poses challenges that the existing legal framework can address only through interpretation, supplementation, and the gradual development of new norms.

The transition is not merely legal but economic. For decades, space resources were of theoretical interest only—the subject of academic papers and speculative business plans but not of serious commercial investment. The economics of space resource extraction depend on the cost of access to space, which has declined dramatically with the advent of reusable launch vehicles. When launch costs were ten thousand dollars per kilogram to low Earth orbit, the economic case for resource extraction was marginal at best. At one to two thousand dollars per kilogram—the approximate cost achieved by SpaceX's Falcon 9—the economics begin to shift. At the hundreds of dollars per kilogram that Starship targets, resource extraction for in-space use becomes potentially viable. This cost trajectory has transformed space resources from a legal curiosity into a governance imperative within the span of a decade.

The resources at stake are both diverse and potentially transformative. Lunar regolith contains water ice—concentrated in permanently shadowed craters at the lunar poles—that could be electrolyzed into hydrogen and oxygen for rocket propellant, creating in-space refueling capabilities that would dramatically reduce the cost of deep space missions. NASA's Lunar Flashlight and various orbital radar instruments have confirmed the presence of water ice in concentrations potentially sufficient for extraction, and the Artemis III and subsequent missions plan to characterize these deposits in detail. Near-Earth asteroids contain platinum-group metals, iron, nickel, and cobalt in concentrations that dwarf terrestrial deposits. A single metallic asteroid one kilometer in diameter could contain more platinum than has been mined in all of human history—though the economics of returning such materials to Earth remain prohibitive at current launch costs.

The more immediate economic case for asteroid resources lies not in Earth return but in in-space utilization. Water extracted from carbonaceous asteroids could be processed into propellant for spacecraft operating between Earth and Mars, creating "gas stations in space" that fundamentally reshape the economics of interplanetary transportation. Metals from asteroids could be used for in-space construction, reducing the mass that must be launched from Earth. Lunar helium-3, though its energy applications remain speculative and dependent on the development of viable fusion power, has been identified as a potential fuel for future fusion reactors. Mars's subsurface water ice and atmospheric carbon dioxide could support future human habitation through in-situ resource utilization (ISRU)—the production of breathable air, water, and propellant from local materials rather than transporting them from Earth at a cost of thousands of dollars per kilogram.

Article II and the Principle of Non-Appropriation

Article II of the Outer Space Treaty provides that outer space, including the Moon and other celestial bodies, is not subject to national appropriation "by claim of sovereignty, by means of use or occupation, or by any other means." This provision is the cornerstone of space property law and one of the most widely cited—and most diversely interpreted—articles in the entire corpus of international space law. The provision's drafting history reveals that it was negotiated relatively quickly during the Treaty's preparation in 1966–1967, building on the non-appropriation principle already established in the 1963 Declaration of Legal Principles Governing the Activities of States in the Exploration and Use of Outer Space.

The scholarly debate over Article II's scope has produced an extensive literature. Manfred Lachs, the distinguished Polish jurist who served as judge on the International Court of Justice, argued that the non-appropriation principle should be interpreted broadly to encompass any form of exclusive control over celestial body resources. Bin Cheng, another foundational figure in space law, suggested a narrower reading focused on territorial sovereignty. More recent scholars, including Frans von der Dunk and Fabio Tronchetti, have explored the middle ground—arguing that Article II prohibits sovereignty and territorial claims but does not necessarily prohibit property rights over extracted materials, provided that extraction is conducted in accordance with other Treaty obligations.

The scope of Article II is both broad and deliberately open-ended. It clearly prohibits territorial claims and sovereign ownership of celestial bodies: no state may declare the Moon, Mars, or any asteroid to be its sovereign territory, and no state may exclude others from accessing these bodies. At the same time, Article II does not explicitly address private ownership of materials extracted from celestial bodies. This omission has given rise to two fundamentally divergent interpretations that define the contemporary legal debate.

> ■ **The Non-Appropriation Principle: Article II of the Outer Space Treaty**
>
> "Outer space, including the Moon and other celestial bodies, is not subject to national appropriation by claim of sovereignty, by means of use or occupation, or by any other means."
>
> This provision prohibits territorial sovereignty but does not explicitly address ownership of extracted resources—an ambiguity that drives the central legal debate over space resource utilization.

One interpretation holds that any assertion of ownership over space resources constitutes appropriation by another name, undermining the Treaty's core principle. Under this view, the prohibition on appropriation "by any other means" is broad enough to encompass not only territorial claims but also the assertion of property rights over materials derived from celestial bodies. Proponents of this interpretation often point to the language's breadth and to the Treaty's underlying purpose of preventing the extension of national power into outer space. If states or their nationals can claim exclusive ownership of extracted resources, the argument runs, the prohibition on appropriation is hollow—because the economically valuable component of celestial bodies (their resources) can be privatized even if the territory itself cannot.

The opposing interpretation distinguishes between ownership of territory and ownership of materials removed from that territory. Under this view—which has gained significant support among spacefaring states—Article II prohibits sovereignty over celestial bodies but does not prohibit ownership of resources that have been extracted through lawful activity. Proponents analogize space resources to fish caught on the high seas: no state may claim sovereignty over the ocean, yet fish lawfully caught become the property of the fisher. Similarly, minerals lawfully extracted from an asteroid become the property of the entity that extracted them, without any claim to the asteroid itself. This interpretation treats resource utilization as an exercise of the freedom of use guaranteed under Article I rather than an act of appropriation prohibited by Article II.

The high seas analogy is influential but imperfect. In the law of the sea, the right to fish on the high seas is explicitly provided for in the UN Convention on the Law of the Sea (Article 87) and is subject to conservation obligations and regional fisheries management agreements. No comparable explicit authorization exists in space law for resource extraction, and no comparable management framework governs the sustainability of extraterrestrial resource use. Moreover, the deep seabed mining regime—established by Part XI of UNCLOS and administered by the International Seabed Authority—provides a contrasting model in which resources in areas beyond national jurisdiction are subject to collective governance and benefit-sharing rather than free appropriation. The deep seabed precedent suggests that the "fishing" analogy may be too permissive: it assumes a regime of free access that the international community has explicitly rejected in the closely analogous context of deep seabed mineral resources.

The distinction between the deep seabed and outer space regimes is partly historical. The deep seabed regime was negotiated during the same 1970s era that produced the Moon Agreement, when developing states had sufficient political leverage to insist on collective governance structures. The Moon Agreement's common heritage provision reflects the same normative impulse. But whereas UNCLOS attracted near-universal ratification (including eventual U.S. acceptance of a modified Part XI), the Moon Agreement failed to secure the participation of spacefaring states. The result is a governance gap: the most closely analogous international precedent (deep seabed mining) favors collective governance, but the applicable legal instrument (the Outer Space Treaty) is ambiguous, and the instrument that would have resolved the ambiguity (the Moon Agreement) lacks the ratification needed for broad legal effect.

Freedom of Use and Its Limits

Article I of the Outer Space Treaty guarantees freedom of exploration and use of outer space by all states. Proponents of resource utilization argue that extraction constitutes a legitimate form of "use" provided it does not involve sovereignty claims or territorial exclusion. According to this interpretation, resource utilization is lawful so long as it respects the due regard, cooperation, and non-interference obligations established by the Treaty's other provisions.

Critics caution that unchecked extraction risks transforming freedom of use into de facto appropriation, particularly if technologically advanced actors monopolize access to valuable sites. Without regulatory constraints, freedom may entrench inequality rather than promote shared benefit—a concern that echoes the equity debates discussed in Chapter 8. The concentration of resource activity at specific locations—such as the permanently shadowed craters at the lunar south pole, where water ice deposits are concentrated—could create de facto exclusive zones even without formal territorial claims, particularly if the first mover establishes infrastructure that physically prevents or discourages others from operating in the same area.

The lunar south pole concentration problem is particularly acute because the resource targets are geographically limited. Unlike terrestrial mining, where mineral deposits are distributed across vast continental areas, lunar water ice is concentrated in a small number of permanently shadowed craters within a few degrees of the south pole. The total area of permanently shadowed terrain at the lunar south pole is estimated at approximately 13,000 square kilometers—roughly the size of Montenegro—but the areas with confirmed high ice concentrations are far smaller. If the first operators to establish extraction facilities at these sites can effectively exclude competitors through safety zones, infrastructure placement, or operational interference, the result could be a first-come, first-served allocation of the Moon's most valuable resource—an outcome that many states would view as inconsistent with the Outer Space Treaty's principle of exploration for the benefit of all countries.

The due regard obligation of Article IX provides an important constraint. States must conduct their activities "with due regard to the corresponding interests of all other States Parties." In the resource context, this requires that extraction activities not unduly interfere with other states' ability to access and use the same celestial body. However, the practical application of "due regard" to resource extraction—at what point does one state's mining operation interfere with another's access?—raises questions for which no authoritative answers yet exist.

Common Heritage of Mankind Revisited

The Moon Agreement of 1979 represents the most explicit attempt to regulate space resources under international law. By designating the Moon and its natural resources as the "common heritage of mankind," the Agreement sought to prevent unilateral exploitation and ensure equitable benefit-sharing through an international regime that would govern resource extraction once it became feasible. Article 11 provides that the Moon's natural resources "in place" shall not become the property of any state, organization, or natural person, and envisions an international authority to manage exploitation and distribute benefits equitably.

The Moon Agreement's failure to attract major spacefaring states' ratification—with only eighteen parties as of 2025, none of them leading space powers—severely limits its direct legal impact. The United States, Russia, China, India, Japan, and European Space Agency member states have all declined to ratify, citing concerns about the common heritage principle's perceived threat to commercial incentives and technological innovation. As a result, the Agreement's provisions do not bind the states most likely to conduct resource activities.

Nevertheless, the common heritage concept retains significant normative influence. It has shaped the vocabulary and expectations of space governance debates, informing discussions within COPUOS and influencing the positions of developing states that view unilateral resource exploitation as inconsistent with the inclusive spirit of the Outer Space Treaty. The Hague International Space Resources Governance Working Group, a multistakeholder initiative that operated from 2016 to 2019, produced Building Blocks for the Development of an International Framework on Space Resource Activities that explicitly engaged with common heritage concerns while seeking to bridge the gap between states favoring permissive resource regimes and those advocating collective governance. The Building Blocks proposed principles including adaptive governance, respect for existing international law, benefit-sharing, and environmental protection that have influenced subsequent COPUOS discussions. The tension between common heritage and commercial exploitation—between collective ownership and individual initiative—remains one of the defining fault lines of space resource governance.

■ **Key Legal Principles Governing Space Resources**

Non-appropriation (Art. II OST): No state may claim sovereignty over celestial bodies or outer space by any means.

Freedom of use (Art. I OST): All states have the right to explore and use outer space freely.

Benefit-sharing (Art. I OST): Exploration shall be carried out for the benefit of all countries.

Due regard (Art. IX OST): Activities must not unduly interfere with other states' interests.

Common heritage (Art. 11 Moon Agreement): Moon's resources are the common heritage of mankind (limited ratification).

State responsibility (Art. VI OST): States must authorize and supervise national resource activities.

Customary Law and Interpretive Evolution

In the absence of clear treaty rules on extracted resource ownership, attention has turned to customary international law and interpretive practice. State statements, national legislation, multilateral agreements, and operational practice all contribute to an evolving understanding of what space law permits. The Apollo precedent is frequently invoked: when the United States returned lunar samples to Earth during the Apollo missions (1969–1972), no state objected to American possession and use of those materials. Similarly, the Soviet Luna missions returned lunar samples without international protest. These precedents suggest that at least limited extraction and appropriation of space resources has been accepted in practice, though the scale of contemplated commercial extraction far exceeds anything the Apollo-era actors envisioned.

Whether a customary norm recognizing ownership of extracted resources will crystallize depends on the consistency and breadth of state practice and the extent to which that practice is accompanied by opinio juris—the belief that the practice is required or permitted by law. At present, practice is concentrated among a handful of technologically advanced states, and opinio juris is contested by states that favor multilateral solutions. The legal landscape is therefore best characterized as transitional: a new norm may be emerging, but it has not yet achieved the universality and consistency required for full customary status.

The speed at which custom can form in international law is itself debated. Traditional doctrine requires extensive and virtually uniform practice over a substantial period. However, the International Court of Justice recognized in the North Sea Continental Shelf cases that custom can form relatively rapidly if practice is extensive and uniform and is accompanied by clear opinio juris. The proliferation of national resource legislation and the Artemis Accords' growing membership suggest rapid accumulation of practice, but the absence of major spacefaring states from this consensus—particularly Russia and China—and the vocal dissent of some developing countries undermine claims of universality. The formation of customary law on space resources is therefore likely to be a prolonged, contested process rather than a rapid crystallization.

■ **Legal Ambiguity as Deliberate Strategy**

The ambiguity surrounding space resources is not merely a legal deficiency; it reflects a deliberate strategy of deferral. By postponing definitive answers, early space law preserved cooperation in an era of geopolitical tension. The Treaty's drafters chose broad principles over detailed rules, preferring to leave future generations the flexibility to adapt the law to circumstances that could not be foreseen. Today, that ambiguity enables innovation but also generates contestation—precisely the dynamic the drafters sought to avoid but could not permanently prevent.

***

Part 11

National Space Resource Laws and Unilateral Interpretation

As international space law has remained deliberately ambiguous on the question of resource ownership, several states have moved to clarify their positions through national legislation. These unilateral legal developments represent one of the most significant—and most controversial—evolutions in contemporary space governance. By asserting that the extraction and ownership of space resources are lawful under international law, states are actively shaping interpretive practice and testing the limits of the non-appropriation principle.

The United States: Commercial Space Launch Competitiveness Act

The United States became the first state to enact space resource legislation with Title IV of the Commercial Space Launch Competitiveness Act (CSLCA), signed into law on November 25, 2015. The Act provides that "a United States citizen engaged in commercial recovery of an asteroid resource or a space resource" shall be "entitled to any asteroid resource or space resource obtained, including to possess, own, transport, use, and sell the asteroid resource or space resource." The legislation includes an explicit disclaimer that it does not constitute a claim of sovereignty, and it affirms U.S. obligations under the Outer Space Treaty.

The CSLCA's legal reasoning rests on the distinction between territorial appropriation and resource ownership. By declaring that resource extraction is consistent with U.S. obligations under the Outer Space Treaty, the legislation advances the interpretation that Article II's prohibition on national appropriation does not extend to extracted materials. The Act does not establish a licensing regime specifically for resource extraction; rather, it provides a legal guarantee that the fruits of lawful commercial activity will be recognized as private property under U.S. law.

The CSLCA's adoption generated immediate international reaction. Some commentators praised it as a necessary clarification that would encourage commercial investment in space resource activities. Others criticized it as a unilateral reinterpretation of a multilateral treaty—an assertion of national policy preferences disguised as legal interpretation. The Brazilian delegate to COPUOS described the legislation as potentially inconsistent with the Outer Space Treaty, while Russia expressed concern about unilateral action outside multilateral channels. Belgium's representative raised questions about the legislation's compatibility with international law, and several developing country delegations expressed concern about the precedent of unilateral norm-creation. No state, however, filed a formal legal protest or initiated dispute resolution proceedings—a silence that itself contributes to the interpretive landscape.

The CSLCA's legislative history reveals the domestic dynamics that shaped it. The Act emerged from lobbying by the nascent asteroid mining industry, particularly companies such as Planetary Resources and Deep Space Industries (neither of which ultimately survived as resource-focused enterprises), which argued that legal uncertainty about resource ownership deterred the investment needed to develop extraction technology. Congressional supporters framed the legislation as promoting American commercial competitiveness and technological leadership while remaining consistent with international obligations. The Act's bipartisan passage—with minimal floor debate—reflected a political consensus that the United States should actively shape the legal environment for space resource activities rather than waiting for international consensus to emerge.

Luxembourg, UAE, and Other National Approaches

Luxembourg became the second state to adopt space resource legislation, enacting a comprehensive law on the exploration and use of space resources in July 2017. Luxembourg's approach was explicitly commercial: the legislation was part of a broader SpaceResources.lu initiative launched in 2016, which included a dedicated fund of 200 million euros to support companies engaged in space resource exploration and utilization. The government established Luxembourg as an alternative to the United States for companies seeking a regulatory environment favorable to resource activities, successfully attracting ispace Europe, Planetary Resources (before its acquisition), and other companies to establish operations in the Grand Duchy. The law provides that space resources are capable of being owned and establishes a licensing framework under which companies authorized by Luxembourg may conduct resource activities. Notably, Luxembourg's law is more permissive than the CSLCA in one important respect: it does not require the operator to be a Luxembourg citizen, only that the company be authorized under Luxembourg law—a provision designed to attract international companies.

Japan followed in 2021 with the Act on Promotion of Business Activities Related to the Exploration and Development of Space Resources, reflecting Japan's growing ambitions in lunar exploration. The Act recognizes property rights over extracted space resources and establishes a permitting framework administered by the government. Japan's legislation was closely linked to its partnership with the United States through the Artemis Accords and its contributions to the Artemis program, including the development of the pressurized lunar rover and various scientific instruments for lunar missions. The Japanese company ispace—which attempted the first commercial lunar landing in 2023 with its Hakuto-R mission—is among the companies that benefit from the legal certainty provided by Japan's resource legislation.

The United Arab Emirates enacted its Federal Decree-Law on the Regulation of the Space Sector (2020), which includes provisions addressing space resource activities as part of a comprehensive space law framework. The UAE's approach reflects its broader strategy of positioning the country as a leading space nation, complementing its Mars exploration program (the Hope mission), its astronaut program, and its growing satellite manufacturing capabilities. India's draft Space Activities Bill has included resource-related provisions, though as of 2025 comprehensive legislation has not yet been enacted. Several other states—including Belgium, Greece, Saudi Arabia, and the Czech Republic—have signaled interest in developing resource-specific legislation or have included resource provisions in broader space law frameworks.

Jurisdiction	Legislation	Year	Key Features
United States	CSLCA Title IV	2015	Property rights for US citizens; no sovereignty claim; no specific licensing regime
Luxembourg	Law on Space Resources	2017	Property rights; licensing framework; investment promotion strategy
Japan	Space Resources Act	2021	Permitting framework; property rights recognition; business promotion
UAE	Federal Decree-Law on Space Sector	2020	Comprehensive space law including resource provisions
Artemis Accords signatories	Bilateral agreements	2020–	Affirm resource extraction consistent with OST; 40+ signatories
Moon Agreement parties	Moon Agreement Art. 11	1979	Common heritage; international regime envisioned; 18 parties only

Common Legal Reasoning and Strategic Objectives

National space resource laws share several common features despite their jurisdictional diversity. Each explicitly affirms compliance with international law, particularly the Outer Space Treaty. Each recognizes property rights over extracted resources while disclaiming any claim of territorial sovereignty. Each establishes or contemplates a licensing and supervision framework consistent with Article VI obligations. And each is motivated, at least in part, by the strategic objective of attracting commercial investment by providing legal certainty for private actors.

The shared legal reasoning underlying these laws—that non-appropriation of celestial bodies does not prohibit ownership of extracted resources—draws on the high seas analogy and on the Apollo/Luna precedents discussed in Part I. This reasoning has been described as an exercise in "coordinated unilateralism": multiple states independently arriving at the same legal interpretation and codifying it in national law, creating a convergent pattern of practice that may influence the development of customary international law.

The strategic dimension should not be understated. For Luxembourg, a small European state with no indigenous launch capability, space resource legislation is primarily an instrument of economic policy—a means of attracting high-technology companies and positioning the country at the forefront of an emerging industry, much as Luxembourg used favorable financial regulation to become a leading center for European investment fund management. For the United States, the CSLCA reflects a broader commitment to commercial space development and a policy judgment that legal certainty is necessary to mobilize the private investment that resource exploitation will require. For Japan, resource legislation serves both its Artemis partnership objectives and its domestic ambition to develop a competitive space industry that can compete with American and European firms. For the UAE, resource provisions within its comprehensive space law signal the country's transformation from a space newcomer to a serious player in the emerging lunar economy, complementing its Mars exploration achievements and its plans for lunar rover missions.

The coordination among these states—while not formally orchestrated—is visible in the consistent legal reasoning, the temporal clustering of legislation, and the alignment with the Artemis Accords framework. Whether this coordination constitutes evidence of a genuinely shared legal conviction (opinio juris) or merely parallel strategic positioning is a question that international lawyers will debate for years. The answer has significant implications for the formation of customary international law: if coordinated legislation reflects genuine legal conviction, it strengthens the case for an emerging norm; if it reflects strategic convenience, its normative weight is diminished.

Legal Controversies and International Reactions

Unilateral space resource laws have generated significant debate within international forums. Critics raise several substantive concerns. First, they argue that national legislation erodes the non-appropriation principle through economic control: even if territorial sovereignty is formally disclaimed, the assertion of property rights over extracted resources creates exclusive economic entitlements that are functionally indistinguishable from appropriation. Second, critics contend that unilateral legislation marginalizes developing states by establishing interpretive precedents that favor technologically advanced actors without multilateral consultation or consent. Third, opponents warn that national legislation fragments space governance by creating parallel domestic regimes that may conflict with each other or with future international agreements.

The absence of formal legal challenges to national resource legislation is significant but ambiguous. It may reflect tacit acquiescence—a silent acceptance that resource extraction is consistent with international law. Alternatively, it may reflect political caution: states may disagree with the legislation but choose not to challenge it diplomatically or legally for reasons unrelated to their legal assessment. The persistent objector doctrine in customary international law allows states that consistently and publicly oppose an emerging norm to exempt themselves from its application—

but this requires affirmative objection, not mere silence. The current landscape of partial support, partial silence, and partial criticism complicates the assessment of whether a customary norm is forming.

Regulatory Fragmentation and Coordination Challenges

The proliferation of national space resource laws risks creating a fragmented regulatory environment in which different jurisdictions impose different requirements for authorization, environmental protection, benefit-sharing, and dispute resolution. A company authorized to extract resources under U.S. law operates under different conditions than one authorized under Luxembourg law, and neither framework addresses the interaction between competing operations at the same site or the relationship between resource activities conducted under different national jurisdictions.

Fragmentation creates both practical and normative challenges. Practically, it complicates coordination at sites where multiple operators may seek to exploit the same deposits. If a U.S.-licensed company and a Luxembourg-licensed company both seek to extract water ice from the same permanently shadowed crater, no international mechanism exists to allocate access, resolve disputes, or coordinate operations. The Artemis Accords' safety zone concept provides a partial answer for Accords signatories, but it does not apply to non-signatories and lacks binding enforcement mechanisms even among participants.

Normatively, fragmentation undermines the universality of space law. If different states apply different interpretations of the Outer Space Treaty to resource activities—with some recognizing property rights and others rejecting them—the Treaty's function as a universal framework for space governance is weakened. The risk is not merely legal uncertainty but the erosion of the cooperative ethos that has sustained space governance since 1967. Addressing fragmentation requires either convergence of national approaches (potentially through multilateral guidelines) or coordination mechanisms that manage divergence without requiring uniformity.

> *"National space resource laws represent a calculated gamble: that unilateral assertion of property rights, if sufficiently widespread and consistent, will establish the customary international law that multilateral negotiation has been unable to produce."*
>
> – On the strategy of coordinated unilateralism

***

Part III

The Artemis Accords and Evolving International Practice

As national space resource laws redefined expectations at the domestic level, a parallel development emerged on the international stage: the Artemis Accords. Announced in 2020 in connection with the United States–led Artemis lunar program, the Accords represent a novel governance instrument—neither a treaty nor a purely political declaration, but a plurilateral framework designed to shape state practice through shared principles and operational norms. Their significance for space resource governance extends far beyond their immediate operational content.

Origins and Objectives

The Artemis Accords were conceived against a backdrop of renewed global interest in lunar exploration and resource utilization. NASA's Artemis program aims to return humans to the Moon and establish a sustained presence, with resource utilization—particularly the extraction of water ice for propellant production—as a central element of mission architecture. Unlike the Apollo program, which was a national demonstration of technological capability, Artemis is designed as a multinational, commercially supported endeavor requiring cooperative frameworks that the existing treaty regime does not provide in operational detail. The program envisions a lunar Gateway orbital station, surface habitation systems, rovers, and ISRU infrastructure that will support continuous human and robotic operations at the lunar south pole.

The Accords were negotiated bilaterally between the United States and individual partner states, bypassing the multilateral, consensus-based process of COPUOS. This approach was deliberate: it allowed rapid adoption of operational principles among like-minded states without the delays and compromises inherent in multilateral negotiation involving over 100 COPUOS member states. The bilateral structure also gave the United States significant influence over the Accords' content, framing the normative landscape in terms consistent with American legal interpretations and policy objectives. By 2025, over forty states had signed the Accords, including traditional U.S. allies (United Kingdom, Japan, Canada, Australia, South Korea), emerging space nations (UAE, Nigeria, Rwanda, Bahrain, Colombia), and several European states (France, Italy, Spain, Poland, Romania). China's and Russia's absence from the Accords is the most significant gap, creating a bifurcated governance landscape for lunar activity.

Resource Utilization and Safety Zones

Section 10 of the Artemis Accords addresses space resource extraction directly, affirming that "the extraction of space resources does not inherently constitute national appropriation under the Outer Space Treaty." This provision aligns with the legal reasoning of national resource legislation, extending it to a plurilateral context. By including this affirmation, the Accords create a coordinated expression of state practice that strengthens the interpretive foundation for resource property rights.

The concept of "safety zones" introduced in Section 11 has attracted particular attention and controversy. Safety zones are described as areas around operations where coordination is needed to avoid harmful interference. Signatories commit to providing notification of their activities and the extent of safety zones, and to respecting other signatories' safety zones. The Accords emphasize that safety zones are coordination mechanisms rather than territorial claims and that they should be temporary, proportionate, and consistent with the Outer Space Treaty.

Critics argue that safety zones risk becoming de facto exclusion areas, particularly if established around resource-rich sites such as the permanently shadowed craters at the lunar south pole where water ice deposits are concentrated. If the first state to establish operations at a particular location designates a safety zone that physically or operationally prevents others from accessing the same area, the distinction between coordination and appropriation becomes difficult to maintain. The practical implementation of safety zones—their size, duration, enforcement, and relationship to other operators' activities—will determine whether they function as legitimate coordination tools or as instruments of de facto territorial control.

The concern is not hypothetical. The lunar south pole's water ice deposits are concentrated in a relatively small number of permanently shadowed craters, primarily in the Shackleton, Haworth, Faustini, and Cabeus crater regions. NASA's Artemis III landing site selection has focused on the Shackleton crater rim and the connecting ridge to de Gerlache crater—the same areas of greatest scientific and resource interest. If the United States establishes extensive safety zones around its initial operations in this region, the practical effect could be to limit other states' access to the most valuable resource sites, regardless of the Accords' formal disclaimer of territorial claims.

Proponents respond that safety zones are no different from safety exclusion areas around terrestrial industrial operations—necessary measures to protect personnel, equipment, and mission integrity that do not imply ownership of the surrounding territory. They note that the Accords require safety zones to be temporary, proportionate to the activity, and periodically reviewed—features designed to prevent their transformation into permanent exclusion areas. The resolution of this debate will depend on operational practice: how safety zones are defined, how broadly they extend, how long they persist, and whether they are applied in a manner that genuinely accommodates other states' access rights.

■ Key Provisions of the Artemis Accords

Section 1: Affirms commitment to peaceful purposes and the Outer Space Treaty.

Section 3: Transparency – signatories commit to sharing information about policies and plans.

Section 5: Registration – commitment to register space objects consistent with the Registration Convention.

Section 9: Preservation of heritage – protection of historically significant sites (e.g., Apollo landing sites).

Section 10: Space resources – extraction does not inherently constitute national appropriation.

Section 11: Safety zones – notification and coordination to prevent harmful interference.

Section 12: Orbital debris – commitment to debris mitigation consistent with guidelines.

Non-binding, implemented through bilateral arrangements; 40+ signatories as of 2025.

International Reception: Support and Criticism

The reception of the Artemis Accords has been divided along lines that reflect both geopolitical alignment and differing conceptions of legitimate governance. Supporters view the Accords as a pragmatic framework that operationalizes existing space law principles and enables collaborative lunar exploration. For emerging space nations that have signed—including the UAE, Nigeria, Colombia, and Rwanda—the Accords offer partnership opportunities, technology access, and a seat at the table of lunar governance that COPUOS deliberations have not provided.

Critics raise several objections. Russia and China—both planning independent or collaborative lunar programs—have declined to join, arguing that the Accords were negotiated outside the United Nations system and reflect American rather than universal interests. Roscosmos Director Dmitry Rogozin described the Accords in 2020 as an effort to establish an American-centric framework for lunar governance, comparing the bilateral approach to NATO's expansion—a politically charged comparison that signaled deep opposition. Chinese officials have expressed similar concerns through diplomatic channels and COPUOS deliberations, emphasizing the importance of multilateral consensus in developing rules for celestial body activities.

Some developing countries view the Accords as an attempt by spacefaring states to establish rules of the road for lunar activity that favor their interests before the broader international community has had an opportunity to participate in norm development. The fact that the Accords were largely finalized before being presented to potential signatories—rather than being co-developed through inclusive negotiation—reinforces concerns about the legitimacy of their norm-setting function.

Legal scholars have questioned whether a bilateral instrument negotiated by the United States can legitimately shape the interpretation of a multilateral treaty to which all COPUOS members are party. Others counter that the Accords are merely an expression of how signatory states understand their existing obligations—no different in principle from any other form of subsequent practice relevant to treaty interpretation under the Vienna Convention on the Law of Treaties.

The COPUOS Legal Subcommittee's Working Group on the Legal Aspects of Space Resource Activities, established in 2022, represents the multilateral response to the Accords and to national resource legislation. The Working Group's mandate is to develop a framework of principles for space resource activities—potentially a set of guidelines or principles that could complement or compete with the Artemis Accords' provisions. The Working Group operates under the consensus rule that governs all COPUOS deliberations, meaning that any member state can effectively block outcomes that it considers adverse to its interests.

The Working Group's deliberations reflect the broader geopolitical fault lines of space resource governance. The United States and its Artemis Accords partners advocate principles that affirm the lawfulness of resource extraction and property rights, consistent with their national legislation. Russia and China—which are pursuing their own International Lunar Research Station (ILRS) partnership—advocate a more cautious approach that preserves the possibility of collective governance mechanisms. Many developing states emphasize benefit-sharing, equity, and inclusive participation as essential elements of any framework. Whether this multilateral process will produce results that influence the trajectory of resource governance, or whether the Accords' growing membership will establish the dominant normative framework before COPUOS reaches consensus, remains one of the most consequential open questions in contemporary space law.

The Russia-China ILRS initiative represents an alternative governance trajectory that may develop principles different from those of the Artemis Accords. Announced in 2021, the ILRS envisions a permanent lunar research station developed jointly by Russia and China, with invitations extended to other partners. As of 2025, the ILRS has attracted expressions of interest from several states, including Pakistan, Belarus, South Africa, and Venezuela. While the ILRS framework has not yet articulated detailed resource governance principles, its development outside the Artemis partnership suggests that lunar governance may bifurcate into competing normative frameworks—each with its own member states, principles, and operational practices—rather than converging toward a single universal regime.

The Accords as State Practice

From the perspective of customary international law formation, the Artemis Accords' significance lies in their contribution to state practice and opinio juris. Over forty states have explicitly articulated their understanding that space resource extraction is consistent with the Outer Space Treaty—a significant accumulation of interpretive practice that strengthens the case for an emerging customary norm. Each signature represents a state-level endorsement of the proposition that non-appropriation does not prohibit resource ownership.

At the same time, the existence of vocal dissent—particularly from Russia and China, which together account for a substantial portion of global space activity—prevents the immediate consolidation of a universal norm. The Accords thus operate in a contested legal space: they advance one vision of space resource governance while provoking debate over alternatives. The outcome of this contest will depend not only on the number of signatories but on the operational practice that follows—whether and how states actually conduct resource activities, establish safety zones, and share benefits from extraction.

The temporal dimension of norm formation is significant. As of 2025, no state or company has conducted commercial resource extraction on a celestial body. The Artemis Accords' resource provisions are therefore anticipatory: they establish principles for activities that have not yet occurred. Once actual extraction begins—likely in the late 2020s or early 2030s with lunar water ice experiments—the legal significance of state practice will increase dramatically. How the first resource operators conduct their activities, how other states respond, and whether disputes arise at contested sites will determine whether the Accords' principles are validated by practice or challenged by operational reality. The transition from anticipatory norm-setting to operational implementation will be a defining moment for space resource law.

■ **The Accords as Norm-Setting Instrument**

The Artemis Accords represent a new mode of international norm development: pragmatic, operational, and coalition-based rather than universal and treaty-driven. Their significance lies not in their legal binding force—they have none—but in their capacity to coordinate state practice around a particular interpretation of existing law. If the Accords' provisions become the operational standard for lunar activity, they may establish customary norms regardless of their formal non-binding status. This represents a fundamental shift in how international space law develops—from top-down treaty negotiation to bottom-up practice consolidation.

***

Part IV

Equity, Sustainability, and Future Governance Pathways

The accelerating pursuit of space resource utilization has transformed long-standing legal ambiguities into pressing governance challenges. While national legislation and plurilateral initiatives such as the Artemis Accords have advanced practical frameworks for resource activity, they have also intensified concerns about equity, environmental sustainability, and long-term governance. The future of space resource law will depend on how these competing imperatives are reconciled.

Equity and Access in Resource Utilization

At the heart of the resource governance debate lies the question of who benefits from space resources. Technologically advanced states and well-capitalized private actors are best positioned to exploit extraterrestrial materials. The companies developing lunar landers, asteroid mining technology, and ISRU systems—SpaceX, Blue Origin, ispace, AstroForge, Intuitive Machines, Astrobotic—are based in the United States, Japan, and other advanced economies. Without corrective mechanisms, early movers may secure disproportionate advantages—access to the most favorable sites, establishment of infrastructure that creates barriers to entry, and accumulation of technical knowledge that widens rather than narrows the participation gap.

The economics of space resource utilization reinforce equity concerns. The initial investment required for resource extraction is enormous: developing a lunar mining system capable of extracting and processing water ice requires billions of dollars in launch systems, landing technology, excavation equipment, processing facilities, and storage infrastructure. Only states and companies with access to substantial capital can participate as developers. The revenues from space resources—whether from selling propellant to other operators, providing consumables to lunar habitats, or eventually returning materials to Earth—will flow initially to these investors and their home states. The question is whether market forces alone will distribute benefits broadly or whether deliberate governance mechanisms are needed to ensure that the global community shares in the returns from resources that international law designates as open to all.

The International Seabed Authority (ISA) provides the closest institutional precedent for collective governance of resource exploitation in areas beyond national jurisdiction. Under UNCLOS Part XI, the ISA regulates deep seabed mining in the "Area" (the seabed beyond national jurisdiction), requiring mining contractors to share financial benefits with the international community, to transfer technology to the Authority's mining arm (the Enterprise), and to reserve mining sites for developing country use. While the ISA model has been criticized for bureaucratic complexity, slow progress, and environmental concerns, it demonstrates that institutional mechanisms for benefit-sharing in global commons resource exploitation are technically and politically feasible. The question is whether a comparable mechanism—adapted to the unique characteristics of celestial body resource exploitation—is politically achievable in the space domain.

Equity does not necessarily require equal outcomes. No credible proposal envisions requiring that every state receive an equal share of lunar water ice or asteroid metals. But the principle that space exploration shall be carried out "for the benefit and in the interests of all countries"—enshrined in Article I of the Outer Space Treaty—creates a legitimate expectation that resource activities will not exclusively benefit those who conduct them. Translating this principle into operational terms remains a central challenge, particularly because the Article I language is aspirational rather than prescriptive: it does not specify how benefits should be shared, what form benefits should take, or who bears the obligation to ensure sharing occurs. Potential approaches include open access to scientific data derived from resource activities, shared infrastructure at lunar sites that any authorized operator can use, capacity-building programs linked to resource missions that train developing country scientists and engineers, and voluntary contribution mechanisms through which resource operators support development programs benefiting the broader international community.

The COPUOS Working Group on Space Resource Activities provides the most important multilateral forum for addressing equity concerns. If the Working Group produces guidelines or principles that include benefit-sharing provisions—even non-binding ones—these could establish normative expectations that influence state practice and commercial behavior. The challenge is to develop benefit-sharing mechanisms that are meaningful enough to address equity concerns without being so onerous that they deter the commercial investment needed to make resource utilization economically viable.

Environmental Sustainability and Planetary Stewardship

Resource extraction inevitably alters the environments in which it occurs. On celestial bodies, these environments are scientifically valuable and potentially unique. The permanently shadowed craters at the lunar south pole—the primary targets for water ice extraction—are also sites of extraordinary scientific interest, preserving a four-billion-year record of the inner solar system's bombardment history in their pristine regolith. Extraction activities that disturb these deposits before they are scientifically characterized would represent an irreversible loss of knowledge.

International space law contains only limited environmental provisions applicable to celestial body resource activities. Article IX of the Outer Space Treaty requires states to avoid "harmful contamination" of celestial bodies and "adverse changes in the environment of the Earth resulting from the introduction of extraterrestrial matter." These provisions were designed primarily to address biological contamination—the risk that terrestrial microorganisms might compromise the search for extraterrestrial life, or that extraterrestrial materials might introduce hazards to Earth's biosphere. They were not designed to regulate the large-scale physical alteration of celestial body surfaces through mining, excavation, or industrial processing.

The concept of planetary stewardship—the idea that humanity has an ethical and legal obligation to protect extraterrestrial environments from irreversible degradation—provides a normative framework for addressing this gap. While not yet codified in binding law, planetary stewardship draws on principles of intergenerational equity and environmental precaution that are well-established in terrestrial environmental law. Operational expressions of planetary stewardship might include environmental impact assessments for resource activities, designation of protected scientific sites (analogous to terrestrial nature reserves), limits on surface disturbance, contamination prevention requirements, and phased development approaches that prioritize scientific characterization before industrial exploitation.

Heritage site protection represents a related but distinct concern. The Apollo landing sites, with their footprints, artifacts, and scientific instruments, hold extraordinary historical and cultural significance—they are the only places beyond Earth where humans have walked. The Artemis Accords include a commitment to preserving heritage sites (Section 9), and NASA has published recommendations for protecting Apollo landing sites from disturbance by future missions. However, no binding international framework governs heritage protection on celestial bodies, and the legal basis for excluding other operators from areas surrounding heritage sites is uncertain under the non-appropriation principle. The protection of culturally and scientifically significant sites on the Moon and other celestial bodies—from the Apollo landing areas to Curiosity's tracks on Mars—will require governance mechanisms that balance preservation with the freedom of access that space law guarantees.

The ISRU Challenge: In-Situ Resource Utilization and Legal Frameworks

In-situ resource utilization represents the most technically ambitious and legally novel form of space resource activity. ISRU involves processing extraterrestrial materials at their point of origin—extracting water from lunar regolith, producing oxygen from Mars's carbon dioxide atmosphere, or manufacturing construction materials from asteroid metals. Unlike the extraction and return of samples (as in the Apollo missions), ISRU contemplates sustained industrial operations on celestial body surfaces—operations that will require infrastructure, energy systems, waste management, and continuous access to resource deposits.

The legal framework for ISRU is largely undefined. Existing space law addresses the extraction and ownership of resources but provides no guidance on the regulatory framework for industrial operations on celestial bodies. Questions that will require resolution include the authorization and supervision of ISRU facilities under Article VI, the liability regime for damage caused by industrial operations to other states' facilities or personnel, the environmental standards applicable to surface operations, the coordination of competing claims to the same resource deposits, and the governance of shared infrastructure (such as power systems or transportation networks) that may serve multiple operators at a single site.

NASA's MOXIE experiment on the Perseverance rover, which successfully produced oxygen from the Martian atmosphere in 2021, demonstrated the technical feasibility of ISRU at a small scale. The experiment generated approximately ten grams of oxygen per hour—a tiny amount, but a proof of concept that validated the chemistry and engineering needed for larger-scale operations. Multiple lunar lander missions planned for the late 2020s include ISRU demonstration payloads designed to test water ice extraction techniques, including NASA's VIPER rover (Volatiles Investigating Polar Exploration Rover), which will map water ice distribution and test drilling techniques at the lunar south pole. As these demonstrations progress toward operational systems, the need for legal frameworks governing industrial activities on celestial bodies will become increasingly urgent.

ISRU also raises novel questions about the relationship between resource extraction and the prohibition on national appropriation. Continuous extraction from a fixed site requires continuous access to and control over that site—a form of occupation that, while not involving sovereignty claims, creates exclusive physical presence that may be difficult to distinguish from the "occupation" that Article II prohibits as a means of appropriation. The longer an ISRU operation continues at a particular site, and the more infrastructure it accumulates, the more its physical presence resembles permanent occupation. Whether Article II's prohibition on appropriation "by means of use or occupation" applies to sustained industrial operations—as opposed to temporary scientific missions—is a question that will require resolution as ISRU moves from demonstration to production scale.

Governance Beyond Unilateralism: Future Pathways

The current trajectory of space resource governance is characterized by incremental unilateralism tempered by coordination among like-minded states through instruments such as the Artemis Accords. While this approach has enabled rapid progress and provided legal certainty for early commercial activities, it risks entrenching fragmentation and exclusion if left unchecked. Long-term stability will likely require multilateral accommodation, even if comprehensive treaties remain politically infeasible in the near term.

Several governance pathways are under active consideration. The COPUOS Working Group on Space Resource Activities could produce multilateral guidelines or principles that complement national legislation and the Artemis Accords, providing a universal reference point that reflects the interests of the broader international community. The Working Group's 2024 progress report identified areas of convergence among member states—including agreement that space resource activities should be conducted in accordance with international law, that transparency and information-sharing are essential, and that benefit-sharing warrants further discussion—alongside areas of persistent disagreement over the scope of property rights and the role of international institutions.

Issue-specific agreements could address particular challenges—such as the governance of water ice extraction at the lunar south pole—without requiring comprehensive regime development. A "lunar south pole coordination agreement" that established access procedures, notification requirements, environmental protections, and dispute resolution mechanisms for the most contested resource site could be negotiated more rapidly and with greater specificity than a comprehensive resource governance treaty. International registries or notification mechanisms for resource operations could enhance transparency and reduce the risk of conflict by ensuring that all states have visibility into planned resource activities, even if they do not participate in those activities directly.

Benefit-sharing frameworks, modeled on precedents from the law of the sea (the International Seabed Authority) or biodiversity (the Nagoya Protocol on access and benefit-sharing), could operationalize the equity principles of the Outer Space Treaty. A resource benefit-sharing mechanism need not replicate the ISA's institutional complexity: it could be as simple as a voluntary contribution fund, financed by resource operators, that supports capacity-building and space access programs for developing countries. Such a mechanism would address equity concerns while minimizing the regulatory burden on commercial operators—potentially securing broader international acceptance for resource activities than unilateral legislation alone can achieve.

The most promising approach may be layered governance: a combination of treaty principles, national regulation, soft-law guidelines, plurilateral coordination, and industry practice that collectively create a functional governance framework without requiring a single comprehensive instrument. This approach acknowledges political realities—the improbability of a new binding treaty, the irreversibility of national legislation already enacted, and the need for operational flexibility as technology evolves. It also recognizes that effective governance in a complex domain rarely emerges from a single source but rather from the interaction of multiple normative layers that reinforce and check each other.

A layered governance framework for space resources might include: the Outer Space Treaty's foundational principles (non-appropriation, freedom of use, benefit-sharing, due regard) as the constitutional layer; COPUOS guidelines on resource activities as the multilateral soft-law layer; the Artemis Accords and similar plurilateral frameworks as the operational coordination layer; national legislation as the domestic implementation layer; industry standards and best practices as the technical layer; and bilateral or site-specific agreements as the conflict resolution layer. Each layer serves a different function and operates at a different scale, but together they create a governance architecture that is more resilient, adaptive, and inclusive than any single instrument could be.

> *"Space resource governance will not be defined by a single treaty or doctrine. It will emerge through layered governance—combining foundational treaty principles, national regulation, soft-law guidelines, and operational practice into a functional framework that balances innovation with equity and sustainability."*

– On the future architecture of space resource law

Space Resources and the Evolution of Space Law

Space resource utilization represents a turning point in the evolution of international space law. It challenges the field to move beyond foundational principles—non-appropriation, freedom of use, benefit-sharing—toward detailed governance of complex commercial and industrial activities that the Treaty's drafters could not have anticipated. The transition from exploration to utilization tests whether a legal framework designed to keep space open and peaceful can also govern the economic exploitation of extraterrestrial resources in a manner that is equitable, sustainable, and consistent with the interests of all countries.

How the international community responds to this challenge will shape not only economic opportunity but also humanity's ethical and legal relationship with outer space. The choices made in the coming decade—in national legislatures, in COPUOS, in the Artemis partnership, and in the operational practice of resource companies—will establish precedents that endure for generations. The stakes extend beyond commercial profit or legal technicality: they concern the fundamental question of whether outer space will be developed in a manner that reflects the shared aspirations of all humankind or the interests of those few states and companies with the technological capability to get there first.

***

Chapter Summary

Chapter 10 has examined the legal status of space resources, the rise of national resource legislation, the Artemis Accords' approach to emerging norms, and the equity and sustainability challenges that will define the governance of extraterrestrial resources.

Part I established the foundational legal framework, tracing the tension between the non-appropriation principle of Article II and the freedom of use guaranteed by Article I. The divergent interpretations of these provisions—one viewing resource extraction as prohibited appropriation, the other treating it as lawful use analogous to fishing on the high seas—define the parameters of the contemporary debate. The Moon Agreement's common heritage principle, while not binding on major spacefaring states, continues to shape normative expectations and equity discourse.

Part II examined the national space resource laws adopted by the United States, Luxembourg, Japan, the UAE, and others. These laws share a common legal reasoning—that non-appropriation of celestial bodies does not prohibit ownership of extracted resources—and a common strategic objective of providing legal certainty for commercial investment. Their coordinated adoption constitutes a significant accumulation of state practice that may contribute to the formation of customary international law, though the absence of universal acceptance and the persistence of dissenting views complicate this trajectory.

Part III analyzed the Artemis Accords as a novel governance instrument that combines resource utilization principles with operational norms for lunar activity. The Accords' growing membership—over forty states—strengthens the interpretive practice supporting resource property rights, while the concept of safety zones raises concerns about de facto exclusion at resource-rich sites. The COPUOS Working Group on Space Resource Activities represents the multilateral response to these developments and may produce guidelines that complement or challenge the Accords' framework.

Part IV addressed the equity, sustainability, and governance challenges that space resource utilization presents. The concentration of resource capability among a few states and companies creates risks of entrenched inequality that the benefit-sharing principles of the Outer Space Treaty were intended to prevent. Environmental sustainability requires frameworks that do not yet exist for managing the physical alteration of celestial body surfaces. The most promising governance pathway is layered governance—combining treaties, national law, soft-law guidelines, plurilateral coordination, and industry practice—that provides functional regulation without requiring political consensus that does not presently exist.

In the next chapter, we turn to the environmental dimensions of space activity closer to home: space debris, orbital sustainability, and the emerging concept of space traffic management.

***

End of Chapter 10

Part IV
CONTEMPORARY CHALLENGES, CYBERSECURITY AND ARTIFICIAL INTELLIGENCE

Chapter 11

ENVIRONMENTAL PROTECTION, SUSTAINABILITY, AND SPACE TRAFFIC MANAGEMENT

Outer space was once perceived as vast, empty, and essentially limitless. That perception no longer holds. Orbital regions essential for communications, navigation, and Earth observation are congested, contested, and increasingly fragile. Tens of thousands of satellites share orbits with millions of debris fragments, any of which can destroy critical infrastructure in a microsecond. This chapter examines how the international community has responded to the environmental challenge of space—through debris mitigation, sustainability frameworks, and the emerging concept of space traffic management—and asks whether existing governance mechanisms are adequate for an era of unprecedented orbital activity.

Part 1

Space as an Environment: Legal Recognition and Emerging Risks

For much of the space age, outer space was treated primarily as a strategic and technological domain, not as an environment requiring protection. Early legal frameworks focused on preventing conflict, allocating responsibility, and enabling exploration. Environmental considerations were secondary, largely confined to avoiding biological contamination of celestial bodies and preventing immediate physical harm. As space activity expands in scale and intensity, this perspective is no longer adequate. Outer space is increasingly understood as a shared, finite, and vulnerable environment, requiring deliberate legal and institutional protection.

Reconceptualizing Outer Space as an Environment

The notion of "environment" in international law traditionally evokes terrestrial ecosystems—oceans, atmosphere, forests, and polar regions. Outer space was long excluded from this conceptual framework, perceived as vast, empty, and resilient to human activity. This perception shaped early governance, which emphasized freedom of use and technological progress without significant constraints related to environmental impact.

Today, this assumption has been fundamentally challenged. Orbital regions essential for communication, navigation, and Earth observation are limited and congested. Low Earth orbit (LEO)—the shell between approximately 200 and 2,000 kilometers altitude—hosts the vast majority of operational satellites, the International Space Station, and the densest concentrations of debris. Certain altitude bands within LEO, particularly those around 800 to 850 kilometers, are already critically congested, with debris density high enough that cascading collisions could render these altitudes increasingly hazardous for decades. The geostationary orbit (GEO), at approximately 35,786 kilometers, functions as irreplaceable infrastructure for telecommunications, broadcasting, and weather observation. These orbital regions are not boundless frontiers; they are finite, shared resources whose degradation has tangible consequences for economic development, security, scientific research, and the daily lives of billions of people who depend on satellite services.

Recognizing outer space as an environment does not imply treating it identically to terrestrial ecosystems. Orbital space lacks biological life, and its "degradation" takes the form of congestion, debris accumulation, and interference rather than pollution, habitat loss, or species extinction. Rather, environmental recognition acknowledges that space activities produce cumulative effects that can impair long-term usability, requiring stewardship rather than unchecked exploitation.

The geostationary orbit provides a particularly clear illustration of orbital space as a finite resource. GEO is a unique orbital position where a satellite's orbital period matches Earth's rotation, allowing it to remain stationary relative to a point on the ground—an irreplaceable characteristic for telecommunications broadcasting, weather observation, and early warning systems. The GEO belt can accommodate only a limited number of satellites before electromagnetic interference between adjacent systems becomes unacceptable. The International Telecommunication Union (ITU) manages GEO orbital slot allocations through a coordination process that, in effect, treats GEO positions as a shared resource requiring collective management—one of the few examples of functional resource management in space governance. The ITU's experience with GEO allocation offers lessons for the broader challenge of managing LEO congestion, though the technical characteristics of the two domains differ significantly.

Early Legal Foundations for Environmental Protection

International space law contains implicit environmental obligations, even if it lacks comprehensive environmental regulation. Article IX of the Outer Space Treaty requires states to conduct activities "with due regard to the corresponding interests of all other States Parties" and to avoid "harmful contamination" of celestial bodies and "adverse changes in the environment of the Earth resulting from the introduction of extraterrestrial matter." These provisions reflect early awareness of environmental risk, particularly in the context of planetary protection—the risk that terrestrial microorganisms might compromise the search for extraterrestrial life.

The Liability Convention contributes indirectly to environmental protection by creating financial consequences for damage caused by space objects. The Registration Convention enhances transparency by requiring states to register objects launched into orbit, creating a record that supports tracking, identification, and accountability. However, none of these instruments was designed to address the systemic environmental challenges of contemporary space activity: orbital congestion, debris proliferation, electromagnetic interference, atmospheric effects of satellite re-entry, or the cumulative degradation of shared orbital resources.

The planetary protection framework represents the most developed environmental mechanism in space governance, though it operates through institutional practice rather than binding treaty obligation. COSPAR (the Committee on Space Research) maintains the Planetary Protection Policy, which categorizes space missions by their potential to contaminate celestial bodies with terrestrial biological material or to bring extraterrestrial material back to Earth. Mars missions, in particular, are subject to stringent contamination control requirements that add significant cost and complexity to mission design. The planetary protection framework demonstrates that environmental principles can be operationalized in space governance when the scientific community and space agencies agree on the necessity—a precedent that sustainability advocates seek to extend to the orbital environment.

General international environmental law provides additional normative resources that could be applied to space activities. The precautionary principle—the idea that lack of full scientific certainty should not postpone measures to prevent environmental degradation—has been recognized in numerous international environmental instruments (the Rio Declaration, the Stockholm Convention, the Cartagena Protocol) and could inform approaches to uncertain but potentially irreversible environmental risks in orbit. The polluter pays principle—which holds that the entity responsible for environmental harm should bear the costs of remediation—resonates with the Liability Convention's allocation of liability to launching states but has not been extended to long-term debris remediation obligations. The principle of environmental impact assessment, well-established in terrestrial environmental law through instruments such as the Espoo Convention, has no counterpart in space law despite the increasingly significant environmental effects of large-scale space activities.

■ Environmental Provisions in Space Treaties

OST Article IX: Due regard obligation; avoidance of harmful contamination of celestial bodies; avoidance of adverse changes to Earth's environment from introduction of extraterrestrial matter.

OST Article III: Activities must be conducted in accordance with international law, including the UN Charter—potentially incorporating environmental principles from general international law.

Liability Convention: Creates financial liability for damage caused by space objects, incentivizing precautionary behavior.

Registration Convention: Requires registration of space objects, supporting tracking and identification essential for environmental monitoring.

The Kessler Syndrome and Systemic Risk

The most consequential environmental risk in orbital space is the Kessler syndrome—a theoretical scenario, first described by NASA scientist Donald Kessler in 1978, in which the density of objects in certain orbital regions becomes high enough that collisions between objects produce debris fragments that cause further collisions, creating a self-sustaining cascade that renders entire orbital bands unusable for generations. The Kessler syndrome is not a sudden catastrophic event but a gradual degradation: as debris density increases, collision probability rises, each collision generates additional debris, and the process feeds upon itself.

Current estimates suggest that LEO already contains sufficient mass in debris objects that cascading collisions will occur even without additional launches—the so-called "critical density" threshold may have been crossed in the most congested altitude bands. NASA's Orbital Debris Program Office tracks approximately 36,500 objects larger than 10 centimeters, approximately one million objects between 1 and 10 centimeters, and an estimated 130 million objects between 1 millimeter and 1 centimeter. Even millimeter-sized fragments at orbital velocities (7–8 kilometers per second in LEO) carry kinetic energy sufficient to damage satellite components, solar panels, and thermal protection systems.

The mathematical models underlying the Kessler syndrome have been refined over four decades by researchers at NASA, ESA, and national space agencies. The MASTER (Meteoroid and Space Debris Terrestrial Environment Reference) model maintained by ESA and the ORDEM (Orbital Debris Engineering Model) maintained by NASA provide probabilistic assessments of the debris environment at various altitudes. Both models project that the debris population in the 800–850 kilometer altitude band will continue to grow over the coming century even with no further launches, driven by fragmentation of large intact objects already in orbit. The implication is stark: debris mitigation—preventing new debris from being created—is necessary but insufficient. Active removal of existing debris is required to stabilize the orbital environment in the most congested regions.

The 2009 collision between the operational Iridium 33 communications satellite and the defunct Russian Cosmos 2251 military satellite demonstrated the Kessler mechanism in action. The collision, at approximately 789 kilometers altitude and a relative velocity of over 11 kilometers per second, generated over 2,300 trackable debris fragments, most of which remain in orbit as of 2025 and will persist for decades to centuries. The event was particularly significant because it was the first accidental hypervelocity collision between two intact satellites—proving that debris-generating events could occur through simple orbital mechanics in crowded altitude bands without any deliberate human action. The Cosmos 2251 satellite had been defunct since 1995; no Russian entity was monitoring its trajectory or capable of maneuvering it to avoid collision. The Iridium 33 satellite was operational, but its operator had not received a conjunction warning from the U.S. Space Surveillance Network in time to execute an avoidance maneuver.

Together with the debris from China's 2007 ASAT test (over 3,500 fragments from the Fengyun-1C satellite at 865 kilometers), India's 2019 ASAT test (approximately 400 fragments from the Microsat-R satellite at 300 kilometers, most of which re-entered quickly due to the low altitude), and Russia's 2021 ASAT test (over 1,500 fragments from Cosmos 1408 at 480 kilometers), deliberate and accidental events have substantially increased debris density in the most congested altitude bands. Each of these events created debris clouds that will persist for years to centuries, depending on altitude, and each has increased the probability of future collisions that will generate yet more debris.

■ The Orbital Debris Environment: Key Statistics (2025)

Tracked objects (>10 cm): ~36,500, of which ~10,000 are active satellites.

Estimated objects 1–10 cm: ~1,000,000 (untrackable by most systems).

Estimated objects 1 mm–1 cm: ~130,000,000.

Major debris-generating events: 2007 Chinese ASAT (3,500+), 2009 Iridium/Cosmos collision (2,300+), 2021 Russian ASAT (1,500+).

ISS collision avoidance maneuvers: ~30 per year (increasing trend).

Starlink conjunction warnings: ~10,000 per week (estimated).

Orbital velocity in LEO: ~7.5 km/s; collision energy equivalent: 1 cm fragment = hand grenade.

New Risk Profiles: Mega-Constellations and Atmospheric Effects

The deployment of mega-constellations—systems comprising thousands of satellites in coordinated orbital shells—has introduced environmental challenges that existing frameworks did not anticipate. SpaceX's Starlink constellation, with over 6,000 satellites operational and regulatory approval for up to 12,000 (with applications pending for an additional 30,000), occupies orbital shells between approximately 340 and 570 kilometers. Amazon's Project Kuiper has authorization for 3,236 satellites. OneWeb operates over 600 satellites at approximately 1,200 kilometers. Chinese constellations (Guowang, G60) plan thousands more. The cumulative effect is a transformation of the orbital environment from one populated by hundreds of satellites to one populated by tens of thousands—an increase that strains conjunction assessment systems, debris mitigation capacity, and the fundamental sustainability of shared orbital regions.

Beyond orbital congestion, mega-constellations raise environmental concerns that extend to the terrestrial atmosphere. The de-orbiting of thousands of satellites at end-of-life deposits aluminum oxide and other metallic particulates in the upper atmosphere. Recent research published in scientific journals has raised concerns about cumulative atmospheric effects, including potential impacts on stratospheric ozone chemistry and Earth's albedo. The scale is unprecedented: replacing a constellation of 12,000 satellites every five to seven years means de-orbiting approximately 2,000 satellites annually—each depositing metallic residue in the mesosphere and stratosphere. No environmental impact assessment framework addresses these atmospheric effects, and the intersection of space law with atmospheric environmental regulation remains largely unexplored.

The light pollution effects of mega-constellations have generated significant concern among the astronomical community and raised governance questions that straddle the boundary between space and environmental law. Starlink satellites, particularly during their orbit-raising phase when they travel in closely spaced "trains," are visible to the naked eye and leave bright streaks across astronomical observations. Professional surveys—particularly wide-field surveys searching for near-Earth asteroids, transient astronomical phenomena, and faint distant objects—can be significantly degraded by satellite trails. The Vera C. Rubin Observatory in Chile, which will conduct the Legacy Survey of Space and Time beginning in the mid-2020s, is expected to be particularly affected, with satellite trails potentially contaminating a substantial fraction of its exposures.

SpaceX has responded to astronomical concerns with iterative design modifications—VisorSat, DarkSat, and laser-based inter-satellite links that reduce reflected sunlight—demonstrating that private operators can mitigate adverse effects when sufficiently motivated. However, the mitigation has been voluntary and incomplete. The International Astronomical Union's Centre for the Protection of the Dark and Quiet Sky from Satellite Constellation Interference coordinates advocacy and research, while the UNOOSA-supported Dark and Quiet Skies initiative has issued recommendations. No binding framework requires commercial operators to limit their satellites' brightness or to compensate the astronomical community for degraded observations. The issue illustrates a broader governance challenge: mega-constellations impose costs on third parties—astronomers, indigenous communities with cultural connections to the night sky, amateur observers—who have no seat at the regulatory table that authorizes these activities.

> *"The orbital environment is not infinitely resilient. Every satellite launched, every upper stage abandoned, and every collision fragment generated contributes to a cumulative degradation that, if unchecked, will render essential orbital regions increasingly hazardous for all users."*

– On the finite nature of orbital space

> ■ **From Freedom of Use to Environmental Stewardship**
>
> The evolution of space activity demands a recalibration of legal priorities. Freedom of use remains a foundational principle, but it must be balanced against stewardship obligations that preserve the orbital environment for current and future users. This balance does not require abandoning openness; it requires redefining it to include the collective responsibility that shared, finite resources demand. The concept of sustainability—maintaining the usability of orbital regions for future generations—provides the normative bridge between freedom and stewardship.

***

Part II

Space Debris and Long-Term Sustainability Frameworks

Among all environmental challenges facing outer space, space debris represents the most immediate and widely recognized threat to the long-term sustainability of space activities. Unlike many issues in space law that remain speculative, debris is a present and growing problem with measurable consequences. It has transformed sustainability from a normative aspiration into an operational necessity, compelling states and institutions to develop frameworks that emphasize prevention, coordination, and shared responsibility.

Legal Characterization of Space Debris

International space law does not define space debris explicitly. Under existing treaties, debris remains legally classified as a "space object"—a term that encompasses all objects launched into outer space, regardless of whether they are functional. This classification has important implications for responsibility and liability. The launching state retains jurisdiction and control over a space object under the Outer Space Treaty (Article VIII) and bears liability for damage it causes under the Liability Convention, even if the object is no longer functional and the launching state has no ability to control it.

This legal framework creates a paradox: states bear responsibility for debris they cannot control. A defunct satellite or spent rocket stage may orbit for centuries, generating collision risk and potentially causing damage for which the launching state is liable—but the launching state has no practical means of mitigating that risk once operational control is lost. The framework was designed for an era when the number of objects in orbit was small enough that the risk of uncontrolled collisions was negligible. In today's congested environment, the gap between legal responsibility and operational capability is a central governance challenge.

The registration and identification of debris compounds the legal complexity. The Registration Convention requires states to register objects launched into outer space, but registration requirements apply to the initial object—the satellite or launch vehicle stage—not to the fragments generated by its subsequent breakup. When a registered satellite explodes and generates hundreds of fragments, each fragment is technically a "space object" associated with the original launching state, but individual fragments are often too small to identify or attribute. The U.S. Space Surveillance Network can track objects as small as 10 centimeters in LEO, but objects between 1 and 10 centimeters—which are large enough to destroy a satellite but too small to be reliably tracked—constitute a lethal, invisible hazard for which no attribution and therefore no liability enforcement is possible.

The question of consent for active debris removal (ADR) illustrates the legal complexity at its sharpest. Under Article VIII, a launching state retains jurisdiction over its space objects in perpetuity. No other state may remove, relocate, or interfere with a space object without the consent of its owner state. This means that a state or company wishing to remove dangerous debris must obtain permission from the debris's launching state—a requirement that may be politically difficult or diplomatically sensitive, particularly when the debris is of military origin (and the launching state may deny that it is debris at all), when the launching state no longer exists as a political entity (as with debris from the Soviet Union, which is attributed to the Russian Federation as successor state but was launched under different political circumstances), or when geopolitical tensions make cooperation between the debris owner and the ADR operator impractical. Proposals for streamlined consent mechanisms—such as advance waivers, multilateral agreements, or deemed consent for objects exceeding a specified age or orbital residency—are under discussion but have not yet achieved international agreement.

The IADC and COPUOS Debris Mitigation Guidelines

The international community's response to the debris challenge has centered on prevention rather than remediation, primarily through non-binding guidelines developed within two institutional frameworks: the Inter-Agency Space Debris Coordination Committee (IADC) and the United Nations Committee on the Peaceful Uses of Outer Space (COPUOS).

The IADC, established in 1993, comprises thirteen national space agencies (including NASA, ESA, JAXA, CNSA, Roscosmos, ISRO, and others) that coordinate research and develop consensus technical guidelines for debris mitigation. The IADC's Space Debris Mitigation Guidelines (2002, revised 2007) established the technical foundation that subsequent COPUOS guidelines built upon. Key measures include limiting debris released during normal operations (such as lens caps, deployment mechanisms, and separation devices), preventing on-orbit explosions by passivating spacecraft at end of life (venting fuel tanks, discharging batteries, deactivating pressurized systems), and post-mission disposal—either de-orbiting satellites into the atmosphere within a specified time period or moving them to graveyard orbits above the operational altitude band.

Passivation—the process of removing all stored energy from a spacecraft at end of life—addresses one of the most significant historical sources of debris. Upper stages and spacecraft that retain residual propellant or charged batteries after their missions end can explode years or decades later, generating debris clouds that persist for centuries. The explosion of a single rocket upper stage can produce hundreds of trackable fragments. The IADC guidelines' passivation requirement has been widely implemented by responsible operators, but historical objects launched before the guidelines were adopted—including hundreds of spent upper stages from Soviet, American, and European launch vehicles—remain in orbit with residual energy, creating an ongoing risk of spontaneous fragmentation.

The graveyard orbit concept applies primarily to geostationary satellites, which at end of life are raised to a disposal orbit approximately 300 kilometers above the GEO belt rather than de-orbited (de-orbiting from GEO altitude would require impractical amounts of propellant). The graveyard orbit approach effectively parks defunct GEO satellites in a region that does not interfere with operational spacecraft, though the long-term sustainability of the graveyard orbit itself—which will accumulate defunct satellites indefinitely—has not been assessed. For LEO satellites, the preferred disposal method is controlled or uncontrolled re-entry into the Earth's atmosphere, where the satellite burns up (or, for larger objects, has surviving fragments impact unpopulated areas).

COPUOS adopted its own Space Debris Mitigation Guidelines in 2007, endorsed by the UN General Assembly in Resolution 62/217. These guidelines largely mirror the IADC standards but carry greater political weight due to their adoption by a universal membership body. The guidelines include seven specific measures: limiting debris released during normal operations, minimizing the potential for break-ups during operational phases, limiting the probability of accidental collision in orbit, avoiding intentional destruction and other harmful activities, minimizing the potential for post-mission break-ups, limiting the long-term presence of spacecraft and launch vehicle orbital stages in the LEO region after end of mission, and limiting the long-term interference of spacecraft and launch vehicle orbital stages with the GEO region after end of mission.

Framework	Year	Scope	Status	Key Contribution
IADC Guidelines	2002/2007	Debris mitigation technical measures	Non-binding; agency consensus	Technical foundation for all subsequent guidelines
COPUOS Debris Guidelines	2007	7 specific debris mitigation measures	Non-binding; UNGA endorsed	Universal political endorsement of mitigation norms
ISO 24113	2011/2019	Detailed technical debris mitigation standard	Voluntary industry standard	Operational specificity for satellite manufacturers
COPUOS LTS Guidelines	2019	21 guidelines on sustainability broadly	Non-binding; COPUOS consensus	Broadened agenda beyond debris to systemic sustainability
FCC 5-Year Rule	2022	LEO satellites must deorbit within 5 years	Binding on FCC licensees	First major regulatory tightening of disposal timeline
ESA Zero Debris Charter	2023	Commitment to generate zero debris by 2030	Voluntary industry commitment	Aspirational target beyond existing guidelines

The Long-Term Sustainability Guidelines

In 2019, COPUOS adopted the Guidelines for the Long-term Sustainability (LTS) of Outer Space Activities, representing the most comprehensive multilateral effort to address space environmental governance. The LTS guidelines go beyond debris mitigation to address the systemic conditions needed for sustainable space activity. The twenty-one guidelines are organized into four groups: policy and regulatory framework for space activities, safety of space operations, international cooperation and capacity-building, and scientific and technical research and development.

The LTS guidelines address issues including the sharing of space situational awareness data, the coordination of conjunction assessment and collision avoidance, the development of national regulatory frameworks incorporating sustainability requirements, the promotion of international cooperation in space debris research, and the investigation of measures to manage the space debris population. They represent a qualitative shift from debris mitigation—which focuses on preventing individual actors from making the problem worse—to sustainability governance, which addresses the systemic conditions needed for the orbital environment to remain usable for all actors over the long term.

Compliance with debris mitigation guidelines has improved significantly since their adoption but remains imperfect. ESA's Annual Space Environment Report tracks global compliance rates and reports that approximately 60 to 80 percent of recent LEO missions attempt post-mission disposal, with roughly 30 to 40 percent successfully achieving disposal within the twenty-five-year guideline period. These compliance rates represent substantial progress from the pre-guidelines era, when post-mission disposal was virtually nonexistent, but they leave a significant number of new objects in orbit beyond their intended disposal timeline. Compliance rates for GEO satellites are somewhat higher for the graveyard orbit maneuver, though not all operators achieve the recommended disposal altitude. The gap between guideline adoption and full compliance reflects both technical failures (spacecraft malfunctions that prevent end-of-life maneuvers) and economic decisions (operators choosing to extend missions beyond planned lifetimes to maximize revenue, consuming propellant reserves that would otherwise be available for disposal).

The LTS guidelines' effectiveness depends on implementation. Their voluntary character means that compliance relies on national political will and regulatory capacity. The COPUOS Working Group on the Long-term Sustainability of Outer Space Activities, reconvened in 2022, is tasked with reviewing implementation, identifying challenges, and potentially developing additional guidelines. Early assessments suggest that implementation is uneven: technologically advanced states with established regulatory frameworks have incorporated LTS principles into licensing requirements, while states with less developed space programs may lack the institutional capacity to implement them effectively.

The Twenty-Five-Year Rule and Its Evolution

The post-mission disposal timeline has become the most visible and contested element of debris mitigation policy. The IADC guidelines established a twenty-five-year maximum for post-mission disposal from LEO—a compromise between the technical feasibility of ensuring de-orbit within a reasonable time and the cost of propulsion systems capable of achieving earlier disposal. For two decades, the twenty-five-year guideline served as the de facto international standard, incorporated into national regulations and satellite design requirements worldwide.

However, the twenty-five-year timeline has come under increasing criticism as inadequate for the contemporary debris environment. With mega-constellations deploying thousands of satellites, even high compliance rates with the twenty-five-year rule would leave hundreds of defunct satellites in orbit at any given time—each representing a collision risk during its decades-long disposal period. Modeling by ESA and NASA suggests that shorter disposal timelines would significantly reduce the long-term debris population growth rate. The FCC's September 2022 rule requiring LEO satellites to de-orbit within five years of end of mission represented the most significant tightening of disposal standards by any national regulator, prompting intense debate about technical feasibility, cost implications, and competitive effects on operators licensed under less demanding jurisdictions.

The five-year rule illustrates both the promise and limits of national regulatory action as a tool for environmental governance. By tightening standards for the world's largest satellite licensing authority, the FCC created a new benchmark that other regulators will face pressure to match. SpaceX's Starlink satellites, designed with electric propulsion for active de-orbit, already comply with even shorter disposal timelines. But operators without onboard propulsion—including many CubeSat and small satellite developers—face significant cost increases to comply with a five-year disposal requirement, potentially creating barriers to entry that conflict with the goal of expanding space access to new actors. Balancing environmental ambition with equitable access remains a persistent tension in debris governance.

ASAT Testing and the Debris Legacy

Anti-satellite weapons testing has produced some of the most consequential debris-generating events in history, directly undermining the sustainability of the orbital environment. China's January 2007 destruction of the Fengyun-1C weather satellite at approximately 865 kilometers altitude generated over 3,500 trackable fragments—the single largest debris-generating event in the history of spaceflight—in an altitude band that is already critically congested. Many of these fragments will remain in orbit for centuries. Russia's November 2021 destruction of the Cosmos 1408 satellite at approximately 480 kilometers generated over 1,500 trackable fragments, some of which threatened the International Space Station and forced its crew to shelter in their return vehicles.

The United States conducted its last kinetic ASAT test in 2008 (Operation Burnt Frost), deliberately targeting a malfunctioning reconnaissance satellite at a low altitude where debris would re-enter relatively quickly—a design choice that reflected growing awareness of debris consequences. In April 2022, Vice President Kamala Harris announced that the United States would not conduct destructive direct-ascent ASAT missile testing and called on other nations to adopt similar commitments. Several states have endorsed this moratorium, and the UN General Assembly adopted a resolution in December 2022 (76/231) encouraging all states to commit to not conducting destructive ASAT tests. However, the resolution is non-binding, and the states most likely to conduct ASAT tests—China and Russia—did not support it.

"Debris mitigation prevents individual actors from making the problem worse. Sustainability governance addresses whether the orbital environment will remain usable for all actors over the long term. The shift from mitigation to sustainability marks a fundamental evolution in how the international community conceives its responsibility for the space environment."

– On the evolution from mitigation to sustainability

***

Part III

Space Traffic Management: Concepts, Models, and Challenges

As orbital regions become increasingly congested, the challenge of ensuring safe and sustainable operations has moved beyond debris mitigation to encompass the broader concept of Space Traffic Management (STM). STM refers to the coordination, regulation, and management of space activities to prevent collisions, interference, and environmental degradation. While still an emerging concept without an agreed international definition, STM is rapidly becoming a central pillar of future space governance.

The Aviation Analogy and Its Limits

The concept of STM draws inspiration from air traffic management (ATM), where centralized coordination, shared information, and standardized procedures enable safe operation in a crowded environment. The International Civil Aviation Organization (ICAO) administers a comprehensive framework of Standards and Recommended Practices (SARPs) that states adopt into national law, creating a harmonized global system that manages over 40 million flights annually with an extraordinary safety record. ICAO's framework includes standardized flight plans, common communication protocols, mandatory transponder requirements, defined airways and altitude assignments, separation standards, and emergency procedures—a comprehensive regulatory architecture developed incrementally over eight decades since the Chicago Convention of 1944. The aviation model demonstrates that complex, multi-actor traffic management in a shared domain is technically and institutionally feasible.

However, direct analogy between ATM and STM has significant limits that space governance practitioners must understand. Unlike airspace, outer space lacks territorial sovereignty—no state has jurisdiction over the orbital shells through which satellites pass, and the sovereignty-based jurisdictional framework that underpins ICAO's authority does not exist in space. Aviation depends on active human control: pilots make real-time decisions based on air traffic controller instructions, and aircraft can change course, speed, and altitude rapidly. Satellites travel at orbital velocities of 7 to 8 kilometers per second, making real-time intervention impossible in the way that air traffic controllers redirect aircraft. Trajectories are governed by orbital mechanics rather than pilot discretion: a satellite cannot simply change course to avoid another object without expending finite propellant resources that directly reduce its operational lifetime. Communication delays complicate coordination, particularly for objects in higher orbits. And unlike aircraft, which land after each flight, satellites remain in orbit for years or decades, accumulating in a shared environment rather than cycling through it.

These differences require STM models that are distributed, cooperative, and data-driven rather than centralized and command-based. The most promising STM concepts envision shared data infrastructure, common operational standards, and coordination protocols that enable operators to make informed decisions autonomously, rather than a central authority directing traffic in real time.

Space Situational Awareness: The Foundation of STM

Any STM system requires comprehensive, accurate, and timely knowledge of the positions and trajectories of objects in orbit—a capability known as space situational awareness (SSA). SSA is the foundation on which all other STM functions depend: conjunction assessment, collision avoidance, anomaly investigation, re-entry prediction, and debris tracking all require knowing where objects are and where they are going.

The United States has historically provided the world's most comprehensive SSA capability through the U.S. Space Surveillance Network (SSN), a global system of radar and optical sensors operated by the U.S. Space Force. The SSN includes the Space Fence—a powerful S-band radar on Kwajalein Atoll in the Marshall Islands that became operational in 2020 and can detect objects as small as 10 centimeters in LEO—as well as older radars, optical telescopes, and ground-based electro-optical deep space surveillance systems distributed across multiple continents. The SSN tracks over 47,000 objects and provides conjunction warnings to satellite operators worldwide through the 18th Space Defense Squadron's public catalog and conjunction data messages distributed via Space-Track.org.

This service—provided free of charge to all operators, including those of other states—has made the United States the de facto global SSA provider, a role that carries both benefits and concerns. The benefit is global safety enhancement: operators worldwide receive conjunction warnings that enable collision avoidance decisions. The concerns are multiple: dependence on a single state creates vulnerability if that state reduces, restricts, or politicizes the service; the military's control of the SSA mission means that tracking data for some objects (classified military satellites) is withheld from the public catalog; and the data's accuracy and timeliness may not meet the operational needs of all users, particularly those operating in the most congested orbital regimes where even small positional uncertainties can produce misleading collision probability assessments.

Recognizing the limitations and risks of dependence on a single provider, multiple states and organizations have developed independent or complementary SSA capabilities. The European Union's Space Surveillance and Tracking (EU SST) consortium, comprising sensors in France, Germany, Italy, Poland, Portugal, Romania, and Spain, provides an independent European conjunction assessment capability. Japan's JAXA operates radar and optical tracking systems. India's ISRO has developed domestic SSA capabilities. Commercial SSA providers—including LeoLabs (which operates a global network of phased-array radars), ExoAnalytic Solutions (optical tracking), and Slingshot Aerospace (data fusion and analytics)—offer services that complement governmental capabilities and are increasingly used by commercial operators for operational decision-making.

■ **Space Situational Awareness: Key Providers (2025)**

U.S. Space Force (18th SDS): Tracks 47,000+ objects; provides free conjunction warnings globally via Space-Track.org.

EU SST Consortium: 7 European nations; independent European tracking and conjunction assessment since 2016.

LeoLabs: Commercial; global phased-array radar network; real-time LEO tracking with high accuracy.

ExoAnalytic Solutions: Commercial; global optical telescope network for GEO and higher orbit monitoring.

JAXA (Japan): National SSA system including radar and optical sensors.

ISRO (India): Developing comprehensive national SSA capability.

Slingshot Aerospace: Commercial data fusion platform integrating multiple sensor sources.

Conjunction Assessment and Collision Avoidance

Conjunction assessment—the process of identifying potential close approaches between objects in orbit—is the operational core of current STM practice. The U.S. Space Force issues conjunction data messages (CDMs) when tracked objects are predicted to pass within specified distance thresholds. Satellite operators evaluate these warnings and decide whether to execute avoidance maneuvers, a process that involves assessing collision probability, weighing the operational cost of maneuvering (propellant expenditure, mission disruption) against the risk of inaction, and coordinating with other operators whose satellites may be affected.

The conjunction assessment process reveals the limitations of current STM practice. Collision probability calculations are inherently uncertain, depending on the accuracy of tracking data, atmospheric density models (which affect drag predictions), and the propagation of orbital state vectors over time. Operators must make maneuver decisions based on probabilistic rather than deterministic information, under time pressure, with commercial consequences for every propellant-expending maneuver. When two operators both receive conjunction warnings about the same close approach, coordination is essential to ensure that their maneuvers do not create new hazards—but no standardized protocol exists for such coordination, and communication between operators is often ad hoc.

The scale of the conjunction assessment challenge is growing exponentially. SpaceX reported that its Starlink constellation generates approximately 10,000 conjunction warnings per week—a volume that exceeds the capacity of manual review and requires automated maneuver planning systems. As additional mega-constellations become operational, the total volume of conjunction events will increase further, potentially overwhelming existing SSA infrastructure and operator decision-making capacity. The transition from manual to automated conjunction assessment and collision avoidance is not merely a technical challenge; it raises governance questions about accountability, liability, and transparency when algorithms rather than humans make safety-critical decisions.

The absence of standardized coordination protocols between operators is a critical gap. When two satellite operators receive conjunction warnings about the same close approach, each must decide independently whether to maneuver—and if both maneuver without coordination, their actions may create a new close approach rather than resolving the original one. The Space Data Association, a nonprofit industry consortium, facilitates data sharing among commercial operators, but participation is voluntary and does not include all operators. NASA and ESA have established bilateral agreements for conjunction assessment data sharing, but no multilateral mechanism exists for coordinating collision avoidance maneuvers among the full range of operators—government, commercial, and international—that share congested orbital regions.

The "screening volume" problem illustrates the technical complexity. When an operator screens its constellation against the catalog of tracked objects, the number of potential conjunctions grows geometrically with the number of objects on each side. A constellation of 12,000 satellites screened against a catalog of 47,000 objects generates a vast number of potential close approaches, most of which are false alarms that require no action. Distinguishing genuine collision risks from statistical noise requires sophisticated algorithms, high-quality tracking data, and near-real-time processing capability—resources that not all operators possess equally. The result is an information asymmetry in which large, well-resourced operators have better situational awareness than smaller operators, creating differential safety levels within shared orbital regions.

Private Actors and STM Responsibilities

Commercial operators are increasingly central to STM. Mega-constellation operators conduct the majority of collision avoidance maneuvers in LEO, making safety-critical decisions that affect the entire orbital environment. SpaceX's autonomous collision avoidance system maneuvers Starlink satellites thousands of times per year based on conjunction data and probability thresholds—a volume of operational decision-making that exceeds any government operator. This reality challenges the traditional assumption that traffic management is a purely governmental function and raises questions about accountability, transparency, and the public interest when private companies make decisions that affect a shared global resource.

The proprietary nature of commercial SSA data and collision avoidance algorithms creates transparency concerns. SpaceX's maneuver decisions are based on its own tracking data and algorithms, which are not publicly available or independently verifiable. Other operators—including government agencies operating scientific or national security satellites—must trust that SpaceX's autonomous system will behave predictably and safely, but they have no means of verifying this trust. The dependence of the global space community on the collision avoidance decisions of a single private company operating a majority of active LEO satellites is an unprecedented governance situation that existing frameworks do not address.

Incorporating private actors into STM frameworks requires clear expectations about data sharing, operational transparency, and accountability. Potential mechanisms include mandatory reporting of conjunction events and avoidance maneuvers to a central registry, publication of collision avoidance protocols and probability thresholds, certification of automated maneuver planning systems by independent technical authorities, and liability frameworks that assign responsibility for collision damage resulting from inadequate avoidance actions. These mechanisms would preserve operational autonomy while ensuring that private STM decisions serve collective safety interests.

Equity and Access in STM

STM raises significant equity concerns that mirror the broader participation gap discussed in Chapter 8. States and operators with advanced SSA capabilities, sophisticated maneuver planning systems, and direct relationships with tracking providers have a substantial safety advantage over those without. A developing country operating a single Earth observation satellite may receive conjunction warnings but lack the technical capacity to evaluate them, the propulsion capability to execute avoidance maneuvers, or the communication infrastructure to coordinate with other operators. The result is differential safety: some actors operate in a well-monitored, actively managed environment, while others—particularly smaller operators from developing countries—operate with significantly less awareness and fewer options.

Addressing this equity dimension requires capacity-building, data sharing, and institutional support. UNOOSA's UN-SPIDER program provides disaster management support but has no counterpart for conjunction assessment assistance. The EU SST provides conjunction warnings to European operators but not globally. Commercial SSA providers offer services at prices that may be prohibitive for developing country operators. A genuinely global STM framework must include mechanisms for ensuring that all operators—regardless of their national origin, financial resources, or technical sophistication—have access to the information and support needed for safe operations in shared orbital regions.

National and International STM Initiatives

In the absence of a global STM authority, states have developed national initiatives that contribute to an evolving patchwork of STM capabilities. The United States designated the Department of Commerce as the lead agency for providing civil space traffic coordination services through Space Policy Directive-3 (2018), separating the civil STM function from the military's space surveillance mission. The transition has been slow: as of 2025, the Department of Commerce's Office of Space Commerce is still developing its Traffic Coordination System for Space (TraCSS), which is intended to provide enhanced conjunction assessment services to all operators.

The European Union has adopted a Space Traffic Management approach emphasizing civil autonomy and multi-provider data fusion. France has integrated STM principles into its Space Operations Act, requiring licensed operators to comply with collision avoidance and disposal requirements. The United Kingdom's Space Industry Act incorporates sustainability provisions that function as STM requirements at the licensing stage. Japan, India, and Australia have all developed or are developing national STM-related capabilities.

At the international level, COPUOS has discussed STM within the framework of the LTS guidelines but has not established a dedicated working group or negotiating mandate. The ITU manages radiofrequency coordination and orbital slot allocation for GEO satellites—a form of traffic management for the electromagnetic spectrum and geostationary positions—but does not address physical traffic management in LEO or other orbital regimes. The absence of an international institution with a clear STM mandate means that coordination remains bilateral, ad hoc, and dependent on the goodwill of operators and the capabilities of a few major SSA providers.

■ The STM Gap

Space traffic management represents the most significant governance gap in contemporary space law. No international authority coordinates orbital operations. No binding rules establish right of way, minimum separation standards, or mandatory collision avoidance procedures. No common data infrastructure ensures that all operators have access to the information needed for safe operations. The gap is not merely institutional; it is normative—there is no agreed framework of principles that defines what STM should accomplish, who should be responsible for it, or how it should be governed. Filling this gap is the most urgent governance challenge of the commercial space era.

***

Part IV

Future Regulatory Pathways and Institutional Reform

The challenges posed by space debris, orbital congestion, and the rapid expansion of space activities have revealed the limits of existing governance mechanisms. While soft-law instruments and national initiatives have advanced sustainability and safety, they remain fragmented and unevenly implemented. The future of environmental protection and space traffic management will depend on whether the international community can move toward more coherent regulatory pathways and institutional adaptation, without undermining the flexibility that has enabled innovation.

The Case for Regulatory Evolution

International space law was crafted for an era of limited activity and state dominance. Its foundational principles—freedom of use, non-appropriation, and state responsibility—remain relevant, but their application must evolve to accommodate environmental sustainability and traffic management as core governance objectives. Regulatory evolution does not necessarily mean new comprehensive treaties. The record of the Moon Agreement demonstrates that politically ambitious treaties face significant resistance, and the pace of technological change means that detailed regulatory instruments risk obsolescence before they enter into force. Instead, adaptive governance mechanisms—capable of responding to technological change and incorporating new knowledge—are increasingly favored by both practitioners and scholars.

The ICAO model of Standards and Recommended Practices (SARPs) offers the most frequently cited precedent for adaptive space governance. ICAO's SARPs are adopted by the ICAO Council (a technical body of thirty-six states elected by the ICAO Assembly) rather than through treaty negotiation, allowing relatively rapid updating as technology and operational practices evolve. States are required to incorporate SARPs into national law or file "differences" explaining their divergence—a mechanism that creates transparency about non-compliance while respecting sovereignty. This model creates convergence without requiring unanimity and allows standards to evolve incrementally rather than through periodic comprehensive negotiation.

Whether a comparable institution could be established for space faces several fundamental obstacles. First, ICAO's authority rests on the Chicago Convention of 1944, which established both the organization and the principle that states have sovereignty over their airspace. No equivalent constitutional instrument exists for space: the Outer Space Treaty establishes principles but does not create an implementing institution with regulatory authority. Second, aviation operates within sovereign airspace where states have undisputed jurisdiction; space operations traverse orbital regimes over which no state has sovereignty, making jurisdictional authority for regulation ambiguous. Third, military space operations—which are deeply intertwined with civilian space activity through shared orbits, dual-use tracking systems, and dual-use satellite technology—create sensitivities that would complicate any international regulatory authority's mandate. Military operators are unlikely to accept international oversight of their orbital operations, yet their objects contribute to congestion and their maneuvers affect the safety of all other operators.

Despite these obstacles, elements of the ICAO model can be adapted for space governance without replicating the full institutional structure. Technical standards development through expert bodies (analogous to ICAO's technical panels), national implementation with transparency about divergences (analogous to the "differences" filing system), and periodic review mechanisms that allow standards to evolve (analogous to ICAO's continuous amendment process) could all be incorporated into space governance through existing institutions such as COPUOS, the IADC, and national regulatory agencies. The goal need not be an "ICAO for space" but rather an ICAO-inspired approach to standard-setting that achieves practical convergence through technical excellence, transparency, and sustained institutional engagement.

Active Debris Removal: Technical Promise and Legal Challenges

Active debris removal (ADR)—the physical capture and de-orbiting of defunct satellites and debris—represents the only approach that can reduce existing debris populations rather than merely slowing their growth. Several ADR concepts are under development: ESA's ClearSpace-1 mission, planned for 2026, will attempt to capture and de-orbit a spent Vega upper stage (VESPA) using a four-armed robotic capture system—the first-ever active debris removal mission by any space agency.

The mission is structured as a commercial service contract: ESA has contracted ClearSpace SA, a Swiss startup, to perform the removal, establishing a model in which debris removal is procured as a commercial service rather than conducted as a government program. Astroscale, a Japanese-headquartered company, demonstrated magnetic capture technology with its ELSA-d mission in 2021 and is developing ADRAS-J, a mission to characterize and approach a large piece of debris as a precursor to removal. Other concepts include capture nets, harpoons, ion beam shepherd systems that use ion thruster exhaust to push debris objects to lower orbits, laser ablation systems that vaporize surface material to create thrust, and electrodynamic tethers that use interaction with Earth's magnetic field to generate drag.

The economic case for ADR is strengthening. Studies by ESA, NASA, and academic researchers estimate that the economic value of the orbital environment—the satellite services that depend on safe access to congested orbital regions—exceeds one trillion dollars over the coming decades. The cost of removing the most dangerous debris objects (large, intact defunct satellites and upper stages in congested orbits) is estimated at tens of millions to hundreds of millions of dollars per object using current technology, with costs expected to decrease as ADR technology matures and economies of scale develop. The cost of not removing these objects—measured in increased collision risk, debris generation, and eventual inaccessibility of critical orbital altitudes—is potentially orders of magnitude higher. The economic case for ADR is therefore compelling, but the question of who pays remains unresolved: the launching states that created the debris, the operators whose satellites are threatened by it, or the international community as a whole.

ADR raises novel legal challenges that existing frameworks do not adequately address. The consent requirement under Article VIII means that any ADR operator must obtain permission from the debris's launching state before removing it—a requirement that may be politically difficult or diplomatically sensitive, particularly for debris of military origin. The dual-use character of ADR technology is also concerning: a spacecraft capable of capturing and de-orbiting debris is also capable of capturing and disabling an operational satellite, creating potential ASAT applications that complicate international trust. The liability framework for ADR operations is uncertain: if an ADR mission accidentally damages a third party's satellite while attempting to remove debris, the allocation of liability between the ADR operator, the debris's launching state, and the damaged satellite's operator is unclear under existing law.

Despite these challenges, ADR is increasingly recognized as essential to long-term sustainability. Modeling by NASA, ESA, and other agencies suggests that even with perfect compliance with debris mitigation guidelines, the debris population in the most congested LEO altitudes will continue to grow due to collisions among existing objects. Removing approximately five to ten large defunct objects per year from the most congested altitudes could stabilize the debris environment; without such removal, cascading collisions will gradually degrade these orbital regions regardless of mitigation efforts. Developing the legal, institutional, and commercial frameworks for ADR is therefore not merely a technical or policy challenge but an environmental imperative.

Integrating Sustainability into Licensing and Authorization

One of the most promising near-term pathways for environmental governance lies in strengthening the sustainability requirements embedded in national licensing regimes. States already possess the legal authority under Article VI to authorize and supervise space activities, and licensing conditions provide a direct mechanism for imposing environmental requirements on operators. The FCC's 2022 adoption of a five-year post-mission disposal rule for LEO satellites—replacing the previous twenty-five-year guideline—demonstrates that national regulators can unilaterally raise environmental standards within their jurisdictions. France's Space Operations Act mandates specific debris mitigation measures with the force of law. The UK's Space Industry Act incorporates sustainability considerations into licensing decisions.

If major licensing jurisdictions converge on common sustainability standards—through mutual recognition, model legislation, or coordinated regulatory action—the effect could be equivalent to binding international regulation without the political difficulty of treaty negotiation. Since the United States, France, the United Kingdom, Luxembourg, and a handful of other states license the vast majority of commercial satellite operations, convergence among these jurisdictions would establish de facto global standards that operators must meet regardless of where they are headquartered.

Economic Instruments and Market Mechanisms

Traditional regulatory approaches—licensing requirements, technical standards, disposal mandates—can be supplemented by economic instruments that create market incentives for environmentally responsible behavior. Orbital use fees—charges levied on satellite operators for occupying orbital capacity—have been proposed by economists as a mechanism for internalizing the externalities of orbital congestion. Just as road congestion pricing charges drivers for using crowded roads during peak hours, orbital use fees would charge satellite operators for the collision risk their presence creates in shared orbital regions. Modeling by researchers at the University of Colorado and elsewhere suggests that optimally calibrated orbital use fees could dramatically reduce long-term debris growth by incentivizing operators to minimize their orbital presence and invest in reliable de-orbit capabilities.

Insurance mechanisms provide another market-based pathway. If space insurers systematically price collision risk based on operators' debris mitigation practices, constellation management procedures, and disposal reliability, the insurance market would create financial incentives for environmental responsibility. Operators with superior debris mitigation records would enjoy lower premiums, while operators with poor compliance records would face higher costs or inability to obtain coverage. Since most licensing regimes require insurance as a condition of authorization, the insurance market effectively functions as a private-sector enforcement mechanism for environmental standards. The challenge is ensuring that insurers have access to the data needed for accurate risk assessment—a requirement that reinforces the case for transparency and information sharing in space operations.

Deposit-refund schemes represent a third economic mechanism. Under such a scheme, satellite operators would pay a deposit at the time of launch, refundable upon demonstrated successful de-orbit at end of mission. Operators who fail to de-orbit their satellites—whether due to malfunction, negligence, or financial insolvency—forfeit their deposit, which is used to fund debris removal operations. This mechanism aligns private incentives with public environmental objectives and creates a financial reserve for remediation activities that would otherwise require public funding.

Institutional Reform: Toward Coordinated Governance

The institutional landscape for space environmental governance is fragmented across multiple bodies with overlapping mandates, limited authority, and insufficient coordination. COPUOS provides the primary multilateral forum for policy development but lacks enforcement authority and operates by consensus, which prevents action over any member state's objection. The IADC provides technical expertise but comprises only space agency members and has no formal role in governance. The ITU manages spectrum and orbital slot allocation for GEO but does not address physical traffic management. National regulators exercise jurisdiction over their licensees but cannot coordinate with operators licensed by other states. Commercial SSA providers offer valuable services but operate outside any regulatory framework.

Several institutional reform options have been proposed. The creation of a dedicated international STM authority—analogous to ICAO for aviation—is the most ambitious proposal, envisioning an institution with the mandate, expertise, and resources to develop, implement, and enforce traffic management standards. This option faces enormous political obstacles: states are reluctant to delegate sovereign authority over their space activities to an international body, particularly when space operations have military and intelligence dimensions. A more modest option involves strengthening existing institutions by enhancing COPUOS's technical capacity, establishing formal linkages between COPUOS and the IADC, and creating dedicated working groups for STM and active debris removal. A third option—a network-of-networks approach—would coordinate existing national and commercial capabilities through agreed data standards, communication protocols, and operational procedures without creating a new institution.

"The orbital environment is a global commons that no single state created, no single state controls, and no single state can protect alone. Its governance requires collective action mechanisms that match the scale and interconnectedness of the risks that space activity creates."

– On the governance imperative for orbital sustainability

Sustainability as a Shared Responsibility

Ultimately, environmental protection and space traffic management reflect a broader shift in space law—from individual freedom toward collective responsibility. Space activities generate benefits that transcend borders, but they also impose risks shared by all users of the orbital environment. A debris fragment generated by one state's satellite threatens every other state's space assets. An uncoordinated maneuver by one operator can create collision risk for dozens of others. An abandoned upper stage in a congested orbit reduces the usable capacity of that orbit for all future users. Managing these interconnected risks requires cooperation, trust, and institutions capable of facilitating collective action in a domain that international law has traditionally governed through individual state responsibility.

The transition from freedom of use to environmental stewardship is not yet complete. The legal and institutional frameworks examined in this chapter—debris mitigation guidelines, LTS principles, national licensing requirements, SSA services, and STM concepts—provide the building blocks for a sustainable space governance architecture. But building blocks are not a building. Assembling them into a coherent, effective, and equitable governance framework will require sustained political commitment, institutional innovation, and the willingness to accept constraints on individual freedom in the interest of collective sustainability. The orbital environment's future—and with it, the future of the satellite services on which modern civilization depends—hangs in the balance.

The generational dimension of this challenge deserves emphasis. Decisions made today about debris mitigation standards, disposal timelines, constellation sizes, and environmental safeguards will determine the orbital conditions that future generations inherit. Unlike many environmental challenges, where degradation can potentially be reversed through remediation, orbital debris cannot be easily cleaned up once created: fragments traveling at seven kilometers per second cannot be swept away, and each collision generates more fragments in an exponential process. The precautionary principle—acting to prevent irreversible harm even in the presence of scientific uncertainty—has particular force in the orbital context, where the consequences of inaction may be irreversible on timescales measured in centuries. The responsibility that today's space actors bear to future generations of space users is one of the most compelling moral arguments for strengthening environmental governance of the orbital commons.

***

Chapter Summary

Chapter 11 has examined the environmental dimensions of space activity, tracing the evolution of space governance from a domain characterized by unconstrained freedom of use toward one requiring deliberate environmental stewardship.

Part I established the conceptual foundations for treating outer space as an environment. The finite character of orbital regions, the Kessler syndrome's cascading collision threat, the growing debris population, and the atmospheric effects of mega-constellation operations all demonstrate that the orbital environment is vulnerable to degradation. Existing treaty provisions—Article IX's due regard and harmful contamination obligations—provide implicit environmental protection but were not designed for the systemic challenges of contemporary space activity.

Part II examined the debris mitigation and sustainability frameworks that constitute the international community's primary response to the orbital environment challenge. The IADC and COPUOS debris mitigation guidelines, now reinforced by ISO standards and national regulatory requirements, have established a consensus approach to prevention. The LTS guidelines broadened the agenda from debris-specific mitigation to systemic sustainability governance. The voluntary character of these instruments is both their strength (enabling adoption by consensus) and their weakness (permitting uneven implementation).

Part III analyzed the emerging concept of space traffic management, examining the aviation analogy and its limits, the essential role of SSA infrastructure, the operational challenges of conjunction assessment and collision avoidance at mega-constellation scale, and the patchwork of national and commercial STM initiatives. The absence of an international STM authority, common data standards, or binding operational rules constitutes the most significant governance gap in contemporary space law.

Part IV considered future regulatory pathways, including the ICAO model for adaptive standards, the legal and technical challenges of active debris removal, and the potential for convergence among national licensing regimes to create de facto global environmental standards. The chapter concluded that the transition from freedom of use to environmental stewardship is underway but incomplete, and that the orbital environment's long-term sustainability depends on political commitment to collective action that the existing governance framework can facilitate but not compel.

In the next chapter, we turn to the mechanisms available when cooperation fails: dispute resolution and conflict management in international space law.

***

End of Chapter 11

Chapter 12

DISPUTE RESOLUTION AND CONFLICT MANAGEMENT IN INTERNATIONAL SPACE LAW

When a defunct Russian satellite collides with an American communications satellite, who pays? When one state's signals jam another's navigation system, where is the forum for redress? When a private company's debris damages a government satellite, what law applies? These questions—deceptively simple in formulation, extraordinarily complex in resolution—define the challenge of dispute resolution in international space law. This chapter examines how space disputes have been managed, why formal adjudication has been remarkably rare, the structural limits of existing mechanisms, and the innovative models that may be needed as space becomes more congested, commercialized, and contested.

Part 1

The Nature of Space Disputes and Diplomatic Settlement

Dispute resolution in international space law occupies a paradoxical position. On one hand, space activities are deeply intertwined with national security, commercial interests, and critical infrastructure—factors that make disputes highly sensitive and potentially destabilizing. On the other hand, formal legal disputes in space law have been remarkably rare. In over six decades of space activity, no case has been adjudicated before an international court, no arbitration has been concluded under space-specific rules, and the Liability Convention's Claims Commission has never been constituted. This absence of litigation does not indicate an absence of conflict; rather, it reflects the preference for diplomatic settlement, informal negotiation, and political accommodation that has characterized space governance since its inception.

The rarity of formal dispute resolution in space law is striking when compared to other domains of international law. International trade law has generated thousands of WTO panel and Appellate Body reports. International investment law has produced hundreds of investor-state arbitration awards. The law of the sea has been shaped by dozens of ITLOS cases and ICJ judgments on maritime delimitation. Even international humanitarian law—another domain where enforcement is inherently difficult—has been developed through proceedings before international criminal tribunals. Space law stands alone in having produced virtually no formal adjudication, despite governing activities worth hundreds of billions of dollars annually and affecting the national security of every spacefaring state. Understanding why this is so—and whether it should change—is essential to assessing the future of space governance.

Why Space Disputes Are Different

Disputes arising from space activities differ from those in many other areas of international law in ways that profoundly shape how they are managed. Several characteristics distinguish space disputes and explain the persistent preference for informal resolution over formal adjudication.

First, the strategic stakes are exceptionally high. Space systems support military command and control, intelligence gathering, nuclear deterrence, precision navigation, and secure communications. A dispute involving interference with military satellite systems can escalate rapidly from a technical disagreement to a strategic confrontation. States are therefore reluctant to submit such disputes to external adjudication, where outcomes cannot be controlled and where the proceedings themselves may reveal sensitive capabilities or vulnerabilities.

Second, technical complexity pervades space disputes. Determining the cause of satellite damage, attributing interference, assessing whether a conjunction resulted from negligence or unavoidable orbital mechanics, or evaluating whether a state's supervision of its operators was "appropriate" under Article VI requires specialized scientific and engineering knowledge that few legal institutions possess. The gap between legal expertise and technical knowledge creates barriers to effective adjudication and favors resolution mechanisms that can integrate technical assessment without the formalities of judicial procedure.

Third, attribution challenges are pervasive. In the terrestrial context, identifying the party responsible for harm is usually straightforward—the source of an oil spill, the manufacturer of a defective product, or the state that violated a treaty can typically be identified with reasonable confidence. In space, attribution is far more difficult. A satellite may fail due to a debris impact, but the debris fragment may be too small to track or attribute to a specific launching state. Signal interference may originate from multiple potential sources across different countries. A conjunction between two satellites may result from one operator's failure to maneuver, but the operator may lack the tracking data to prove it. These attribution difficulties undermine the factual foundation on which legal claims depend.

Fourth, the interdependence of space systems creates systemic risks from disputes. Space systems operate in shared orbital environments where one actor's behavior affects all others. Escalating a dispute—through sanctions, retaliatory interference, or hostile action—could disrupt services on which states, militaries, and billions of civilians depend. This systemic risk creates powerful incentives for quiet resolution and strong disincentives for confrontation.

Categories of Space-Related Disputes

Space-related disputes can be grouped into several overlapping categories, each with distinctive characteristics that influence the choice of resolution mechanism. Damage and liability disputes arise from physical harm caused by space objects—collisions, uncontrolled re-entries, debris impacts—and are governed primarily by the Liability Convention. Frequency and orbital slot conflicts concern competing claims to radiofrequency spectrum and geostationary orbital positions, addressed through ITU coordination procedures. Interference and harmful use disputes involve deliberate or negligent disruption of satellite signals, including jamming, spoofing, and cyber interference—activities that may violate the Outer Space Treaty's due regard obligation but are extraordinarily difficult to prove and attribute. Interpretive disputes concern the meaning of treaty provisions—such as the scope of "peaceful purposes," the boundary of "appropriate" supervision, or the limits of "non-appropriation"—and arise when states adopt conflicting interpretations that create operational friction. Commercial disputes with international dimensions involve private actors (launch providers, satellite operators, data companies) but engage state responsibility when the dispute implicates international obligations or when the private party's state must exercise diplomatic protection.

Emerging categories of disputes reflect the evolution of space activity. Resource utilization disputes—concerning competing claims to extraction sites, the adequacy of safety zones, or the interpretation of benefit-sharing obligations—are likely to increase as lunar and asteroid resource activities advance. Environmental disputes—concerning debris generation, atmospheric pollution from satellite re-entries, light pollution affecting astronomical observations, or failure to comply with debris mitigation guidelines—represent a growing area of potential conflict. On-orbit servicing and active debris removal disputes—concerning consent for proximity operations, liability for accidental damage during servicing, or the dual-use implications of rendezvous and capture technology—are already generating regulatory and diplomatic discussions. Cybersecurity disputes—concerning attacks on satellite ground systems, data theft, or interference with command and control links—straddle the boundary between space law and international law on cyber operations.

Dispute Type	Typical Parties	Primary Framework	Resolution Mechanism
Damage/liability	State vs. state (or via diplomatic protection)	Liability Convention	Diplomatic negotiation; Claims Commission (unused)
Frequency/ orbital slot	States; operators via national authorities	ITU Radio Regulations	ITU coordination; Radiocommunication Bureau mediation
Signal interference/ jamming	State vs. state	OST Art. IX; ITU Constitution	Bilateral consultation; ITU complaint procedures
Treaty interpretation	State vs. state	Outer Space Treaty; relevant treaties	COPUOS discussion; diplomatic channels; ICJ (theoretically)
Commercial/ mixed	Private actors; states as responsible parties	National law; contracts; Liability Convention	Arbitration; national courts; diplomatic protection
Military/security	State vs. state	OST; customary int'l law; UN Charter	Bilateral channels; UNSC; confidence-building measures

Diplomatic Settlement: The Dominant Mode

The peaceful settlement of disputes is a cornerstone of international law, enshrined in Article 33 of the UN Charter, which calls on states to seek solutions through negotiation, enquiry, mediation, conciliation, arbitration, judicial settlement, or other peaceful means. In space law, diplomacy has been overwhelmingly dominant—not merely as a first resort but as the only resort. This preference is reflected explicitly in the Liability Convention, which requires that claims be presented through diplomatic channels and that the parties attempt resolution through negotiation before any escalation to a Claims Commission.

Diplomatic settlement offers several advantages that explain its dominance. Flexibility allows outcomes to be tailored to the specific circumstances of each dispute, accommodating technical uncertainty, political sensitivities, and commercial confidentiality that formal legal proceedings may struggle to manage. Confidentiality protects sensitive information about capabilities, vulnerabilities, and operational practices. Preservation of relationships is critical in a domain where the same states must continue to cooperate on ISS operations, launch services, frequency coordination, and debris mitigation regardless of any particular disagreement. And the capacity to accommodate technical uncertainty allows parties to reach pragmatic solutions without requiring the definitive factual findings that judicial proceedings demand but that the evidentiary challenges of space disputes often preclude.

The Liability Convention's diplomatic framework illustrates how space law structures the interaction between negotiation and escalation. Under the Convention, a claim must be presented through diplomatic channels within one year of the damage or the identification of the responsible launching state. The parties then have one year to negotiate a settlement. Only if negotiations fail within this period may either party request the establishment of a Claims Commission. This structured timeline creates incentives for resolution: the claimant knows that it has a fallback if negotiation fails, while the respondent knows that stonewalling will lead to a more formal process. Yet the Claims Commission's recommendatory character (unless the parties agree otherwise) limits its deterrent effect, as states can accept or disregard its recommendations without legal consequence.

Frequency coordination disputes within the ITU framework provide the most active, if little-known, example of space-related dispute management. The ITU's Radio Regulations allocate radiofrequency spectrum and orbital positions through a coordination process that requires states to negotiate with all potentially affected parties before activating a satellite network. When coordination fails—because states cannot agree on acceptable interference levels, or because one state activates a satellite network without completing coordination—the Radiocommunication Bureau mediates, and the Radio Regulations Board may intervene. These disputes are technical rather than geopolitical in character, but they involve billions of dollars in commercial value and can delay or prevent satellite deployments. The ITU's institutional capacity to resolve frequency disputes through technical expertise and established procedures offers a model for other areas of space dispute resolution.

Signal jamming represents one of the most politically sensitive categories of space disputes and illustrates the limits of existing resolution mechanisms. Multiple states have been accused of deliberately jamming satellite signals—including GPS navigation signals, satellite television broadcasts, and communications links. Iran has been accused of jamming satellite television broadcasts from foreign providers. North Korea has been accused of jamming GPS signals affecting South Korean aviation. Russia has been accused of jamming GPS signals in the Baltic region and in conflict zones. In each case, the accused state has either denied responsibility or remained silent, and no formal legal proceedings have been initiated. The ITU Constitution prohibits harmful interference with radio signals, and Article IX of the Outer Space Treaty requires states to avoid harmful interference with other states' activities. Yet the practical difficulty of proving attribution, the geopolitical sensitivity of the accusations, and the absence of compulsory dispute resolution procedures have meant that signal jamming disputes remain in the diplomatic sphere—resolved, if at all, through bilateral pressure and public criticism rather than legal process.

> **■ The Cosmos 954 Incident: Space Law's Most Prominent Dispute**
>
> On January 24, 1978, the Soviet nuclear-powered Kosmos 954 satellite re-entered Earth's atmosphere and scattered radioactive debris across approximately 124,000 square kilometers of Canada's Northwest Territories.
>
> Canada presented a formal claim to the Soviet Union under the Liability Convention, seeking CAD 6,041,174.70 for search, recovery, and cleanup costs.
>
> After prolonged diplomatic negotiations, the dispute was settled in 1981 for CAD 3,000,000—approximately half of Canada's claim—through a diplomatic protocol rather than a Claims Commission.
>
> The case remains the only formal international claim ever presented under the Liability Convention. Its resolution through negotiated compromise rather than adjudication set a precedent that has shaped expectations about how space disputes are managed.

Informal Conflict Management and Confidence-Building

Beyond formal diplomatic claims, many space-related disagreements are managed through informal channels that never reach the level of a formal "dispute" in the legal sense. Technical consultations between space agencies, data-sharing arrangements between satellite operators, frequency coordination discussions within the ITU framework, and bilateral military-to-military communication channels all serve to defuse tensions before they escalate. The U.S.-Russia bilateral space security dialogues (when active), NASA-Roscosmos operational coordination for ISS operations, and multilateral discussions within COPUOS all function as conflict prevention mechanisms.

Confidence-building measures—transparency measures, notification of planned activities, voluntary restraints on certain behaviors—play a particularly important role in preventing military space disputes. The Prevention of an Arms Race in Outer Space (PAROS) discussions at the Conference on Disarmament, the UN General Assembly's transparency and confidence-building measures (TCBMs) resolutions, and bilateral agreements such as the U.S.-Russia notifications on launches of ballistic missiles all contribute to a framework that reduces the risk of misunderstanding and miscalculation. While these mechanisms do not resolve disputes in a legal sense, they address the conditions that give rise to disputes—mistrust, uncertainty, and misperception—making formal resolution less frequently necessary.

Specific incidents illustrate how informal conflict management operates in practice. When Russia's Luch satellite maneuvered between two Intelsat satellites in geostationary orbit in 2014 and 2015, the unusual proximity operations generated concern about potential intelligence-gathering or interference. The incidents were addressed through diplomatic channels and public commentary rather than formal legal proceedings, though they prompted increased attention to the absence of norms governing proximity operations. When China tested a ground-based missile that destroyed a satellite in 2007, the debris generated by the test threatened satellites of multiple nations, but no state filed a formal legal claim—instead, the international community responded through diplomatic criticism, COPUOS discussions, and strengthened advocacy for debris mitigation guidelines and ASAT test moratoria.

The 2021 Russian ASAT test that destroyed the Cosmos 1408 satellite and generated debris threatening the ISS crew represents a particularly stark example of the gap between the severity of harm and the modesty of the response. Despite the fact that the test created debris that endangered the lives of astronauts and cosmonauts aboard the ISS (including Russian cosmonauts), forced the crew to shelter in their return vehicles, and will continue to endanger space activities in the affected altitude band for years, the international response was limited to diplomatic condemnation, a U.S.-led initiative for a moratorium on destructive ASAT testing, and UN General Assembly resolutions. No formal legal claim was filed, no liability proceeding was initiated, and no reparation was sought. The incident demonstrates that even egregious conduct that creates immediate danger to human life and long-term environmental harm may not trigger the formal dispute resolution mechanisms that international space law provides.

The limits of diplomatic settlement should not be overlooked. Power asymmetries influence outcomes: a small developing country whose satellite is damaged by debris from a major spacefaring state may lack the political leverage to secure adequate compensation through negotiation. The smaller state may also face a stark choice between pursuing its legal claim and maintaining the broader diplomatic relationship with a state on which it depends for trade, aid, or security cooperation. Confidentiality, while protecting sensitive information, may also conceal unjust outcomes from public scrutiny and prevent the development of precedent that could guide future cases. The absence of authoritative legal rulings leaves contested interpretations unresolved, perpetuating ambiguity that may eventually generate more serious disputes. And reliance on diplomacy offers no recourse to private actors, whose commercial losses may be substantial but who have no standing to pursue claims through diplomatic channels unless their home state chooses to exercise diplomatic protection on their behalf—a discretionary decision that the state is under no obligation to make and that may be influenced by considerations entirely unrelated to the merits of the claim.

The growing volume and diversity of space activities will test the limits of diplomatic settlement with increasing urgency. When space was the domain of a small number of states operating a modest number of satellites, disputes could be managed through the close personal and institutional relationships that characterized the space community. As the number of spacefaring states grows to over seventy, the number of satellite operators reaches thousands, and the volume of conjunction events reaches millions per year, the informal, relationship-based dispute management that has served the community well may prove insufficient. The question is not whether more formal dispute resolution mechanisms will be needed, but whether they will be developed proactively—through deliberate institutional design—or reactively, in response to a crisis that exposes the inadequacy of existing approaches.

> *"The remarkable rarity of formal space disputes is both a testament to the success of cooperative governance and a warning sign that legitimate grievances may go unaddressed. The absence of adjudication preserves diplomatic harmony but at the cost of legal development, authoritative interpretation, and accountability."*
>
> – On the paradox of dispute resolution in space law

***

Part 11

Arbitration, Adjudication, and Quasi-Judicial Mechanisms

While diplomacy has dominated the resolution of space-related disputes, international law provides a spectrum of formal dispute-resolution mechanisms that may be invoked when negotiation fails or proves insufficient. These mechanisms—ranging from arbitration to judicial settlement—offer legal certainty, procedural structure, and authoritative interpretation of contested obligations. In the context of space law, however, their use has been remarkably limited, reflecting both practical constraints and political caution.

Arbitration: Flexibility and Expertise

Arbitration occupies a productive middle ground between diplomacy and adjudication. It allows parties to submit disputes to an independent tribunal while retaining significant control over the process, including the selection of arbitrators, the applicable law, the procedural rules, and the confidentiality of proceedings. These features make arbitration particularly attractive for space disputes, where technical complexity, commercial sensitivity, and the involvement of both state and private actors create needs that neither pure diplomacy nor judicial proceedings can fully serve.

The Permanent Court of Arbitration (PCA) adopted the Optional Rules for Arbitration of Disputes Relating to Outer Space Activities in 2011—the first international arbitration rules specifically designed for the space sector. Developed under the leadership of PCA Secretary-General Hugo Hans Siblesz and informed by consultations with space law experts and industry practitioners, the rules adapt the PCA's Arbitration Rules to the specific characteristics of space disputes. They permit the appointment of arbitrators with technical and scientific expertise, accommodate the participation of both states and private entities, address confidentiality concerns arising from sensitive commercial or national security information, and allow for expedited proceedings when urgency requires rapid resolution.

Despite their availability since 2011, the PCA Optional Rules have never been formally invoked in a space dispute. This non-use does not necessarily reflect inadequacy; rather, it reflects the broader pattern of space disputes being resolved through informal channels before they reach the stage where formal arbitration would be appropriate. The rules' existence may nonetheless have a "shadow effect"—influencing negotiations by providing a credible fallback that motivates parties to reach agreement rather than risk the costs and uncertainties of arbitration.

Commercial arbitration under established institutional rules—the International Chamber of Commerce (ICC), the London Court of International Arbitration (LCIA), or the Singapore International Arbitration Centre (SIAC)—plays a significant role in resolving private disputes arising from space activities. Launch service contracts, satellite manufacturing agreements, in-orbit insurance claims, ground station leases, and satellite capacity purchase agreements routinely include arbitration clauses. These disputes are resolved within commercial arbitration frameworks rather than space-specific mechanisms, applying the law chosen by the parties (typically the governing law of the contract) rather than public international space law. The vast majority of space-related commercial arbitrations are confidential, making it difficult to assess the volume or nature of disputes being resolved through this channel.

The space insurance market provides a distinctive dispute resolution ecosystem that operates largely outside both diplomatic and judicial frameworks. When a satellite fails in orbit or during launch, the financial consequences—often hundreds of millions of dollars—are allocated through insurance contracts governed by the London market's established practices. Disputes between insurers and insured operators are resolved through expert claims adjustment, negotiation, and, when necessary, arbitration under the contractual terms of the policy. The insurance market has developed substantial expertise in evaluating technical causation—determining whether a satellite failure resulted from a manufacturing defect, a launch anomaly, a debris impact, or an operational error—that would be valuable if applied to the broader challenge of space dispute resolution. Indeed, the insurance market's private claims adjustment process is arguably the most active and sophisticated space dispute resolution mechanism in operation today, even though it operates entirely within commercial law rather than public international law.

The relationship between commercial dispute resolution and public international law creates a potential gap. A commercial arbitration tribunal resolving a launch failure dispute will apply contract law and may not address the international law questions that the failure raises: whether the launching state fulfilled its supervision obligations under Article VI, whether the debris generated by the failure was properly reported under the Registration Convention, or whether the state's licensing regime met international standards. These public law questions may go unresolved even as the private law dispute is settled, leaving the international legal framework uninterpreted and undeveloped.

The International Court of Justice

The International Court of Justice (ICJ), as the principal judicial organ of the United Nations, has jurisdiction to hear contentious cases between states and to issue advisory opinions on legal questions referred by authorized UN organs and agencies. In theory, the ICJ could adjudicate any dispute concerning the interpretation or application of the Outer Space Treaty, the Liability Convention, the Registration Convention, or other space law instruments. Several of these treaties contain dispute resolution provisions that could lead to ICJ jurisdiction: the Outer Space Treaty itself contains no compulsory jurisdiction clause, but states that have accepted the ICJ's compulsory jurisdiction under Article 36(2) of the ICJ Statute could, in principle, bring space law cases before the Court.

In practice, no state has ever brought a space law case to the ICJ, and the Court has never issued an advisory opinion on space law questions. Several factors explain this reluctance. States are unwilling to establish binding precedents that might constrain their future freedom of action in a strategically important domain. Judicial proceedings are public, creating risks that sensitive information about military space capabilities, operational practices, or intelligence activities could be disclosed. The ICJ's general jurisdiction means that its judges may lack the technical expertise needed to evaluate complex space engineering questions. And the Court's proceedings are lengthy—typically spanning several years—while many space disputes require rapid resolution to prevent ongoing harm.

Despite these obstacles, the ICJ's potential contribution to space law should not be entirely discounted. An advisory opinion—which does not require the consent of any state and does not create binding obligations—could provide authoritative interpretation of contested provisions such as the meaning of "peaceful purposes" in the Outer Space Treaty, the scope of "appropriate" supervision under Article VI, or the relationship between non-appropriation and resource extraction. Advisory opinions by the ICJ on other subjects—including the legality of nuclear weapons (1996), the legal consequences of Israel's wall in occupied Palestinian territory (2004), and the Chagos Archipelago (2019)—have significantly influenced the development of international law even without binding force. A well-crafted request for an advisory opinion on a space law question could provide normative guidance that decades of diplomatic discussion have failed to produce.

The procedure for obtaining an advisory opinion requires that a request be made by the UN General Assembly, the Security Council, or another authorized UN body or specialized agency. COPUOS itself does not have standing to request advisory opinions directly, but the General Assembly could do so based on a recommendation from COPUOS or the Fourth Committee. The strategic value of an advisory opinion would depend on the question posed: a narrowly framed question about a specific provision—such as whether the extraction of space resources constitutes "appropriation" under Article II—could provide focused guidance, while a broadly framed question about the legal framework for commercial space activities could invite a comprehensive assessment of the Treaty's contemporary relevance. The risk, of course, is that an advisory opinion could produce an interpretation that some states find unacceptable, potentially undermining rather than strengthening the cooperative framework. This risk explains why no state has yet advocated for an ICJ advisory opinion on space law, despite the acknowledged need for authoritative interpretation.

The Liability Convention Claims Commission

The Liability Convention establishes the most detailed dispute resolution mechanism in space law: a Claims Commission that may be constituted when diplomatic negotiations fail to resolve a liability claim within one year. The Commission comprises three members—one appointed by the claimant state, one by the launching state, and the third (the chairman) selected by agreement or, failing agreement, by the UN Secretary-General. The Commission's decision is binding if the parties have so agreed; otherwise, it constitutes a "final and recommendatory" award that the parties are to consider "in good faith."

The Claims Commission mechanism has never been constituted. The Cosmos 954 incident—the only formal claim ever presented under the Convention—was resolved through diplomatic negotiation before the Commission stage was reached. This non-use raises questions about the Commission's practical viability. The appointment process, which gives each party effective veto power over the chairman's selection through the requirement of agreement, could create deadlock. The Commission's recommendatory (rather than binding) character reduces its deterrent effect, as states know that unfavorable recommendations need not be accepted. And the Convention's limitation to interstate claims—private parties have no standing—means that the growing category of commercial space disputes falls outside the Commission's jurisdiction entirely.

The Claims Commission's design reflects the political compromises of the early 1970s when the Liability Convention was negotiated. The Soviet Union and other socialist states insisted on a non-binding mechanism that would not subject them to compulsory adjudication; Western states sought a more robust procedure that would ensure accountability. The result was a compromise that created a formal mechanism with limited practical authority—a pattern that characterizes much of space law's dispute resolution architecture. The Commission exists as a legal option but lacks the compulsory jurisdiction, binding authority, and enforcement mechanisms that would make it a credible deterrent or an effective resolution tool.

The question of whether the Claims Commission should be reformed or replaced has been debated by space law scholars for decades. Proposals have included making Commission decisions binding by default (rather than merely recommendatory), extending standing to private parties alongside or in place of states, reducing the appointment process's susceptibility to deadlock by providing for automatic third-party appointment of the chairman, and expanding the Commission's jurisdiction to cover not only physical damage but also interference, contamination, and environmental harm. None of these proposals has gained political traction, reflecting the broader reluctance of states to strengthen compulsory dispute resolution in the space domain.

> ■ **Dispute Resolution Mechanisms in Space Law Treaties**
>
> OST Article III: Activities must conform to international law, including the UN Charter's peaceful settlement obligations (Art. 33).
>
> Liability Convention Art. XIV–XX: Claims presented through diplomatic channels; if unresolved within one year, either party may request a Claims Commission (never constituted).
>
> Registration Convention: No specific dispute resolution provision.
>
> Moon Agreement Art. 15: Disputes to be settled by negotiation; failing that, other peaceful means including good offices, mediation, conciliation, arbitration, or judicial settlement.
>
> ITU Constitution Art. 56: Disputes on interpretation may be settled by negotiation, mediation, or arbitration.

Quasi-Judicial and Administrative Mechanisms

Beyond formal arbitration and adjudication, space governance relies on a range of quasi-judicial and administrative mechanisms that resolve disputes through technical expertise rather than legal authority. The ITU's Radiocommunication Bureau mediates frequency coordination disputes through technical analysis and administrative procedures, resolving conflicts over spectrum use and orbital slot allocation that affect satellite operations. The ITU's Radio Regulations Board adjudicates disputes that the Bureau cannot resolve, issuing decisions that carry significant practical authority even if their formal legal status is debated.

The ISS Intergovernmental Agreement (IGA) and its associated Memoranda of Understanding include dispute resolution provisions tailored to the unique challenges of multinational space station operations. The IGA provides for consultation and negotiation, with the possibility of referral to an agreed arbitration procedure. The IGA's cross-waiver of liability—under which each partner bears its own losses from ISS-related activities, waiving claims against other partners regardless of fault—has been particularly significant in preventing disputes by removing the most common basis for claims: damage caused by one partner's activities to another partner's assets or personnel.

These provisions have functioned primarily as a framework for operational disagreements—concerning resource allocation (crew time, power, data bandwidth), module utilization priorities, experiment scheduling, and crew procedures—rather than as formal legal dispute resolution. The ISS partnership's success in managing operational friction across fifteen partner nations and five space agencies over more than two decades of continuous habitation, including through periods of severe geopolitical tension (such as the Russia-Ukraine conflict beginning in 2022), is itself a testament to the effectiveness of informal, relationship-based conflict management in space operations. The ISS experience suggests that operational partnerships with shared infrastructure create strong mutual dependence that motivates cooperative dispute management—a dynamic that may become increasingly relevant as commercial space stations, lunar surface operations, and other multinational facilities develop.

***

Part III

Structural Limits of Existing Frameworks

Despite the availability of diplomatic, arbitral, and judicial mechanisms, dispute resolution in international space law remains underdeveloped and underutilized. This is not merely a matter of institutional design but a reflection of deeper structural, political, and technical constraints. As space activity becomes more congested, commercialized, and strategically sensitive, these limitations become increasingly consequential.

State-Centric Design in a Multi-Actor Environment

International space law was constructed around the assumption that states are the primary actors in outer space. Dispute-resolution mechanisms reflect this assumption by privileging interstate claims and diplomatic protection. The Liability Convention allows only states to present claims for compensation; private parties must rely on their home state to exercise diplomatic protection on their behalf—a decision that lies within the state's sovereign discretion and may be influenced by political, commercial, or strategic considerations entirely unrelated to the merits of the private party's claim.

This state-centric design is increasingly misaligned with operational reality. Private companies now own and operate a majority of active satellites, conduct a majority of orbital launches, and make the collision avoidance decisions that determine whether conjunctions result in avoidance maneuvers or collisions. SpaceX, Amazon, OneWeb, and other commercial operators have commercial interests that may diverge from their home states' diplomatic priorities. A launch failure that destroys a commercial payload creates a dispute between the launch provider and the satellite operator that is fundamentally commercial in character, even though the underlying activity is governed by international space law and the responsible states bear international liability for any third-party damage. The Sea Launch venture, which conducted launches from a floating platform in international waters, demonstrated the jurisdictional complexity when multinational commercial operations intersect with the state-centric liability framework: identifying the "launching state" for a Sea Launch mission involved determining which of several jurisdictions—the United States, Russia, Norway, or Ukraine—bore international responsibility.

The absence of direct access for private parties to international dispute resolution mechanisms creates a governance gap that commercial arbitration partially fills but that leaves public international law questions—about the adequacy of state supervision, the reasonableness of due regard obligations, or the allocation of liability for debris damage—unresolved. This gap will widen as private actors assume greater roles in activities with international law dimensions: commercial lunar operations under the Artemis Accords, private space station operations, on-orbit servicing and manufacturing, and mega-constellation management all generate potential disputes that may require resolution at the intersection of private commercial law and public international law.

Evidentiary and Technical Barriers

Effective dispute resolution depends on evidence. In space-related disputes, evidence is often technical, complex, and asymmetrically distributed. Determining the cause of a satellite failure may require access to telemetry data that only the operator possesses, tracking data that only the U.S. Space Force provides with sufficient accuracy, and engineering analysis that requires specialized expertise. Attributing signal interference requires direction-finding capabilities, spectrum monitoring equipment, and technical analysis that many states lack. Proving that a conjunction resulted from one operator's negligent failure to maneuver requires conjunction data, maneuver history, and probability assessments that are often proprietary or classified.

These evidentiary barriers create asymmetries that systematically disadvantage less technologically advanced states and smaller commercial operators. A developing country whose satellite is damaged by debris from a major space power may be unable to prove attribution—not because it lacks a valid legal claim, but because it lacks the tracking data and technical capability needed to establish the factual foundation for that claim. The U.S. Space Surveillance Network is the only system capable of tracking objects as small as 10 centimeters in LEO, and its data is provided voluntarily through Space-Track.org with caveats about accuracy and completeness. A state that does not operate its own tracking systems must rely on this American-provided data to support any claim—data that may not be sufficiently precise or detailed for legal purposes and that is controlled by a state that may have its own interests in the outcome.

The attribution challenge is particularly acute for debris-related damage. When a satellite ceases functioning, the cause may be a debris impact—but distinguishing debris impact from component failure, design defect, or radiation damage requires detailed telemetry analysis that the satellite's operator may or may not be able to perform. Even if a debris impact is confirmed, identifying the specific fragment—and hence the launching state responsible under the Liability Convention—may be impossible if the fragment is too small to have been tracked. The result is a legal framework that assigns liability to launching states but an operational reality in which liability cannot be enforced because the responsible party cannot be identified. This enforcement gap undermines the deterrent function of the liability regime and means that the costs of debris damage are borne by the victim rather than the polluter—a perverse incentive structure that contradicts the polluter-pays principle established in other areas of environmental law.

Without shared data frameworks, independent verification mechanisms, or technical assistance programs, formal dispute resolution may be practically inaccessible to precisely those parties who need it most. The establishment of independent, multilateral tracking and attribution capabilities—analogous to the OPCW's investigation capacity for chemical weapons or the IAEA's safeguards inspections for nuclear facilities—could address this evidentiary gap. However, the military sensitivity of space tracking data (which reveals the capabilities and limitations of surveillance systems) has prevented the development of such independent capabilities.

Political Sensitivity and Strategic Restraint

Many space-related disputes implicate national security, critical infrastructure, or strategic advantage. Signal jamming of GPS or communications satellites, close approaches by military inspection satellites, and ASAT weapon testing all generate disputes that states prefer to manage quietly through intelligence channels and diplomatic communications rather than through public legal proceedings. Formal dispute resolution risks revealing classified capabilities or vulnerabilities, establishing precedents that constrain future freedom of action, and escalating political tensions at moments when restraint may be more prudent.

This strategic restraint is understandable but carries costs. By avoiding formal legal resolution, states prevent the development of jurisprudence that could clarify contested norms, establish expectations about acceptable behavior, and create deterrents against future violations. The absence of authoritative legal interpretation means that states can maintain contradictory positions on questions such as whether ASAT testing violates the Outer Space Treaty's peaceful purposes obligation, whether signal jamming constitutes "harmful interference" under Article IX, or whether a satellite's proximity operations constitute a threat of force under the UN Charter. These ambiguities may preserve diplomatic flexibility in the short term, but they erode the normative framework that makes cooperation possible in the long term.

Power Asymmetries and Access to Justice

Reliance on diplomatic settlement systematically favors states with greater political, economic, and technological power. A major spacefaring state that causes debris damage to a smaller country's satellite can offer a negotiated settlement that reflects its bargaining position rather than the legal merits of the claim. The smaller state, lacking the political leverage to insist on full compensation and lacking the technical capacity to prove its case in a formal proceeding, may accept an inadequate settlement—or may decline to pursue its claim at all. The Cosmos 954 settlement, in which Canada accepted approximately half of its documented costs, may reflect this dynamic: Canada, while a technologically advanced state, was negotiating with a nuclear-armed superpower during the Cold War and may have prioritized diplomatic relations over full financial recovery.

Access to justice is further limited by the requirement that claims be channeled through states. A private satellite operator whose asset is destroyed by debris from another state's launch vehicle cannot bring a claim directly; it must persuade its home government to exercise diplomatic protection. The government may decline for reasons entirely unrelated to the merits: diplomatic relations with the launching state may be more important than one company's commercial loss; the government may lack the resources to pursue the claim; or political considerations may counsel restraint. The result is a dispute resolution system in which the strength of one's claim matters less than the willingness and capacity of one's government to advocate for it.

The Risk of Normative Stagnation

Perhaps the most significant long-term consequence of the current dispute resolution landscape is normative stagnation. In other areas of international law, adjudication has played a transformative role in developing the law. The ICJ's decisions in cases such as the Nicaragua case (1986), the Nuclear Weapons advisory opinion (1996), and the Pulp Mills case (2010) established important precedents that shaped state behavior and scholarly understanding. The WTO Dispute Settlement Body has produced hundreds of panel and Appellate Body reports that have interpreted and developed international trade law in ways that diplomatic negotiation alone could never have achieved. ITLOS has developed the law of the sea through cases on provisional measures, maritime delimitation, and deep seabed mining.

Space law has no comparable body of jurisprudence. After more than six decades, the fundamental provisions of the Outer Space Treaty—"peaceful purposes," "due regard," "harmful contamination," "appropriate supervision"—remain without authoritative judicial interpretation. Their meaning is contested among scholars, debated in diplomatic forums, and asserted unilaterally by states. This normative uncertainty is not merely an academic concern; it has practical consequences for operators who must determine what "due regard" requires in planning a mega-constellation deployment, for regulators who must determine what constitutes "appropriate" supervision of private space activities, and for states that must assess whether another state's military space activities are consistent with "peaceful purposes." The absence of authoritative interpretation creates a permissive environment in which states can claim compliance with vaguely defined obligations while engaging in conduct that other states consider inconsistent with those obligations.

> ■ **The Paradox of Non-Litigation**
>
> The absence of space law adjudication is both a strength and a weakness of the current governance system. It is a strength because it reflects a successful culture of cooperation and informal conflict management that has prevented disputes from escalating into confrontations. It is a weakness because it deprives space law of the jurisprudential development that other areas of international law have benefited from. Maritime law, trade law, investment law, and human rights law have all been shaped significantly by judicial and arbitral decisions that clarified ambiguous provisions, established precedents, and created expectations about state behavior. Space law lacks this jurisprudential foundation, leaving its most contested provisions—peaceful purposes, due regard, appropriate supervision, non-appropriation—without authoritative interpretation after more than sixty years.

Jurisdictional Fragmentation and Legal Uncertainty

Space disputes frequently implicate multiple legal regimes simultaneously. A single incident may engage international space law (the Liability Convention's allocation of responsibility), telecommunications law (the ITU's frequency coordination framework), environmental principles (debris mitigation obligations), domestic regulatory law (licensing conditions), contractual obligations (launch service or insurance agreements), and potentially human rights law (if harm to individuals results). This multi-layered legal landscape complicates forum selection, creates risks of inconsistent outcomes, and generates uncertainty about applicable law.

The fragmentation problem is compounded by the absence of hierarchy among forums. There is no space law equivalent of the WTO's Dispute Settlement Body, which provides a single forum for trade disputes with clear rules about applicable law and appellate review. A party to a space dispute must choose among diplomatic channels, national courts, commercial arbitration, the PCA Optional Rules, and (theoretically) the ICJ—each with different jurisdictional requirements, procedural rules, and legal frameworks. The result is a dispute resolution landscape that is simultaneously rich in options and poor in coherence.

Consider a hypothetical but realistic scenario: a Chinese launch vehicle fails during ascent and its debris damages a European telecommunications satellite insured by a London market syndicate. The European satellite operator has a contractual claim against its insurer (governed by English law), a contractual claim against the Chinese launch provider (governed by the launch contract's chosen law, possibly Chinese or Swiss), and a potential international law claim under the Liability Convention (requiring its home state to exercise diplomatic protection against China as the launching state). The insurer, having paid the claim, may be subrogated to the operator's rights against the launch provider. The operator's home state may have political reasons for not pursuing a diplomatic claim against China. The resulting jurisdictional fragmentation means that different aspects of the same incident may be addressed in different forums, applying different laws, potentially reaching inconsistent results—or may not be addressed at all if no single forum has both jurisdiction and practical viability.

> *"Space law has mechanisms for resolving disputes but not a system for resolving disputes. The distinction matters: mechanisms are available individually, but they are not integrated into a coherent framework that guides parties from disagreement to resolution through a predictable, principled process."*
>
> – On the absence of systemic dispute resolution in space law

***

Part IV

Future Models for Space Dispute Resolution

As space activity enters a phase marked by congestion, commercialization, and strategic competition, the limitations of existing dispute-resolution mechanisms have become increasingly apparent. Preventing conflict and managing disputes in outer space will require innovative, adaptive, and hybrid models that reflect the unique characteristics of the space domain while remaining grounded in international legal principles.

From Reactive Resolution to Preventive Governance

The most effective dispute resolution mechanism is one that prevents disputes from arising in the first place. A defining feature of future space governance is likely to be a shift from reactive adjudication toward preventive frameworks that reduce the probability of conflict through transparency, coordination, and pre-established protocols. Mandatory notification of potentially hazardous activities—such as planned de-orbits, proximity operations, or ASAT-capable maneuvers—can prevent misunderstandings that might otherwise escalate into disputes. Shared conjunction assessment and warning systems provide common situational awareness that enables coordinated responses to collision risks. Pre-established protocols for resolving close-approach incidents—analogous to the "rules of the road" that prevent collisions at sea—create predictable behavioral expectations that reduce both the probability of harm and the likelihood of disputes about responsibility.

The space traffic management concepts discussed in Chapter 11 are essentially preventive dispute resolution mechanisms. By establishing shared data infrastructure, common operational standards, and coordination protocols, STM frameworks address the conditions that generate disputes—information asymmetry, conflicting operational decisions, and uncertainty about other actors' intentions. Investing in STM is therefore an investment in dispute prevention: the more transparent, coordinated, and predictable orbital operations become, the fewer disputes will arise from the ambiguities and miscommunications that currently characterize shared orbital environments.

The concept of "rules of the road" for orbital operations—analogous to the International Regulations for Preventing Collisions at Sea (COLREGs)—would constitute a form of preventive dispute resolution by establishing clear expectations about who maneuvers, when, and how. COLREGs specify which vessel gives way in various encounter scenarios, reducing both the probability of collision and the potential for disputes about responsibility when collisions occur. Comparable rules for orbital operations—specifying which operator maneuvers in a conjunction, the minimum acceptable miss distance, the required lead time for maneuver notification, and the communication protocols for coordination—would serve a dual function: preventing the physical events that generate disputes and providing the normative baseline against which responsibility can be assessed when prevention fails.

Hybrid Diplomatic-Legal Mechanisms

Purely diplomatic approaches and purely judicial proceedings each have significant limitations for space disputes. Diplomacy lacks the authority to produce binding outcomes, develop precedent, or provide access to private parties; adjudication lacks the flexibility, confidentiality, and speed that space disputes often require. Hybrid mechanisms that combine elements of both offer a promising path forward.

A standing mediation panel for space disputes, composed of experts in space law, orbital mechanics, telecommunications, and international relations, could provide a permanent institutional framework for resolving disputes that diplomacy alone cannot address. Unlike ad hoc arbitration, which requires parties to agree on a tribunal for each dispute, a standing panel would develop institutional expertise, accumulate knowledge, and provide a readily accessible forum that reduces the transaction costs of initiating dispute resolution. The panel's proceedings could be confidential, its recommendations non-binding (preserving diplomatic flexibility), but its composition and expertise would lend its recommendations significant persuasive authority.

A graduated escalation model could structure the progression from informal consultation through mediation to binding arbitration, with each stage providing appropriate incentives for resolution while preserving the option of escalation if earlier stages fail. The Liability Convention already contemplates a two-stage process (negotiation, then Claims Commission), but this model could be refined and expanded. A well-designed graduated model would include mandatory good-faith consultation within specified time limits (for example, sixty days for initial response, six months for substantive negotiation), with failure to respond in good faith triggering automatic escalation; optional mediation by a standing panel of experts, available to either party and conducted within a defined timeframe; binding arbitration if mediation fails (with the parties' advance consent, provided through a standing agreement or treaty provision); and technical fact-finding procedures—conducted by independent experts with access to tracking data, telemetry, and operational records—to address evidentiary challenges that would otherwise prevent effective dispute resolution.

The WTO's Dispute Settlement Understanding provides an instructive model for graduated escalation. WTO members must first attempt consultations; if consultations fail within sixty days, a panel is established automatically upon request; panel decisions may be appealed to the Appellate Body; and enforcement is backed by the threat of trade sanctions. This system has been criticized on various grounds, but it demonstrates that graduated escalation can function effectively in a domain involving sensitive sovereign interests and substantial economic stakes. Adapting its key features—mandatory consultations, automatic panel establishment, independent fact-finding, and credible enforcement—to the space context would require overcoming states' reluctance to accept compulsory jurisdiction, but the WTO precedent demonstrates that such reluctance can be overcome when the benefits of a rules-based system are sufficiently compelling.

Expanding Access for Non-State Actors

The growing role of private actors in space activities makes their exclusion from international dispute resolution mechanisms increasingly untenable. Several approaches could expand access without fundamentally restructuring the state-centric framework of international space law. Arbitration clauses in international space agreements—including the Artemis Accords, future resource governance frameworks, and bilateral space cooperation agreements—could provide for the participation of private entities in dispute resolution alongside or in place of their home states.

National space legislation could require domestic dispute resolution mechanisms for private space disputes, with international coordination to prevent jurisdictional conflicts. Several states have already incorporated dispute resolution provisions into their space laws: France's Space Operations Act provides for administrative review of licensing decisions, the UK's Space Industry Act establishes regulatory appeal mechanisms, and the United States has well-developed administrative and judicial review processes for FAA and FCC decisions affecting space operators. Harmonizing these domestic mechanisms—through mutual recognition agreements, common procedural standards, or model legislation—could create a more coherent landscape for commercial space dispute resolution.

Industry-led dispute resolution mechanisms—such as those developed by the space insurance market for claims adjustment, the Space Data Association's coordination protocols, and commercial arbitration under standard industry contracts—could be formalized and strengthened to provide reliable, efficient resolution of commercial space disputes. The space insurance market, in particular, has developed sophisticated claims assessment procedures that evaluate technical causation, allocate responsibility, and determine compensation with an expertise that few legal institutions can match. Formalizing these procedures, ensuring their transparency, and linking them to international legal frameworks could create a hybrid system that combines industry expertise with legal authority.

The investment arbitration model offers a particularly instructive precedent. Bilateral investment treaties (BITs) and multilateral instruments such as the ICSID Convention allow private investors to bring claims against states directly, without requiring their home state to exercise diplomatic protection. A comparable mechanism for space activities—allowing private operators to bring claims against states for inadequate supervision, excessive interference, or failure to fulfill treaty obligations—would transform the accountability landscape of space governance. Whether states would accept such constraints on their sovereignty in the space domain is uncertain, but the precedent of investment arbitration demonstrates that it is possible.

The investment arbitration analogy also carries cautionary lessons. The investor-state dispute settlement (ISDS) system has been criticized for creating a chilling effect on regulation, as states may hesitate to adopt environmental, health, or safety measures that could trigger investor claims. A comparable system in space governance could discourage states from tightening debris mitigation requirements, imposing stricter licensing conditions, or restricting access to congested orbital regimes if such measures might expose them to claims from commercial operators. Any mechanism for private access to international dispute resolution in space would need safeguards to ensure that it promotes accountability without undermining the regulatory autonomy that states need to fulfill their environmental and safety obligations.

Building a Culture of Legal Accountability

Ultimately, dispute-resolution mechanisms are only as effective as the political and institutional culture in which they operate. Building a culture of legal accountability in space governance requires sustained commitment to several principles: transparency about space activities, so that disputes can be identified and evidence assembled; good faith engagement with dispute resolution processes, so that mechanisms on paper become mechanisms in practice; willingness to accept independent assessment of contested questions, even when outcomes may be unfavorable; and consistency between stated legal positions and actual operational behavior, so that the legal framework retains credibility and predictive value.

The space governance community has largely succeeded in maintaining a culture of cooperation, but cooperation and accountability are not the same thing. Cooperation may involve avoiding difficult questions, accommodating violations through diplomatic silence, and prioritizing relationships over principles. Accountability requires confronting difficult questions, addressing violations through legitimate processes, and applying principles consistently even when doing so creates diplomatic friction. As space activity intensifies and the stakes—economic, environmental, and strategic—continue to rise, the adequacy of a governance culture based primarily on cooperation and accommodation will be increasingly tested. The challenge for the next generation of space governance is to build institutions that can provide accountability without sacrificing the cooperative foundations that have served the space community well.

Specialized Institutions: Feasibility and Design

Some scholars have proposed the creation of a specialized international space tribunal—a permanent court with jurisdiction over space law disputes, staffed by judges with relevant expertise and supported by technical advisory capacity. Such a tribunal could develop coherent jurisprudence, resolve contested interpretations, and provide authoritative guidance on emerging questions about resource rights, debris liability, traffic management obligations, and the scope of state responsibility. Proponents point to the International Tribunal for the Law of the Sea (ITLOS) as a precedent: ITLOS was established under UNCLOS to adjudicate maritime disputes and has developed a significant body of jurisprudence on maritime delimitation, provisional measures, prompt release of vessels, and deep seabed mining advisory opinions.

The ITLOS analogy is instructive but imperfect. ITLOS was created as part of a comprehensive new convention (UNCLOS) that included its own dispute resolution system; no comparable comprehensive space treaty is on the horizon. ITLOS's jurisdiction extends to disputes between states parties to UNCLOS, but space law lacks a single comprehensive instrument that could provide the jurisdictional foundation for a comparable tribunal. ITLOS has been criticized for underutilization (receiving relatively few cases compared to the ICJ), suggesting that even domain-specific tribunals face acceptance challenges. And the military sensitivities of space operations create additional political obstacles that maritime law's predominantly civilian and commercial character does not share.

The political obstacles to establishing a new international tribunal are formidable. States are reluctant to create institutions with binding authority over sensitive space activities, particularly when military equities are involved. The establishment of new international courts and tribunals has slowed dramatically since the proliferation of institutions in the 1990s and 2000s; states have become more cautious about creating institutions whose jurisdiction and precedential authority they cannot fully control. More feasible intermediate steps include establishing a specialized chamber within the Permanent Court of Arbitration dedicated to space disputes, creating a standing expert roster from which arbitrators with relevant technical and legal expertise can be selected, seeking advisory opinions from the ICJ on contested space law questions to provide authoritative interpretive guidance, and strengthening the PCA Optional Rules through outreach, training, and model clause development to make them the default arbitration framework for space disputes.

Mechanism	Advantages	Limitations	Feasibility
Standing mediation panel	Expert, accessible, confidential, low cost	Non-binding; depends on party cooperation	High – can be established by agreement
Graduated escalation model	Structured process; incentivizes resolution	Requires advance consent; complex design	Medium – needs treaty amendment or new agreement
Private actor access	Addresses governance gap; enhances accountability	States resist sovereignty constraints	Medium – precedent in investment arbitration
Specialized tribunal	Authoritative jurisprudence; permanent expertise	High political obstacles; costly; slow to establish	Low – long-term aspiration
ICJ advisory opinion	Authoritative interpretation; no state consent needed	Non-binding; narrow scope per request	Medium – requires UNGA or authorized body request
Enhanced PCA Optional Rules	Existing framework; flexible; space-specific	Unused so far; requires party agreement	High – institutional infrastructure exists

Technology and Dispute Resolution

Technological innovation can support more effective dispute resolution by addressing the evidentiary and attribution challenges that currently impede formal proceedings. Improved space situational awareness—through commercial tracking networks, shared data platforms, and advanced analytics—can provide the factual foundation needed for legal claims. The development of persistent, high-accuracy tracking systems by commercial providers such as LeoLabs and ExoAnalytic Solutions means that independent, non-governmental evidence about satellite positions, maneuver histories, and conjunction circumstances is increasingly available—reducing the dependence on military tracking data that has historically limited the evidentiary basis for space disputes.

Blockchain-based registries could create tamper-proof records of satellite operations, maneuver commands, and conjunction data that reduce evidentiary disputes about what happened and when. If satellite operators were required to log operational data to a distributed ledger accessible to authorized dispute resolution bodies, the factual foundation for liability claims and interference allegations would be substantially strengthened. Digital communication platforms could facilitate real-time consultation between operators and between states, enabling rapid resolution of close-approach incidents before they escalate. Machine learning applied to conjunction data could produce more accurate collision probability assessments, reducing the uncertainty that complicates liability determinations.

Forensic analysis of satellite damage is another area where technology could transform dispute resolution. When a satellite fails in orbit, determining whether the failure was caused by a debris impact, a component malfunction, radiation damage, or external interference currently requires access to telemetry data that only the operator possesses. Advanced onboard diagnostic systems, combined with ground-based analysis tools, could enable more definitive determination of failure causes—providing the causal evidence that liability claims require. If standardized diagnostic protocols were adopted across the industry, the evidentiary foundation for space disputes would be significantly strengthened.

Technology does not replace law, but it can enhance its implementation by reducing the information asymmetries, attribution challenges, and evidentiary barriers that currently make formal dispute resolution impractical for many space disputes. As tracking capabilities improve, data sharing becomes more standardized, and analytical tools become more sophisticated, the practical obstacles to formal dispute resolution will diminish—creating conditions in which legal mechanisms that currently exist only on paper may become operationally viable.

> *"The future of space dispute resolution lies not in choosing between diplomacy and adjudication but in building integrated systems that combine preventive governance, technical support, diplomatic flexibility, and legal authority into a coherent framework capable of managing conflict in an increasingly complex and contested domain."*

– On the future architecture of space dispute resolution

***

Chapter Summary

Chapter 12 has examined how disputes in outer space are managed, highlighting both the achievements and shortcomings of existing mechanisms.

Part I explored the distinctive nature of space disputes—their strategic sensitivity, technical complexity, attribution challenges, and systemic risks—and the dominance of diplomatic settlement as the primary resolution mechanism. The Cosmos 954 incident remains the only formal claim ever presented under the Liability Convention, and its resolution through negotiated compromise established a precedent of pragmatic settlement over legal adjudication.

Part II analyzed the formal dispute resolution mechanisms available under international law, including arbitration (particularly the PCA Optional Rules), the ICJ, and the Liability Convention's Claims Commission. Despite their availability, these mechanisms have been remarkably underutilized, reflecting the practical constraints and political caution that characterize space governance.

Part III identified the structural limits of existing frameworks: the state-centric design that excludes private actors, evidentiary and technical barriers that impede attribution, political sensitivity that discourages formal proceedings, jurisdictional fragmentation that complicates forum selection, and the normative stagnation that results from the absence of adjudicated decisions.

Part IV explored future models for space dispute resolution, including preventive governance mechanisms that reduce the probability of disputes arising, hybrid diplomatic-legal models that combine flexibility with authority, expanded access for non-state actors drawing on investment arbitration precedents, and the institutional innovations that could provide space law with the jurisprudential development it currently lacks.

In the next chapter, we turn to the convergence of air and space law, examining how technological innovation is eroding the boundary between atmospheric and orbital operations and the governance challenges this convergence creates.

***

End of Chapter 12

Chapter 13

THE FUTURE OF INTERNATIONAL AIR AND SPACE LAW: CONVERGENCE, CHALLENGES, AND OPPORTUNITIES

"The law cannot anticipate every horizon, but it can ensure that those who reach it do so with shared purpose and mutual restraint."

Introduction

International air and space law stand at a pivotal juncture. The legal frameworks that have governed human activity above the Earth's surface for more than a century are now being tested by a confluence of forces: **rapid technological innovation, commercial expansion, geopolitical competition, and the prospect of permanent human presence beyond Earth.** What began as two distinct legal regimes—air law rooted in sovereignty and space law built on freedom—are converging in ways that challenge long-standing assumptions and demand new thinking.

For much of the twentieth century, the separation between air law and space law was both conceptually clear and practically workable. Aircraft operated within the atmosphere under regimes of state sovereignty, governed by the Chicago Convention and its extensive regulatory apparatus. Satellites, by contrast, orbited well above, in a domain declared free for exploration and use by all states under the Outer Space Treaty of 1967. Few technologies straddled both realms, and the legal distinction, however imprecise at its boundary, served its purpose.

Today, that clarity is eroding. Suborbital vehicles traverse the atmosphere and the edge of space in a single flight. Reusable launch systems operate like rockets on ascent and like aircraft on descent. Hypersonic vehicles move at speeds and altitudes that confound traditional jurisdictional categories. Mega-constellations of thousands of satellites crowd low Earth orbit, raising questions that echo aviation's early regulatory challenges: safety, traffic management, environmental impact, and equitable access. Meanwhile, ambitious programs aimed at the Moon and Mars—driven by both states and private enterprises—push space law into domains it was never designed to regulate.

This chapter examines the future trajectory of international air and space law through four interconnected lenses. Part I explores the technological drivers of convergence between the two regimes. Part II analyses the legal challenges that arise at the air–space interface, including sovereignty, delimitation, and regulatory overlap. Part III looks outward, addressing the governance challenges posed by activities beyond Earth orbit—from cislunar operations to Mars settlement. Part IV considers the normative future of international governance, asking what principles, institutions, and frameworks will be needed to manage humanity's expanding presence in space.

Throughout, this chapter draws on the legal foundations explored in preceding chapters while engaging with the most significant contemporary developments: the rise of the Artemis Accords, the proliferation of national space legislation, the emergence of space sustainability as a governance priority, and the deepening geopolitical rivalry between competing visions of space order. The aim is not to predict the future with certainty, but to identify the structural forces, unresolved questions, and normative choices that will shape the legal architecture of air and space governance in the decades ahead.

The stakes of this inquiry are high. The decisions made by states, institutions, and private actors in the coming decades will determine whether the legal order for air and space remains coherent, adaptive, and equitable—or whether it fragments under the weight of technological disruption, geopolitical competition, and institutional inertia. As the distinguished space law scholar Bin Cheng observed, law must serve not merely the interests of the present but the needs of those who will inherit the consequences of today's choices. In few domains is this observation more relevant than in the governance of air and space.

***

Part 1

Convergence of Air and Space Law—Technological Drivers

For much of the twentieth century, air law and space law evolved as distinct legal regimes, shaped by different technologies, geopolitical contexts, and regulatory objectives. Air law focused on sovereignty, safety, and commercial aviation within Earth's atmosphere, while space law emphasized freedom of use, non-appropriation, and peaceful exploration beyond it. Today, however, technological innovation is eroding the practical and conceptual boundaries between air and space, forcing a reconsideration of this long-standing legal separation.

1. Historical Separation of Legal Regimes

The separation of air and space law reflects a fundamental legal distinction: **state sovereignty over airspace** versus the **freedom of outer space.** This dichotomy was embedded early in international law, most notably through the Chicago Convention of 1944, which affirms complete and exclusive sovereignty over national airspace, and the Outer Space Treaty of 1967, which rejects sovereignty claims beyond Earth.

For decades, this distinction was workable. Aircraft operated within the atmosphere, satellites orbited well above it, and few technologies traversed both domains. Legal certainty was achieved by drawing a conceptual line—albeit an undefined one—between airspace and outer space. The International Civil Aviation Organization (ICAO) governed the skies below, while the United Nations Committee on the Peaceful Uses of Outer Space (COPUOS) addressed matters above. Each regime operated with its own treaties, institutions, norms, and constituencies.

This dual structure was not an accident of history. It reflected deliberate choices made in specific geopolitical contexts. Air law emerged from the experience of two world wars, where control of the sky was synonymous with national security. The sovereignty principle was absolute and non-negotiable. Space law, by contrast, was shaped by the Cold War imperative to prevent the weaponization of orbit and to establish outer space as a domain of peaceful competition rather than territorial conquest. The freedom principle served strategic stability by ensuring that neither superpower could claim exclusive control over orbital pathways.

The conceptual architecture was elegant in its simplicity: below a certain undefined altitude, sovereignty governed; above it, freedom prevailed. But this simplicity depended on a technological reality that no longer holds. As new vehicles and activities blur the operational boundary between atmosphere and orbit, the legal boundary between the two regimes is increasingly strained.

2. Technological Erosion of the Boundary

Recent technological developments have begun to blur the boundary between air and space with increasing urgency. Suborbital vehicles, reusable launch systems, hypersonic aircraft, and spaceplanes operate across altitudes traditionally associated with both air and space. These vehicles challenge the assumption that air and space are separate operational domains governed by distinct legal regimes.

Suborbital flights, for example, may resemble space missions in trajectory and purpose while raising aviation-like concerns regarding safety, licensing, and passenger protection. A vehicle that reaches an altitude of one hundred kilometres before descending back to Earth traverses both regimes within minutes. At what point does it leave the domain of air law and enter that of space law? At what point does it return? These questions have no settled answers, yet they have practical consequences for regulation, liability, and jurisdiction.

Hypersonic vehicles present even more complex challenges. Operating at speeds exceeding Mach 5, these vehicles can traverse national airspaces at altitudes and velocities previously associated only with spaceflight. A hypersonic glide vehicle launched from one continent could reach another in under an hour, passing through the upper atmosphere at altitudes where the boundary between airspace and outer space is most ambiguous. The legal implications extend beyond regulatory classification to encompass security, arms control, and early warning systems.

High-altitude platforms—stratospheric balloons, solar-powered unmanned vehicles, and other systems designed to operate in the upper atmosphere for extended periods—add another dimension to the challenge. These platforms perform functions traditionally associated with satellites, such as communications relay and Earth observation, but they operate within or near sovereign airspace. Their regulatory classification determines which legal regime applies, with significant consequences for authorization, liability, and oversight.

3. Reusable Launch Systems and Hybrid Operations

Reusable launch systems exemplify convergence in practice. These vehicles launch vertically like rockets, operate briefly in outer space, and return through controlled atmospheric descent. Companies such as SpaceX, with its Falcon 9 and Starship vehicles, and Blue Origin, with its New Shepard and New Glenn rockets, have demonstrated that reusability is no longer experimental but **operationally routine.** Their operations implicate both space law principles and aviation safety standards.

Regulatory responses have been pragmatic rather than doctrinal. States apply aviation-style licensing and safety oversight to launch and reentry operations while maintaining compliance with international space law obligations. In the United States, the Federal Aviation Administration's Office of Commercial Space Transportation manages both launch licences and airspace integration, effectively straddling the two regimes. This hybrid approach reflects functional necessity rather than legal clarity.

The challenge is not merely administrative. Reusable systems require coordinated airspace management during launch and reentry, temporary flight restrictions for conventional aircraft, and real-time coordination between aviation and space authorities. As launch frequency increases—SpaceX alone conducted over one hundred orbital launches in a single year—the interaction between space operations and air traffic becomes a systemic concern rather than an occasional event.

Europe, Japan, and other jurisdictions are developing their own regulatory approaches to reusable vehicles, but no international consensus exists on how these systems should be classified and governed. The absence of harmonized rules creates potential for regulatory fragmentation, competitive distortion, and liability gaps.

4. Commercial Spaceflight and Human Carriage

The emergence of commercial human spaceflight further accelerates convergence. Passenger-carrying suborbital flights occupy a regulatory grey zone, neither fully aviation nor traditional space missions. Issues of passenger rights, liability, certification, and safety oversight demand regulatory frameworks that draw from both air and space law traditions.

This development raises fundamental questions about the adequacy of existing legal categories. Should passengers on suborbital flights be treated as airline passengers, spaceflight participants, or a new legal category altogether? Current regulatory approaches vary, reflecting experimentation rather than settled doctrine. In the United States, the informed consent regime allows participants to accept elevated risks, deferring full certification requirements to allow industry maturation. Other jurisdictions, particularly within the European Union, are considering more prescriptive approaches aligned with aviation safety culture.

The distinction matters enormously for liability. Under aviation law, carriers bear strict or near-strict liability for passenger harm, supported by mandatory insurance and robust compensation regimes. Under space law, liability operates primarily at the state level, with the launching state bearing international responsibility for damage caused by space objects. Suborbital passengers fall awkwardly between these frameworks, and no international agreement addresses their specific situation.

As commercial human spaceflight matures—with companies like SpaceX, Blue Origin, and Virgin Galactic expanding their operations—the pressure to develop coherent, internationally harmonized passenger protection standards will intensify. The question is not whether such standards will emerge, but whether they will be developed proactively through international cooperation or reactively in response to a catastrophic incident.

5. Mega-Constellations and Orbital Congestion

Perhaps the most transformative technological development affecting both air and space governance is the deployment of **mega-constellations**—vast networks of thousands of satellites operating in low Earth orbit. SpaceX's Starlink network, with over six thousand satellites in orbit, exemplifies a trend that will only accelerate as Amazon's Project Kuiper, OneWeb, and other operators deploy their own constellations.

Mega-constellations challenge space governance in ways that echo the early challenges of aviation. Just as the proliferation of aircraft demanded traffic management, safety standards, and environmental regulations, the crowding of low Earth orbit demands analogous responses: space traffic management, collision avoidance protocols, spectrum coordination, and debris mitigation. The parallels between early twentieth-century air law and early twenty-first-century orbital governance are striking and instructive.

The environmental dimension is equally significant. Satellite reentry produces aluminium oxide particles in the upper atmosphere, the long-term effects of which on ozone chemistry and atmospheric composition remain under investigation. The light pollution caused by satellite reflections has prompted concern from the astronomical community and spurred initiatives such as the International Astronomical Union's campaign for dark and quiet skies. In 2025, the British Standards Institution published new principles to promote space sustainability standards, reflecting growing institutional attention to the environmental externalities of orbital activity.

6. Point-to-Point Suborbital Transport

Among the most disruptive applications of convergence technology is point-to-point suborbital transport—the concept of using rocket-powered vehicles to carry passengers between cities across the globe in under an hour. Companies and agencies have invested heavily in this vision, which promises to compress intercontinental travel from twelve or fourteen hours to thirty or forty minutes by launching passengers to the edge of space and allowing the vehicle to descend at a distant spaceport.

The legal challenges are formidable. Point-to-point transport combines elements of aviation and spaceflight in a single commercial operation. The departure and arrival resemble airport operations, but the intervening trajectory passes through sovereign airspace at hypersonic speeds and potentially through the legal grey zone at the edge of outer space. Passengers expect the safety standards and consumer protections associated with airline travel, but the vehicles operate in an environment far more hazardous and less regulated than conventional aviation.

No existing international framework governs this activity comprehensively. The Chicago Convention applies to civil aviation but does not clearly encompass vehicles that exit the atmosphere. The Outer Space Treaty applies to space activities but was not designed for routine commercial passenger transport. Bilateral or multilateral agreements between departure and arrival states would be necessary, but the terms of such agreements—including overflight rights, liability allocation, safety certification, and passenger protection—remain largely undefined.

The development of point-to-point suborbital transport thus represents a microcosm of the broader convergence challenge. It is simultaneously an aviation problem, a space problem, a consumer protection problem, and a sovereignty problem. Its resolution will require creative legal thinking that transcends traditional boundaries between air and space law.

7. The Proliferation of National Space Legislation

Alongside technological convergence, the proliferation of national space legislation represents a significant structural change in the legal landscape. States across the world are adopting or updating domestic legal frameworks to govern an expanding range of space activities. In 2025 alone, Italy adopted a comprehensive national space law; Japan announced amendments to its Space Activities Act to cover suborbital flights and human spaceflight; and the United Kingdom continued to refine its regulatory framework with new sustainability standards and debris removal contracts.

This wave of national legislation reflects several trends. First, it responds to the growth of commercial space activity and the need for clear licensing, liability, and insurance frameworks at the domestic level. Second, it implements international obligations under the Outer Space Treaty, which requires states to authorise and continuously supervise national space activities. Third, it creates competitive regulatory environments intended to attract space industry investment. Fourth, and perhaps most importantly, it contributes to the development of state practice that may, over time, crystallise into customary international law.

The diversity of national approaches, however, raises concerns about regulatory fragmentation. Different states may impose different requirements on operators for similar activities, creating compliance burdens and potential forum shopping. Harmonisation efforts—whether through COPUOS, bilateral agreements, or industry standards—will be essential to ensure that the proliferation of national legislation strengthens rather than fragments the international legal order.

8. Technological Convergence as a Legal Catalyst

Technological convergence acts as a **catalyst for legal change.** It exposes the limitations of rigid doctrinal boundaries and demands adaptive governance. Rather than choosing between air law and space law, regulators increasingly blend elements of both, guided by risk profiles and operational realities.

This convergence does not imply the disappearance of air or space law as distinct regimes. Instead, it suggests the emergence of what scholars have termed interface governance—a hybrid regulatory space where principles from both domains are applied flexibly to activities that defy traditional classification. Interface governance is pragmatic, activity-based, and risk-responsive. It recognizes that legal categories are tools, not ends in themselves, and that the ultimate objective is the safe, sustainable, and equitable management of human activity above the Earth's surface.

9. Implications for International Governance

At the international level, convergence challenges existing institutional arrangements. Aviation and space governance have historically been managed by different organizations with distinct mandates—ICAO for aviation and COPUOS for space. Hybrid activities require coordination across institutional boundaries, raising questions about jurisdiction, competence, and cooperation.

The International Telecommunication Union (ITU) adds a third dimension, managing the radio frequency spectrum on which both aviation and space operations depend. The increasing overlap between these institutional domains suggests the need for enhanced inter-institutional coordination, if not structural reform. Whether this takes the form of joint working groups, memoranda of understanding, or more fundamental institutional realignment will depend on political will and practical necessity.

Part I has examined how technological innovation drives convergence between air and space law, destabilizing traditional legal distinctions. In the next part, we explore the legal challenges at the air–space interface, including sovereignty, delimitation, and regulatory overlap.

***

Part II

Legal Challenges at the Air–Space Interface

As technological convergence accelerates, the air–space interface has emerged as one of the most contested and conceptually challenging areas of international law. Activities that traverse or operate within this interface strain legal categories built on assumptions of separation and exclusivity. The resulting challenges are not merely technical; they implicate sovereignty, jurisdiction, safety, security, and the coherence of international governance.

1. The Enduring Problem of Delimitation

At the core of the air–space interface lies the unresolved issue of **delimitation**: where does airspace end and outer space begin? Despite decades of debate within COPUOS and among legal scholars, international law has never established a legally binding boundary. This ambiguity was once manageable, as few activities occupied the grey zone. Today, it creates legal uncertainty for hybrid vehicles and operations.

Two broad approaches have been proposed. Spatial delimitation advocates establishing a fixed altitude boundary—the Kármán line at approximately one hundred kilometres is the most commonly cited candidate. Functional delimitation, by contrast, distinguishes activities based on their purpose and nature rather than their altitude: an activity is governed by air law if it exhibits the characteristics of aviation and by space law if it exhibits the characteristics of spaceflight.

Neither approach has achieved consensus. Spatial boundaries risk arbitrariness and technological obsolescence. The Kármán line, while scientifically grounded in the concept of aerodynamic lift, does not correspond to any sharp physical transition. The atmosphere does not end abruptly; it thins gradually over hundreds of kilometres. Moreover, advances in propulsion and materials science may enable sustained flight at altitudes above the Kármán line, further undermining its utility as a legal boundary.

Functional approaches, while more flexible, introduce subjectivity and unpredictability. Classifying an activity as aviation or spaceflight based on its characteristics requires judgements about intent, capability, and operational profile that may not be clear in advance. A suborbital tourism vehicle, for instance, has characteristics of both: it carries passengers like an aircraft but follows a ballistic trajectory like a spacecraft.

In practice, states have avoided formal delimitation, relying instead on pragmatic regulatory responses. This pragmatism has served reasonably well in the short term, but it carries risks. Without a clear boundary, sovereignty disputes could arise over activities in the upper atmosphere. A state might claim sovereign authority over a vehicle transiting at eighty or ninety kilometres—an altitude where the legal status of the space is genuinely uncertain. As the frequency of such transits increases, the absence of an agreed boundary becomes a source of potential conflict rather than mere academic debate.

2. Sovereignty and Overflight Rights in the Hybrid Zone

Air law is grounded in the principle of **complete and exclusive sovereignty** over national airspace. Space law, by contrast, is founded on freedom of access and non-appropriation. Hybrid activities that pass through upper airspace raise difficult questions about overflight rights and state consent.

Suborbital flights, in particular, challenge traditional sovereignty concepts. A vehicle that traverses the upper atmosphere at hypersonic speeds may cross multiple national airspaces in minutes. Requiring individual overflight permissions for each state could be impractical, introducing delays and uncertainties that undermine the commercial viability of suborbital transport. Yet unrestricted passage risks eroding sovereignty norms that states have consistently defended since the Paris Convention of 1919.

The analogy to innocent passage in the law of the sea has been suggested but remains imperfect. Maritime innocent passage applies to a defined zone—the territorial sea—whose limits are established by treaty. No equivalent exists for the upper atmosphere. Moreover, innocent passage is subject to conditions, including the requirement that passage be continuous, expeditious, and non-threatening to the coastal state. Translating these conditions to hypersonic overflight would require careful adaptation.

States have thus far addressed this issue through bilateral arrangements and licensing practices, but the absence of clear international rules leaves room for dispute. As hypersonic and suborbital technologies mature and the number of operations increases, the need for multilateral agreement on overflight rights in the hybrid zone will become increasingly acute.

3. Jurisdiction and Applicable Law

Determining which legal regime applies to hybrid operations is another major challenge. Air law governs aircraft operations, certification, and liability within airspace, while space law addresses launch, reentry, and activities in outer space. Hybrid vehicles may fall under both regimes at different phases of flight.

This **segmented jurisdiction** complicates regulatory oversight and enforcement. Operators must comply with multiple regulatory frameworks, and states must coordinate across agencies with differing mandates. At the international level, institutional fragmentation mirrors this complexity—ICAO, COPUOS, and the ITU each claim competence over aspects of hybrid operations, yet no mechanism ensures coherent regulation across institutional boundaries.

The practical implications are significant. An operator planning a point-to-point suborbital flight from Abu Dhabi to London would need to navigate the aviation and space regulations of the departure state, the arrival state, every state whose airspace is overflown, and the international rules applicable to the space segment of the flight. The licensing requirements, safety standards, insurance obligations, and liability frameworks could vary at each stage, creating a regulatory patchwork that increases costs, delays operations, and creates gaps in oversight.

Several proposals have been advanced to address this challenge. One approach advocates for a unified regulatory framework that applies to all vehicles operating above a certain altitude, regardless of their classification as aircraft or spacecraft. Another proposes a vehicle-based approach, classifying the regulatory regime based on the predominant characteristics of the vehicle rather than the phase of flight. A third, more pragmatic approach relies on bilateral or multilateral agreements to harmonize rules for specific types of operations.

4. Safety Regulation and Risk Management

Safety considerations are central to both air and space law, but the approaches differ significantly. Aviation safety is highly standardized, with detailed technical regulations and centralized oversight through ICAO's Standards and Recommended Practices. Space safety regulation, by contrast, relies more heavily on national licensing and operator responsibility, with international coordination limited to general principles of due regard and harmful interference avoidance.

Hybrid operations challenge these paradigms. Applying aviation-style certification to space vehicles may be impractical given the pace of innovation and the diversity of vehicle designs. Conversely, relying solely on operator self-regulation may be insufficient for activities involving human passengers or operations over populated areas.

The challenge is particularly acute for reusable vehicles that operate from spaceports integrated into aviation infrastructure. Managing the interaction between launch and reentry operations and conventional air traffic requires coordination, communication, and safety standards that neither regime adequately provides in isolation. In 2025, growing concerns about rocket debris landing in populated areas—including incidents involving SpaceX and Blue Origin components falling in the Bahamas, Florida, and Poland—highlighted the practical urgency of improved safety regulation at the air–space interface.

5. Liability Gaps and Insurance Challenges

The liability frameworks of air and space law differ fundamentally. Aviation liability is governed by the Montreal Convention and related instruments, which establish a comprehensive regime of carrier liability for passenger injury and cargo damage. Space liability operates under the Liability Convention of 1972, which addresses damage caused by space objects and assigns fault-based or absolute liability depending on the location of the damage.

Hybrid activities can fall into gaps between these frameworks. A suborbital vehicle carrying passengers may not qualify as an aircraft under the Montreal Convention if it does not meet the treaty's definition of aircraft, yet it may not be covered by the Liability Convention if the damage occurs within the atmosphere rather than being caused by a space object in the conventional sense.

Insurance markets reflect this uncertainty. Insurers accustomed to aviation risk pricing have limited experience with space vehicle operations, while space insurance underwriters may lack expertise in passenger liability. The emerging suborbital tourism industry thus faces challenges in securing adequate insurance coverage at reasonable premiums, a situation that could constrain commercial development or leave passengers inadequately protected.

6. Security Dimensions of the Air–Space Interface

The security implications of the air–space interface add a further layer of complexity. Hypersonic glide vehicles and fractional orbital bombardment systems operate in the grey zone between airspace and outer space, evading traditional early warning and missile defence systems designed for ballistic trajectories. These capabilities challenge existing arms control frameworks and raise questions about the applicability of both air and space law to dual-use technologies.

The militarisation of the air–space interface is already underway. The United States Space Force received nearly forty billion dollars in funding for fiscal year 2026, reflecting the strategic significance of space and near-space operations. Other states—including China, Russia, India, France, and the United Kingdom—are investing in similar capabilities. Japan's 2025 Space Domain Defence Guidelines, which emphasise satellite protection and countermeasures against anti-satellite threats, signal a broader trend toward integrating space into national security strategy.

The legal governance of these activities remains underdeveloped, caught between arms control regimes designed for traditional weapons systems and space law principles emphasising peaceful use. The Outer Space Treaty prohibits the placement of nuclear weapons and other weapons of mass destruction in orbit, but it does not prohibit the placement of conventional weapons. The ambiguity surrounding dual-use technologies—systems that serve both civilian and military functions—further complicates the legal analysis.

Confidence-building measures, transparency mechanisms, and norms of responsible behaviour in space have been proposed as interim solutions. The United Nations General Assembly has endorsed the development of such norms, and several states have unilaterally committed to practices such as not conducting destructive anti-satellite tests. But these commitments remain voluntary and partial. The gap between the strategic significance of the air–space domain and the legal framework governing it is one of the most concerning asymmetries in contemporary international law.

7. The Role of Private Actors in Shaping the Air–Space Interface

Private actors have become central to the air–space interface in ways that challenge traditional governance models. Historically, air and space law were state-centric: states made the rules and bore primary responsibility for compliance. The rise of commercial space companies—many of which now rival or surpass state agencies in technological capability and operational tempo—has introduced new dynamics.

Companies like SpaceX, Blue Origin, Rocket Lab, and Relativity Space drive innovation at a pace that regulators struggle to match. Their business models encompass launch services, satellite manufacturing, space tourism, in-orbit servicing, and planetary exploration—activities that span the full spectrum of air and space law. Their influence extends beyond technology to norm-setting: SpaceX's operational practices in collision avoidance, for instance, effectively establish standards that others follow, even in the absence of binding rules.

The challenge for international law is to ensure that the growing influence of private actors is channelled within a framework of public accountability. The Outer Space Treaty assigns international responsibility to states for national space activities, including those of non-governmental entities. This principle ensures that states retain ultimate legal responsibility, but it also creates a governance gap: states that lack the technical expertise to supervise advanced commercial operations may struggle to fulfil their supervisory obligations.

Future governance frameworks will need to accommodate the reality of private sector leadership while preserving the public interest. This may involve enhanced industry participation in standard-setting processes, mandatory reporting and transparency requirements, and mechanisms for holding private actors accountable for harm caused by their activities—whether through strengthened national legislation or through innovative international arrangements.

8. Toward a Coherent Framework

The challenges at the air–space interface are not merely theoretical. They have practical consequences for operators, regulators, passengers, and states. Addressing them requires a combination of pragmatic national regulation, bilateral cooperation, and gradual multilateral norm development.

Several pathways offer promise. First, enhanced coordination between ICAO and COPUOS could ensure that regulatory responses to hybrid activities are complementary rather than contradictory. Joint working groups, shared data platforms, and coordinated standard-setting processes could bridge the institutional divide. Second, model legislation and regulatory guidelines—developed through multilateral forums or by leading regulatory states—could provide templates for national implementation, reducing fragmentation while preserving flexibility. Third, the insurance industry, which has a direct financial interest in clarity and predictability, could play a constructive role in developing risk assessment frameworks and liability standards for hybrid operations.

What is clear is that the air–space interface will not govern itself. The experience of early aviation—where unregulated flight quickly proved untenable and states were compelled to develop rules—is instructive. The same imperative is emerging today, driven not by balloons or biplanes but by reusable rockets, hypersonic vehicles, and commercial spaceplanes. The question is not whether governance will emerge, but whether it will emerge proactively through deliberate international cooperation or reactively in response to accidents, disputes, and crises.

Part II has examined the legal challenges arising from the convergence of air and space activities. In Part III, we turn outward, examining the governance challenges that arise as human activity extends beyond Earth orbit into cislunar space and toward Mars.

***

Part III

Beyond Earth Orbit—Governance Challenges of Deep Space

While convergence challenges near Earth demand immediate attention, the most profound governance questions lie beyond Earth orbit. As states and private actors plan missions to the Moon, asteroids, and Mars, international law must grapple with activities it was never designed to regulate in detail. The expansion of human activity into cislunar space and beyond raises novel legal questions that test the adaptability of existing frameworks and the imagination of lawmakers.

1. The Artemis Accords and the New Governance Landscape

No development better illustrates the shifting landscape of space governance than the **Artemis Accords.** Launched in October 2020 by NASA and the United States Department of State, the Accords are a set of non-binding principles designed to guide civil space exploration and use in the twenty-first century. As of early 2026, sixty-one countries have signed the Accords, including the UAE, Japan, India, the Republic of Korea, and most European states.

The Artemis Accords represent a deliberate effort to operationalise the principles of the Outer Space Treaty in the context of contemporary exploration activities. They address transparency, interoperability, emergency assistance, registration, scientific data sharing, heritage preservation, space resource utilisation, deconfliction through safety zones, and orbital debris mitigation. While explicitly grounded in the Outer Space Treaty, the Accords go beyond its general principles by articulating specific expectations for cooperative behaviour.

The Accords are significant for several reasons. First, they represent a form of norm development outside the traditional UN treaty-making process. Rather than negotiating a new multilateral treaty through COPUOS—a process that has not produced a binding space law instrument since 1979—the United States has pursued a coalition-based approach, building consensus among like-minded states through bilateral signature. This approach is faster and more flexible than multilateral negotiation, but it raises questions about inclusivity and universal applicability.

Second, the Accords address issues that existing treaties leave unresolved, most notably the extraction and utilisation of space resources. By affirming that resource extraction does not constitute national appropriation, the Accords adopt a position consistent with the United States' 2015 Commercial Space Launch Competitiveness Act and similar legislation in Luxembourg, the UAE, and Japan. This position is not universally accepted, however, and several states—including Russia and China—have criticised the Accords as a unilateral attempt to reshape space law outside the multilateral framework.

Third, the concept of safety zones introduced by the Accords has generated significant debate. While proponents argue that safety zones are a practical mechanism for implementing the Outer Space Treaty's requirement of due regard and avoidance of harmful interference, critics contend that they could function as de facto exclusive zones, advantaging early arrivals and conflicting with the principle of non-appropriation.

2. The Competing Vision: China's International Lunar Research Station

The Artemis Accords do not represent the only vision for lunar governance. China and Russia have jointly proposed the International Lunar Research Station (ILRS), an alternative framework for lunar exploration that emphasises state-led cooperation, comprehensive planning, and a more cautious approach to commercial resource utilisation. While the ILRS has attracted fewer signatories than the Artemis Accords, it represents a genuine alternative that appeals to states sceptical of the US-led framework.

The emergence of two competing frameworks for lunar governance raises the spectre of a **bifurcated space order**—one in which the principles, norms, and institutional arrangements governing activities on the Moon differ depending on which coalition a state belongs to. This is a departure from the universalist model of space governance that prevailed during the International Space Station era and echoes terrestrial geopolitical alignments in ways that previous space law sought to transcend.

Whether these competing visions can be reconciled—or whether they will harden into rival blocs—is one of the defining questions of contemporary space governance. The answer will depend not only on diplomatic engagement but also on the practical experience of lunar operations, which may reveal shared interests in coordination, safety, and environmental protection that transcend geopolitical competition.

3. Cislunar Governance and the New Operational Domain

The space between Earth and the Moon—cislunar space—is rapidly emerging as a new operational domain. Lunar orbits, Lagrange points, and transit corridors are becoming strategically significant for navigation, communication relay, scientific observation, and resource transport. Yet this vast domain remains largely ungoverned, with no dedicated legal framework and only limited surveillance capability.

Cislunar governance presents challenges that differ qualitatively from those of near-Earth orbit. Distances are greater, communication delays are longer, and the ability of states to monitor and control activities diminishes significantly. Traditional space situational awareness systems, designed for tracking objects in low Earth orbit and geostationary orbit, have limited capability beyond geostationary altitude. The absence of comprehensive cislunar surveillance means that activities in this domain may occur with little visibility to the broader international community, raising concerns about transparency, verification, and the potential for undetected interference.

Several states and organisations have begun to address this gap. The United States Space Force has identified cislunar domain awareness as a strategic priority, investing in sensing capabilities and command structures adapted to deep space operations. The European Space Agency has proposed programmes for cislunar navigation and communication infrastructure, including the Moonlight initiative to provide positioning and communication services for lunar missions. NASA's Lunar Gateway—a small space station in a near-rectilinear halo orbit around the Moon—will provide a permanent human presence in cislunar space for the first time, serving as a staging point for lunar surface operations and a testbed for technologies needed for Mars missions.

The governance implications of these developments are profound. As cislunar space transitions from a scientific domain to an operational one, questions of coordination, traffic management, environmental protection, and security governance will multiply. The principles applicable in low Earth orbit—freedom of use, non-interference, and state responsibility—provide a starting point, but they must be adapted to the unique characteristics of cislunar operations. The absence of atmospheric drag means that objects in cislunar space do not naturally deorbit, making debris management a permanent concern. The strategic significance of Lagrange points, which offer energetically favourable positions for observation and transit, may create competition for positional advantage. The development of cislunar governance frameworks—before competition intensifies and precedents harden—is one of the most pressing tasks facing the international space law community.

4. Mars and the Prospect of Human Presence

Mars represents the most ambitious frontier of space activity. Unlike the Moon or asteroids, Mars is a planet with its own environment, geological history, and potential for long-term human habitation. Governance questions extend beyond resource use to encompass **jurisdiction over habitats, the application of human rights, environmental protection, and long-term sustainability.**

Existing space law provides only a skeletal framework for addressing these issues. The Outer Space Treaty establishes that states cannot claim sovereignty over celestial bodies, that activities must be conducted for the benefit and in the interests of all countries, and that states bear international responsibility for their national activities. These principles provide a normative foundation, but they do not address the practical realities of permanent settlement: governance within habitats, criminal jurisdiction, property rights over constructed infrastructure, dispute resolution between co-located settlements, or the legal status of individuals born on Mars.

The prospect of Mars settlement forces a fundamental rethinking of space governance. Exploration-era legal concepts—designed for short-duration missions by state actors—are inadequate for communities that may eventually develop their own social, economic, and political dynamics. The history of human settlement on Earth suggests that governance structures will evolve organically as communities grow, but space law must provide a framework that channels this evolution in directions consistent with shared principles of justice, sustainability, and non-appropriation.

5. Planetary Protection and the Duty of Environmental Care

Planetary protection—the prevention of biological contamination between Earth and other celestial bodies—has emerged as a critical governance challenge. As missions to Mars become more frequent and ambitious, the risk of introducing terrestrial microorganisms to the Martian environment grows. If life exists on Mars, even in microbial form, contamination could compromise one of the most profound scientific discoveries in human history.

The Committee on Space Research (COSPAR) has established planetary protection guidelines that classify missions by category and impose corresponding contamination controls. These guidelines are widely followed but not legally binding. As mission frequency increases and private actors pursue their own Mars ambitions, the adequacy of voluntary guidelines comes into question.

The Outer Space Treaty requires states to conduct space exploration in a manner that avoids harmful contamination. This obligation, while general in its formulation, provides a legal basis for more specific planetary protection requirements. The challenge lies in translating a broad treaty obligation into operational standards that are scientifically rigorous, practically enforceable, and applicable to both state and private actors.

The reverse dimension—protecting Earth from potential extraterrestrial hazards—adds further complexity. Sample return missions from Mars and other bodies require strict biocontainment protocols to prevent the release of unknown biological agents. These protocols intersect with biosafety regulations, public health law, and environmental law, creating cross-cutting governance challenges that no single legal regime adequately addresses.

6. Resource Governance Beyond Earth Orbit

The governance of space resources—water ice on the Moon, minerals on asteroids, and potentially subsurface materials on Mars—constitutes one of the most consequential legal questions of the twenty-first century. As discussed in earlier chapters, the legal status of space resources remains contested. The Outer Space Treaty prohibits national appropriation of celestial bodies but does not explicitly address the extraction and use of resources found on those bodies.

The Artemis Accords take the position that resource extraction, conducted in accordance with the Outer Space Treaty, does not constitute national appropriation. This interpretation is supported by national legislation in the United States, Luxembourg, the UAE, and Japan, but it is not universally accepted. Some states and scholars argue that resource extraction without an internationally agreed framework risks de facto appropriation and could advantage early-arriving, technologically advanced states at the expense of the broader international community.

The challenge of resource governance beyond Earth orbit is compounded by the absence of detailed rules on coordination, dispute resolution, and benefit-sharing. The safety zones concept in the Artemis Accords provides a partial answer for operational deconfliction, but it does not address the broader distributional and ethical questions. Ultimately, resource governance will require a framework that balances incentives for investment with obligations of fairness and sustainability—flexible enough to accommodate diverse activities and actors while robust enough to prevent the emergence of exclusionary practices.

7. Jurisdiction Without Territory

One of the defining features of space law is jurisdiction without territorial sovereignty. States retain jurisdiction over their space objects and personnel, not over land. This model works reasonably well for spacecraft and space stations, where the nationality of the object provides a clear jurisdictional basis. But it becomes increasingly complex in the context of permanent or semi-permanent settlements.

A Mars habitat constructed by a multinational consortium, inhabited by nationals of multiple states, and supported by private companies incorporated in different jurisdictions presents a jurisdictional puzzle of extraordinary complexity. Which state's laws apply within the habitat? Who exercises criminal jurisdiction if an offence is committed? How are civil disputes between inhabitants resolved? The International Space Station provides a partial precedent through its Intergovernmental Agreement, which assigns jurisdiction based on the nationality of personnel and the registration of modules. But a Mars settlement would be far more complex, involving permanent residents, economic activity, and potentially the birth of children who hold no terrestrial nationality.

Future governance may require hybrid jurisdictional arrangements, combining state responsibility with cooperative management structures agreed upon by participating states. Such arrangements would need to preserve the non-appropriation principle while enabling effective governance—a balance that will test legal creativity and diplomatic skill.

8. Governance Through Coordination Rather Than Control

Deep space governance is likely to rely on **coordination rather than centralised control.** The political feasibility of creating new supranational authorities remains low. States are unlikely to cede sovereignty to an international body with binding authority over activities on the Moon or Mars. Instead, governance may emerge through shared standards and protocols, transparency and notification mechanisms, cooperative management of shared resources, and voluntary codes of conduct.

This approach aligns with the historical evolution of space law, which has consistently emphasised flexibility, consensus, and incremental norm development over rigid codification. The Artemis Accords themselves exemplify this model: they are non-binding, voluntary, and open to adaptation through practice. Their influence derives not from legal enforceability but from the collective commitment of their signatories and the practical utility of their principles.

The risk of coordination-based governance is that it may prove insufficient in the face of serious disputes, environmental harm, or the accumulation of competing claims. Without binding rules and enforcement mechanisms, there is a danger that governance will default to power rather than principle—that those with the greatest technological capability will set the rules while others are marginalised. Preventing this outcome is one of the central challenges of twenty-first-century space governance.

9. Normative Implications of Expansion

Expansion beyond Earth orbit challenges the normative foundations of space law. Concepts such as peaceful use, benefit of all mankind, and due regard acquire new meanings when applied to sustained human presence. The risk of replicating terrestrial patterns of competition, exclusion, and environmental degradation looms large.

The normative implications extend to questions of identity, community, and political legitimacy. A human settlement on Mars, sustained over generations, will inevitably develop its own culture, institutions, and sense of identity. The relationship between such a settlement and the Earth-based legal order that authorised its creation will evolve in ways that are difficult to predict but essential to consider. Will Martian communities accept indefinite governance by distant Earth-based authorities? Will the principles of self-determination, enshrined in international human rights law, apply to extraterrestrial communities? These questions may seem remote, but they are implicit in every vision of permanent human presence beyond Earth, including the UAE's Vision 2117.

Part III has examined how governance challenges evolve as humanity moves beyond Earth orbit. In the final part of this chapter, we synthesise these developments, exploring normative futures and the shape of a global legal order for air and space in the decades ahead.

***

Part IV

Normative Futures and the Global Legal Order

As air and space activities converge near Earth and expand outward into cislunar space and beyond, international law faces a defining moment. The future of international air and space law will not be determined solely by technological capability, but by the normative choices made by states, institutions, and private actors. These choices will shape whether outer space evolves as a cooperative global commons or becomes fragmented by competing interests and unequal access.

1. From Rule-Based Order to Normative Governance

Traditional international law relies on formal rules expressed through treaties and binding agreements. In space governance, however, the pace of technological change has outstripped formal lawmaking. The last binding multilateral space law treaty—the Moon Agreement of 1979—was adopted more than four decades ago and has been ratified by only a handful of states, none of which are major spacefaring nations. Since then, the legal landscape has evolved through softer instruments: UN General Assembly resolutions, guidelines, best practices, bilateral agreements, and national legislation.

As a result, the legal order is increasingly shaped by **normative governance**—a blend of treaty principles, soft law, state practice, and ethical commitments. This shift does not signal the decline of law, but its adaptation. Norms such as sustainability, transparency, and due regard now function as guiding principles that influence behaviour even in the absence of binding obligations. Their strength lies in shared acceptance rather than enforcement.

The proliferation of national space legislation illustrates this trend. In 2025, Italy adopted a comprehensive national space law introducing licensing, liability, insurance, and sustainability obligations. Japan announced plans to amend its 2016 Space Activities Act to regulate suborbital flights, reusable launch systems, and human spaceflight. The United Kingdom expanded its regulatory framework with new principles for space sustainability. These national frameworks, while varying in detail, reflect converging normative commitments to responsible space activity.

2. Balancing Freedom, Equity, and Responsibility

The foundational principle of freedom of use remains central to space law, but it must be balanced against emerging demands for equity and responsibility. Freedom without restraint risks congestion, environmental degradation, and exclusion. Conversely, excessive regulation risks stifling innovation and access.

The normative future of space law depends on achieving a **dynamic equilibrium**: freedom to explore and innovate; responsibility to avoid harm and preserve access for future generations; and equity in opportunity, participation, and benefit-sharing. This balance cannot be imposed unilaterally; it must be cultivated through dialogue, cooperative practice, and institutional innovation.

The tension between these values is already visible in contemporary debates. The Artemis Accords emphasise freedom of resource utilisation and operational flexibility, while the Long-term Sustainability Guidelines adopted by COPUOS prioritise environmental protection and equitable access. Reconciling these perspectives requires not a zero-sum negotiation but a recognition that freedom, equity, and responsibility are mutually reinforcing in the long term: unsustainable exploitation diminishes future freedom, and inequitable access undermines the legitimacy on which cooperative governance depends.

3. Inclusivity and the Global South

As space activity expands, inclusivity becomes a defining normative concern. Many states remain excluded from meaningful participation in space activities due to technological and financial constraints. Without deliberate efforts to promote capacity-building and access, the benefits of space may accrue disproportionately to a small group of technologically advanced actors.

Significant initiatives are emerging to address this gap. The inauguration of the African Space Agency in 2025, together with the Africa–EU Space Partnership Programme, represents a landmark effort to integrate African states into the global space ecosystem. Regional organisations such as the Asia-Pacific Space Cooperation Organization (APSCO) are expanding their membership and activities. The growing number of Artemis Accords signatories from the Global South—including Nigeria, Rwanda, Bangladesh, and Ecuador—reflects a broadening of participation, though the depth of that participation varies widely.

International air and space law has long affirmed that space activities shall be carried out for the benefit and in the interests of all countries, irrespective of their degree of economic or scientific development. Operationalising this commitment remains a challenge. Normative leadership will require integrating capacity-building into governance frameworks, ensuring that emerging norms do not entrench existing inequalities, and creating genuine pathways for developing states to transition from passive beneficiaries to active participants and contributors.

4. The Geopolitics of Space Governance

Any discussion of the normative future of space law must reckon with the geopolitical realities that shape governance possibilities. The current landscape is characterised by competition between two principal coalitions: the Artemis Accords coalition, led by the United States and comprising over sixty signatories as of early 2026, and the International Lunar Research Station framework, led jointly by China and Russia.

This bifurcation represents a departure from the universalist tradition of space governance. The International Space Station, despite its origins in Cold War competition, ultimately became a model of inclusive international cooperation—a platform shared by the United States, Russia, Europe, Japan, and Canada. The fracturing of this cooperative model into rival frameworks raises the prospect that governance norms will diverge along geopolitical lines, creating a fragmented legal landscape for lunar and deep space activities.

The implications extend beyond diplomatic posturing. If the Artemis coalition and the ILRS coalition adopt different norms regarding resource extraction, safety zones, transparency, and environmental protection, operators and states may face conflicting expectations. A dispute between entities operating under different normative frameworks would lack a common legal basis for resolution. The risk of misunderstanding, miscalculation, and conflict increases in the absence of shared rules.

Yet the picture is not entirely bleak. Several developments suggest that pragmatic cooperation remains possible even amid strategic competition. The International Telecommunication Union continues to manage spectrum allocation through a universal framework. COPUOS, despite its limitations, provides a forum where all states can contribute to norm development. And the shared interest in avoiding catastrophic orbital debris—which threatens all operators regardless of geopolitical alignment—creates a basis for cooperation on sustainability even when broader relations are strained.

The challenge for the legal community is to maintain pathways for universal governance while respecting the reality of competing coalitions. This may require distinguishing between issues where geopolitical competition is inevitable and issues where cooperation is essential—and investing diplomatic capital in the latter.

5. Space Sustainability as a Governance Priority

The concept of **space sustainability** has moved from the margins to the centre of international space governance. The 2025 United Nations Conference on Space Law and Policy, held under the theme "Operationalising Space Sustainability: Legal and Regulatory Approaches Across the Lifecycle of Space Debris," signalled the mainstreaming of sustainability concerns in multilateral space forums.

Sustainability encompasses multiple dimensions: orbital debris mitigation and remediation; responsible end-of-life disposal of satellites; management of the radio frequency spectrum; protection of the space environment from contamination; and preservation of the outer space domain for future generations. The Long-term Sustainability Guidelines, adopted by COPUOS in 2019, provide a voluntary framework, but their implementation varies across states and operators.

Active debris removal is emerging as both a technological possibility and a governance challenge. The United Kingdom has awarded multi-million-pound contracts to ClearSpace and Astroscale for missions to de-orbit non-operational satellites by 2026. These initiatives raise legal questions about who authorises the removal of another state's space object, how liability is apportioned if removal operations cause damage, and whether a duty to remove debris will eventually crystallise as a norm of customary international law.

The environmental dimension of space activity also extends to planetary protection—the prevention of biological contamination of celestial bodies and the protection of Earth from potential extraterrestrial biological hazards. As missions to Mars and other potentially habitable environments increase, planetary protection standards will need to evolve from guidelines into binding obligations.

6. Ethics, Intergenerational Justice, and Stewardship

Beyond legal doctrine, ethical considerations are increasingly influential in shaping space governance. Sustainability is not merely a technical issue; it reflects concerns about intergenerational justice. Decisions made today regarding debris generation, resource extraction, orbital slot allocation, and planetary protection will shape the opportunities available to future generations.

In this sense, space law is evolving from a framework of **access** to a framework of **stewardship.** Stewardship emphasises care, restraint, and long-term responsibility—values that transcend national interest and commercial gain. The stewardship model draws on environmental law, indigenous rights frameworks, and intergenerational equity principles to argue that the current generation holds outer space in trust for humanity as a whole, including those who have not yet been born.

This ethical shift has practical implications. It supports arguments for debris remediation obligations, sustainability assessments for new constellations, heritage protection for historic lunar sites, and limits on irreversible alteration of celestial environments. It also reinforces the case for inclusive governance: if outer space belongs to all humanity, all humanity should have a voice in how it is managed.

7. Institutional Adaptation and Legal Pluralism

The future legal order is likely to be **pluralistic rather than unified.** Different regimes, institutions, and instruments will coexist, interacting through coordination rather than hierarchy. COPUOS will remain the primary multilateral forum for space law development, but it will operate alongside the Artemis Accords signatory group, national regulatory agencies, regional organisations, industry consortia, and civil society networks. This pluralism reflects political reality and allows governance to adapt to diverse activities and contexts.

Institutional adaptation—rather than wholesale reform—offers a pragmatic path forward. COPUOS has demonstrated its ability to produce influential soft law instruments, even as its capacity for binding treaty development has stalled. ICAO is increasingly engaging with space-related issues, particularly those arising from the air–space interface. The ITU continues to manage spectrum allocation with growing attention to the needs of mega-constellations and next-generation satellite systems.

The key to effective pluralistic governance lies in coherence, complementarity, and communication. Different institutions and instruments need not duplicate one another's work, but they must avoid contradictions and ensure that gaps are identified and addressed. Regular inter-institutional dialogue, joint working groups, and shared information platforms can facilitate this coordination without requiring structural integration.

8. Law as an Enabler of Human Expansion

Ultimately, international air and space law must be judged by whether it enables peaceful, sustainable, and inclusive human expansion. Law cannot eliminate competition or conflict, but it can shape incentives, manage risk, and provide shared expectations that reduce uncertainty. At its best, law serves as a civilising framework, channelling ambition toward collective benefit and constraining the exercise of power through agreed principles.

As humanity moves beyond Earth—building stations in orbit, habitats on the Moon, and eventually communities on Mars—the need for law becomes not less but more urgent. The distances are greater, the stakes are higher, and the consequences of legal failure are potentially irreversible. A generation of debris in low Earth orbit could deny access to space for decades. Unchecked exploitation of lunar or Martian resources could foreclose opportunities for states that arrive later. Jurisdictional conflicts in extraterrestrial habitats could endanger lives.

The choices made in the coming decades will determine whether space becomes a domain of cooperation or contention, of shared opportunity or entrenched inequality, of sustainable development or environmental degradation. The legal foundations laid in the twentieth century—sovereignty over airspace, freedom in outer space, peaceful use, and benefit of all mankind—remain sound. But they must be reinterpreted, extended, and supplemented to meet the challenges of a new era.

***

Conclusion: Setting the Stage for the Future

This chapter has explored how convergence, expansion, and normative evolution are reshaping international air and space law. Technological innovation is dissolving the boundary between air and space, creating hybrid activities that strain established legal categories. Beyond Earth orbit, the expansion of human activity into cislunar space and toward Mars raises governance questions of unprecedented complexity. The proliferation of actors—states, private companies, international organisations, and emerging spacefaring nations—makes governance both more difficult and more necessary.

Several key themes emerge from this analysis. First, convergence between air and space law is not a future possibility but a present reality. Suborbital vehicles, reusable launch systems, hypersonic platforms, and mega-constellations are already operating in the regulatory grey zone between the two regimes. The legal community's response has been pragmatic but fragmented—a patchwork of national regulations, bilateral agreements, and industry practices that lacks coherence at the international level. The need for harmonised principles, if not harmonised rules, is increasingly urgent.

Second, the expansion of human activity beyond Earth orbit introduces governance challenges that existing law is not equipped to address in detail. The Artemis Accords represent the most significant normative development in space governance in decades, but they remain non-binding, coalition-based, and incomplete. The emergence of competing frameworks—most notably the International Lunar Research Station—raises the prospect of a bifurcated space order that could undermine the universalist aspirations of the Outer Space Treaty.

Third, the concept of space sustainability has matured from an aspirational ideal to a governance priority. Orbital debris, spectrum congestion, light pollution, and planetary protection are now recognised as shared challenges that demand collective action. The 2025 United Nations Conference on Space Law and Policy, national legislative developments in Italy, Japan, the United Kingdom, and elsewhere, and the growing number of active debris removal initiatives all signal a deepening institutional commitment to sustainability.

Fourth, inclusivity remains both a normative imperative and a practical challenge. The broadening of the Artemis Accords coalition, the inauguration of the African Space Agency, and the expansion of regional cooperation frameworks are positive developments. But meaningful participation requires more than signature on an agreement; it demands investment in education, technology transfer, institutional capacity, and the creation of genuine opportunities for developing states to contribute to and benefit from space activities.

Fifth, the role of private actors in shaping the air–space environment has transformed the governance landscape. States remain the primary subjects of international law, but commercial entities now drive innovation, set operational precedents, and influence norm development in ways that traditional legal frameworks struggle to accommodate. The relationship between state responsibility and private enterprise—always a central feature of space law—has become more complex and consequential as private capabilities expand.

The normative future of international air and space law will be determined by the interplay of several forces: the pace and direction of technological development; the geopolitical dynamics between competing space coalitions; the willingness of states to invest in inclusive governance; the capacity of existing institutions to adapt; and the depth of commitment to sustainability, equity, and intergenerational responsibility.

No single treaty, institution, or state can address these challenges alone. The future legal order will be built incrementally, through practice, negotiation, and the gradual accumulation of shared expectations. It will be pluralistic, adaptive, and imperfect—but it need not be inadequate. The experience of the past century demonstrates that international law, when supported by political will and sustained engagement, can govern even the most challenging domains. The sky was once ungoverned; today it is one of the most regulated environments on Earth. Outer space, though vast and complex, need not remain a domain of legal improvisation.

In the concluding chapter, we turn from theory to practice, examining how individual states contribute to the emerging legal order. We focus on a state that has embraced this future-oriented vision: the United Arab Emirates. Through its space programme and Mars ambitions, the UAE offers a compelling case study of how law, policy, and aspiration converge in shaping humanity's next frontier.

***

End of Chapter 13

Chapter 14

ARTIFICIAL INTELLIGENCE AND AUTONOMOUS SYSTEMS IN SPACE

"As machines assume greater autonomy in the orbital domain, the question is no longer whether artificial intelligence will reshape space law, but whether space law will reshape itself quickly enough to govern it."

– Adapted from contemporary space governance scholarship

Introduction

Artificial intelligence and autonomous systems are transforming virtually every dimension of space activity. From **satellite constellation management and autonomous collision avoidance to robotic planetary exploration and AI-driven mission planning,** the integration of machine intelligence into space operations represents one of the most consequential technological developments since the dawn of the space age. Yet the international legal framework governing outer space was designed for a fundamentally different era—one in which human operators made critical decisions, state actors dominated the domain, and the pace of orbital activity permitted deliberation.

Figure 21: Artificial Intelligence and Autonomous Systems in Future Space Operations

Source: Generated using OpenAI Sora.

Today, that framework confronts a reality in which algorithms execute collision avoidance manoeuvres in milliseconds, autonomous spacecraft dock with uncooperative debris objects, and AI systems manage fleets of thousands of satellites simultaneously. The International Institute of Space Law published its landmark report on the legal aspects of AI in space in December 2024, acknowledging that existing treaties and regulatory instruments are inadequate to address the challenges posed by autonomous space systems. Stanford Law School launched a dedicated policy lab in 2025 to examine how governance should evolve to manage AI-driven autonomy in orbit. These initiatives reflect a growing consensus that the intersection of artificial intelligence and space law constitutes one of the most urgent governance challenges of the twenty-first century.

This chapter examines the legal implications of artificial intelligence and autonomous systems in the space domain. Part I surveys the technological landscape, tracing the proliferation of AI across space operations. Part II analyses the core legal challenges, focusing on liability, accountability, and the erosion of meaningful human control. Part III examines space traffic management and autonomous collision avoidance as a case study in governance urgency. Part IV considers the military and security dimensions of AI in space. Part V explores emerging governance frameworks and proposes principles for the responsible development of autonomous space systems.

The analysis draws on the foundational treaties examined in preceding chapters—particularly the Outer Space Treaty, the Liability Convention, and the Registration Convention—while engaging with the most significant contemporary developments: the IISL Working Group's 2024 report on AI regulation in space, the European Union's AI Act, national regulatory initiatives, and the rapidly evolving operational practice of satellite constellation operators. The chapter demonstrates that the challenge is not merely technical but fundamentally normative: the choices made about governing AI in space will reflect and shape broader assumptions about the relationship between human authority, machine autonomy, and international responsibility.

***

Part 1

The Technological Landscape—AI Across the Space Domain

The integration of artificial intelligence into space operations is not a future prospect but a present reality. AI systems are already embedded in virtually every stage of the space value chain, from satellite design and manufacturing to launch operations, on-orbit management, and end-of-life disposal. Understanding the scope and depth of this integration is essential to appreciating the legal challenges it generates.

The transformation is being driven by two converging forces: the exponential growth of objects in orbit, which makes human-paced decision-making inadequate for safe operations, and the rapid maturation of AI and machine learning technologies, which makes autonomous operations technically feasible at scale. Together, these forces are creating an orbital environment in which AI is not merely an efficiency tool but an operational necessity—and in which the governance of AI becomes inseparable from the governance of space itself.

1. Satellite Operations and Constellation Management

The most immediate and widespread application of AI in space concerns the management of satellite constellations. As of 2025, SpaceX's Starlink constellation alone comprises over six thousand satellites in low Earth orbit, with Amazon's Project Kuiper and other mega-constellations in active deployment. Managing fleets of this scale is beyond the capacity of traditional human-operated ground control. AI systems now handle orbit maintenance, station-keeping, power management, communication routing, and—critically—collision avoidance for thousands of spacecraft simultaneously.

These AI-driven management systems operate with increasing autonomy. Starlink satellites, for example, execute autonomous collision avoidance manoeuvres based on onboard algorithms that evaluate conjunction data and calculate optimal evasion trajectories without human intervention. The European Space Agency has similarly developed machine learning systems to automate collision risk assessment and manoeuvre planning, acknowledging that the sheer volume of conjunction alerts—now numbering in the thousands per day—makes human evaluation of each event impractical.

Figure 22: Global Satellite Networks and Space Traffic Management

Source: Generated using OpenAI Sora.

The operational implications are substantial. AI systems now determine not only whether a manoeuvre is necessary but when to execute it, how much fuel to expend, and what trajectory to adopt—decisions that directly affect the satellite's operational capacity, mission lifetime, and interaction with other objects in orbit. For Earth observation satellites, every collision avoidance manoeuvre means lost data; for communications satellites, it means service interruption. AI optimisation of these trade-offs increasingly operates beyond the scope of real-time human review, raising fundamental questions about the legal meaning of 'continuing supervision' in the age of autonomous operations.

2. Robotic Exploration and Planetary Operations

AI plays an increasingly central role in robotic space exploration. NASA's Mars rovers, including Perseverance, employ autonomous navigation systems that enable the spacecraft to traverse the Martian surface, identify scientifically interesting targets, and select optimal driving paths without waiting for instructions from Earth—a necessity given the communication delay of up to twenty-two minutes each way. These systems represent a form of operational autonomy in which the machine makes consequential decisions about movement, resource allocation, and scientific prioritisation.

The trend toward greater autonomy in exploration missions is accelerating. Future missions to the outer solar system, where communication delays extend to hours, will require spacecraft capable of making complex decisions about scientific observation, hazard avoidance, and even self-repair without any possibility of real-time human oversight. The legal implications of such operational independence—particularly regarding liability for damage caused by autonomous decisions—are profound and largely unaddressed by existing instruments.

3. Active Debris Removal and On-Orbit Servicing

Among the most legally consequential applications of AI in space is active debris removal. Companies such as ClearSpace and Astroscale are developing autonomous spacecraft designed to rendezvous with, capture, and deorbit defunct satellites and debris. ESA's ClearSpace-1 mission, planned for the second half of 2026, will demonstrate autonomous approach, capture, and controlled re-entry of a debris object using robotic arms guided by machine vision and AI-driven guidance, navigation, and control systems.

These operations involve autonomous decision-making in safety-critical contexts. An active debris removal spacecraft must identify and approach a non-cooperative, potentially tumbling target, execute physical capture using robotic mechanisms, and manage the controlled deorbit of a combined mass through the atmosphere. Each stage involves decisions that could, if erroneous, generate additional debris, damage operational spacecraft, or cause uncontrolled re-entry over populated areas. The question of who bears legal responsibility when an autonomous system makes a consequential error during such operations lies at the heart of the AI-space law challenge.

On-orbit servicing—the refuelling, repair, or upgrade of operational satellites by autonomous robotic spacecraft—raises analogous legal issues with additional complications. A servicing spacecraft that autonomously docks with a client satellite must make real-time decisions about approach trajectory, docking mechanism engagement, and force application, any of which could damage the client spacecraft if executed incorrectly. The contractual and tortious liability implications of autonomous on-orbit servicing are complex, involving interactions between international space law, domestic contract law, and emerging norms of due diligence for autonomous operations.

> ■ **AI Applications in Space—Current Operational Scope**
>
> Constellation management: autonomous orbit maintenance for 6,000+ Starlink satellites • Collision avoidance: AI-driven manoeuvre planning processing thousands of conjunction alerts daily • Planetary exploration: autonomous navigation on Mars rovers • Debris removal: machine vision and robotic capture for ClearSpace-1 (2026) • Earth observation: AI-powered image analysis and data processing • Space situational awareness: machine learning for debris tracking and trajectory prediction

4. AI-Powered Space Situational Awareness

Space situational awareness—the ability to detect, track, and predict the movements of objects in orbit—is increasingly reliant on artificial intelligence. With over 140 million pieces of debris larger than one millimetre estimated to be in orbit, traditional tracking methods are insufficient. Machine learning algorithms now process radar, optical, and infrared sensor data to catalogue orbital objects, predict trajectories, and assess collision probabilities with far greater speed and accuracy than conventional methods.

AI is also transforming downstream space applications, particularly Earth observation. Machine learning algorithms analyse satellite imagery for environmental monitoring, disaster response, agricultural assessment, and urban planning with capabilities that far exceed human visual analysis. These applications generate their own legal questions—concerning data privacy, surveillance, intellectual property in AI-generated analysis, and the responsibilities of operators whose AI systems produce actionable intelligence from satellite data. While these downstream applications fall partially outside the scope of space law proper, they illustrate the breadth of legal challenges that AI integration creates across the space value chain.

Space situational awareness—the ability to detect, track, and predict the movements of objects in orbit—is increasingly reliant on artificial intelligence. With over 140 million pieces of debris larger than one millimetre estimated to be in orbit, traditional tracking methods are insufficient. Machine learning algorithms now process radar, optical, and infrared sensor data to catalogue orbital objects, predict trajectories, and assess collision probabilities with far greater speed and accuracy than conventional methods.

The legal significance of AI-enhanced space situational awareness extends beyond technical efficiency. Reliable tracking data forms the basis for conjunction warnings, collision avoidance decisions, and post-incident attribution of responsibility. If an AI system incorrectly assesses a collision probability—either triggering an unnecessary manoeuvre that disrupts satellite services or, conversely, failing to detect a genuine threat—the consequences may involve significant economic loss or physical damage. The reliability, transparency, and accountability of these AI systems are therefore matters of direct legal concern.

***

Part II

Legal Challenges—Liability, Accountability, and Human Control

The proliferation of AI in space operations generates legal challenges that cut across the foundational principles of international space law. The existing framework was designed around assumptions of human decision-making, state responsibility, and identifiable chains of command. Autonomous systems disrupt each of these assumptions, creating gaps and ambiguities that demand urgent attention.

1. The Liability Framework and Autonomous Decisions

The international liability regime for space activities rests on two pillars: **absolute liability for damage caused on the surface of the Earth and fault-based liability for damage caused in space,** as established by the Liability Convention of 1972. Under this framework, the 'launching State' bears responsibility for damage caused by its space objects. The Convention was drafted with the assumption that space objects are inert or human-controlled; it did not contemplate objects capable of making autonomous decisions that independently cause or avoid harm.

When an AI system aboard a satellite autonomously executes a collision avoidance manoeuvre that inadvertently causes damage to another spacecraft, the existing framework provides an answer—the launching State is liable—but the answer is mechanically derived rather than normatively satisfying. The launching State may have had no knowledge of the specific decision, no ability to prevent it, and no control over the algorithm that generated it. The gap between formal liability and operational responsibility creates perverse incentives: states and operators may avoid deploying beneficial autonomous safety systems if doing so increases their liability exposure without commensurate control.

The complexity deepens when multiple actors contribute to an autonomous system's decision chain. A satellite may be manufactured in one state, launched from another, operated by a private company incorporated in a third, and equipped with AI software developed by a fourth. When the AI system makes an erroneous decision, allocating responsibility among these parties under existing international law is extraordinarily difficult. The Liability Convention's focus on the 'launching State' provides a point of entry, but it does not resolve the internal allocation of responsibility among designers, manufacturers, operators, and software developers—an allocation that domestic legal systems are only beginning to address.

Furthermore, the fault-based liability standard applicable to damage caused in outer space raises particular challenges for autonomous systems. Establishing 'fault' requires demonstrating that the responsible party failed to meet an applicable standard of care. But what standard of care applies to an AI system? In the absence of internationally agreed performance benchmarks for autonomous spacecraft, determining whether an AI-driven decision constituted a failure of due diligence or a reasonable response to uncertain data becomes a matter of contested interpretation rather than objective assessment.

The insurance industry is already responding to these uncertainties. Satellite insurers are placing increasing emphasis on collision avoidance measures and AI system reliability as conditions of coverage, effectively creating private governance mechanisms that supplement public regulatory frameworks. As the space debris monitoring and removal market grows—projected to expand significantly through 2033 driven by AI-enabled tracking and active removal solutions—insurance standards may emerge as important de facto regulators of autonomous system design and performance. This market-driven governance, while valuable, cannot substitute for the international legal clarity that only state-level engagement can provide.

2. The Erosion of Meaningful Human Control

The concept of meaningful human control—drawn from debates over lethal autonomous weapons systems—is increasingly relevant to civilian space operations. As spacecraft become more autonomous, the role of human operators shifts from direct control to supervisory oversight, and in some cases to post-hoc review. For mega-constellation management, the volume and speed of decisions required makes meaningful human involvement in each individual manoeuvre physically impossible.

International space law has not yet established clear standards for the degree of human oversight required in autonomous space operations. Article VI of the Outer Space Treaty requires states to ensure that national space activities are carried out in conformity with the Treaty, including through 'authorization and continuing supervision.' The question is whether 'continuing supervision' can be satisfied when the supervised entity is an AI system making thousands of operational decisions daily, many of which may not be individually reviewed by human operators until after execution.

The challenge is particularly acute for deep-space operations, where communication delays make real-time human control physically impossible. A spacecraft operating autonomously at Mars or beyond the Moon must make safety-critical decisions—collision avoidance, system reconfiguration, resource management—without the possibility of human intervention. In these contexts, 'continuing supervision' must be reinterpreted to encompass the design, programming, testing, and monitoring of autonomous systems rather than direct control of individual decisions. This reinterpretation has not yet been formally articulated by COPUOS or any other authoritative body, leaving a significant normative gap.

3. Attribution and the Opacity of AI Decision-Making

Machine learning systems, particularly deep neural networks, are often characterised by opacity—the inability of external observers, and sometimes even developers, to fully explain why a particular decision was made. In space operations, this opacity creates challenges for post-incident investigation. If an autonomous collision avoidance system fails to manoeuvre, leading to a collision, determining whether the failure resulted from a design defect, inadequate training data, sensor malfunction, or an unforeseeable edge case may be extremely difficult.

This opacity complicates both liability attribution and regulatory oversight. The IISL Working Group on Legal Aspects of AI in Space, in its December 2024 report, identified transparency and explainability as critical requirements for AI systems deployed in the space domain. The report recommended that AI systems used in safety-critical space operations should be auditable, with decision logs that enable post-incident reconstruction of the reasoning process. This recommendation, if implemented, would represent a significant new regulatory requirement for space operators.

■ **The IISL Report: Balancing Innovation and Responsibility (December 2024)**

The International Institute of Space Law's Working Group published its final report recommending: transparency and auditability for AI in safety-critical space operations; adaptation of liability frameworks to account for autonomous decision-making; alignment with ICAO and IMO regulatory models; ethical guidelines for AI deployment; and international cooperation frameworks for responsible AI governance in space.

***

Part III

Space Traffic Management and Autonomous Collision Avoidance

Space traffic management represents the most urgent governance challenge at the intersection of AI and space law. The orbital environment is increasingly congested, contested, and dependent on automated systems for safe operation. The near-collision between a Starlink satellite and a OneWeb spacecraft in 2021—in which both operators' automated systems detected a potential collision but lacked coordinated deconfliction protocols—exemplified the governance gap that autonomous operations create.

Unlike aviation, which developed comprehensive traffic management systems over decades of regulated growth, space operations have grown explosively without a comparable governance infrastructure. The number of conjunction alerts has increased exponentially, yet there is no international equivalent of air traffic control for orbit. The 18th Space Defense Squadron of the United States Space Force currently provides the primary global conjunction screening service, but this arrangement is neither institutionally sustainable nor politically neutral. The transition from a US military-provided service to a more inclusive, internationally governed system is widely recognised as necessary but has proven politically difficult to achieve.

1. The Scale of the Congestion Problem

As of 2025, approximately ten thousand active satellites orbit the Earth, a number projected by the European Space Agency to grow nearly tenfold by 2030. These spacecraft must navigate an environment containing over 34,000 tracked objects larger than ten centimetres and an estimated 130 million objects larger than one millimetre. ESA reports that it must perform more than one collision avoidance manoeuvre per satellite per year, with the vast majority triggered by debris encounters. Each manoeuvre disrupts operational schedules, consumes scarce fuel, and reduces mission lifetime.

The congestion problem is self-reinforcing. The Kessler Syndrome—a theoretical cascade in which debris collisions generate additional fragments, triggering further collisions in an exponential chain—represents the nightmare scenario that underscores the urgency of effective space traffic management. AI-driven systems offer the most promising technical solution: they can process vast volumes of conjunction data, evaluate collision probabilities in real time, and execute avoidance manoeuvres at speeds far beyond human capability. But the very features that make AI essential—speed, scale, and autonomy—also generate the governance challenges that law must address.

2. Machine-to-Machine Coordination

As autonomous collision avoidance systems proliferate across different operators' constellations, the need for machine-to-machine coordination becomes acute. When two autonomous systems simultaneously detect a conjunction risk involving their respective satellites, their independent avoidance manoeuvres may be contradictory—both moving into the same evasion trajectory, for example, or one manoeuvring into the path of a third object. Without shared protocols for autonomous coordination, the proliferation of independent AI systems could paradoxically increase collision risk.

This challenge mirrors the development of air traffic control in aviation, a comparison that space governance scholars have increasingly drawn. The International Civil Aviation Organization developed standardised communication, navigation, and surveillance protocols that enable aircraft to operate safely in shared airspace. An analogous framework for space—establishing common data formats, communication protocols, and deconfliction algorithms for autonomous spacecraft—is urgently needed but does not yet exist in binding form. The IISL report explicitly recommended drawing on ICAO and International Maritime Organization models to develop such frameworks.

The technical foundations for machine-to-machine coordination are emerging. Industry initiatives to develop common data standards for conjunction assessment and manoeuvre notification are underway, and the Space Data Association provides a voluntary framework for operators to share operational data. However, these initiatives are voluntary, partial in coverage, and lack the regulatory authority to compel participation. A mandatory international framework for autonomous coordination—analogous to aviation's Traffic Collision Avoidance System—would require political will, institutional capacity, and a level of data transparency that many operators, particularly those with military or dual-use missions, may resist.

3. Regulatory Gaps and the Need for Standards

Current international space law provides no specific standards for autonomous collision avoidance systems. There are no requirements for minimum response times, algorithm validation, decision transparency, or coordination protocols. The United States Space Policy Directive-5, issued during the first Trump administration, recognised the need for updated approaches to space system cybersecurity and automated processes, but concrete regulatory implementation has lagged behind policy aspiration.

The absence of standards creates both operational risk and legal uncertainty. When an autonomous system causes damage, the lack of agreed performance benchmarks makes it difficult to determine whether the operator acted with due diligence. Establishing internationally recognised standards for autonomous space systems—addressing algorithm validation, testing, transparency, and coordination—would provide the normative infrastructure necessary for both safety and accountability.

National regulatory approaches are beginning to address these gaps, though inconsistently. The United States, through the Federal Aviation Administration's Office of Commercial Space Transportation and the Federal Communications Commission's licensing requirements for satellite constellations, imposes certain operational obligations on constellation operators, including debris mitigation commitments. However, these requirements do not specifically address the design or performance of autonomous systems. The European Union's Space Surveillance and Tracking programme provides conjunction data and warning services, but does not regulate the autonomous systems that respond to those warnings.

The regulatory challenge is compounded by the rapid pace of technological development. AI capabilities are advancing faster than regulatory frameworks can evolve through traditional treaty-based or even national legislative processes. This temporal mismatch suggests that governance approaches emphasising adaptable standards, industry best practices, and regularly updated technical guidelines may be more effective than rigid regulatory instruments that risk obsolescence before implementation.

***

Part IV

Military and Security Dimensions

The integration of AI into military space operations raises a distinct set of legal challenges, implicating not only international space law but also international humanitarian law, arms control norms, and the law governing the use of force. The intersection of AI, autonomy, and military space activity is among the most sensitive and least regulated domains in international law.

1. AI in Military Space Operations

Major space powers are investing heavily in AI for military space applications. The United States Space Force, with a fiscal year 2026 budget of approximately forty billion dollars, has prioritised cislunar domain awareness, autonomous satellite operations, and AI-driven intelligence processing. China and Russia are similarly developing AI-enhanced space capabilities for reconnaissance, navigation warfare, and space situational awareness. These developments transform space from a domain of passive observation into one of active, AI-mediated operational engagement.

The deployment of AI-enabled spacecraft for military purposes raises questions about the applicability of the Outer Space Treaty's peaceful use provisions. Article IV prohibits the placement of weapons of mass destruction in orbit but does not specifically address AI-enabled conventional weapons systems or autonomous military spacecraft. The treaty's requirement that outer space be used exclusively for peaceful purposes provides a broad normative framework, but its application to AI-driven military operations in the grey zone between peaceful and hostile activity remains contested.

Autonomous proximity operations—in which military spacecraft manoeuvre close to foreign satellites for inspection, intelligence gathering, or potential disruption—represent a particularly challenging application. Several states have demonstrated rendezvous and proximity operations capabilities, and AI systems are essential for the precise orbital mechanics involved. These operations exist in a legal grey zone: they may constitute legitimate space situational awareness activities, or they may amount to harmful interference with other states' space operations under Article IX of the Outer Space Treaty. When conducted by autonomous systems without real-time human oversight, the potential for misinterpretation and escalation is particularly acute.

2. Autonomous Weapons and the Space Domain

The debate over lethal autonomous weapons systems, conducted primarily within the framework of the Convention on Certain Conventional Weapons, has direct implications for space. If autonomous weapons systems are deployed in or through space—whether for anti-satellite operations, orbital interception, or space-based missile defence—the existing legal framework may be inadequate to govern their use. International humanitarian law's requirements of distinction, proportionality, and precaution in attack assume human decision-makers capable of exercising judgement. Autonomous systems that select and engage targets without meaningful human control challenge these foundational requirements.

The unique characteristics of the space environment amplify these concerns. The speed of orbital mechanics, the difficulty of distinguishing military from civilian satellites, and the cascading debris consequences of any kinetic engagement make the space domain particularly ill-suited to autonomous targeting decisions. The potential for AI-driven escalation—where autonomous systems interpret benign activities as hostile and respond with counterforce measures—represents a strategic stability risk that existing governance mechanisms do not adequately address.

The absence of agreed norms for AI in military space operations creates a dangerous governance vacuum. Without shared understandings of how autonomous systems should behave in ambiguous situations—for instance, when an unknown spacecraft approaches a military satellite—the risk of miscalculation and unintended escalation increases significantly. Confidence-building measures, transparency agreements, and crisis communication protocols specifically designed for autonomous military space systems are urgently needed, yet international discussions on these issues remain in their early stages.

> **■ The Dual-Use Challenge**
>
> Most space technologies are inherently dual-use: the same autonomous systems used for civilian collision avoidance can be adapted for military proximity operations; AI-driven debris removal spacecraft could theoretically be repurposed as anti-satellite weapons. This dual-use character complicates governance, as restrictions on military applications may inadvertently constrain civilian innovation, while permissive civilian frameworks may enable military exploitation.

***

Part V

Emerging Governance Frameworks and Principles

The challenges identified in preceding sections are not insurmountable, but they require proactive governance rather than reactive adaptation. Several emerging frameworks and principles offer pathways toward the responsible integration of AI and autonomous systems into the space domain.

1. Adapting Existing Legal Instruments

The most pragmatic approach to AI governance in space is to adapt existing legal instruments rather than negotiate entirely new treaties. The Outer Space Treaty's provisions on state responsibility, continuing supervision, and due regard for the interests of other states provide a normative foundation that can accommodate autonomous systems through interpretation and supplementary regulation. The challenge is to develop authoritative interpretations that clarify how these provisions apply to AI-mediated activities.

The Liability Convention, similarly, does not require fundamental revision but would benefit from supplementary guidelines addressing autonomous decision-making. Establishing that launching States bear responsibility for the autonomous systems deployed aboard their space objects—and that this responsibility extends to ensuring adequate testing, validation, and monitoring of AI systems—would close the most significant governance gap without requiring new treaty negotiations.

The Registration Convention provides another avenue for governance adaptation. Requiring states to include information about the autonomous capabilities of registered space objects—such as the degree of onboard decision-making authority, the types of autonomous manoeuvres the spacecraft can execute, and the protocols for human override—would enhance transparency and facilitate accountability. Such requirements could be implemented through COPUOS recommendations without amending the Convention itself, demonstrating how existing instruments can be adapted to accommodate technological change through interpretive development.

2. Cross-Sectoral Regulatory Models

The IISL report's recommendation to draw on ICAO and IMO regulatory models is well-founded. Both organisations have developed sophisticated frameworks for governing automated and semi-autonomous systems in shared domains. Aviation's Traffic Collision Avoidance System provides a particularly instructive precedent: a standardised onboard system that enables automated coordination between aircraft to prevent mid-air collisions, operating within a framework of internationally agreed protocols, performance standards, and regulatory oversight.

Developing an analogous space traffic management system would require international agreement on data sharing, common algorithmic standards, and coordination protocols. The European Union's AI Act, adopted in 2024, provides another cross-sectoral reference, establishing risk-based regulatory requirements for AI systems across domains. High-risk AI systems—a category that would encompass autonomous spacecraft operations—are subject to requirements for risk assessment, documentation, human oversight, and transparency. Adapting these terrestrial regulatory models to the unique features of the space environment offers a pathway toward governance that is both technically informed and legally robust.

3. Principles for Responsible Autonomy in Space

Drawing on the analysis presented in this chapter, several principles can be identified as foundational for the responsible governance of autonomous systems in space: **state responsibility for autonomous systems, meaningful human oversight, transparency and auditability, interoperability and coordination, proportionate regulation, and international cooperation.**

State responsibility for autonomous systems affirms that the deployment of AI does not diminish the launching State's international obligations. Meaningful human oversight requires that, even where individual decisions are automated, the overall system operates within parameters established, monitored, and adjustable by human operators. Transparency and auditability demand that AI systems in safety-critical space operations maintain decision logs sufficient for post-incident investigation. Interoperability and coordination require that autonomous systems from different operators can communicate and deconflict their actions. Proportionate regulation ensures that governance frameworks are calibrated to the risk level of specific applications, avoiding over-regulation of low-risk uses while imposing stringent requirements on safety-critical systems.

International cooperation, the sixth principle, is perhaps the most essential. The orbital environment is a shared commons; the actions of any operator's autonomous systems affect all others. Unilateral governance approaches, however well-intentioned, cannot address the coordination challenges inherent in a multi-actor, multi-constellation orbital environment. Developing shared norms, common standards, and cooperative institutions for AI governance in space is not merely desirable but necessary for the long-term sustainability of the space domain.

4. The Role of Soft Law and Technical Standards

Given the difficulty of negotiating new binding treaties, soft law instruments and technical standards are likely to play a leading role in AI governance in space. COPUOS guidelines, IISL recommendations, industry best practices, and national regulatory standards can collectively establish normative expectations that shape state and operator behaviour even without formal legal obligation. The 2019 COPUOS Guidelines for the Long-term Sustainability of Outer Space Activities already address some relevant issues, including the need for improved conjunction assessment and safe space operations, though they do not specifically address AI.

Technical standards bodies, including the International Organization for Standardization and national standards institutions, can develop performance benchmarks for autonomous space systems that regulatory authorities then reference in licensing and oversight decisions. This approach—combining normative frameworks with technical standards—has proven effective in aviation and maritime governance and offers a realistic pathway for space AI governance.

The European Union's approach to AI governance is particularly instructive. The AI Act's risk-based classification system—which subjects high-risk AI systems to stringent requirements for testing, documentation, transparency, and human oversight while imposing lighter obligations on lower-risk applications—provides a model that could be adapted for the space domain. Autonomous collision avoidance systems and active debris removal operations would likely qualify as high-risk applications under such a framework, warranting rigorous pre-deployment validation and ongoing monitoring. Lower-risk applications, such as AI-assisted ground-based data analysis, might require less intensive oversight. This calibrated approach avoids the twin dangers of regulatory overreach and regulatory absence, both of which could undermine the sustainable development of AI in space.

> ■ **Toward a Governance Architecture for AI in Space**
>
> The emerging consensus points toward a layered governance approach: existing treaty obligations interpreted to encompass autonomous systems; supplementary guidelines developed through COPUOS and the IISL; cross-sectoral regulatory adaptation from aviation and maritime models; industry-developed technical standards for algorithm validation and coordination; and national legislation incorporating AI-specific requirements into space licensing regimes.

***

Conclusion

Artificial intelligence and autonomous systems are not merely enhancing space operations; they are fundamentally altering the governance landscape. The speed, scale, and autonomy of AI-driven space activities outpace the legal frameworks designed to govern them, creating gaps in liability attribution, accountability, transparency, and coordination that demand urgent attention. The orbital environment is becoming too congested, too fast-moving, and too commercially competitive for governance structures designed around human-paced, state-dominated operations.

The legal challenges are significant but not unprecedented. Aviation, maritime operations, and terrestrial AI governance have all confronted analogous questions about responsibility for automated decisions, the role of human oversight, and the need for international coordination. The space domain can and should learn from these precedents, adapting proven governance models to the unique features of the orbital and deep-space environment.

What is required is neither regulatory paralysis nor hasty over-regulation, but a principled, adaptive approach that preserves the benefits of AI-driven innovation while ensuring that autonomous systems operate within frameworks of accountability, transparency, and safety. States, international organisations, industry, and the scholarly community all have roles to play in developing this governance architecture. The IISL's 2024 report, COPUOS deliberations, and academic initiatives such as Stanford's policy lab represent important contributions, but they are beginnings rather than conclusions.

The fundamental insight is that AI does not diminish the relevance of law—it amplifies it. As machines assume greater operational authority in the space domain, the need for clear legal rules, transparent processes, and enforceable accountability mechanisms becomes more acute, not less. The international community has an opportunity to shape the governance of autonomous space systems proactively, drawing on the principles of cooperation, responsibility, and due regard that have sustained international space law for more than half a century. Whether that opportunity is seized will determine not only the safety and sustainability of the orbital environment but the credibility of international law itself in the face of transformative technological change.

The path forward requires collaboration across traditional boundaries: between space lawyers and AI engineers, between national regulators and international organisations, between military and civilian stakeholders, and between established space powers and emerging actors. The IISL's 2024 report, with its emphasis on balancing innovation and responsibility, captures the essential challenge. Artificial intelligence offers extraordinary benefits for space safety, sustainability, and scientific discovery. Realising those benefits while managing the risks they entail is the defining governance task of the current generation of space law—a task that demands both urgency and wisdom.

***

End of Chapter 14

Part V
FUTURE FRONTIERS, FROM THE CISLUNAR ECONOMY TO HUMAN SETTLEMENT ON MARS

Chapter 15

CONVERGENCE, EXPANSION, AND THE FUTURE LEGAL ORDER

"The law of air and space is not a monument to be preserved but a living architecture—one that must be continuously rebuilt to shelter the ambitions, anxieties, and responsibilities of each new generation."

– Synthesis of the themes of this volume

Introduction

This book has traced the evolution of international air and space law from its earliest foundations to its most contemporary challenges. Beginning with the **sovereignty-based architecture of the Paris Convention and the Chicago Convention**, through the **freedom-based principles of the Outer Space Treaty**, and onward to the governance dilemmas posed by commercial spaceflight, mega-constellations, resource exploitation, artificial intelligence, and interplanetary settlement, the preceding chapters have demonstrated that the law governing human activity above the Earth's surface is undergoing a period of transformation as profound as any in its history.

This concluding chapter draws together the principal themes that have emerged across the volume, identifies the structural forces shaping the future of air and space law, and offers a framework for understanding how the legal order might evolve in the decades ahead. It does not attempt to predict specific outcomes—the interplay of technology, politics, economics, and human ambition defies precise forecasting. Instead, it identifies the fault lines along which the existing legal order is being tested and the normative choices that will determine whether the governance of air and space remains coherent, adaptive, and equitable.

Three overarching dynamics structure this concluding analysis: convergence, the erosion of boundaries between previously distinct legal regimes; expansion, the extension of human activity into domains that existing law was never designed to govern; and the emergence of a new legal order, characterised by pluralism, complexity, and the coexistence of multiple governance mechanisms operating at different scales and levels of formality.

The year 2025 provided striking evidence of each dynamic. Record-breaking orbital launches underscored the commercial transformation of space. COPUOS advanced draft principles for space resource governance while the Artemis Accords expanded to over sixty signatories. Italy enacted comprehensive national space legislation and the European Commission proposed the EU Space Act. China and the United States coordinated for the first time to prevent a satellite collision—a quiet milestone in operational cooperation. And across the globe, from Abu Dhabi's Space Debate to Vienna's UN Conference on Space Law and Policy, practitioners and policymakers grappled with the realisation that the governance frameworks inherited from the twentieth century require fundamental renewal.

***

Part 1

Convergence—The Dissolution of Legal Boundaries

The separation between air law and space law—between sovereignty and freedom, between the atmosphere and outer space—has served as the organising principle of international aviation and space governance for more than a century. As examined in the preceding chapters, that separation is now eroding under the pressure of technological innovation, commercial ambition, and operational reality.

I. Technological Drivers of Convergence

Suborbital vehicles traverse both domains in a single flight. Reusable launch systems operate as rockets on ascent and aircraft on descent, challenging the applicability of both air law and space law to different phases of the same operation. Hypersonic vehicles move at speeds and altitudes that confound jurisdictional categories derived from an era of subsonic aviation and orbital satellites. Mega-constellations of thousands of satellites raise operational challenges—traffic management, debris mitigation, spectrum coordination—that echo aviation's regulatory history rather than the diplomatic traditions of space law.

These technological developments do not merely create boundary cases requiring classification; they challenge the coherence of the binary framework itself. The question is no longer whether a particular vehicle is an aircraft or a spacecraft, subject to one regime or the other. The question is whether the legal architecture premised on this distinction remains fit for purpose. As this volume has argued, the answer is increasingly that it does not—at least not without substantial adaptation.

2. Institutional Convergence

The institutional landscape is evolving to reflect technological convergence. The International Civil Aviation Organization and the United Nations Committee on the Peaceful Uses of Outer Space—historically operating as separate institutional universes with distinct memberships, mandates, and working methods—are increasingly confronting overlapping issues. Space traffic management, which draws directly on aviation precedents, exemplifies the need for institutional coordination that transcends the air-space divide. National regulatory authorities, too, are being compelled to develop integrated frameworks: the United States Federal Aviation Administration, for instance, licenses both commercial aviation and commercial space launches, bridging the institutional boundary in practice even where it persists in legal theory.

The convergence challenge is not merely administrative. It is normative. Air law and space law embody different foundational principles—sovereignty versus freedom, bilateral versus multilateral governance, safety-focused regulation versus exploration-oriented principles. Integrating these regimes requires normative choices about which principles should prevail in the zones of overlap. These choices are political as much as legal, and they will shape the rights and obligations of states, operators, and individuals for decades to come.

The emerging field of space traffic management illustrates this normative tension with particular clarity. Aviation traffic management operates within a sovereignty framework: each state controls airspace above its territory and delegates management functions to designated authorities. Space traffic management, by contrast, must operate in a domain where sovereignty does not apply and where no single state has legitimate authority to direct the movements of another's spacecraft. Developing a governance model that achieves aviation-level safety coordination without importing aviation's sovereignty assumptions is one of the most challenging institutional design problems in contemporary international law.

3. The Delimitation Question Revisited

The enduring failure of the international community to agree on a boundary between airspace and outer space—examined in detail in earlier chapters—takes on new urgency in the context of convergence. The spatial approach, which would fix a boundary at a defined altitude such as the Kármán line, and the functional approach, which would classify activities based on their purpose and characteristics, each have strengths and limitations. Neither has commanded sufficient consensus for adoption.

The pragmatic reality is that the absence of a formal boundary has been managed through practical accommodation. But as hybrid operations multiply and the commercial stakes increase, the costs of ambiguity are rising. An operator launching a suborbital tourism vehicle needs to know which regulatory regime applies, which liability rules govern, and which state has jurisdiction at each phase of flight. The current answer—that it depends on interpretation, context, and bilateral arrangement—is becoming less sustainable as operations scale.

> ■ **Key Convergence Pressures**
>
> Suborbital flights: single operations crossing regulatory regimes · Reusable launch systems: aircraft-like re-entry under space law launch · Space traffic management: aviation models for orbital congestion · Mega-constellations: aviation-scale safety regulation for space objects · Hypersonic vehicles: dual-domain operations at unprecedented speed · National regulators: FAA, CAA, and others bridging air–space mandates

***

Part II

Expansion—Law Beyond Its Original Horizons

If convergence challenges the internal coherence of existing law, expansion challenges its external reach. Human activity is extending into domains—cislunar space, the lunar surface, Mars, the asteroid belt—that the framers of the Outer Space Treaty contemplated only in the most general terms. The legal framework built for exploration is now being asked to govern exploitation, habitation, and commerce.

1. The Commercialisation Imperative

The most transformative development in contemporary space activity is the shift from state-led exploration to commercially driven operations. Private companies now launch the majority of orbital missions, operate the largest satellite constellations, and are developing capabilities for lunar landing, asteroid mining, and eventually Mars settlement. This commercialisation is not a peripheral development—it is reshaping the fundamental character of space activity, shifting the centre of gravity from public agencies to private enterprises.

International space law was designed for a state-dominated domain. The Outer Space Treaty assigns responsibility to states, not companies. The Liability Convention attributes liability to launching States. The Registration Convention requires states to maintain registries. When the primary actors in space were government agencies, this state-centric framework was both normatively appropriate and practically workable. As private actors assume an ever-larger role, the framework must accommodate entities that are motivated by profit, governed by corporate boards, and responsive to market dynamics rather than diplomatic considerations.

National space legislation—proliferating rapidly across jurisdictions, as examined in earlier chapters—provides the primary mechanism for extending state responsibility to private actors. Italy's comprehensive space law enacted in June 2025, Japan's amendments to its Space Activities Act, and the proposed European Union Space Act all reflect this trend. Yet national approaches vary significantly in stringency, scope, and enforcement capacity, creating a fragmented regulatory landscape that operators must navigate and that competing states may exploit through regulatory arbitrage.

The scale of commercialisation compounds the governance challenge. In 2025, the space industry saw the highest number of orbital launches in history, with private companies accounting for the overwhelming majority. SpaceX alone operates a constellation exceeding six thousand satellites while simultaneously providing the primary launch capability for both commercial and government customers worldwide. This concentration of operational capacity in private hands raises profound questions about the adequacy of state-centred governance mechanisms: when a single company controls more space objects than most nations, the assumption that states are the primary actors requiring regulation no longer reflects operational reality.

2. Resource Activities and the Sovereignty Prohibition

The governance of space resource activities represents the most contested legal frontier of contemporary space law. The COPUOS Working Group on Legal Aspects of Space Resource Activities circulated an initial draft set of recommended principles in March 2025, including preambles emphasising responsible use, peaceful purposes, sustainability, cooperation, and equitable benefit-sharing. These principles seek to operationalise the Outer Space Treaty's provisions without resolving the underlying disagreement about whether resource extraction constitutes permissible use or impermissible appropriation.

The Artemis Accords framework, endorsed by over sixty signatories, affirms that resource extraction is consistent with the Outer Space Treaty. National legislation in the United States, Luxembourg, Japan, and the UAE codifies this interpretation domestically. But this position is not universally accepted. China and Russia, pursuing their own lunar and planetary programmes through the International Lunar Research Station initiative, have not endorsed the Accords' resource interpretation. The result is a bifurcated normative landscape in which competing legal interpretations coexist—a situation that could produce practical conflicts as lunar and Martian resource activities intensify.

The stakes of this disagreement extend beyond legal theory. Lunar water ice, concentrated at the poles, is both scientifically valuable and operationally essential for sustained human presence.

The first actors to extract and utilise lunar water will establish operational facts that shape subsequent governance arrangements. Whether these arrangements are developed cooperatively—through the COPUOS principles process or bilateral agreements—or emerge from uncoordinated unilateral action will significantly affect the long-term character of lunar governance. The analogy to terrestrial resource governance, particularly the deep seabed mining regime under the United Nations Convention on the Law of the Sea, offers both instructive parallels and cautionary lessons about the difficulty of establishing equitable resource-sharing frameworks in the face of powerful economic incentives and divergent national interests.

3. Human Presence Beyond Earth

The prospect of sustained human presence beyond Earth—explored in this volume through the lens of the UAE's Vision 2117 and the broader Mars governance discourse—represents the most profound expansion of the legal frontier. Permanent or semi-permanent settlements on the Moon or Mars will generate governance needs that existing law cannot fulfil: jurisdiction over multinational habitats, the legal status of persons born off-Earth, dispute resolution in isolated communities, environmental stewardship of planetary surfaces, and the protection of human rights in extreme environments.

These challenges are not merely theoretical. NASA's Artemis programme, the Lunar Gateway station, and China's planned lunar research base are designed to support extended human presence on the Moon within the current decade. The governance frameworks developed for these early outposts will establish precedents that shape the legal architecture of human expansion for generations. Getting them right—ensuring that they are inclusive, sustainable, and consistent with the foundational principles of international law—is a responsibility that the current generation of policymakers cannot defer.

The International Space Station Intergovernmental Agreement has provided a valuable, if imperfect, precedent. Its provisions for jurisdiction, intellectual property, criminal law, and liability in a multinational facility have been tested over more than two decades of continuous occupation. The Lunar Gateway's governance arrangements, building on this experience with contributions from multiple nations including the UAE's habitation module commitment, will extend these precedents to cislunar space. But the challenges of lunar and Martian settlement will far exceed those of orbital stations: the distance from Earth, the duration of habitation, the potential for economic self-sufficiency, and the eventual emergence of communities with distinct identities and interests will strain any governance framework designed for temporary, mission-based presence.

> ■ **The Expansion Frontier: Unresolved Legal Questions**
>
> Resource governance: permissible use or impermissible appropriation? • Safety zones: operational necessity or de facto sovereignty? • Jurisdiction: nationality-based or territory-based governance for settlements? • Birth rights: citizenship and legal status of persons born off-Earth • Environmental law: planetary protection standards for sustained habitation • Human rights: application of terrestrial instruments to extraterrestrial communities

***

Part III

The Emerging Legal Order—Pluralism, Complexity, and Adaptation

The convergence of air and space law and the expansion of human activity into new domains are generating a legal order that is fundamentally different from the treaty-based architecture of the twentieth century. This emerging order is characterised by pluralism, complexity, and the coexistence of multiple governance mechanisms operating at different levels of formality and authority.

1. The Treaty Impasse and the Rise of Soft Law

The era of comprehensive space treaty-making appears to have ended. The five United Nations space treaties—negotiated between 1967 and 1979—remain the constitutional foundation of international space law, but no new binding multilateral treaty has been concluded in nearly half a century. The COPUOS Legal Subcommittee has been unable to achieve consensus on new comprehensive agreements, and major spacefaring nations show little appetite for negotiations that might constrain their operational flexibility.

In the absence of new treaties, soft law has emerged as the primary vehicle for normative development. COPUOS guidelines, the Artemis Accords, the IISL's recommendations on AI governance, the ESA Zero Debris Charter, COSPAR planetary protection guidelines, and numerous bilateral cooperation agreements collectively shape the normative landscape of space governance. These instruments lack the binding force of treaties, but they establish expectations, build consensus, and create political and reputational incentives for compliance.

The soft law approach offers flexibility and speed, avoiding the consensus paralysis that afflicts formal treaty negotiations. But it also carries risks: soft law can be ignored without legal consequence, may reflect the preferences of powerful actors rather than the international community as a whole, and can fragment into competing normative frameworks—as the coexistence of the Artemis Accords and the ILRS framework demonstrates.

A critical question is whether soft law instruments can mature into customary international law. State practice, when accompanied by a sense of legal obligation, can crystallise into binding custom—but the process is slow, contested, and uncertain. National legislation that implements soft law principles contributes to state practice; consistent adherence to voluntary guidelines builds expectations of compliance. Over time, the soft law of today may become the hard law of tomorrow, not through formal treaty negotiation but through the organic process of norm development that has always been central to public international law.

2. National Legislation as Global Governance

As multilateral treaty-making stalls, national space legislation has assumed a de facto global governance role. When the United States, Luxembourg, or Japan enacts legislation authorising space resource extraction, the domestic law creates international facts: it establishes legal certainty for operators, generates state practice that may crystallise into customary international law, and shapes the interpretive environment in which treaty provisions are understood.

The proliferation of national space laws observed throughout 2024 and 2025—including Italy's comprehensive space law, Japan's regulatory amendments, and the proposed EU Space Act—reflects this dynamic. Each national framework implements international obligations while simultaneously interpreting and extending them. The aggregate effect is a form of decentralised norm-making in which the content of international space law is shaped as much by domestic legislative choices as by multilateral negotiation.

This decentralised approach has both strengths and vulnerabilities. It enables regulatory innovation, allows experimentation with different governance models, and permits rapid response to technological change. But it also creates risks of fragmentation, inconsistency, and competitive deregulation. When states compete for commercial space investment by offering lighter regulatory burdens, the result may be a 'race to the bottom' that undermines safety, sustainability, and the equitable distribution of benefits. Preventing this outcome requires, at minimum, internationally agreed baseline standards that establish a regulatory floor below which no national framework should fall—a function that the COPUOS guidelines process and the proposed EU Space Act's extraterritorial elements are beginning to address.

3. Geopolitical Competition and Normative Fragmentation

The most significant structural challenge facing the future legal order is **the deepening bifurcation between competing governance frameworks.** The Artemis Accords, led by the United States and endorsed by over sixty signatories, and the International Lunar Research Station programme, led by China and Russia, represent not merely different mission architectures but different normative visions for the governance of space. They differ on resource utilisation, safety zones, data sharing, and the relative authority of multilateral institutions versus plurilateral arrangements.

This bifurcation echoes broader geopolitical tensions but is particularly consequential in the space domain, where the physical environment is shared and the actions of one actor directly affect all others. Orbital debris generated by any nation threatens all satellites. Resource extraction on the Moon or Mars by any entity shapes the governance environment for all future activities. The absence of a unified governance framework risks producing a patchwork of competing norms, conflicting safety zones, and uncoordinated resource claims—an outcome that would undermine the foundational principle of space as a domain for cooperative endeavour.

Yet grounds for cautious optimism exist. The first known instance of operational space traffic management coordination between China and the United States, which occurred in 2025 to prevent a potential satellite collision, suggests that practical necessity can drive cooperation even where political relationships are strained. If expanded, such operational coordination mechanisms could provide a foundation for broader normative convergence—building trust through practice rather than through the formal negotiations that political conditions currently preclude.

4. Institutional Adaptation

The institutional architecture of air and space governance will need to evolve to match the complexity of the emerging legal order. COPUOS, operating on a consensus basis with a membership that now includes over one hundred states, has proven effective at developing guidelines but slow to address urgent governance challenges. ICAO's mandate is limited to civil aviation within the atmosphere. Neither institution is designed to govern the hybrid, multi-domain, commercially driven activities that characterise contemporary space operations.

Several institutional innovations are being explored. COPUOS has agreed to establish a working group on space traffic management, to be convened during its sixty-eighth session, which will examine national and regional frameworks, best practices, and regulatory coordination. The 2025 UN Conference on Space Law and Policy, themed 'Operationalising Space Sustainability,' sought to bridge legal principles with real-world operations. Regional organisations, including the African Space Agency and the Asia-Pacific Space Cooperation Organization, are developing governance capacity that complements multilateral frameworks.

The most likely institutional evolution is not the creation of a single comprehensive space governance body but the development of a networked governance architecture in which multiple institutions, operating at different scales and with different mandates, coordinate their activities through shared norms, mutual recognition, and cooperative mechanisms. This pluralistic model is messy, imperfect, and slow—but it may be the most realistic pathway for governance in a domain characterised by diverse actors, competing interests, and rapid technological change.

> ■ **The 2025 COPUOS Space Resource Principles (Draft)**
>
> COPUOS's Working Group on Legal Aspects of Space Resource Activities circulated draft recommended principles in March 2025, emphasising: responsible use of space resources; peaceful purposes; sustainability and environmental protection; international cooperation and information sharing; equitable benefit-sharing; compatibility with the Outer Space Treaty. These principles, if adopted, would represent the most significant multilateral normative development in space resource governance since the Moon Agreement of 1979.

***

Part IV

Principles for the Future

The preceding analysis suggests that the future legal order for air and space will be shaped not by a single grand design but by the accumulation of choices made by states, institutions, operators, and communities across multiple domains and over extended time. Nevertheless, certain principles can be identified as essential to ensuring that this evolving order serves humanity's collective interests.

1. Stewardship Over Sovereignty

The most important normative shift required is the evolution from a framework centred on state prerogatives to one centred on collective stewardship. The orbital environment, the lunar surface, and the Martian landscape are shared resources whose long-term viability depends on responsible management by all actors. The principle of stewardship—which encompasses environmental protection, intergenerational equity, and the duty not to foreclose future options—provides a normative foundation that transcends the sovereignty-freedom dichotomy and speaks to the shared interest of humanity in the sustainable governance of domains beyond Earth.

UNOOSA's 2026 Issues Note on 'Safeguarding Space: Environmental Issues, Risks and Responsibilities' and COPUOS conference room papers on dark and quiet skies reflect the growing institutional recognition that stewardship must become a central organising principle of space governance. The concept extends beyond environmental protection to encompass the preservation of scientific opportunity, the prevention of irreversible harm, and the obligation to consider the interests of future generations in present decision-making. As human activities in space intensify and expand, stewardship provides the normative compass that neither sovereignty nor freedom alone can supply.

2. Inclusivity and Equity

The benefits of space activity must not accrue exclusively to those with the technological and financial capacity to exploit them. The Outer Space Treaty's declaration that space shall be the 'province of all mankind' and that its exploration shall be carried out 'for the benefit and in the interests of all countries' establishes a normative expectation of inclusivity that emerging governance frameworks must operationalise. The growing participation of emerging space nations—from the UAE's Mars mission to the African Space Agency's inauguration—demonstrates that space governance is no longer the exclusive domain of traditional powers. Ensuring that new voices are heard in norm-making processes is essential to the legitimacy and durability of the future legal order.

3. Adaptive Governance

The pace of technological change in the space domain outstrips the capacity of traditional legal mechanisms to respond. Governance frameworks must therefore be designed for adaptation: incorporating review mechanisms, sunset clauses, and iterative revision processes that allow norms to evolve as technology and operational practice change. The 2019 COPUOS Long-term Sustainability Guidelines, which were explicitly designed to be revisited and updated, provide a model for this approach. Rigid instruments that cannot accommodate unforeseen developments will become obstacles rather than enablers of responsible space activity.

The preceding chapters' examination of artificial intelligence in space operations illustrates the urgency of adaptive governance. AI capabilities are advancing at a pace that would render any fixed regulatory instrument obsolete within years of its adoption. The governance challenge is to establish enduring principles—transparency, accountability, human oversight, interoperability—while leaving the technical specifications flexible enough to accommodate technological evolution. This principle-based approach, familiar from data protection law and financial regulation on Earth, offers the most promising model for governing rapidly changing technologies in the space domain.

4. The Rule of Law as Enabler

Throughout this volume, a consistent theme has emerged: law is not an impediment to human expansion into space but its essential enabler. Legal certainty attracts investment. Liability frameworks manage risk. Safety regulations protect lives. Property rights—however they are ultimately defined for space resources—create the conditions for sustainable economic activity. Dispute resolution mechanisms prevent conflicts from escalating. The rule of law, applied to the space domain with wisdom and flexibility, enables the very activities that some fear regulation would constrain.

This enabling function extends to the relationship between established and emerging space actors. As this volume has demonstrated through the case study of the UAE—an emerging space power that has consciously integrated legal compliance and normative leadership into its space programme—the rule of law provides a framework within which new actors can participate on equal terms, build confidence with established partners, and contribute to the development of governance norms. A rules-based order, unlike a power-based one, can accommodate the arrival of new actors without destabilising existing arrangements. This is precisely the kind of legal environment that the expansion of space activity into new domains and among new participants demands.

***

Conclusion: The Architecture Ahead

International air and space law stands at a crossroads. The legal architecture inherited from the twentieth century—the Chicago Convention for aviation, the Outer Space Treaty for space, the sharp line between sovereignty and freedom—has served humanity remarkably well. It enabled the growth of global aviation into the safest mass transportation system in history. It preserved outer space from the nuclear arms race and established the foundational principle that the cosmos belongs to all humankind. These are extraordinary achievements, and they deserve recognition even as the framework that produced them comes under unprecedented strain.

The strain is real and accelerating. Technological convergence is dissolving the boundary between air and space. Commercialisation is transforming the actor landscape. Artificial intelligence is redefining the meaning of human control. Geopolitical competition is fragmenting the normative consensus that sustained the treaty regime. And the prospect of permanent human presence on the Moon and Mars is raising questions that existing law was never designed to answer.

Yet the history traced in this volume offers grounds for confidence. International air and space law has always evolved in response to new challenges. The Chicago Convention emerged from the wreckage of world war. The Outer Space Treaty was negotiated at the height of Cold War rivalry. The Long-term Sustainability Guidelines were developed in an era of commercial disruption. Each generation has found ways to adapt the legal order to the demands of its time, preserving continuity while accommodating change.

The current generation faces its own defining challenge: to build a governance architecture that can manage the convergence of air and space operations, accommodate the expansion of human activity to the Moon and beyond, harness the transformative potential of artificial intelligence while maintaining accountability, and preserve the principles of cooperation, equity, and stewardship in an era of geopolitical competition. This is not a challenge that can be met by any single treaty, institution, or nation. It requires the collaborative effort of states, international organisations, industry, academia, and civil society—precisely the kind of collective endeavour that the best traditions of international law have always sought to enable.

The future legal order for air and space will not be monolithic. It will be layered, pluralistic, and adaptive—combining binding treaties with soft law guidelines, multilateral institutions with bilateral cooperation, international standards with national legislation, and formal rules with operational practice. This complexity is not a weakness but a reflection of the complexity of the domain itself. The task is not to simplify governance into a single instrument but to ensure coherence among its many components: that the pieces fit together, that gaps are identified and filled, and that the whole serves the interests not only of those who are exploring space today but of those who will inherit the consequences of today's choices.

As the distinguished space law tradition has long maintained, the law must serve not merely the interests of the present but the needs of future generations. In few domains is this obligation more relevant than in the governance of air and space. The decisions made in the coming decades—about delimitation, resource governance, AI accountability, planetary protection, settlement jurisdiction, and the architecture of international cooperation—will determine whether humanity's expansion beyond Earth is governed by principle or by power, by foresight or by accident, by shared purpose or by fragmented self-interest. This volume has sought to illuminate the choices that lie ahead. The making of those choices falls to all of us.

***

End of Chapter 15

Chapter 16

THE CISLUNAR ECONOMY: GOVERNANCE BEYOND LOW EARTH ORBIT

"The cislunar frontier is where the abstract principles of space law will first be tested by the concrete demands of commerce, habitation, and sustained human presence."

– Adapted from contemporary cislunar governance scholarship

Introduction

Cislunar space—the vast region extending from geosynchronous Earth orbit outward to and including the Moon—is rapidly emerging as the **next operational frontier for human activity in space.** After decades of near-exclusive focus on low Earth orbit, the international community is now investing heavily in cislunar infrastructure, lunar exploration, and the institutional foundations of what many anticipate will become a cislunar economy. NASA's Artemis programme, with crewed flights scheduled from 2026 and a crewed lunar landing targeted for mid-2027, and China's International Lunar Research Station, planned for operational establishment by the early 2030s, represent competing but parallel efforts to establish sustained human presence beyond Earth orbit.

Yet the governance framework for cislunar space remains embryonic. The Outer Space Treaty provides foundational principles—non-appropriation, freedom of exploration, state responsibility—but was not designed to govern the sustained economic activity, infrastructure development, and multi-actor coordination that cislunar operations demand. The emergence of a cislunar economy, however nascent, raises governance questions that are both urgent and largely unresolved: who coordinates traffic and operations in cislunar space, how are resources on the lunar surface governed, what rules apply to permanent infrastructure, and how are competing national programmes reconciled within a cooperative legal framework?

This chapter examines the legal and governance dimensions of the emerging cislunar economy. Part I maps the cislunar landscape, tracing the infrastructure programmes and commercial initiatives that are shaping this new domain. Part II analyses the legal framework applicable to cislunar activities, identifying the gaps between existing law and operational needs. Part III examines the critical governance challenges of cislunar space traffic management, resource utilisation, and infrastructure coordination. Part IV considers the geopolitical dynamics shaping cislunar governance, and Part V proposes principles for developing a coherent cislunar governance architecture.

***

Part I

The Cislunar Landscape—Programmes, Infrastructure, and Ambitions

The transformation of cislunar space from an empty transit corridor into an active operational domain is being driven by a convergence of government programmes, commercial ambitions, and strategic competition. Understanding the emerging landscape is essential to appreciating the governance challenges it generates.

1. The Artemis Architecture

NASA's Artemis programme represents the most ambitious cislunar initiative since the Apollo era. The programme aims to return astronauts to the lunar surface, establish a sustained presence, and build infrastructure that supports eventual crewed missions to Mars. Artemis II, a crewed circumlunar flight, is scheduled for March 2026. Artemis III, the first crewed lunar landing in over five decades, is targeted for mid-2027. Subsequent missions—Artemis IV through VI—will construct the Lunar Gateway, a multinational space station in near-rectilinear halo orbit around the Moon, and establish a regular cadence of surface operations.

The Lunar Gateway is the centrepiece of the cislunar infrastructure vision. Developed by NASA in partnership with the European Space Agency, the Japan Aerospace Exploration Agency, the Canadian Space Agency, and the UAE's Mohammed Bin Rashid Space Centre, the Gateway will serve as a communications hub, science laboratory, habitation module, and staging point for lunar surface missions. Its Power and Propulsion Element and Habitation and Logistics Outpost are scheduled for launch together on a Falcon Heavy rocket in 2027, with crewed assembly beginning during Artemis IV in late 2028. The station, weighing approximately forty metric tons when complete, will accommodate crews of four for missions lasting up to ninety days.

The Artemis programme's reliance on commercial partners represents a distinctive feature of the cislunar economy model. The Commercial Lunar Payload Services programme contracts private companies to deliver instruments and cargo to the lunar surface. The Human Landing System, developed by SpaceX using its Starship vehicle, and the Lunar Terrain Vehicle, developed by a team led by Intuitive Machines with Northrop Grumman, are owned by their commercial developers rather than by NASA. This public-private architecture is explicitly designed to seed a commercial cislunar ecosystem in which companies serve multiple government and private customers, creating the foundations for a self-sustaining lunar economy.

2. China's International Lunar Research Station

China's parallel cislunar programme follows a different architectural and governance model. The International Lunar Research Station, planned in cooperation with Russia and a growing number of partner nations, envisions a permanent research base in the Moon's south polar region. The programme's construction timeline is divided into three phases: reconnaissance through uncrewed Chang'e missions, which has been underway since 2021; construction of core infrastructure in the late 2020s; and operational capability with crewed landings planned by 2030. Supporting infrastructure includes a cislunar transportation facility, communications relay satellites, and surface logistics systems.

The ILRS represents not merely a different mission architecture but a different governance model. Where the Artemis programme operates under the Artemis Accords framework and emphasises commercial participation and interoperability, the ILRS operates through bilateral agreements between China and partner states, with governance structures that reflect different assumptions about resource utilisation, data sharing, and operational transparency. The coexistence of these two architectures in cislunar space—potentially operating in close proximity at the lunar south pole—creates governance challenges that existing international law is poorly equipped to resolve.

3. Commercial Cislunar Ventures

Beyond government programmes, a growing ecosystem of commercial ventures is targeting cislunar space. Companies are developing capabilities for lunar resource extraction, including water ice processing and regolith utilisation; cislunar logistics and transportation services; lunar communications and navigation infrastructure, including ESA's Moonlight programme and its Lunar Pathfinder data relay satellite; and in-space manufacturing and recycling, with companies like CisLunar Industries exploring the conversion of space debris into usable materials and fuel. The helium-3 isotope, rare on Earth but abundant on the lunar surface and valued at approximately twenty million dollars per kilogram for potential use in quantum computing, illustrates the economic drivers motivating commercial lunar interest.

The commercial cislunar economy remains, however, fundamentally government-dependent. As analysts have observed, there is currently no market-based cislunar economy; nearly all cislunar activities are tied to government funding and support, even when executed by private companies. The transition from government-anchored to commercially self-sustaining activity—the point at which cislunar operations generate sufficient commercial value to attract private investment independent of public funding—remains an aspiration rather than a near-term reality. Dramatically lowering launch and transportation costs, potentially through SpaceX's Starship and other next-generation vehicles, may eventually enable this transition, but the timeline remains uncertain.

The economic structure of the emerging cislunar economy therefore resembles frontier development more than mature market activity. Government programmes provide anchor demand that de-risks private investment, while blended financing models combining public funding, private capital, and international partnerships distribute the substantial technical and market risks involved. The legal framework for this economic model—encompassing government procurement contracts, intellectual property rights in cislunar innovations, liability allocation between public and private partners, and the regulatory conditions for commercial operations on the lunar surface—is being developed in real time, largely through national legislation and bilateral agreements rather than through multilateral negotiation.

■ **Cislunar Infrastructure Timeline (2026–2030)**

2026: Artemis II crewed circumlunar flight (March) · 2027: Artemis III crewed lunar landing; Gateway PPE/HALO launch · 2028: Artemis IV—first crewed Gateway docking; I-Hab module delivery · 2029: China Chang'e-8 ILRS construction phase begins · 2030: Artemis V—ESPRIT, Canadarm3 delivery; China targeted crewed lunar landing; ESA Argonaut first landing (early 2030s)

***

Part 11

The Legal Framework—Principles and Gaps

Cislunar activities are governed by the same international legal framework that applies to all space activities: principally the Outer Space Treaty of 1967 and its associated instruments. However, the specific characteristics of cislunar operations—proximity to a celestial body with exploitable resources, the establishment of permanent infrastructure, and the sustained presence of human communities—expose significant gaps between the existing framework's general principles and the operational realities of the emerging cislunar domain.

1. Applicable Legal Principles

The foundational principles of international space law apply fully to cislunar space. The Outer Space Treaty's provisions on freedom of exploration, non-appropriation of celestial bodies, state responsibility for national space activities, the requirement of due regard for the interests of other states, and the obligation to conduct activities for the benefit of all countries constitute the normative framework within which all cislunar operations must be conducted. The Liability Convention's provisions on damage caused by space objects, the Registration Convention's requirements for cataloguing space objects, and the Rescue Agreement's obligations regarding astronaut assistance all extend to cislunar activities without geographical limitation.

The Moon Agreement of 1979 specifically addresses the governance of activities on the Moon and other celestial bodies, establishing the principle that the Moon and its natural resources are the 'common heritage of mankind' and calling for an international regime to govern resource exploitation. However, the Agreement has been ratified by only a small number of states, none of which are major spacefaring nations. Its practical influence on cislunar governance is therefore limited, though its normative aspiration—that lunar resources should be governed for the collective benefit of humanity—continues to inform international discussions.

2. The Resource Governance Gap

The most consequential gap in the existing legal framework concerns the governance of lunar resources. As examined in preceding chapters, the Outer Space Treaty prohibits national appropriation of the Moon but does not explicitly address whether the extraction and use of lunar resources by states or their nationals constitutes permissible 'use' or impermissible appropriation. This ambiguity has produced competing interpretations and fragmented governance responses.

The United States, through the 2015 Commercial Space Launch Competitiveness Act and the 2020 Executive Order on space resource utilisation, has adopted the position that resource extraction is lawful under the Outer Space Treaty. The Artemis Accords, now endorsed by over sixty signatories, affirm this interpretation while emphasising transparency, interoperability, and the avoidance of harmful interference. The COPUOS Working Group on Legal Aspects of Space Resource Activities circulated draft recommended principles in March 2025, including preambles emphasising responsible use, sustainability, cooperation, and equitable benefit-sharing. These principles, if adopted, would represent the most significant multilateral normative development in lunar resource governance since the Moon Agreement.

Yet the governance gap remains open. China and Russia, the other major cislunar actors, have not endorsed the Artemis Accords' resource interpretation. The risk of conflicting resource claims or operational interference at lunar sites of particular value—notably the permanently shadowed craters at the south pole, where water ice is concentrated—grows as both programmes advance toward surface operations in the same region. Without an agreed framework for resource governance, the cislunar economy risks developing under competing legal regimes that could produce practical conflicts and undermine the cooperative foundation of international space law.

Environmental sustainability adds another dimension to the resource governance challenge. Lunar resources, while substantial, are not unlimited. Permanently shadowed craters, once disturbed by extraction activities, may lose their scientific value irreversibly. Regolith disturbance creates dust that can contaminate equipment and degrade solar panels across wide areas. The absence of an atmosphere means that environmental impacts, once created, persist indefinitely. Developing environmental standards for lunar resource extraction—addressing site preservation, dust mitigation, cumulative impact assessment, and the protection of scientifically valuable areas—is a governance requirement that existing space law acknowledges in principle but has not yet operationalised.

3. Safety Zones and Operational Coordination

The Artemis Accords introduced the concept of 'safety zones' around lunar operations—areas in which operators notify others of their activities and request avoidance of potentially harmful interference. These zones are explicitly distinguished from territorial claims and are intended to be temporary, proportionate, and transparent. The concept addresses a genuine operational need: lunar surface operations involving habitats, power systems, and resource extraction equipment require protection from dust contamination, communications interference, and physical proximity hazards.

However, safety zones remain controversial. Critics argue that they risk creating de facto territorial claims by establishing exclusive operational areas that, even if formally temporary, may in practice become permanent as infrastructure investment deepens. The absence of an agreed international mechanism for establishing, modifying, and resolving disputes about safety zones creates the potential for unilateral claims that other actors may challenge. The governance of safety zones—who establishes them, how large they can be, what obligations they create for third parties, and how disputes are resolved—is among the most pressing practical challenges of cislunar governance.

- **The Lunar South Pole Challenge**

Both the Artemis and ILRS programmes target the Moon's south polar region, where permanently shadowed craters contain water ice essential for sustained operations. The concentration of interest in a limited geographic area amplifies governance challenges: competing safety zones, overlapping resource claims, communications interference, and the need for operational coordination between programmes that operate under different governance frameworks.

***

Part III

Governance Challenges—Traffic, Resources, and Infrastructure

The operational realities of the cislunar domain generate governance challenges that are qualitatively different from those of low Earth orbit. The distances involved, the proximity to a resource-rich celestial body, the establishment of permanent infrastructure, and the coexistence of competing national programmes create a governance environment of unprecedented complexity.

1. Cislunar Space Traffic Management

Space traffic management, already challenging in the congested low Earth orbit environment, takes on new dimensions in cislunar space. Spacecraft transiting between Earth and the Moon, stations in lunar orbit, landers descending to and ascending from the lunar surface, and robotic systems operating on the surface must all be coordinated to prevent collisions, communications interference, and operational conflicts. The United States National Cislunar Science and Technology Strategy, released in 2022 and supplemented by an action plan, explicitly identifies the extension of space situational awareness into cislunar space as a strategic priority.

The technical challenges are formidable. Ground-based radar and optical sensors that track objects in low Earth orbit have limited capability in cislunar space, where distances are orders of magnitude greater. Dedicated cislunar tracking infrastructure—including space-based sensors in lunar orbit and at Lagrange points—will be required to maintain situational awareness. The United States Air Force Research Laboratory's Oracle programme and commercial initiatives are beginning to address this gap, but comprehensive cislunar situational awareness remains years away.

The governance dimension is equally challenging. No international institution currently has the mandate, capability, or authority to manage traffic in cislunar space. The coordination mechanisms that function, however imperfectly, in low Earth orbit—including conjunction screening services and voluntary data-sharing arrangements—do not extend to the cislunar domain. Developing an international framework for cislunar traffic management that accommodates both the Artemis and ILRS programmes, and that integrates commercial operators with government missions, is essential but politically difficult given the broader geopolitical competition between the programmes' leading states.

2. Lunar Resource Governance

The governance of lunar resources—particularly water ice, regolith, and potentially helium-3—will define the character of the cislunar economy. Water ice, concentrated in the permanently shadowed craters of the lunar south pole, is the most strategically significant resource in the near term. It can be processed into drinking water, breathable oxygen, and rocket propellant, making it essential for sustained human presence and for reducing the cost of cislunar transportation by enabling refuelling in lunar orbit rather than launching all propellant from Earth.

The legal framework for lunar resource governance remains contested, as analysed in preceding chapters. The practical question is how extraction rights are allocated, how competing claims to the same deposit are resolved, and how the benefits of resource utilisation are shared—particularly with states that lack the capability to extract resources themselves. The COPUOS draft principles of March 2025 address some of these questions at the normative level, but operationalising principles of 'equitable benefit-sharing' and 'responsible use' into concrete governance mechanisms will require sustained diplomatic effort and creative institutional design.

The precedent of deep seabed mining governance under the United Nations Convention on the Law of the Sea is frequently invoked in this context. The International Seabed Authority administers mineral resources in areas beyond national jurisdiction, balancing commercial exploitation with benefit-sharing obligations. While the analogy is imperfect—the Moon lacks the legal designation of 'common heritage of mankind' that applies to the deep seabed for most spacefaring nations—the institutional model demonstrates that governance mechanisms for resource exploitation in shared domains are feasible when political will exists. Developing a comparable mechanism for lunar resources, or ensuring that national regulatory approaches achieve functionally equivalent outcomes, is among the most important governance tasks of the coming decade.

3. Infrastructure Coordination and Standards

The construction of permanent infrastructure in cislunar space—orbital stations, surface habitats, communications networks, navigation systems, and transportation nodes—raises governance questions that have no precedent in space law. The Lunar Gateway's governance draws on the International Space Station Intergovernmental Agreement model, establishing jurisdiction, intellectual property, and liability arrangements among partner states. But the Gateway is a single facility with a defined set of partners; the broader cislunar infrastructure landscape will involve multiple facilities operated by different states and commercial entities, potentially with different technical standards, communication protocols, and operational procedures.

Interoperability—the ability of systems from different operators to work together—is essential for safety, efficiency, and the development of a functioning cislunar economy. The U.S. National Cislunar Strategy emphasises the development of common reference systems, including a standardised lunar coordinate framework and celestial time standards, as foundational requirements for cislunar operations. ESA's Moonlight programme, developing communications and navigation services for the lunar environment including the Lunar Pathfinder relay satellite scheduled for launch in 2027, represents a European contribution to this infrastructure. Ensuring that these systems are interoperable across national and commercial boundaries requires international standards that do not yet exist in authoritative form.

***

Part IV

Geopolitical Dynamics—Competition and Cooperation

The cislunar domain is shaped by geopolitical dynamics that both complicate and motivate governance development. The relationship between the Artemis and ILRS programmes, the role of emerging space nations, and the tension between competition and cooperation define the political environment in which cislunar governance must evolve.

1. Moon Race 2.0

The parallel pursuit of lunar programmes by the United States and China has been widely characterised as a second Moon race. Unlike the Cold War space race, which was primarily a bilateral competition between two superpowers, the contemporary cislunar competition involves a broader constellation of actors: the Artemis Accords coalition of over sixty signatories, the ILRS partnership led by China and Russia, and independent programmes pursued by India, Japan, and others. The competition is not purely symbolic; it involves concrete strategic interests in resource access, technological leadership, commercial advantage, and the capacity to shape governance norms for the cislunar domain.

The geopolitical dimension introduces both urgency and difficulty into governance discussions. Urgency, because the absence of agreed rules increases the risk of operational conflicts, misunderstandings, and escalatory dynamics as both programmes converge on the lunar south pole. Difficulty, because the broader political relationship between the United States and China constrains the scope for bilateral or multilateral negotiation on cislunar governance. U.S. legislation, including the Wolf Amendment, restricts NASA cooperation with China, limiting the institutional channels through which governance coordination could occur.

The budget politics surrounding the Artemis programme illustrate the domestic dimension of cislunar competition. The Trump administration's fiscal year 2026 budget proposal sought to cancel the Lunar Gateway and the SLS rocket after Artemis III, proposing a shift toward commercial alternatives. Congress, through the One Big Beautiful Bill Act signed in July 2025, allocated 2.6 billion dollars to preserve the Gateway programme through fiscal year 2032. These domestic political dynamics—in which cislunar investment competes with other priorities and is subject to shifting presidential and congressional preferences—inject uncertainty into both the pace of cislunar development and the governance frameworks that depend on sustained commitment. International partners, having invested years and significant resources in Gateway contributions, face the additional governance challenge of ensuring that bilateral commitments are honoured despite fluctuations in the leading partner's domestic politics.

Figure 23: Human Exploration and Infrastructure Development on the Moon

Source: Generated using OpenAI Sora.

2. The Role of Middle Powers and Emerging Actors

Middle powers and emerging space nations play an increasingly significant role in cislunar governance. The UAE's contribution to the Lunar Gateway through the Mohammed Bin Rashid Space Centre, India's successful Chandrayaan programme and its plans for crewed lunar landings by 2040, Japan's contributions to the Gateway and its partnership with India on a lunar lander, and the growing African engagement with space science all diversify the cislunar actor landscape beyond the US-China binary.

These actors bring perspectives that can enrich governance discussions. Emerging space nations have a particular interest in ensuring that cislunar governance frameworks are inclusive and equitable, reflecting the Outer Space Treaty's principle that exploration shall benefit all countries. Their participation in governance development can enhance the legitimacy of resulting frameworks and guard against outcomes that serve only the interests of the most technologically advanced states. The Abu Dhabi Space Debate, the 2025 UN Conference on Space Law and Policy, and COPUOS deliberations provide forums in which these perspectives can be heard and integrated.

Figure 24: Mohammed Bin Rashid Space Centre, United Arab Emirates

Source: Mohammed Bin Rashid Space Centre.

3. Precedent from Antarctica and the ISS

Historical precedents offer partial guidance for cislunar governance. The Antarctic Treaty System, which suspends territorial sovereignty claims, prohibits military activity, and establishes the continent as a preserve for scientific research, provides a model for governance of a shared domain beyond national jurisdiction. The ISS Intergovernmental Agreement, which allocates jurisdiction by module, establishes intellectual property protections, and provides for criminal jurisdiction and liability, demonstrates how multinational cooperation can function in a hostile extraterrestrial environment.

Neither precedent is directly transferable. Antarctica lacks the resource exploitation dimension that drives cislunar interest. The ISS involves a defined, fixed-membership partnership rather than the open, multi-actor environment anticipated in cislunar space. But both precedents illustrate that international cooperation in challenging domains is achievable when participants perceive shared interests, and that governance frameworks can evolve from initial arrangements designed for limited, specific activities to more comprehensive systems as activity expands. The challenge for cislunar governance is to learn from these precedents while adapting to the unique characteristics of the lunar domain.

> **▪ Cislunar Governance Models Under Discussion**
>
> Antarctic Treaty System: suspended sovereignty, science preserve, environmental protocol · ISS Intergovernmental Agreement: jurisdiction by module, IP protection, liability allocation · Artemis Accords: safety zones, transparency, interoperability, resource utilisation · ILRS bilateral agreements: state-to-state partnerships, centralised coordination · COPUOS draft principles: responsible use, sustainability, benefit-sharing · Hybrid models: layered governance combining binding obligations, soft law, and operational protocols

***

Part V

Toward a Cislunar Governance Architecture

The analysis presented in this chapter suggests that cislunar governance cannot rely solely on the general principles of existing space law, nor can it await the negotiation of a comprehensive new treaty. A pragmatic, incremental approach is needed—one that builds governance capacity through layered mechanisms operating at different levels of formality and authority.

1. Operationalising Existing Principles

The first layer of cislunar governance should involve the operationalisation of existing treaty principles for the specific conditions of the cislunar domain. The Outer Space Treaty's requirement of 'due regard' for other states' activities, for example, can be given concrete content through agreed protocols for operational coordination, advance notification of activities, and procedures for addressing harmful interference. The COPUOS Long-term Sustainability Guidelines, though developed primarily for low Earth orbit, provide a normative model that can be adapted for cislunar operations. Extending and specifying these principles for the cislunar context does not require new treaty negotiation; it requires authoritative interpretation and supplementary guidelines.

The Registration Convention offers a particularly straightforward opportunity for operational adaptation. Requiring comprehensive registration of cislunar objects—including orbital stations, landers, surface infrastructure, and robotic systems—with enhanced information about operational parameters, autonomous capabilities, and intended duration would provide the transparency foundation upon which other governance mechanisms can be built. Similarly, the Rescue Agreement's obligations regarding astronaut assistance can be operationalised for the cislunar domain through protocols for emergency coordination between missions operating in lunar orbit or on the lunar surface, regardless of their programmatic affiliation.

2. Developing Technical Standards

Technical standards are the connective tissue of any functioning economy. For the cislunar domain, standards for communications protocols, navigation reference frames, data formats, docking interfaces, and resource processing specifications are essential prerequisites for interoperability and commerce. The U.S. National Cislunar Strategy's emphasis on reference systems and time standardisation, and ESA's Moonlight infrastructure programme, represent important national and regional contributions. Elevating these into internationally recognised standards—through bodies such as the Consultative Committee for Space Data Systems, the International Organization for Standardization, or dedicated cislunar technical working groups—would provide the infrastructure layer upon which commercial activity can develop.

3. Establishing Coordination Mechanisms

Operational coordination between cislunar actors—whether through multilateral institutions, bilateral agreements, or industry-led initiatives—is essential for safety and efficiency. At minimum, a cislunar traffic coordination service providing conjunction assessment, manoeuvre notification, and deconfliction support is urgently needed. More ambitiously, a cislunar resource coordination mechanism could provide transparency about planned extraction activities, mediate competing claims, and develop equitable benefit-sharing arrangements. These mechanisms need not be created from scratch; they can build on existing institutional infrastructure, including COPUOS, the Space Data Association, and the bilateral coordination channels that, as the 2025 US-China collision avoidance incident demonstrated, can function even between strategic competitors.

4. Ensuring Inclusivity

The legitimacy and durability of cislunar governance will depend on its inclusivity. A framework designed by and for the most technologically advanced states will lack the broad acceptance necessary for universal adherence. The Outer Space Treaty's declaration that space activities shall be carried out for the benefit of all countries creates a normative obligation to ensure that the cislunar economy does not become an exclusive domain of the wealthy and powerful. Practical mechanisms for inclusivity—capacity-building programmes, data-sharing arrangements, technology transfer frameworks, and participation in governance institutions—must be built into cislunar governance from the outset rather than added as afterthoughts.

The experience of the International Space Station provides both positive and negative lessons on this front. The ISS partnership, while remarkably successful in sustaining multinational cooperation over more than two decades, was limited to a small number of advanced space powers. The broader international community participated primarily through visiting astronaut programmes and secondary research opportunities rather than as equal governance partners. The cislunar domain, with its greater economic potential and longer time horizon, demands a more genuinely inclusive governance model—one that gives developing states meaningful voice in decisions about resource allocation, environmental standards, and benefit distribution. The Africa-EU Space Partnership Programme launched in 2025 and the growing engagement of Gulf states in lunar programmes represent encouraging steps toward this more inclusive vision.

***

Conclusion

The cislunar economy is emerging at the intersection of technological capability, strategic ambition, and governance uncertainty. The infrastructure being built today—the Lunar Gateway, the ILRS, commercial lunar services, communications and navigation networks—will define the operational environment for decades. The governance frameworks developed alongside this infrastructure will determine whether the cislunar domain becomes a space of cooperative development or competitive fragmentation.

The legal foundations are sound. The Outer Space Treaty's principles of freedom, non-appropriation, state responsibility, and due regard provide a normative framework that remains relevant and adaptable. But principles alone are insufficient for the operational complexities of sustained cislunar activity. They must be supplemented by specific governance mechanisms—for traffic coordination, resource management, safety zone administration, infrastructure interoperability, and dispute resolution—that translate abstract obligations into practical rules.

The window for proactive governance is narrowing. As infrastructure is deployed, operations commence, and investment deepens, the governance choices made—or deferred—will create path dependencies that become increasingly difficult to reverse. The international community has an opportunity to shape the cislunar economy as a domain of shared benefit, responsible stewardship, and cooperative endeavour. Seizing that opportunity requires political will, institutional creativity, and a commitment to the foundational insight that has sustained international space law for over half a century: that the governance of domains beyond Earth is too important to be left to power alone, and must be guided by principle, sustained by cooperation, and accountable to all humanity.

***

End of Chapter 16

Chapter 17

THE UNITED ARAB EMIRATES AND THE FUTURE OF MARS

"If it is God's will, man can achieve anything; nothing is impossible."

– Sheikh Zayed bin Sultan Al Nahyan, Founding Father of the UAE

Introduction

Few nations in history have traversed the distance from subsistence to space exploration in so compressed a timeframe as the United Arab Emirates. A federation of seven emirates established in 1971 on the shores of the Arabian Gulf, the UAE has, within a single human lifetime, evolved from a desert economy dependent on pearl diving and modest trade into a global centre of aviation, technology, and—increasingly—space exploration. The trajectory is extraordinary not merely for its speed but for its deliberateness: at every stage, the UAE's engagement with aviation and space has been the product of strategic vision, sustained investment, and a determination to diversify the national economy beyond hydrocarbons.

The story begins with a founding father's fascination with the heavens, traces through the building of one of the world's most formidable aviation industries, accelerates through the establishment of a national space programme, and arrives at a destination that would have seemed implausible even a generation ago: the UAE as a Mars-faring nation with a century-long strategy to establish a human settlement on the Red Planet. This chapter examines that remarkable journey, situating the UAE's space ambitions within the broader evolution of international air and space law and assessing the legal, institutional, and geopolitical dimensions of its contribution to the future of Mars exploration.

The chapter proceeds in five parts. Part I traces the UAE's aviation heritage and the foundational vision of Sheikh Zayed bin Sultan Al Nahyan. Part II examines the growth of the UAE's space industry, from its first satellites to the establishment of the UAE Space Agency. Part III chronicles the UAE's human spaceflight programme and its historic milestones. Part IV analyses the Emirates Mars Mission and the Mars 2117 strategy that positions the UAE as a leading actor in Martian exploration. Part V considers the legal and normative dimensions of the UAE's space programme, examining how a relatively young nation is shaping the future of international space governance.

***

Part 1

Foundations—Aviation Heritage and the Vision of Sheikh Zayed

1. The Rise of UAE Aviation

The United Arab Emirates' engagement with the skies began not in the realm of outer space but in the development of one of the world's most dynamic civil aviation industries. The story starts modestly. Dubai's first airport was built in 1959, a simple facility serving a city whose economy still revolved around maritime trade and the remnants of the pearl diving industry. Gulf Air, a regional carrier jointly owned by several Gulf states including the UAE, provided the principal air connections. But as Dubai's economy began to diversify in the 1970s and 1980s, the limitations of depending on a shared regional airline became apparent.

Figure 25: Abu Dhabi Airport Terminal and Control Tower, 1968

Source: National Archives and Library of the United Arab Emirates.

The founding of Emirates airline in 1985 was a transformative moment. When Gulf Air reduced services to Dubai, Sheikh Mohammed bin Rashid Al Maktoum, then UAE Minister of Defence, commissioned the establishment of a new carrier. The directive was characteristically bold: 'Look good, be good, and make money.' With an initial investment of just ten million dollars and two leased aircraft, Emirates launched its inaugural flight from Dubai to Karachi on 25 October 1985. In its first year, the carrier transported 260,000 passengers. By the mid-1990s, Emirates was flying to over thirty destinations. By 2000, it had placed orders for the Airbus A380 and Boeing 777 families that would define its fleet identity. By 2025,

Figure 26: Sheikh Shakhbut bin Sultan Al Nahyan Arriving at Das Island, Abu Dhabi, 1962

Source: National Archives of the UAE; © British Petroleum Company Limited.

Emirates operated a fleet of nearly 270 wide-body aircraft, served over 150 destinations in eighty countries, and had recorded its most profitable year in history.

Figure 27: Official Opening Ceremony of Dubai Airport, 30 December 1960

Source: National Archives and Library of the United Arab Emirates; © Edrick Worsnop.

Abu Dhabi followed with the establishment of Etihad Airways in 2003, created by Amiri decree of the late Sheikh Khalifa bin Zayed Al Nahyan. Etihad grew rapidly to serve over 120 destinations with a fleet exceeding one hundred aircraft. The low-cost segment was addressed by Air Arabia, launched in Sharjah in 2003, and flydubai, established in 2008. Together with world-class airport infrastructure—Dubai International Airport, Al Maktoum International Airport, and Abu Dhabi's Zayed International Airport—the UAE built an aviation ecosystem that positioned the nation as a global hub connecting East and West. By 2024, Emirates alone was the world's fourth-largest airline by available seat kilometres, and the Middle East had become the world's second-fastest growing aviation market.

The legal and regulatory framework supporting this growth was equally significant. The UAE developed a comprehensive civil aviation regulatory regime, established the General Civil Aviation Authority, and negotiated an extensive network of bilateral air service agreements that provided the legal foundation for its carriers' global reach. The UAE's open-skies philosophy, though contested by competitors who alleged unfair advantages, created the regulatory environment in which aviation could flourish as a pillar of national economic diversification. This aviation heritage—the institutional capacity, regulatory sophistication, and strategic ambition it cultivated—would prove essential when the UAE turned its gaze from the atmosphere to outer space.

2. Sheikh Zayed's Vision: From the Desert to the Stars

The origins of the UAE's space ambitions can be traced to a single, visionary figure: Sheikh Zayed bin Sultan Al Nahyan, the founding father of the United Arab Emirates and its first president from 1971 until his passing in 2004. Sheikh Zayed's interest in space science was ignited in the early 1970s, in the immediate aftermath of the Apollo Moon landings. In what would become a foundational moment in the UAE's space narrative, Sheikh Zayed met with members of the NASA team responsible for

Figure 28: Sheikh Zayed bin Sultan Al Nahyan Receiving a Delegation of American Astronauts in Abu Dhabi, 12 February 1976

Source: National Archives and Library of the United Arab Emirates.

the Apollo programme, engaging them in detailed discussions about their experiences travelling to and from the Moon.

In 1973, United States President Richard Nixon gifted Sheikh Zayed a fragment of lunar rock collected during the Apollo 17 mission from the Taurus-Littrow Valley—a gesture that symbolised the connection between a young desert nation and the furthest reaches of human exploration. The rock, now displayed at the Al Ain Museum, bears the inscription 'a symbol of the unity of the human endeavour.' In 1976, a particularly significant encounter took place when three astronauts from the Apollo-Soyuz Test Project—Thomas Stafford, Deke Slayton, and Vance Brand—visited Abu Dhabi, bringing with them a scale model of the Space Shuttle. The meeting, which is commemorated on the UAE's one-thousand-dirham banknote alongside images of the Space Shuttle and the Hope Mars Probe, saw Sheikh Zayed engage the astronauts with detailed questions about space technology, human survival in orbit, and the scientific achievements of the Apollo era.

Dr Farouk El-Baz, the Egyptian-American NASA scientist who participated in several of these encounters, later recalled Sheikh Zayed's remarkable curiosity: the founding father wanted to understand how astronauts survived in space, how they conducted experiments, how they managed to collect rocks from the lunar surface. 'He'd ask such fascinating questions about space and space missions,' El-Baz remembered. These were not casual encounters; they represented a deliberate effort by the UAE's leader to understand the frontiers of human knowledge and to envision a role for his nation in their exploration.

Sheikh Zayed's vision extended beyond personal curiosity to national aspiration. He recognised that investment in science, technology, and education was essential for the UAE's long-term prosperity. His conviction—'If it is God's will, man can achieve anything; nothing is impossible'—became the philosophical foundation for the UAE's subsequent space programme. When the UAE named its crewed space missions 'Zayed Ambition,' it was not merely an act of commemoration but an acknowledgement that the nation's space achievements represent the fulfilment of a vision articulated decades earlier by its founding father.

In 1988, Sheikh Zayed met with Prince Sultan bin Salman Al Saud of Saudi Arabia, who in 1985 had become the first Arab and the first Muslim to travel to space aboard the Space Shuttle Discovery. Sheikh Zayed inquired about the smallest details of Prince Sultan's journey, demonstrating his continued engagement with space exploration throughout his leadership. Prince Sultan's experience had a profound impact on the region, and Sheikh Zayed's response to it underscored his belief that Arab nations had both the right and the capability to participate in humanity's exploration of the cosmos. This encounter became another stepping stone in driving the UAE's enthusiasm for space, laying the groundwork for the eventual creation of a national space programme that would honour Sheikh Zayed's legacy by transforming his aspirations into concrete achievements.

Sheikh Zayed and the Stars: Key Encounters

1970s: Sheikh Zayed meets NASA Apollo team members, sparking national interest in space • 1973: President Nixon gifts a fragment of Apollo 17 lunar rock, now at Al Ain Museum • 1974: Meeting with Dr Farouk El-Baz to discuss Apollo scientific results • 1976: Apollo-Soyuz astronauts Stafford, Slayton, and Brand visit Abu Dhabi with Space Shuttle model • 1988: Sheikh Zayed meets Prince Sultan bin Salman Al Saud, the first Arab in space, inquiring about every detail of his journey

***

Part II

Building a Space Nation—Institutions, Satellites, and Strategy

1. Early Satellite Programmes

The UAE's transition from aviation nation to space nation began in the late 1990s with investments in satellite communications. Thuraya Communications Company, established in 1997, launched its first mobile satellite communications satellite in 2000, providing coverage across Europe, the Middle East, and Asia. Al Yah Satellite Communications Company, known as Yahsat, was established in 2007 and developed a fleet of geostationary communications satellites providing broadband and government communications services. These early ventures, while primarily commercial in nature, built the institutional knowledge, technical relationships, and strategic confidence that would underpin more ambitious space endeavours.

Figure 29: Sheikh Mohamed bin Zayed Al Nahyan Listening to UAE Astronaut Hazzaa Al Mansoori Explaining the Soyuz Spacecraft, Abu Dhabi, 12 October 2019

Source: National Archives and Library of the United Arab Emirates; © WAM.

T came with the establishment of the Emirates Institution for Advanced Science and Technology in 2006, launched by Sheikh Mohammed bin Rashid Al Maktoum. Beginning with just five engineers, the institution—which would be merged into the Mohammed bin Rashid Space Centre in 2015—embarked on a systematic programme of capability development. Its first major achievement was DubaiSat-1, the UAE's first Earth observation satellite, launched in 2009 in partnership with South Korea's Satrec Initiative. DubaiSat-2 followed in 2013, with increased Emirati participation in design and manufacture. The progression was intentional: each mission served as a training ground for Emirati engineers, building the human capital necessary for increasingly complex undertakings.

The capstone of this satellite development programme was KhalifaSat, launched in October 2018. Named after the late Sheikh Khalifa bin Zayed Al Nahyan, KhalifaSat was the first satellite designed and manufactured entirely by Emirati engineers at the Mohammed bin Rashid Space Centre in Dubai. Operating in low Earth orbit at approximately 613 kilometres altitude, the satellite provided high-resolution Earth observation imagery with a ground sample distance of 0.7 metres in panchromatic mode. KhalifaSat represented a pivotal achievement: proof that the UAE had progressed from purchasing satellite services to designing and building its own space hardware.

2. The UAE Space Agency and National Space Policy

The establishment of the UAE Space Agency in 2014, by Federal Decree No. 1 of 2014, marked the institutional maturation of the national space sector. The Agency, headquartered in Abu Dhabi with a branch in Dubai, was charged with developing and regulating the UAE's growing space industry. Its mandate encompassed policy development, regulation, international cooperation, research and development investment, and the coordination of national space activities across government and private sector entities.

The regulatory framework was further strengthened by Federal Law No. 12 of 2019 on the Regulation of the Space Sector, which established comprehensive rules governing space activities conducted by UAE entities. The law addressed licensing, registration, liability, data management, environmental protection, and the coordination of military and civilian space activities. Importantly, the law was designed to align with the UAE's obligations under international space treaties, including the Outer Space Treaty, to which the UAE is a signatory. The UAE also signed an agreement with the United States Federal Aviation Administration in 2019 to facilitate cooperation on commercial space transportation and human spaceflight regulation. This agreement reflected the growing convergence of the UAE's aviation and space regulatory ecosystems, as the institutional expertise developed over decades of civil aviation governance was adapted to meet the distinct requirements of the space domain.

Figure 30: Sheikh Mohamed bin Zayed Al Nahyan and Sheikh Mohammed bin Rashid Al Maktoum Signing the Final Panel of the Hope Probe, Abu Dhabi, 5 January 2020

Source: National Archives and Library of the United Arab Emirates; © WAM.

The National Space Programme, launched on 12 April 2017 by Sheikh Mohammed bin Rashid Al Maktoum and Sheikh Mohammed bin Zayed Al Nahyan, established the strategic framework for the UAE's space ambitions over the coming decades. The programme committed the UAE to developing a specialised cadre of Emirati space professionals, expanding satellite manufacturing capability, pursuing interplanetary exploration, and—most ambitiously—overseeing the realisation of the Mars 2117 settlement strategy. By 2025, the UAE Space Agency had assembled approximately 5.2 billion dollars in funding from government, private, and semi-private entities, establishing the financial foundation for one of the most ambitious space programmes of any nation its size.

Figure 31: Sheikh Mohammed bin Rashid Al Maktoum Communicating with UAE Astronaut Hazzaa Al Mansoori on the International Space Station, 27 September 2019

Source: National Archives and Library of the United Arab Emirates; © WAM.

The Arab Space Pioneers Programme, a three-year intensive training initiative, was established to incubate young talents and expand career prospects in space technology across the region. The National Space Academy welcomed its first cohort of fifty-one students in January 2023. These institutional investments reflected a deliberate strategy: building not just missions but a self-sustaining ecosystem of space professionals capable of supporting the UAE's long-term ambitions.

> ■ **UAE Space Sector Milestones**
>
> 1997: Thuraya Communications Company established • 2000–2008: Thuraya and Yahsat satellite launches • 2006: Emirates Institution for Advanced Science and Technology (later MBRSC) founded with 5 engineers • 2009: DubaiSat-1 launched • 2013: DubaiSat-2 launched • 2014: UAE Space Agency established by federal decree • 2017: National Space Programme launched • 2018: KhalifaSat launched—first satellite fully designed and built in UAE • 2019: Federal Law No. 12 on Space Sector Regulation enacted • 2025: UAE space sector investment reaches $5.2 billion

***

Part III

Emiratis in Space—The Human Spaceflight Programme

1. Hazzaa AlMansoori: The First Emirati in Space

Figure 32 Hazzaa Al Mansoori, the First Emirati Astronaut

Source: Mohammed Bin Rashid Space Centre (MBRSC).

On 25 September 2019, Hazzaa AlMansoori launched from the Baikonur Cosmodrome in Kazakhstan aboard a Soyuz MS-15 spacecraft, becoming the first Emirati and the first Arab astronaut to visit the International Space Station. The mission, named 'Zayed Ambition' in tribute to the founding father whose encounters with Apollo astronauts had sparked the nation's space aspirations, lasted eight days. During his time aboard the ISS, AlMansoori conducted sixteen scientific experiments in areas including fluid dynamics, cell biology, and the effects of microgravity on the human body. He also established a live video connection with schoolchildren across the UAE, inspiring a generation of young Emiratis to engage with science and space exploration.

AlMansoori's selection was itself a significant achievement. The UAE Astronaut Programme, established under the Mohammed bin Rashid Space Centre, received over four thousand applications in its first round—a remarkable number for a nation of fewer than ten million residents, reflecting the depth of public enthusiasm for space exploration that Sheikh Zayed's vision had cultivated over decades. The programme's rigorous selection and training process, conducted in partnership with the Russian space agency Roscosmos and NASA's Johnson Space Center, demonstrated the UAE's commitment to developing indigenous human spaceflight capability rather than merely purchasing a seat on someone else's spacecraft. AlMansoori's mission was a national moment of enormous symbolic and practical significance: it demonstrated that the UAE could participate in the most exclusive club in human exploration, and it fulfilled the dream that Sheikh Zayed had first articulated nearly half a century earlier.

2. Sultan AlNeyadi: The Arab World's Longest Space Mission

Figure 33: Sultan Al Neyadi, Emirati Astronaut

Source: Mohammed Bin Rashid Space Centre (MBRSC).

The UAE's second crewed mission represented a dramatic escalation in ambition and duration. On 2 March 2023, Sultan AlNeyadi launched to the International Space Station aboard a SpaceX Crew Dragon spacecraft as part of NASA's Crew-6 mission. The 'Zayed Ambition 2' mission was no brief visit: AlNeyadi spent approximately six months aboard the ISS, making it the longest space mission undertaken by any Arab astronaut. During this extended stay, AlNeyadi conducted dozens of scientific experiments across multiple disciplines, including materials science, fluid physics, and plant growth in microgravity.

On 28 April 2023, AlNeyadi became the first Arab astronaut to conduct a spacewalk, spending approximately seven hours outside the station performing maintenance and equipment installation. The extravehicular activity was a milestone not only for the UAE but for the broader Arab world, demonstrating that Emirati astronauts could perform the most demanding tasks of human spaceflight. AlNeyadi's mission generated extensive scientific data, and his regular communications with the UAE public maintained public engagement with the nation's space programme throughout the six-month mission.

The success of the Zayed Ambition 2 mission prompted the Mohammed bin Rashid Space Centre to announce plans for regular human spaceflight missions on a three-to-five-year cycle. The UAE's fifteen-year commitment to the Lunar Gateway programme, confirmed by a January 2025 agreement witnessed by Sheikh Mohammed bin Rashid Al Maktoum, extends this human spaceflight ambition beyond low Earth orbit. The UAE will contribute an airlock module to the Gateway—the first space station to orbit the Moon—with the component scheduled for delivery in the early 2030s. As Hazzaa AlMansoori observed in early 2026, 'We are transitioning from the concept of temporary visits to a new stage of long-term settlement in space.'

3. Building the Next Generation

The UAE's investment in human spaceflight extends beyond individual missions to the systematic development of a corps of astronaut candidates. Nora AlMatrooshi and Mohammed AlMulla completed NASA astronaut training at the Johnson Space Center in Houston, graduating alongside ten American colleagues and becoming the first Emirati graduates of the NASA astronaut programme. AlMatrooshi, a mechanical engineer, became the first Arab woman to join an astronaut corps. These investments in human capital signal the UAE's intent to maintain a sustained presence in human spaceflight, not as a series of symbolic achievements but as an enduring national capability.

Figure 34: Sheikh Mohammed bin Rashid Al Maktoum Inspecting the KhalifaSat Satellite, 28 January 2018

Source: National Archives and Library of the United Arab Emirates; © WAM.

The UAE Analog Programme further supports long-duration spaceflight preparation. In 2024, Dr Shareef Al Romaithi completed a forty-five-day simulated Mars mission at NASA's Human Exploration Research Analog facility, conducting eighteen scientific experiments under conditions designed to replicate the isolation, confinement, and communication delays of a Mars mission. These analogue missions are directly linked to the Mars 2117 programme, building the physiological and psychological knowledge base necessary for future human missions beyond Earth orbit.

***

Part IV

To Mars and Beyond—The Emirates Mars Mission and the 2117 Vision

1. The Hope Probe: A National Triumph

The Emirates Mars Mission stands as the UAE's most significant scientific achievement and one of the most remarkable feats in the history of space exploration by a developing nation. The Hope Probe—Al Amal in Arabic, meaning 'hope'—was launched on 20 July 2020 from the Tanegashima Space Center in Japan aboard an H-IIA rocket. On 9 February 2021, the probe successfully entered orbit around Mars, making the UAE only the fifth entity in history to reach the Red Planet, after NASA, the Soviet Union, the European Space Agency, and India. The arrival coincided with the fiftieth anniversary of the UAE's founding, a symbolism that was both deliberate and powerful.

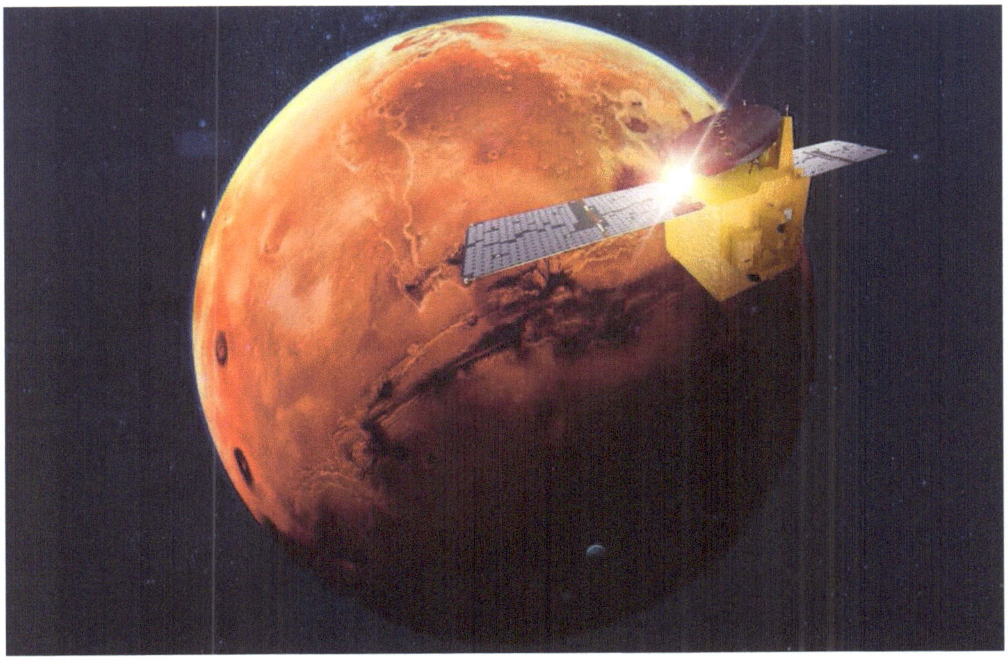

Figure 35: The Emirates Mars Mission "Hope Probe" Orbiting Mars

Source: Mohammed Bin Rashid Space Centre (MBRSC).

The Hope Probe was designed and developed at the Mohammed bin Rashid Space Centre under the leadership of project director Omran Sharaf, with approximately two hundred Emirati scientists and engineers supported by collaborative partnerships with the University of Colorado Boulder's Laboratory for Atmospheric and Space Physics, Arizona State University, and the University of California, Berkeley. The spacecraft carried three scientific instruments: an infrared spectrometer to study the lower atmosphere and surface temperature, an ultraviolet spectrometer to examine the upper atmosphere and hydrogen and oxygen concentrations, and a multi-band camera to capture high-resolution images of Mars.

The mission's scientific objective was to provide the first complete picture of Mars's atmospheric dynamics throughout a full Martian year, studying connections between the planet's current weather patterns and its ancient climate. The data generated by Hope contributed to the global understanding of how Mars lost its atmosphere over geological time—a question with profound implications for understanding the habitability of Mars and, by extension, the long-term prospects for human settlement. The probe's highly elliptical orbit, reaching an apoapsis of approximately 43,000 kilometres above the Martian surface, provided a unique planetary perspective unavailable from other missions in closer orbits.

The Hope Probe's significance transcended its scientific contributions. It demonstrated that the UAE could conceive, design, execute, and manage an interplanetary mission—a capability possessed by only a handful of nations and space agencies worldwide. The knowledge transfer model, in which Emirati engineers worked alongside international partners to build and operate the spacecraft, ensured that the mission's legacy would be measured not only in data but in human capital. The Mohammed bin Rashid Space Centre announced in June 2024 the successful completion of phase two of the Mars mission, cementing Hope's place as one of the most productive Mars orbiters in operation.

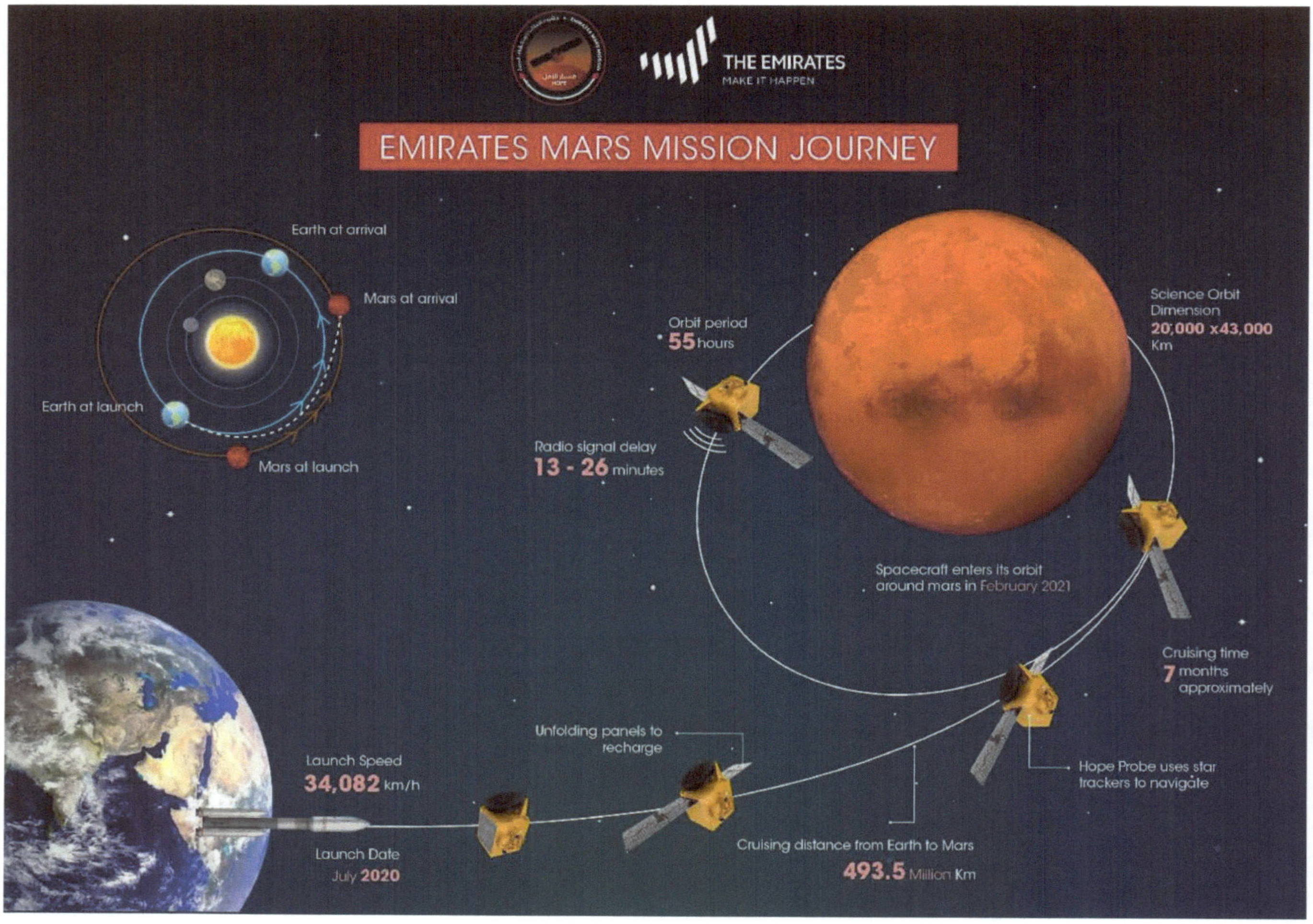

Figure 36: Trajectory and Mission Profile of the Emirates Mars Mission (Hope Probe)

Source: Mohammed Bin Rashid Space Centre (MBRSC).

Equally significant was the UAE's decision to make the Hope Probe's scientific data freely available to the international research community. This open-data policy, consistent with the Outer Space Treaty's principle that space exploration should benefit all countries, established the UAE as a responsible and generous contributor to planetary science. Over two hundred research institutions worldwide accessed Hope's atmospheric data, and the mission's findings were published in leading scientific journals, enhancing the global understanding of Martian climate dynamics. The open-data approach also strengthened the UAE's scientific credibility and diplomatic relationships, demonstrating that national space programmes and international scientific cooperation are complementary rather than competing objectives.

2. The Mars 2117 Strategy

If the Hope Probe represented the UAE's arrival as a Mars-capable nation, the Mars 2117 Project represents its most audacious long-term aspiration. Unveiled on 14 February 2017 by Sheikh Mohammed bin Rashid Al Maktoum and Sheikh Mohammed bin Zayed Al Nahyan during the Fifth World Government Summit in Dubai, Mars 2117 commits the UAE to establishing the first human settlement on Mars within one hundred years. 'The landing of people on other planets has been a longtime dream for humans,' Sheikh Mohammed declared. 'Our aim is that the UAE will spearhead international efforts to make this dream a reality.'

The project is coordinated by the Mohammed bin Rashid Space Centre and the Dubai Future Foundation, with a comprehensive century-spanning implementation plan. The first phase focuses on developing the scientific, technological, and human capabilities required for Mars settlement: advanced propulsion systems, life support technologies, sustainable food and energy production, and the training of a specialised workforce. Subsequent phases will address transportation systems, habitat construction, and the governance frameworks necessary for sustained human presence on another planet.

The Mars Science City project provides a terrestrial proving ground for these technologies. Covering 1.9 million square feet at a cost of approximately 500 million dirhams, Mars Science City is designed to be the largest space simulation facility ever built. The complex encompasses laboratories for food, energy, and water research; agricultural testing facilities; a museum of humanity's space achievements; and an experiential habitat where participants live under simulated Martian conditions. The facility's walls are three-dimensionally printed using sand from the UAE's deserts, a technology that demonstrates approaches to construction using in-situ resources—a capability that will be essential for building habitats on Mars.

Mars 2117 is notable for its explicit acknowledgement that Mars settlement is a multi-generational, multi-national endeavour that no single state can accomplish alone. The project emphasises international collaboration, knowledge sharing, and the development of technologies with dual applications: innovations designed for Mars habitability are intended simultaneously to address terrestrial challenges of food security, renewable energy, and water management. As Sheikh Mohammed bin Zayed Al Nahyan expressed, 'Our goal is to have this programme pioneer breakthroughs that will work towards the betterment of life on Earth.' This dual-use philosophy ensures that investment in Mars exploration generates near-term terrestrial returns while building toward the century-long settlement objective.

3. The Emirati Interplanetary Mission and Lunar Exploration

The UAE's interplanetary ambitions extend beyond Mars. In May 2023, the UAE Space Agency announced an asteroid belt mission planned for launch in 2028. The spacecraft will conduct flybys of six asteroids—including 10253 Westerwald, 623 Chimaera, 88055 Ghaf, and 59980 Moza—before entering orbit around and delivering a landing craft to 269 Justitia, an unusually red asteroid of particular scientific interest, with arrival expected in 2034. This seven-year interplanetary voyage will make the UAE only the fourth entity to land a spacecraft on an asteroid, after Japan, the United States, and the European Space Agency.

Lunar exploration has also featured prominently in the UAE's programme. The Emirates Lunar Mission aimed to deploy the Rashid Rover—named after the late Sheikh Rashid bin Saeed Al Maktoum, architect of modern Dubai—to the lunar surface. The compact rover, designed and built by Emirati engineers, was launched in December 2022 aboard the Hakuto-R Mission 1 lander developed by Japanese company ispace. Although communication with the lander was lost seconds before the attempted landing in April 2023, the mission provided invaluable engineering experience. The Rashid Rover 2 mission is in development, continuing the UAE's commitment to lunar surface exploration and the accumulation of technical knowledge essential for the longer road to Mars.

The UAE's January 2025 agreement to participate in the Lunar Gateway programme represents a further expansion of its exploration footprint. Witnessed by Sheikh Mohammed bin Rashid Al Maktoum, the agreement between the Mohammed bin Rashid Space Centre and NASA commits the UAE to contributing to humanity's first space station around the Moon. The UAE's participation in the Gateway, alongside its Artemis Accords membership, positions the nation as a significant partner in the international architecture of cislunar and deep-space exploration—building the institutional relationships and technical capabilities that will underpin its Mars ambitions in the decades ahead.

UAE's Interplanetary Roadmap

2020: Hope Probe launch to Mars • 2021: Hope enters Mars orbit (9 February) • 2022: Rashid Rover launched to the Moon • 2023: Sultan AlNeyadi—6-month ISS mission, first Arab spacewalk • 2024: Hope Mars Mission Phase 2 completed; NASA analog mission • 2025: Lunar Gateway agreement signed; Artemis Accords membership • 2028: Asteroid belt mission launch • 2030s: Gateway airlock module delivery; Rashid Rover 2 • 2034: Arrival at asteroid 269 Justitia with lander • 2117: Target date for first human settlement on Mars

***

Part V

Legal and Normative Dimensions—The UAE's Contribution to Space Governance

1. National Space Legislation

The UAE's development of a comprehensive national space regulatory framework represents an important contribution to the evolving international governance of space activities. Federal Law No. 12 of 2019 on the Regulation of the Space Sector provides the primary legislative foundation, governing the licensing, supervision, and regulation of space activities conducted by UAE entities. The law addresses the registration of space objects, the management of remote sensing data, liability for damage caused by space activities, environmental protection obligations, and the requirements for deorbiting space objects at the end of their operational life. It also establishes the legal foundation for the UAE's participation in international cooperative missions, providing the domestic authorisation framework required by Article VI of the Outer Space Treaty.

The law's scope is notably broad, encompassing not only the launch and operation of space objects but also the management of space-derived data, the provision of specialised space training, and the collection or trade of meteorites within UAE territory. This comprehensive approach reflects an understanding that the space sector encompasses a value chain extending well beyond launch and operations, and that effective governance must address the full range of space-related economic activities.

2. International Treaties and the Artemis Accords

The UAE is a signatory to the Outer Space Treaty of 1967, the foundational instrument of international space law. Its space activities are conducted within the framework of the Treaty's principles: the freedom of exploration and use of outer space, the prohibition of national appropriation, the obligation to conduct activities for the benefit of all countries, and the requirement of state responsibility for national space activities. The UAE's adherence to these principles is reflected in both its national legislation and its operational practice.

The UAE's membership in the Artemis Accords further defines its normative position in the evolving governance of space activities. The Accords' principles—transparency, interoperability, the release of scientific data, the registration of space objects, the protection of space heritage, the extraction and utilisation of space resources consistent with the Outer Space Treaty, and the deconfliction of activities through safety zones—align closely with the UAE's own regulatory approach. The UAE's participation in both the Artemis Accords coalition and the Lunar Gateway programme positions it as a significant normative actor, contributing to the development of governance frameworks that will shape cislunar and Martian exploration for decades to come.

3. The UAE as a Governance Bridge

The UAE's unique position—as a relatively young, non-Western nation with advanced space capabilities and strong relationships with both Western and non-Western partners—gives it potential influence in space governance that exceeds its size. The UAE's Hope Mars Mission established scientific data-sharing partnerships with institutions across multiple continents. Its astronaut programme has operated within both Russian (Roscosmos) and American (NASA/SpaceX) frameworks. Its Lunar Gateway participation places it alongside the United States, Europe, Japan, and Canada in the most ambitious international space infrastructure project since the ISS.

This multilateral positioning allows the UAE to serve as a bridge between different governance approaches and geopolitical groupings. In a space governance landscape increasingly characterised by competition between the Artemis Accords coalition and the China-Russia ILRS framework, middle powers with credibility across multiple partnerships can play a disproportionate role in maintaining channels of communication, promoting inclusive governance norms, and demonstrating that space cooperation need not be constrained by broader geopolitical rivalries. The UAE's emphasis on space activities as a vehicle for international cooperation, scientific advancement, and the benefit of humanity—principles embedded in its national space law and operational practice—positions it as a natural advocate for inclusive governance frameworks.

4. Legal Challenges of the Mars 2117 Vision

The Mars 2117 strategy raises legal questions that push the boundaries of existing international space law. The establishment of a permanent human settlement on Mars will require governance frameworks addressing jurisdiction and legal authority over settlement activities, the legal status of individuals born on Mars, property rights and resource utilisation, environmental protection of the Martian environment, dispute resolution between settlement inhabitants and between settlements and Earth-based authorities, and the application of human rights law in an extraterrestrial context. None of these questions are adequately addressed by the current treaty framework.

The Outer Space Treaty's prohibition on national appropriation of celestial bodies will need to be reconciled with the practical requirements of permanent settlement, which inherently involves the exclusive use of defined areas for habitats, resource extraction, and infrastructure. The Treaty's requirement of state responsibility for national space activities must be adapted for a context in which a Martian community may eventually develop its own governance institutions, economic relationships, and collective identity. The UAE's explicit engagement with these questions through the Mars 2117 programme—and its century-long timeframe for addressing them—positions the nation as a thought leader in what is arguably the most profound governance challenge humanity will face in the coming century.

The UAE's approach is characterised by pragmatism and incrementalism. Rather than waiting for comprehensive international agreement on Mars governance, the UAE is building the technological, institutional, and legal capabilities that will allow it to participate in shaping governance frameworks as they develop. The Emirates Space Law, the Mars Science City research programme, the analogue missions, the interplanetary mission portfolio, and the investment in human capital all represent building blocks of a governance capacity that will be essential when the practical challenges of Mars settlement move from theoretical discussion to operational reality.

***

Conclusion

The trajectory of the United Arab Emirates from a young desert federation to a space-faring nation with a credible Mars settlement strategy is one of the most remarkable narratives in the history of air and space exploration. It is a story that begins with Sheikh Zayed's fascination with the Apollo astronauts, passes through the construction of one of the world's most dynamic aviation industries, accelerates through the rapid development of indigenous space capability, and arrives at the threshold of interplanetary exploration.

The UAE's space programme embodies several principles that resonate throughout this book. It demonstrates the importance of strategic vision sustained across generations—from Sheikh Zayed's

1970s encounters with NASA to the 2117 Mars settlement target. It illustrates the relationship between aviation and space law, with the regulatory sophistication and institutional capacity developed for civil aviation providing the foundation for space governance. It exemplifies the knowledge transfer model, in which international partnerships build indigenous capability rather than creating permanent dependency. And it underscores the role of middle powers in shaping international norms, demonstrating that meaningful contributions to space governance are not the exclusive preserve of the largest space powers.

The challenges ahead are immense. The Mars 2117 vision requires technological breakthroughs that have not yet been achieved, sustained investment over a century-long timeframe that will span multiple generations of leadership, and governance frameworks for human settlement on another planet that do not yet exist in international law. The road from Abu Dhabi to Mars is long, uncertain, and fraught with obstacles both technical and political. Yet the UAE's willingness to articulate a century-long ambition, and to build systematically toward it through investment in education, technology, legislation, and international partnership, sets it apart as a nation that understands space exploration as a civilisational project rather than a series of discrete missions.

But the UAE's history suggests that these challenges should not be underestimated. A nation that built one of the world's great airlines from a ten-million-dollar investment, that progressed from five engineers to an interplanetary mission in less than fifteen years, and that placed its first astronaut in space within fifty years of its founding father's first conversation with Apollo astronauts has demonstrated a capacity for transformation that defies conventional expectations. The UAE's space programme offers a model for other emerging space nations: one grounded in strategic vision, sustained investment, knowledge transfer through international partnership, and the development of comprehensive legal and institutional frameworks that align national ambitions with international obligations.

The words that Sheikh Zayed spoke to the Apollo astronauts remain the guiding philosophy of the UAE's space programme: if it is God's will, man can achieve anything. Nothing is impossible.

***

End of Chapter 17

Chapter 18

CONCLUSION: TOWARD A NEW LEGAL IMAGINATION

"The law must be stable, and yet it cannot stand still."

– Roscoe Pound

Part 1

The Arc of This Book

This book has traced the legal governance of humanity's ascent from Earth's surface to the threshold of interplanetary civilisation. The journey has been both chronological and thematic, moving from the mythological imagination of flight in ancient cultures to the contemporary governance challenges of artificial intelligence in orbit, cislunar economics, and the prospect of human settlement on Mars. At every stage, a single insight has recurred: law does not precede human capability; it responds to it, and its quality depends on the imagination, foresight, and cooperation that its architects bring to the task.

Chapter 1 began where the story must begin—with humanity's dream of flight. From the myth of Icarus to the experiments of Abbas Ibn Firnas, from the Montgolfier balloons to the Wright brothers, the chapter traced the long transformation of the sky from a sacred realm into a space of human action. The legal vacuum that accompanied early flight revealed a fundamental truth: when technology opens new domains, law must follow or chaos will fill the void. The chapter established the philosophical foundations—the tension between aspiration and restraint, between freedom and responsibility—that would animate every subsequent development in air and space law.

Chapters 2 through 4 examined the foundational legal architecture that emerged in response to powered flight and the space age. Chapter 2 traced how sovereignty became the organising principle of airspace governance, from the Paris Convention of 1919 through the Chicago Convention of 1944, establishing the doctrine of complete and exclusive state sovereignty over superjacent airspace that remains the bedrock of international air law. Chapter 3 confronted the boundary problem—the unresolved question of where airspace ends and outer space begins—revealing how pragmatic ambiguity has served the international community even as technological convergence increasingly tests its limits. Chapter 4 explored the competing conceptualisations of outer space as res communis and common heritage of mankind, tracing the philosophical and political currents that shaped the Outer Space Treaty's distinctive legal character: a domain free for exploration and use by all, immune from national appropriation, yet subject to state responsibility.

Chapters 5 through 8 examined the institutional, operational, and political dimensions of the space governance regime. Chapter 5 analysed the United Nations' role in constructing the architecture of space governance, from the establishment of COPUOS to the negotiation of the five UN space treaties. Chapter 6 explored the frameworks of state responsibility and liability that assign accountability for space activities, revealing both the elegance of the existing regime and its growing strain under the weight of commercialisation and autonomous operations. Chapter 7 addressed the military uses of outer space, tracing the delicate balance between the Outer Space Treaty's limitations on weaponisation and the strategic reality of space as a contested domain. Chapter 8 examined the persistent equity challenge—the gap between spacefaring and non-spacefaring nations—and the mechanisms, from technology transfer to capacity-building, through which the international community has sought to ensure that space remains accessible to all.

Chapters 9 through 12 turned to the transformative forces reshaping the space domain in the twenty-first century. Chapter 9 traced the commercialisation revolution, from the rise of private launch providers to the emergence of mega-constellations, examining how private actors are reshaping a legal framework designed for state-led activities. Chapter 10 explored the governance of space resources, from lunar water ice to asteroid minerals, analysing the tension between the non-appropriation principle and the emerging practice of national legislation authorising resource extraction. Chapter 11 addressed the environmental dimension—space debris, orbital congestion, and the urgent need for space traffic management—revealing how sustainability has become both a practical imperative and a normative obligation. Chapter 12 examined dispute resolution mechanisms, from diplomatic channels to the potential for international adjudication, assessing the adequacy of existing tools for a domain of increasing complexity and competition.

The final section of the book—Chapters 13 through 17—turned to the frontiers of air and space law. Chapter 13 surveyed the convergence of air and space operations, the expansion of activities beyond traditional boundaries, and the challenges and opportunities confronting the international legal order. Chapter 14 examined the governance implications of artificial intelligence and autonomous systems in space, from satellite constellation management to military applications, identifying a fundamental tension between machine autonomy and human legal responsibility. Chapter 15 explored how the emerging legal order is being shaped by treaty impasse, soft law proliferation, national legislation, and geopolitical competition. Chapter 16 analysed the cislunar economy—the programmes, legal gaps, and governance challenges of the region from geostationary orbit to the Moon. And Chapter 17 traced the remarkable journey of the United Arab Emirates from its founding father's fascination with Apollo to its century-long strategy for establishing a human presence on Mars.

***

Part II

Recurring Themes: What This Book Has Revealed

1. Law Follows Capability—But the Gap Is Widening

The history examined in this book reveals a consistent pattern: legal frameworks emerge in response to technological capability, often catalysed by crisis. The Paris Convention of 1919 followed the First World War's demonstration of airpower. The Outer Space Treaty of 1967 followed the Cold War's nuclear anxieties and the race to the Moon. The Long-term Sustainability Guidelines of 2019 followed the commercial disruption of the space sector. In each case, law lagged behind technology but eventually caught up, establishing frameworks that enabled sustained, orderly activity.

Today, that pattern continues—but the gap between capability and governance is wider than at any previous point in the history of air and space law. Artificial intelligence makes orbital decisions faster than any human supervisor can review. Commercial operators launch thousands of satellites without comprehensive international traffic management. National legislation authorises resource extraction on the Moon and asteroids without multilateral agreement on the rules. Hypersonic vehicles traverse the ambiguous boundary between airspace and outer space without a settled legal framework for their classification. The pace of technological change has accelerated while the pace of multilateral legal development has, if anything, slowed.

2. The Enduring Power of Foundational Principles

And yet the foundational principles of air and space law have proven remarkably durable. The Chicago Convention's assertion of sovereignty over airspace, though challenged by technological convergence, remains the organising principle of international air law eighty years after its adoption. The Outer Space Treaty's provisions—freedom of exploration, non-appropriation, state responsibility, peaceful use, due regard—continue to provide the normative framework within which all space activities are conducted, even as the specific activities they govern have transformed beyond recognition.

This durability is not accidental. The foundational instruments succeeded because they established principles rather than prescribing specific technological solutions. The Chicago Convention did not specify the types of aircraft to which it applied; it established a sovereignty framework adaptable to any vehicle. The Outer Space Treaty did not define the technologies of space exploration; it established normative commitments applicable to whatever form exploration might take. This principle-based approach has allowed the legal framework to accommodate developments that its drafters could not have imagined: commercial megaconstellations, autonomous spacecraft, lunar resource extraction, artificial intelligence in orbit. The lesson for the future is clear: legal instruments designed around enduring principles, rather than contemporary technologies, have the greatest prospect of relevance across generations.

3. The Sovereignty-Freedom Dialectic

A central tension running through this entire book is the dialectic between sovereignty and freedom. In airspace, sovereignty prevails: states exercise complete and exclusive authority over the air above their territory, permitting transit only through consent. In outer space, freedom prevails: no state may claim sovereignty, and exploration and use are open to all. This binary, established in the mid-twentieth century, provided clarity and stability during the formative decades of both air and space law.

But as this book has documented, the binary is under increasing strain. Suborbital vehicles that launch as rockets and land as aircraft confound the sovereignty-freedom distinction. Mega-constellations create aviation-scale operational demands in a domain governed by space law's freedom principles. Safety zones on the Moon create de facto exclusive areas without sovereignty claims. Military operations in space exploit the absence of sovereignty-based control. The convergence documented throughout this book is not merely technological; it is normative, challenging the fundamental categories through which international law governs the vertical dimension. The next generation of air and space law will need to develop more nuanced frameworks that accommodate the spectrum of activities between sovereignty and freedom, rather than forcing every activity into one category or the other.

The cislunar domain, examined in Chapter 16, illustrates this challenge with particular clarity. Cislunar operations require coordination mechanisms analogous to air traffic control—which in the aviation context rests on sovereignty—yet they occur in a domain where sovereignty is explicitly prohibited. Space traffic management in cislunar space must therefore achieve aviation-level safety and coordination through mechanisms that do not rely on sovereignty-based authority. How this is accomplished will be one of the defining governance innovations of the coming decades, and its resolution will have implications far beyond the technical question of traffic coordination.

4. The Democratisation of Space and Its Governance Implications

One of the most significant transformations documented in this book is the democratisation of space—the expansion of space activities from a duopoly of Cold War superpowers to a diverse ecosystem of state agencies, commercial companies, middle powers, and emerging space nations. The United Arab Emirates' trajectory from Sheikh Zayed's meetings with Apollo astronauts to interplanetary missions exemplifies this transformation. So does the proliferation of national space legislation, the growing membership of the Artemis Accords, and the commercial revolution that has made satellite services accessible to entities that could never have afforded government-scale space programmes.

This democratisation has profound governance implications. A legal framework designed for a handful of spacefaring states must now accommodate hundreds of actors with varying capabilities, resources, and normative commitments. The consensus-based mechanisms of COPUOS, effective when membership was limited, struggle with a membership exceeding one hundred states. The state-centric liability and responsibility frameworks of the space treaties must grapple with commercial operators that may be more technologically capable than the states that authorise them. Ensuring that governance frameworks are both inclusive and effective—that they give voice to emerging actors without paralysing decision-making—is among the most important challenges of the coming decades.

***

Part III

The Challenges Ahead: An Agenda for the Next Generation

1. Closing the Governance Gaps

This book has identified a series of specific governance gaps that demand attention. The delimitation question—where airspace ends and outer space begins—can no longer be indefinitely deferred as suborbital vehicles and hypersonic systems become operational realities. The governance of space resources requires multilateral agreement that moves beyond competing national interpretations to establish international frameworks for allocation, benefit-sharing, and environmental protection. Space traffic management needs an institutional architecture with the authority and capability to coordinate tens of thousands of orbital objects and growing cislunar activity. The governance of artificial intelligence in space demands frameworks that preserve accountability while accommodating the operational necessity of autonomous decision-making. And the cislunar economy requires governance mechanisms for traffic coordination, resource management, safety zone administration, and infrastructure interoperability that do not yet exist.

None of these gaps can be closed by a single legal instrument or institutional reform. Each will require a layered approach combining treaty interpretation, supplementary guidelines, technical standards, bilateral and multilateral agreements, industry best practices, and national legislation.

The governance architecture of the future will be pluralistic rather than monolithic, adaptive rather than static, and networked rather than hierarchical. This is not a deficiency; it reflects the complexity of the domain being governed.

2. Reconciling Competition and Cooperation

The geopolitical context of air and space law has shifted fundamentally since the cooperative optimism of the post-Cold War era. The parallel pursuit of lunar programmes by the Artemis coalition and the China-Russia ILRS framework, the militarisation of space operations, and the broader deterioration of great-power relations constrain the scope for multilateral cooperation. The treaty impasse documented in Chapter 15—the inability of the international community to negotiate a comprehensive new space treaty in nearly fifty years—reflects this reality.

Yet the shared physical environment of outer space imposes cooperation as a practical necessity, regardless of political preferences. Space debris generated by one actor threatens all. Uncoordinated collision avoidance manoeuvres create cascading risks. Competing safety zones at the lunar south pole produce operational hazards. The 2025 US-China coordination to prevent a satellite collision demonstrated that operational cooperation can function even between strategic competitors. The challenge for the next generation of legal architects is to build on these functional necessities—to develop governance mechanisms that preserve cooperation in the shared operational domain even when broader political cooperation is constrained.

3. From State-Centric to Multi-Actor Governance

The existing legal framework is fundamentally state-centric: states bear responsibility for national space activities, states are liable for damage, states register space objects, and states authorise and supervise private operators. This framework was appropriate for an era in which space activities were conducted by or under the close direction of governments. It is increasingly inadequate for an era in which commercial operators launch the majority of satellites, manage the largest constellations, and develop the most innovative technologies.

The transition to multi-actor governance does not require abandoning state responsibility—a principle that remains essential for accountability. But it does require supplementing state-centric frameworks with mechanisms that directly engage commercial operators, international organisations, technical standards bodies, and civil society in governance processes. The aviation model, in which ICAO sets international standards that national regulators implement and airlines operationalise, offers a partial template. Adapting this model for the more diverse and less hierarchical space domain will require institutional creativity and political will.

The role of commercial actors in governance development is particularly important. Companies operating mega-constellations, developing autonomous collision avoidance systems, and building cislunar infrastructure possess technical knowledge and operational experience that are essential inputs to effective governance. The challenge is to harness this expertise without allowing governance to be captured by the commercial interests of the most powerful actors. Mechanisms for structured industry participation in governance processes—modelled on the consultative status arrangements that exist in other international organisations—would help ensure that governance benefits from commercial expertise while remaining accountable to broader public interests.

■ **The Governance Architecture of the Future**

Layer 1: Treaty obligations—foundational principles of freedom, non-appropriation, state responsibility, peaceful use, due regard • Layer 2: COPUOS and IISL guidelines—soft law instruments providing interpretive guidance and operational norms • Layer 3: Cross-sectoral models—adaptation of aviation (ICAO), maritime (IMO), and AI governance frameworks • Layer 4: Technical standards—ISO, CCSDS, national standards bodies providing interoperability and performance benchmarks • Layer 5: Bilateral and plurilateral agreements—Artemis Accords, ISS IGA, bilateral coordination protocols • Layer 6: National legislation—domestic implementation creating state practice and regulatory baseline • Layer 7: Industry practices—voluntary standards, operational protocols, self-regulatory mechanisms

***

Part IV

Toward a New Legal Imagination

The title of this concluding chapter invokes a 'new legal imagination' because the challenges ahead demand more than incremental adjustments to existing frameworks. They require a reimagining of how law relates to the domains beyond Earth's surface—a reimagining that draws on the best traditions of international law while transcending the assumptions of the era in which the current framework was constructed.

1. From Regulation to Stewardship

The dominant mode of air and space law has been regulatory: establishing rules that permit, prohibit, or condition specific activities. This mode has served well for decades, but the emerging challenges of orbital sustainability, planetary protection, and intergenerational equity demand a complementary mode of governance: stewardship. A stewardship orientation recognises that the orbital environment, the lunar surface, and the Martian landscape are not merely resources to be exploited or domains to be regulated, but environments entrusted to the current generation for the benefit of those that follow. The UNOOSA 2026 Issues Note on 'Safeguarding Space' and the COPUOS Dark and Quiet Skies initiative reflect this emerging sensibility. Embedding stewardship as a governing principle alongside sovereignty, freedom, and responsibility would represent a significant evolution in the normative architecture of air and space law.

Stewardship also provides a normative bridge between the various domains examined in this book. The environmental protection imperatives of Chapter 11, the resource governance challenges of Chapter 10, the cislunar sustainability questions of Chapter 16, and the planetary responsibility dimensions of the Mars 2117 vision all converge on a single insight: humanity's expansion into space must be governed not only by the interests of present actors but by obligations to future generations. This intergenerational dimension distinguishes space governance from most other fields of international law, and it demands a legal imagination that thinks in centuries rather than electoral cycles.

2. From Treaties to Ecosystems

The golden age of space treaty-making—the period from 1967 to 1979 that produced the five UN space treaties—is unlikely to be replicated. The consensus requirements of multilateral negotiation, the geopolitical constraints on cooperation, and the speed of technological change make comprehensive new treaties improbable in the near term. But this does not mean that legal development has ceased; it has shifted to different venues and instruments. National legislation, COPUOS guidelines, bilateral accords, industry standards, and customary international law are all contributing to an evolving normative ecosystem.

A new legal imagination must embrace this ecosystem rather than lamenting the absence of traditional treaties. The task is to ensure coherence within the ecosystem—that its various components reinforce rather than contradict each other, that gaps are identified and addressed, and that the foundational principles of the treaty framework continue to provide normative orientation even as the specific instruments of governance diversify. This requires a different kind of legal scholarship: one that is comfortable with pluralism, attentive to practice as well as principle, and capable of seeing connections across institutional and disciplinary boundaries.

3. From Western Centrality to Global Participation

The foundational instruments of air and space law were negotiated primarily among Western and Soviet bloc states, reflecting the geopolitical realities of the mid-twentieth century. The governance challenges of the twenty-first century demand broader participation. The rise of China as a major space power, the emergence of India, the UAE, Japan, and others as significant actors, and the growing engagement of African, Latin American, and Southeast Asian nations with space activities all require governance frameworks that reflect genuinely global perspectives.

The UAE's journey, documented in Chapter 17, illustrates the transformative potential of inclusive governance. A nation that was not yet independent when the Outer Space Treaty was signed is now contributing hardware to the Lunar Gateway, operating a Mars orbiter, and articulating a century-long vision for interplanetary settlement. Similar trajectories are emerging across the Global South. Ensuring that these actors have meaningful voice in governance development—not as passive recipients of rules designed elsewhere, but as active architects of frameworks that reflect their interests, capabilities, and perspectives—is essential for the legitimacy and durability of the emerging legal order.

4. From Present Regulation to Future Preparation

Perhaps the most distinctive demand of a new legal imagination is the capacity to legislate not only for present activities but for future possibilities. The Mars 2117 strategy challenges legal thinkers to contemplate governance for permanent human communities on another planet. The prospect of space-based solar power raises questions about energy governance on a planetary scale. The possibility of contact with extraterrestrial life—however remote—poses questions that existing law has barely begun to consider. Asteroid mining at industrial scale, large-scale orbital manufacturing, and the establishment of self-sustaining off-Earth economies all present governance challenges that will require legal frameworks not yet conceived.

A new legal imagination must be comfortable with uncertainty and capable of building frameworks that are robust to futures that cannot be precisely predicted. This means investing in adaptive governance mechanisms—review clauses, sunset provisions, iterative revision processes—that allow legal frameworks to evolve as circumstances change. It means developing principles that can provide normative guidance even in the absence of specific rules. And it means cultivating a community of legal scholars, policymakers, and practitioners who understand both the possibilities and the limitations of law in governing the domains beyond Earth.

***

Final Reflections

This book opened with the myth of Icarus—a story often read as a warning against the hubris of flight. But as Chapter 1 observed, the deeper lesson of the myth is not that flight is forbidden; it is that unregulated ascent—flight without restraint, foresight, or structure—leads to catastrophe. The entire history of international air and space law can be understood as humanity's effort to provide the restraint, foresight, and structure that Icarus lacked: to enable ascent while preventing harm.

That effort has been remarkably successful. The Chicago Convention created the framework for the safest mass transportation system in human history. The Outer Space Treaty preserved outer space from the nuclear arms race and established it as a domain of exploration rather than conquest. The five UN space treaties, the institutional architecture of COPUOS and ICAO, and the evolving body of guidelines, accords, and national legislation have together enabled decades of sustained activity in the atmosphere and beyond, with benefits that touch nearly every aspect of modern life.

But success is not permanence. The legal architecture that served the twentieth century is under strain from the transformations documented throughout this book: technological convergence, commercial disruption, AI autonomy, geopolitical competition, environmental degradation, and the expansion of human presence into cislunar space and eventually to Mars. The question is not whether the existing framework will evolve—it will—but whether it will evolve through deliberate design or haphazard accumulation, through inclusive cooperation or fragmented competition, through principle or through power.

The history traced in these chapters offers grounds for both caution and confidence. Caution, because the governance gaps are real, the geopolitical constraints are formidable, and the pace of technological change shows no sign of slowing. Confidence, because the international community has repeatedly demonstrated its capacity to develop legal frameworks for new domains under difficult circumstances. The Paris Convention was negotiated in the aftermath of the most devastating war the world had then known. The Outer Space Treaty was negotiated at the height of the Cold War. The Long-term Sustainability Guidelines were developed despite deep disagreements about the commercialisation of space. Each time, the architects of international law found ways to establish common ground, articulate shared principles, and build institutions capable of sustaining cooperation.

The generation now entering the fields of law, policy, science, and technology will face governance challenges more complex than any their predecessors confronted. They will need to manage the convergence of air and space operations, govern the extraction and use of extraterrestrial resources, ensure accountability for autonomous systems that operate beyond direct human control, preserve the space environment for future generations, coordinate activities in cislunar space, and eventually establish governance frameworks for permanent human communities beyond Earth. These challenges are daunting. But they are also exhilarating—opportunities to shape the legal architecture of a multi-planetary civilisation.

The role of education and scholarship in preparing this generation cannot be overstated. The interdisciplinary nature of the challenges ahead—spanning engineering, physics, computer science, environmental science, political science, philosophy, and law—demands training that transcends traditional disciplinary boundaries. The growth of space law programmes at universities worldwide, the expansion of research centres dedicated to space governance, and the increasing engagement of early-career scholars from diverse national backgrounds are encouraging developments. But more is needed: dedicated investment in space law education, particularly in regions and institutions where it has been historically underrepresented, and a scholarly culture that values engagement with practice as well as theoretical rigour.

What is required, above all, is imagination. Not the imagination of Icarus, which was reckless and solitary, but a disciplined, collaborative imagination that can envision legal frameworks adequate to the challenges ahead and muster the political will to bring them into being. The international community must imagine governance architectures that are layered, pluralistic, and adaptive. It must imagine frameworks that balance sovereignty with freedom, national interest with collective benefit, present needs with future obligations. It must imagine a legal order capacious enough to accommodate the full diversity of human aspiration in the domains beyond Earth.

Sheikh Zayed told the Apollo astronauts that if it is God's will, nothing is impossible. The same spirit of ambitious possibility, tempered by responsibility and guided by principle, must animate the legal imagination of those who will build the governance frameworks for the next century of air and space activity. The sky is no longer the limit. The law must not be either.

***

End of Chapter 18

ABOUT THE AUTHOR

Dr. Alsayedissa Alhashmi

Born in Al Ain, United Arab Emirates (1966)

Alsayedissa Alhashmi is a distinguished Emirati expert in International Air and Space Law, combining rigorous academic scholarship with extensive professional experience across the aviation, aerospace, safety, and international legal sectors.

He earned an Advanced LL.M. in International Air and Space Law from Leiden University in the Kingdom of the Netherlands. The program is a postgraduate, research-intensive course of study focused on the preparation of a specialized thesis conducted under rigorous academic and scientific methodology.

Over a professional career spanning more than three decades, Alsayedissa Alhashmi has held leadership and supervisory roles in both civil and military aviation sectors. His expertise includes aviation safety management and investigations, government and international contract administration, and legal practice in matters of strategic significance. His work has encompassed aviation agreements, sovereign contracts, dispute resolution, and arbitration.

Dr. Alhashimi is distinguished by an integrative perspective that bridges deep technical understanding of aviation operations and air systems with precise legal analysis of the international frameworks governing airspace and outer space. His scholarship reflects an acute awareness of the historic transformation currently reshaping the aviation industry and space activities worldwide.

This book represents a national scholarly contribution aimed at documenting the historical evolution of International Air and Space Law and analyzing its contemporary challenges in light of technological and strategic developments. It aligns with the forward-looking vision of the United Arab Emirates to consolidate its position as a global hub in aviation, space, and scientific innovation.

The author dedicates this work to the United Arab Emirates—its leadership and its people—and to its pioneers in the fields of aviation and space, in tribute to a nation that has made the sky and outer space horizons for its civilizational ambition.

***

www.ingramcontent.com/pod-product-compliance
Lightning Source LLC
LaVergne TN
LVHW072314210926
848482LV00021B/230
9798903428526